BABA SAHEB B. R. AMBEDKAR, JUSTICE K. RAMASWAMY AND ROHITH VEMULA

BABA SAHEB B. R. AMBEDKAR, JUSTICE K. RAMASWAMY AND ROHITH VEMULA
(A Study in the National Perspective)

Dr Anirudh Prasad
and
Dr Chandra Sen Pratap Singh

FOREWORD
By
Professor (Dr) Mahendra P. Singh
Chancellor, Central University of Haryana
Former, Vice Chancellor, W.B.N.U.J.S., Kolkata

KALPAZ

ISBN: 978-93-5128-278-5

First Published, 2017

Published by

Kalpaz Publications
C-30, Satyawati Nagar,
Delhi-110052
Ph. : 9212142040
E-mail: kalpaz@hotmail.com

Printed at : G. Print Process, Delhi

Cataloging in Publication Data—DK

Courtesy: D.K. Agencies (P) Ltd. <docinfo@dkagencies.com>

Prasad, Anirudh, author.

Baba Saheb B.R. Ambedkar, Justice K. Ramaswamy and Rohith Vemula : a study in the national perspective / by Dr. Anirudh Prasad & Dr. Chandra Sen Pratap Singh ; foreword by Professor (Dr.) Mahendra P. Singh.

pages cm

Includes bibliographical references and index.

1. Ambedkar, B. R. (Bhimrao Ramji), 1891-1956. 2. Statesmen—India—Biography. 3. Social reformers—India—Biography. 4. Ramaswamy, K., 1932- 5. Judges—India—Biography. 6. Vemula, Rohith, 1989-2016. 7. University of Hyderabad—Students—Biography. 8. Dalits—India—Biography. 9. Dalits—India—Social conditions. I. Singh, Chandra Sen Pratap, 1976- author. II. Title.

DS481.A1P73 2017 DDC 305.5688092254 23

Dedication

Inscribed
In the Honour of
Professor (Dr) Upendra Baxi
The Great Legal Luminary, Living Legend

The Innovative, Dedicated and Revolutionary Ambedkarite Thinker Asserting Emancipation as Justice and Neglected Dimensions of Baba Saheb B. R. Ambedkar's Grand Achievements as Statesman, Jurist and Great Humanitarian

and

Extending the Generous, But, Well Deserved Academic Appreciation to the Exemplary Contribution of Justice K. Ramaswamy, as a Judge of the Apex Court of the Country by Exemplifying His Role as an Activist Judicial Actor "Who Deployed Judicial Activism for the Depressed under classes of Contemporary Indian, Inaugurated New Spheres of Social Action Litigation".

Contents

Part - Three
JUSTICE K. RAMASWAMY AND HIS CONTRIBUTION TO THE NATION

Part - Four
ROHITH VEMULA AND HIS MESSAGE

Part - Five
A CRITICAL APPRAISAL

List of Abbreviations

A.I.R.	All India Reporter
A P H C	Andhra Pradesh High Court
C A D	Constituent Assembly Debates
C L R	Common Wealth Law Report
C W M G	Complete Works of Mahatma Gandhi
C W S V	Complete Works of Swami Vivekananda
E B C	Eastern Book Company
E P W	Economic and Political Weekly
Etc.	Etcetra
I C P S	Institute of Constitutional and Parliamentary Studies
p.	page
pp.	pages
PCR Act	Protection of Civil Right Act, 1955
R C S C S T	Report of the Commissioner for Scheduled Castes and Scheduled Tribes
S.C.	Supreme Court of India
SCC	Supreme Court Cases
SC	Scheduled Castes
S C S T POAA	Scheduled Castes and Scheduled Tribes (Prevention of Atrocities) Act, 1989
ST	Scheduled Tribes
UOA	Untouchability Offences Act, 1955
U.S.	United States
Vol.	Volume
W S B R A	Writing and Speeches of B. R. Ambedkar

Aknowledgements

Writing a book about a great national figure of everlasting impact, compelling even those who disagree, criticise and differ, not to ignore what he has said, a socially transformative justice oriented judge and a brilliant student with spark leaving the world with great message through sacrifice, is in no way, an easy task. In order to be authentic, objective and convincing, one has to gather information from different sources and to be guided by different luminaries in the process of evaluation, adaptation and moderation making it socially relevant, politically approvable and evidentially sound.

The authors have been inspired immensely by the writings and good words of Professor Upendra Baxi whose writings on Dr Ambedkar, particularly 'Emancipation as Justice: Babasaheb's Legacy and Vision' Ambedkar Memorial Lecture, 2013- "Restoring Title Deeds to Humanity : Lawless Law, Living Death, and the Insurgent Reasòn of Babasaheb Ambedkar" and Constitution Days after have given insight to think about Ambedkar and like situated Dalit men with spark. He has been kind enough to provide very thoughtful literature written by him as well as others like Aishway Kumar, "Radical Equality – Ambedkar, Gandhi and Risk of Democracy" (2015). Above all Dr Baxi is an unparallel scholar of such magnitude that he never fails to appreciate the ideas inspite of his difference of opinion on the point, as he did in our approach towards Gandhi-Ambedkar rapprochment. His unmistakable message- let us agree to disagree on the point but continue to search more and more truth through constructive writings, has everlasting value in our life. Dr Baxi has encouraged with appreciative words by writing Preface/ Foreword to our earlier writings on reservation issues. Authors owe a debt to him which mere words are not enough to express.

Authors have been inspired to do something inspite of odds in the life by reading Justice K. Ramaswamy's Ceaseless and Relentless Journey. His life is message for all. Authors express profound sense of gratitude to Justice K. Ramaswamy for additional reason that his autobiography- Ceaseless and Relertless Journey has been profoundly used in study of chapter 10 of the book. The authors put on record the height of academic excellence, integrity and objectivity of Prof. Baxi and Justice Ramaswamy. In our earlier book on reservation in two volumes, Dr Baxi did not agree to write Foreword till his name was not removed from one of dedicatees and Justice Ramaswamy showed disinclination to write the same because some discussion in the proposed book related to him and instead suggested the name of Dr Baxi as most appropriate scholar to write the Foreword which Dr Baxi did but only when we deleted his name from dedicatees. Scholars of such height are constant source of our inspiration.

We express our sincere gratitude to Professor Ram Deo Shukla who inspite of his birth in the Garga Gotriya high caste has always been appreciative of worth with his large-hearted human touch.

Authors express sense of gratitude to Professor P. S. Jaswal, Vice-Chancellor, R.G.N.U.L., Punjab, Patiala for his good appreciative gesture and encouragement. No work can be completed without the help of library staff and therefore, Arjun, Yogendra, Yashpal, Gurjant and other staff of Library, R.G.N.U.L. deserve gratitude for extending their helping hands in search of materials. Dr Anand Pawar, Associate Professor of Law, Mr Sagar, Examination Section, R.G.N.U.L. have helped in one way or the other. Authors are indebted to them for their co-operation. Authors are also thankful to the library staff of Law Department Lucknow University, Lucknow and Professor R. K. Singh, H.O.D. and Dean, Faculty of Law, Lucknow University for their co-operation.

The authors are extremely grateful to Ms Gurmanpreet Kaur, Assistant Professor of Law, RGNUL, Punjab, Patiala for painstaking interest in re-arranging the typed matters, footnotes and photographs with most appropriatness.

Authors are very much thankful to Professor (Dr) Mahendra P. Singh, a well-known authority on Constitutional and

Administrative Law, presently Chancellor, Central University, Haryana, Former, Vice-Chancellor, National University of Juridical Sciences, Kolkata for expressing his grace by writing Foreword to the book.

The authors are also thankful to Mr R. S. Shukla, who has tirelessly typed the manuscript of the book.

Last but not the least; authors are thankful to Kalpaz Publications for publishing the book in the presentable form.

All attempts have been made to make the book upto date, objective and thoughtful to provide food for even future thoughts, Healthy comments and good suggestions are always welcome.

Ano Bhadrah Kratavo Yantu Vishwatah. (Let the noble thoughts come to us from every side).

Shubha Ramanavami, 2017
"Srijan", 107, Indira Nagar,
Gorakhpur

Anirudh Prasad
Chandra Sen Pratap Singh

Foreword

This book from the authors is quite different from the kind of books I have known from them. The earlier books from them known to me have either been purely on law meant primarily, if not only, for lawyers or law students with the addition of social and political perspective in some of them. On my reading, if this book is not purely a study of one of the most striking phenomenon of the Indian society, it could be classified as a book on sociology of law as it happens to examine the legal phenomenon through the life and work of two prominent law persons though the third one does not fall in that category. That phenomenon has been the creation of a birth-based class of persons in the Indian society as excluded section of Indian humanity to be treated as untouchables and subject to every kind of discrimination and humiliation at the hands of the rest of the society since the time immemorial. This social fact has persisted in spite of all efforts of social reformers from time to time including that of the Buddha among the earliest ones who established a new order in society to get rid of this social evil. But instead of banishing this phenomenon from the society Buddhism itself got banished from India in course of time leaving its traces only as part of the existing order now known as Hinduism or Hindu religion. Similarly later efforts of Kabir, Nanak, Dayananda, Vivekananda and others could also not make much difference to this phenomenon until we come to the freedom struggle, its success and making of our Constitution as the founding principle of our society.

The enlightened members of our society constituting the Constituent Assembly, who were almost all for the eradication of this evil from the face of the Indian society, assigned the task of framing the Constitution as its Chief Draftsman to a person who was himself a victim of this phenomenon. The Constitution as it finally emerged incorporated in its body everything possible that it could do for removing this blot from the Indian society. With reference to the lives of three persons one of whom was the chief draftsman of the Constitution, the other held the highest position as the interpreter of the Constitution and the third one was in the process of becoming a crusader of bringing the social life in harmony with the Constitution. This book examines whether the society has actually changed in the direction envisaged by the Constitution and its makers. After carefully examining the life and mission of each one of them separately it arrives at the conclusion that the Constitution has hardly made any visible or substantial difference in the social attitude and behaviour during its operation so far.

Understandably the book has devoted maximum space to the Chief Draftsman, Dr Bimrao Ambedkar major part of whose life was spent in the pre-Constitution days as a victim of the foregoing phenomenon. But braving through all odds pursuing extremely hard work and commitment to change despite all odds he proved that there was no rational basis whatsoever for the birth-based hierarchy in the Indian society in which the creation of an untouchable class was the most pernicious of all. Of course, the life journey of this iconic figure was constantly full of struggles at every step in every walk of life which the authors have depicted with great sensitivity bringing out and highlighting several events in his life which are generally unknown. But after having overcome all kinds of hurdles in life and achieving iconic status not only among the class of people to which he belonged by birth but overall in general, he could never be satisfied with the realities of Indian society which did not appear to him changed in any way or sufficiently and reached the end of life as a quite dissatisfied person. Even though he has successively acquired greater status after his death than before and some progress is visible in some aspects of social and political life of the country, the authors have brought out several facts that point out in the direction that nothing much has changed. His concluding words in the Constituent Assembly that "however good a Constitution may be, it is sure to turn out bad because those who are called to work it happen to be a bad lot" sound prophetic among others in the context of the continuing practice of untouchability and the associated injustice, discrimination and inhumanity against a large section of our society.

The second person through whom the authors have established their point of incompatibility and failure of law and the Constitution vis-a-vis the realities of our society is Justice K. Ramaswamy who having been born to *dalit* parents rose to become a judge of the Supreme Court of the country that has the last word on the interpretation and application of the Constitution. Again with great care and sensitivity the authors describe his childhood, which was even more traumatic than of Dr Ambedkar, his struggle and neglect in the family, the kind of work he did as a child labourer for his survival and for financing his education, humiliation faced in the school and at every stage of education and ultimately at work as a law person and public prosecutor of unmatched merit. In spite of his unmatched hard work, strength of character and excellence in everything that he did, he was persecuted at every stage in his life only because of the accident of his birth in a *dalit* family. For the same reason his appointment as a judge of the High Court and later his elevation to the Supreme Court was delayed time and again for no other reason but his birth as *dalit*. This happened to him after three to four decades of the Constitution having been in operation. In spite of all these hurdles and humiliations Justice Ramaswamy in the midst of his onerous duties as a judge kept on working incessantly towards bringing the life of the downtrodden in our society in line with the words and the ideals of our Constitution. His judgements in the High Court and the Supreme Court as well as his other writings including his autobiography are the living proof of the hardships a *dalit* has to undergo to survive and move forward in life in our country. All this and much more has been brought to our attention by this book.

That even until this day visible signs of any change in the thought and action of the Indian society are not visible is obvious from the birth, growth and ultimate premature end of the life of the third and the last character in the book who unlike the previous two was compelled to lay his life in the formative stage unlike the other two who survived all the trials travails of the life of a *dalit* in India. Rohith Vemula by name this person having been raised by his *dalit* mother did very well in the school and moved to the university for higher studies reaching ultimately the stage of research for PhD supported by statutory grant of scholarship. Unlike the other two previous characters in the book who did not take any activist role during their school or university days, Rohith started raising his voice against the injustices which the *dalits* continued to face in the society and in education institutions. Finding his support for a just cause having sufficient base in the Constitution to be unpalatable to them the university authorities supported by or at the behest of their political bosses started torturing Rohith by ultimately stopping his legitimate stipend for pursuing his PhD which became unbearable for him resulting in the premature end of a promising life.

Besides these three prominent characters the authors have referred to several other instances of unbridled humiliation and torture to which the *dalits* are subjected in the daily life of our society in clear violation of the laws and the Constitution. As much as the authors of the book are puzzled and intellectually as well as emotionally disturbed as law persons I have all my sympathies and support for them in raising their voice against the perpetuation of constitutionally and legally outlawed activities of the individuals and their organised groups either in the form of caste, creed, custom or otherwise. I will rather go a step further in asserting that any failure of any state in the Indian Union in safeguarding the interest of the weaker section of the society in which the *dalits* are the weakest amounts to failure to act according to the Constitution inviting the imposition of the President's rule in that state and also amounts to violation of the fundamental rights to life, liberty and equality which can be invoked against any government. The public spirited persons who resort to the courts for remedy and relief against the violation of the fundamental rights must avail that facility for uprooting this social evil from our society. Only a concerted effort as was done by our freedom fighters and later by the Constitution-makers could finally eradicate this social evil from our society.

The current book takes us a long way in pointing out the evils of our society with due care of not hurting the sensibilities of any section of our society but at the same time pointedly bringing to their notice the injustice and violation of human rights that they are persistently indulging in. They have taken a very conciliatory approach in respect of various social issues on which our predecessors and the Constitution-makers sharply differed. This is what a constitutional scholar is expected to do. In pointing out solutions to the non-implementation or realisation of the goals of the Constitution he is not expected to suggest steps that will shake or uproot the foundations of the Constitution. He should rather search and suggest, even invent suitable constitutional means for achieving the constitutional goals. In the light of my experience with this and other books from the authors I don't expect that they will ever deviate from that path even in the case of grave personal or principled provocation on any constitutional issue. I hope this book will immensely help our society in following the right path towards its goals of a just society based on equality, fraternity and human dignity.

Let me end by thanking the authors for giving me the opportunity of reading the book at pre-published stage and for the honour of writing its foreword.

21.12. 2016, New Delhi **Professor Dr M.P. Singh,**
Chancellor,
Central University of Haryana.

Part One

INTRODUCTION AND GENERAL STUDY

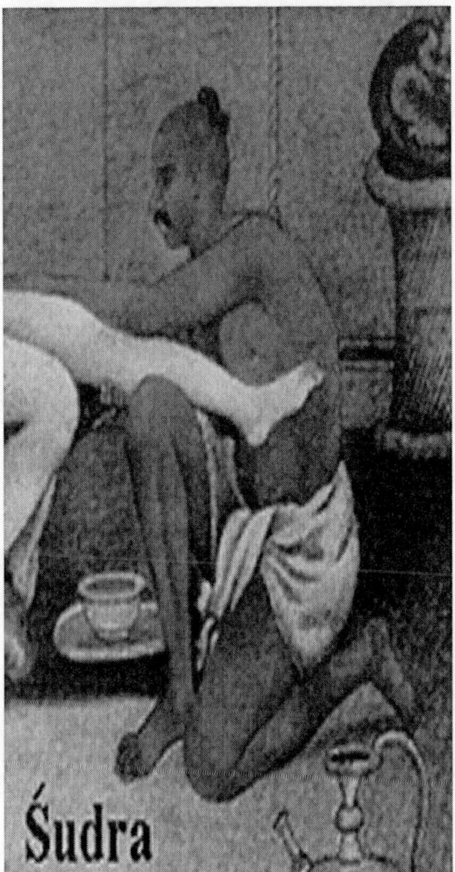

1

Introduction

"A caste is an Enclosed Class. Hindu society is like tower which have several stories without a ladder or an entrance in which one was to die in the story in which one was born."

Dr B.R. Ambedkar

"The struggle begins for Dalits from the cradle to the grave."

Justice K. Ramaswamy

"My birth was a tragic accident".

Rohith Vemula

All the three lamps of the humanity with some ingrained natural spark belonged to the Untouchable families of the Dalit community .The former two fully lighted the society with their luminous flames. The last extinguished in dawn of his life by the wretched hands of the caste-conscious people.

The chronologicl sequence is that Dr Ambedkar was born more than four decades earlier than Justice Ramaswamy and Rohith Vemula was born after more than five decades after Justice Ramaswamy. There is more than a century gap between the birth days of Dr Ambedkar and Ambedkarite Rohith Vemula. But, the agony of the tragic accident of birth and continued discriminatory persecution is the same, though they vary to some extent with varying circumstances. Dr Ambedkar and Justice Ramaswamy enjoyed more than two decades common period. Latter was very much influenced by the Former's visionary philosophy about the Indian graded society divided into privileged and disprivileged groups. A short comparison of Dr Ambedkar and Justice Ramaswamy is presented below.

Dr B.R. Ambedkar and Justice K. Ramaswamy are the two ever shining stars of the Dalit community- a community, deprived, despised, disprivileged, persecuted, discriminated and humiliated at the hands of caste people since time immemorial. Starting from the dust they reached the Himalayan summit of their respective field. Neither of them had come with golden spoon in his mouth, nor with even silver spoon but with iron spoon in the mouth. Both were deprived of the love and affection of mother- Dr Ambedkar from the age of six and Justice Ramaswamy from still earlier age of one and half years. Both had to bear the experience of step mothers as their father remarried after death of their mothers. However Dr Ambedkar was lucky to find the care of his paternal aunt, but Justice Ramaswamy was completely deprived of such caring lady. He had bitter experience of inhumanly treatment at the hands of his step mother as well as the maternal aunt. Dr Ambedkar had most caring father. Justice Ramaswami had most neglecting and uncaring father. Dr Ambedkar faced more severe brunt of the discriminatory treatment at the hands of the graded and degraded Indian society. Both had to face abject poverty and pursued study keeping themselves half fed. Both had utmost eagerness to learning. Dr Ambedkar found opportunity to get financial help from generous and noble king Gaikvad of Baroda and went abroad for higher study. Ramaswmy had to depend totally on self help- learning by earning from labour in agricultural field and some other petty jobs. Both appeared to be inspired by Biblical adage, "Ask and you shall receive; seek and you shall find; and knock the door and it shall be open to you". As to marital engagement and marriage ceremony, both share similar experience of lack means to make it celebrative. Dr Ambedkar married nine years old Ramabai, the daughter of a Mahar labourer, Bhiku Dhutre (already dead before marriage). The marriage was ceremonised in a fish market in Bombay in presence of in-laws when the market was closed for night and all fish mongers had pulled down their shutters. Justice Ramaswamy got his marriage registered in Registrar's Office and in his own words: "I had purchased a sari and blouse for my wife but I could not give her a golden tali as per the custom prevalent among Andhras since I did not have the capacity to purchase one. I gave her a "turmeric piece" tied with thread." Both found full and unconditional supports from their wives in the making of their academic career. Both were fortunate to have the affectionate support from some of their teachers for whom their worth mattered, not the birth. Dr Ambedkar received his name 'Ambedkar' from his merit loving teacher of the same surname. Dr Ambedkar was fortunate to have teachers/ guide Professor R.A. Seligaman and John Dewey. Justice Ramaswamy received the moving touch from dedicated and kind hearted teacher Mallikarjuna Rao who not only saved him from unnecessary humiliation but inspired him to seek proper remedy for partisan act of a teacher favouring rich student and punishing poor. He also received affectionate, judicious and impartial treatment of humane teacher, good administrator and disciplinarian Headmaster K. Sitharama Swamy, who helped him in many ways including helping him in clearance of the result which would not have been clear due to striking of name from register for want of fee. He was immensely helped by Lolla Laxemi Pati Sastry who coming to know his late coming in class due to being dependent on earn to learn arranged required book. He also got help from his History teacher S. Anjjaneyulu and Economics teacher Hanumanta Rao who allowed him to attend their private classes without any charge. Both read in very non-congenial atmosphere. Dr Ambedkar, 'would sit before a flickering kerosene lamp without a chimney and go on reading and writing, doing his class work' and that too in a very small and congested room wherein the father and the son had to sleep by turn (his father had to remain awaken till two in the night, there after he used to sleep and Dr Ambedkar had to be awakened and start study till morning). Justice Ramaswamy remained on pial (outer plate form of a house) and studied under a streetlight. Both studied in adverse situations, sometimes, continued study half- fed. Justice Ramaswamy's financial position was still worse. What a pitiable condition? He himself narrates in autobiography: "I was a paying guest in my father's house. I used to work at night threshing the grain and the wages earned were kept in a sack for financing my studies." Both faced discrimination of one sort or the other- the former as student and teacher/employee and latter in appointment and promotions. All adverse circumstances made them firm, resolute and brave to face the challenges of life undeterred. Their commitment to learning and mission to achieve something significant in life made them broad visioned persons. They achieved name and fame in their respective field of work.

Rohith Vemula succumbed to the treacherous assault of the Indian graded and degraded society. A brilliant Dalit scholar could not bear the hammer of discrimination and continued persecution. The sun of the hope of humanity was eclipsed before shining. Had he been allowed to flourish India would have been benefitted by another Dr Ambedkar or Justice Ramaswamy in the shape of a great thinker.

Dr Ambedkar and Justice Ramaswamy are proof of astonishing success through hard work in adverse circumstances. Their lives themselves are message for posterity. The messages are for all, especially for those, who come from disprivileged and deprived classes; but not the less, to those who are privileged and treat others contemptuously. If talent flourishes society is benefitted, but if choked the society suffers.The main thrust of book is on exposition of facts-situations to show if opportunity given the untouchable community does not lag behind and can serve the society in better way with intelligence coupled with hard work culture.

The Scheme of the Book

The book entitled, "Baba Saheb Ambedkar, Justice Ramaswamy and Rohith Vemula" has been divided into five parts. Part-One contains two chapters. Chapter one deals with introduction and general study and Chapter two deals with the development of the Hindu graded society. An attempt is made to justify the choice of the subject matter of the book and specially, comparison and significance of the book in the present day scenario with our march towards equality, liberty and fraternity through the constitutional commitment to establish a society based on the principles of egalitarianism and distributive justice. It also contains discussion on the development of Hindu society from worth based distinction to the birth based privileges.. Part two of the book contains six chapters veering around the study of the different dimensions of Baba Saheb Bhim Rao Ambedkar's struggleful life. Chapter three presents in brief the life grief of Dr Ambedkar's school days experiences of sitting in the last, deprived of drinking water in absence of peon and other indignities. Chapter four gives an account of his brilliant academic career and postgraduate and doctorate degree from prestigious Universites of U.S.A. and U.K. It also enumerates his distinguished writings and prestigious posts adorned with special note. Chapter five discusses the great personalities contributing in the making of Dr Ambedkar in one way or the other. Chapter six and seven deal with many specialities, innovations and distinctions ignored by critics and not properly appreciated by his admirers. Both Chapters are devoted to dicuss threadbare: Is Dr Ambedkar false worshipped

God, as some motivated comments are read and heard or he is underworshipped, ignored, misunderstood and not properly appreciated. An attempt has also been made to appreciate his innovative jurisprudential contribution as precursor of many new concept which latter jurists have discussed, that is to say the idea of lawless law, demosprudence, duty coinciding with power of the state to secure justice to the disprivileged people and new dimension of the theory of rights addressed more to civil society than to the state. Chapter eight tries to narrate how Dr Ambedkar worked for the abolition of untouchability, the most pernicious old age evil of the the caste-ridden society. An attempt has been made to establish how despite verbal expressions of disagreement and difference of approaches Dr Ambedkar and Gandhi both helped in the eradication of untouchability.Chapter nine presents critical analysis of contribution of Dr Ambedkar in the nation building building as Chairman of the Drafting Committee of the Constituent Assembly and through his vision of politico-economic and social democracy. Part Three of the book contains one big chapter on the brilliant and trend setting performance of Justice K. Ramaswamy as judge of the Andhra Pradesh High Court and the apex court of the country. It discusses in brief his early strurrgle with earning bread and pursuing learning ceaselessly, his impressive and excellent work as an advocate, as government pleader and judge. It also discusses his new dimensions of judicial interpretation with a view to make the aspirations and the commitment envisioned in the Constitution effective and meaningful. Part Four of the book contains one Chapter 11 which relates to the recent past Dalit brilliant chap who fell victim of the graded Indian Society not allowing independent initiative of disprivileged class scholar and flourish him as he liked. Part Five of the book deals with two chapters. Chapter Twelve is devoted to Coda giving appraisal of the book study with dimensional view about the message for posterity anxious to build the nation and develop it with participatory democracy and establish an egalitarian society based on liberty for all, equality without discrimination and fraternity sans any inhibition. The world is moving fast and old orders are changing giving way to new. The book concludes with faith in Mendel's Principle of Heredity that: "There is nothing in the descent of the higher mental qualities to suggest that they follow any single system of transmission." All need be given equal opportunity to contribute towards nation building as nation needs worth not birth. Chapter 13 proffers some valuable and befitting suggestions.

2

Development of the Hindu Graded Society: A Development from Worth to Birth

(God created man in his own image. Man distorted that image for his personal gains. Being the creation of God, all men are equal. It is quite inconceivable from where does come the complex of superiority and inferiority?)

[The most elaborate model of status-oriented society, which much interested Maine, and which anthropologists continue to illuminate, was of course that of the Hindu caste system in its widely variegated tribal and local forms. The democratic Republic of India is still struggling courageously to abolish it by constitutional, legal and economic measures. While the system no longer exists in law (save insofar as it is recognised by legal measures designed to undo its effect) it retains much of its former reality in social arrangements and practice][1]

Julius Stone

General Observations

Every society from primitive to the ultra modern has shown certain pattern of development. In 1861 in his most celebrated book, 'Ancient Law' Sir Henry Sumner Maine passed generalisation about the development of the progressive societies as 'development from status to contract'. Thereafter the development has been in reverse gear with the recognition of the individuals and organisational rights like human rights and trade unions rights. At present social relations are governed by both the status and contract whichever is beneficial to the weaker segments of societies like workers, socially disprivileged and historically persecuted as well as has defiled all women. The development of the Hindu society shows juridical generalisation with its peculiar staticism. Speaking of the special Indian situation Julius Stone remarks:

"... its laws are hostile elements to be shunned. Behind all this lies also perhaps a view of society's material endowment as fixed and stable, a static pie divided up in a manner sanctified by both authority and tradition among the various institutions, caste, classes and families. Equally basic, and complementary to this, is the hope and belief that the oppressed and the dispossessed (similarly accredited) that in the endless ***Samsara*** *the sufferings and frustrations of one existence will be compensated (for whom bear themselves worthily) by the serene blessings in a later incarnation".*

Stone further remarks:

"It is still the **Sadhu,** the itinerant saint, rather than the member of the **Lok Sabha**, or the industrialist of Bombay or Calcutta, who symbolises human achievement for three-quarters of the people of India."[2]

Above comment appears to be reinforced even in case of the working of the governmental organs duly constituted by and under the Constitution. As late as 2016, a Chief Minister offered 3.45 crores to a temple on the occasion of ***Vijayadashami*** *as he thought / believed that the State of Telangana was created as a new state with the blessings of the revered deity.*

The height of superstitious belief is notable in the case of the non-disposal of the dead body of Shri Ashutosh Maharaj, the late head of the Divya Jyoti Jagriti Sansthan whose body has been lying inside a deep freezer at the DJJS ashram since January 2014 in spite of the Sansthan doctors declaring him clinically dead and the order of the High Court dated Dec.1, 2016 to cremate the body within 15 days as per religious rites. The government avoiding taking any measures since three years and seeking adjournment after adjournment under pressure of the so called devotees who inhere blind faith that Ashutosh Maharaj is in meditation and will return to the life someday.[3]

General Trend of Race-Discrimination in Every Society

God created the human creature. There is near unanimity among all the religions that God created the man in his own image. The problem started when man distorted the image of God for his personal end. Dominant people claimed superiority over subservient people. Advantaged group segregated the disadvantaged people, degraded them with a view to exploit them for aggrandisement of the claims of the advantaged people. Where ever white Britishers went, they started segregating others. The racial superiority was superimposed on those over whom they established dominance. Charles F. Andrews candidly admits: "The Christian Church in the west, no less than the Hindu Religion, has sadly failed hitherto to deal justly and act generously with those of another race."[4] It became more obvious in the United States of America where British settlers brought black Negroes from Africa by force and by segregating them started their exploitation degrading and deprive them of human dignity. They justified their unequal and inhuman treatment by creating unscientific dualism between the Whites and the Blacks. Kimberle Crenshaw has very well summarised this dualism between the Black and White images as given below:

Table 1
Black and White Images

White Image	Black Image
Industrious	Lazy
Intelligent	Unintelligent
Moral	Immoral
Knowledgeable	Ignorant
Enabling Culture	Disabling Culture
Responsible	Shiftness
Virtuous/Pious	Lascivious
Law-Abiding	Criminal

Professor Ronald M. Dworkin rightly comments that, "Segregation treats Blacks and Whites differently, and history shows that the seed of the different treatment lies in prejudice.[5] By the middle of the twentieth century and more particularly after the Second World War unequal treatment with Negroes began to be criticised on account of its basis in deep-rooted prejudices and decency of the modern civilised world. To quote Professor Dworkin, "Racial discrimination that disadvantages blacks is unjust, not because people cannot choose their race, but because that discrimination expresses prejudice"[6] and "America's growing sense was that racial segregation was wrong in principle, because it was incompatible with decency to treat one race inherently inferior to another."[7]

Development of Hindu Society- A Development from Worth to Birth and Consequent Vulnerable Status of Untouchables

In comparison to the discrimination in other societies of the world the position of untouchables in the Indian graded society is still worse. It is not so much racial as the caste- based. The discriminators and discriminated both belong to the same soil and more or less of the same origin.Everybody was created by the same Virat Purush/Brahma, therefore, all were equal. Social adjustment was done on the basis of division of labour the Varna system was called **Chaturvarna**- the priestly class was termed as **Brahmin,** the military class as **Kshatriya,** the merchant class as **Vaishya** and the menial class as **Shudra.** This social arrangement was based on the principle of equality and full liberty to choose any calling suitable to one's genius. The Brahmins should cultivate knowledge and guide people; Kshatriyas should bear arms and protect the people of their tribe in case of attack from outside; Vaishya should earn money by engaging in trade and business, and Shudra should serve the other class by constructing houses and doing other services. Earlier there was mention of only three Varnas. Shudras came to be searched later. Anyway, the people of all Varnas could live together happily and the different members of the same family could opt for suitable job according to his ability and natural inclination. Rigveda depicted the prevailing social condition:

We all have various hopes and plan
And many are the ways of men:
The craftsman seeks for job to do,
The priest his folk, the healer the sick.
Flow, Indu, flow for Indra's sake:
The arrow-smith with hard dry reeds
And feathers from the birds of air,
Bronze for the tips, and glowing coals,
Seek out the man who'll pay him best.
Flow, Indu, flow for Indra's sake:

Vedic India was classless and casteless society. There was much flexibility in pursuing jobs according to one's natural inclination and choice. Rig Vedic hymn exemplify the ideal arrangements job adherence without any sense of superiority or inferiority on the basis of doing some jobs.

The Vedic verse says:
A bard am I, my father's a healer,
And mother grinds corn on the quern,
Striving for wealth, with varied plans,
We follow our desires like kine.

Even sons born of the same parents could opt for different callings. Devapi opted to do priestly job and his younger brother became king. There was no bar on the acquisition of the Vedic knowledge for any class of the people. There was no complex. All enjoyed equal status and dignity. King Sudas was Shudra and there was a fierce competition between Bashishtha and Vishvamitra to serve as his purohit. One view is that both Vashishtha and Vishvamitra served as king Sudas's purohit at different times. The other view is that Vishwamitra won over Bashishtha and became the king's purohit. Vishwamitra was Kshatriya. Many scholars who wrote some parts of Vedas were Shudras. The name of Mahidas comes to the forefront. Sage Kavash of **Aitareya Brahmana** was son of a slave girl. Agastya and Vashishtha are said to have been born from Jars, signifying their mysterious parenthood. Worth received recognition and was allowed flourish. The social division of work was good from the point of view of convenience, proper utilisation of talents of different people and social interdependence or what jurisprudentially came to be termed by social thinkers and sociological jurists 'social solidarity.' Such tendencies are found, more or less, in every society in the course of its development. Hindu social system based on Vedic injunctions was accommodative and equalitarian. The Varnashrama Dharma was natural- the Brahmins had to use their mouth to speak to others and communicate or disseminate the acquired knowledge, Kshatriyas had to use their hands for warrior acts of using swords for protection of the people associated with them, Vaishyas had to use thigh and sit for merchandise and Shudras had to use their legs to run for serving other classes. All were discharging essential services and helping each other and balance and social equilibrium was maintained. None was completely self dependent. Each class helped the other and was dependent on the other.

The problem started with the change of time and Brahmin class starting conscious efforts to appropriate Hinduism. No doubt, Brahmins were well-versed in Vedas and were also intelligent. They started exercising their talent to the benefit of their own clan. They constructed certain myths and the natural course of things was diverted towards supernaturalism. The biggest and most powerful myth was the creation of the four Varnas- the root of embracing birth and ignoring worth. After a long gap of the march of society the divine origin of caste structure was searched. It was attributed that according to Purushsukta of Rig-Veda the cosmogenic Male created Brahmana from His mouth; the Kshatriya from His arms; the Vaishya from his thighs; and the Shudra from his feet. This myth was repeated continuously in subsequent scriptures with a view to attach more and more creditability as if it was real. Thus, identical view if divine creation is found in **Vajneya-samhita** of **Ajurveda**; in the Taittiriya-samhita of the Sama-Veda in the Atharva- Veda; and in Brhadaranyaka Upanishad. After a long gap in Dwapar Lord Krishna made some efforts to cut the tightened knot of birth and reestablish worth. In Bhagvad-Gita lord Krishna said '**Chaturvanya Maya Srishtam Guna Karma Vibhagashah** (The four varnas were created by Me, dividing them according to distinct aptitudes and functions)'. The Vagrasuchika gives example of great Indian scholars like Kaushika, Jambuka, Valmiki, Vyasa, Gautam, Vashishtha and Agastya to prove that four-fold orders was based on aptitude, knowledge and conduct of the person and not on the basis of birth.[8] Kashyapa clan of Vedic seers, were well known to absorb, "aborigines who wanted to become Brahmins." (as pointed out by Kaushambi).[9]

Even Manu, who is author of all sorts of inequality, recognised promotion and demotion depending on one's deeds and virtues. He declared, a Shudra attains the rank of a Brahmana and Brahmana sinks to the rank of Shudra (**Shudro Brahmanotomati Brahmanascheti Shudratam**). But, at other places he degraded Shudras to the status of birds. Thus, "if a Brahmin kills a cat or an ichneumon, the bird chasa, or a frog, a dog, a lizard, or a Shudra," he was absolved of his performing a sort of fasting penance. On the other hand, for killing the Brahmin Shudra could be punished with death penalty. The inequality to the absurd stage was prescribed for the punishment of adultery. If Shudra cohabited a Brahmin adultress his life was to be taken away. But, even if Brahmin cohabited the lawful wife of a Shudra, he was exempted from all corporeal punishments. The second myth was created by styling Brahmin as the Lord of the universe, even equal to God Himself. The third myth was created by announcing Brahmin as god on the earth- Bhusur, Bhudev and so on so forth. By one myth God himself lives in Brahmins. Ashwamedhic Parva narrates imputing Lord Krishna to have said, "For many ignorant people do not know, it is I who reside on the earth in the form of the Brahman **(Bahvastu va jananti nara gyan bahishkritah. Yadahan dha Dwijarupena Vasami Vasutale**).[10]

The Aryans' **chaturvana** system based on occupational order projecting the division of labour was reduced into the entrenched caste-system. In words of Professor Harold A. Gould the Brahmins "sacralised the occupational order, and occupationalised the sacred order."[11] The impact of Brahmin sacralisation was two-fold. First, the universal Varnashrama dharma of occupational division was converted into adharma of varna as jati-dharma. As Mahabharata reveals in Satyuga there was only one caste, Brahmin, as they began to degenerate, they became divided into different castes. The second impact was the creation of hierarchy among the different castes- Brahmins at the top and Shudras at the lowest. Inequality was created and hierarchical gradation was enforced. Superiority- inferiority was imposed, Brahmins were declared to be superior to all the three other castes; Kshatriyas were declared to be superior to Vaishyas and Shudras; and Vaishya were declared superior to Shudras. Shudras were lowest and inferior to all the three upper castes. Not only this, Shudras were prohibited from reading scriptures. Certain scriptures mandate; "If Shudra hears Vedas, fill his ears with molten lead, and if he remembers a line cut his tongue out". Even if he uttered to the Brahmin, "You Brahmin" the mandate was to cut his tongue out. There was and there came rampant inequality. Shudras were deprived of livelihood and were compelled to eat carrion.

Manu was sworn leader of Brahminical order. Other Brahmins Smritikars followed him. To cite a few Bhrigu Samhita, Narad Smriti, Kautilya's Arthashashtra. There was concerted design behind securing knowledge reserved for Brahmins and keeping other castes in the abysmal depth of ignorance. That design was to accomplish their selfish ends – privileging ownselves and disprivilrging others. A very vivid picture has been painted by Jotirao Phule who realised that "the seeds of Brahmins' power, supremacy and privileges lay in their scripture and puranas; and these works and the caste system were created to exploit the lower classes". Subsequently, the great propounder of Vedanta philosophy Swami Vivekananda echoed the same harsh truth. Swami Vivekananda said, "Whenever the Brahmins wrote anything they would deny all rights to others and added that Vyasa tried to put meanings upon the Vedas to cheat the poor Shudras."[12] Vivekananda drew the attention towards some experience based realities. Swami Vivekananda made clear; "Brahmins and Kshatriyas have always been our teachers, and most of the Uapnishads were written by Kshatriyas, while ritualistic portions of the Vedas came from the Brahmins. Most of our great teachers through-out India have been Kshatriyas, and were always universal in their teachings; whilst the Brahmins prophets with two exceptions were very exclusive. Rama, Krishna, and Buddha- worshipped as incarnation of God- were Kshatriyas."[13] Result being that good religion was converted into bad living religion. To quote Vivekananda again: "There cannot be any growth without liberty. Our ancestors freed religious thoughts, and we have a wonderful religion; but they put a heavy chain on the feet of society, and our society is, in a word, horrid, diabolical."[14] Abraham Eraly, very succinctly summarises the development of Hindu society starting during Vedic period with the worth and reaching to the birth and stabilising there:

"The basic structure of Ancient Indian society was the **varna** system, which divided people into four classes- Brahmins (priestly class), Kshatriyas (martial class), Vaishyas (producers, farmers, traders and artisans) and Shudras (serfs and labourers) then as society evolved and became progressive more diversified, and professions became hereditary and professional groups lived apart from each other in separate villages or in particular zones in towns, these classes over the centuries split into innumerable **jatis,** hereditary castes. The classes and castes maintained their exclusivity though endogamous marriages and by imposing varius taboos, especially regarding whom they could eat with and what occupations they could take to. One could become a member of a caste only by birth- **jati** means birth-so no one could change his caste."

Efforts to Substitute Birth by Worth and its Failure

There have been many moves to challenge the brahminical authority of entrenched caste hierarchy giving privileges to some and depriving it to many i.e. caste based status or birth based privileges and liabilities. The main challenge came in Mahabharata. Lord Krishna exhorted to live the life of Yogi i.e. to live thoroughly a God-centric life and interpreted Yoga in such a universal way as to be practicable to every man and woman, to the humblest Shudra or labourer as much as to the most learned Brahmin or the most warlike Kshatriya or the most commercialist Vaishya, to a person born in the lowest cadre of the society as much as to an illustrious person occupying the highest position in the society, to an ordinary house-holder as much as to an all-renouncing Sanyasi. He also tried to give rational base to the Chaturvarna Dharma proclaiming Himself to have created it. He also clarified its bases- Guna and deed. Swadharma meant deeds based on one's natural instinct and abilities. The cunning hierarchical structure supporter interpreted that Lord Krishna too supported Chaturvarna. They intelligently blacked out virtues and deeds. So was done with Swadharma. Its individual merit was lost in caste structured obligations as Plato had done – to perform the duties of one's own class and not meddle with the other. Greek discarded Platonic social arrangement. But India is clinging with it still. Mahabharata tried to substitute birth by worth by denouncing the impact of the accident of birth. Repeatedly the position of Brahmana and Shudra was asserted to be decided on the basis of relative conduct. In **Vanaparva** it was made clear that 'it is difficult to determine the **jati** of a person because all the varna have become hopelessly mixed (**jatiratra mahasarpa manusyatve mahamate. Sanskarat sarvavarnanam dushparkshyate me matih-Vanaparva 180.31).** It has been clearly laid down that a Brahmana is one in whom can be seen truth, generosity, forgiveness, humility absence of cruelty, austerity and kindness. But these qualities are found in a shudra as well. It was also made clear that the earlier mentioned qualities are present in a shudra, and are absent in a brahmana, then that shudra is not a shudra, and that brahmana is not a brahmana.[16] And, therefore, only that person who has those qualities is to be regarded as brahmana, and the one who does not have them is to be regarded as a Shudra.[17] Finally, it is ruled that Brahminhood is determined by conduct, and not by family, nor by studies, nor by listening to scriptures-of this there is no doubt.[18] The valid reason was proffered that: 'born of Brahma, all varna are brahmana.[19] Similar observations are available in Shukraniti, that is to say, born of Brahma, all varnas are brahmana[20] and Not by birth one is Brahmin, or Kshatriya, or Vaishya, or Shudra, or Maleccha, but by virtue of one's function and conduct.[21] Anushasanparva of Mahabharata goes a step further and points out that Lord Shiva said that Shudra is a social function and not a person; after delineating the functions of Brahmana, Kashatriya and Vaishya. He declares: "similarly, shudra is the basis of all dharmas: if there were no shudra, there would be no service: other three varnas are founded on shudra and all social functions are shudramulaka.[22] But what was done in Vanaparva and Anushasanaparva was undone in the name of certainty in Ashvamedhikparva. Good or bad; cultured or uncultured was not to be insulted as he was fire concealed under the ash. By his very birth the Brahmin was the abiding symbol of eternal dharma. The myth was created and put in the mouth of the most judicious, objective and worth loving Lord Krishna that where a Brahmana (by birth) is worshipped, He is worshipped too. The believer and benefitted by worship by birth went a step further and put in the mouth of Lord Krishna: "For many ignorant people do not know, it is I who reside on the earth in the form of Brahmana. They further went a step more and attributed to Lord Krishna to declare: 'I fear neither gods nor demons; but I fear when the Veda are recited by the Shudra.' The original text may be interpolation which might have been done later completely ignoring how Lord Krishna loved worth ignoring birth. The story of the non-declaration of the completion of Yudhisthira's Rajsuya yagya by Lord Krishna until the bell of completion of Yagya rang and the bell rang in its full swing when Supana Maharaj his Chandal devotee was served with food prepared by Draupadi and he blessed Yagya by accepting it. The minute study of the different Parvas of the Mahabharata reveals the inconsistency, logical incoherence and unlike God conduct of Lord Krishna and one writer could not be that incoherent, self-contradictory and irrational. Yet it was and is found in Mahabharata. In a nutshell, the efforts to substitute birth by worth was diluted and the emphasis on the worth was swallowed by the latter indomitability of birth. It is also very pertinent to point out that three Gods are imputed to have created Chaturvana. First, Prajapati

(Brahma) from different parts- mouth, arms, thighs and feet without indication of superiority or inferioriry. Second, Lord Krishna with clear indication of the bases of cotegorisation- virtue/ capability and deed. Third, Lord Shiva who attached more importance to Shudras. Thus, there is no convincing reason why Prajapati's creation without superiority –inferiority complex, Lord Krishna's version of Chaturvarna based on capability and deed or Lord Shiva's version of most valuable position of Shudras be not adhered, applied and accepted as norms governing the social interactions.The next challenge to the brahminical construction of entrenched caste-hierarchy came from Tathagat Buddha and Tirthankar Mahabir in the forms of Baudh and Jain dharmas diluting the himsa element of Yagyas and declaring: **Ahimsa Paramo Dharmah** (the principle which had started since Mahabharata). Tathagat Buddha made all efforts to ignore birth and establish the social significance of worth. First, he demolished the theory of Brahminhood or the status of Shudra by birth. Buddha taught that none is Brahmin or Shudra by birth. It is the conduct which makes one Brahmin or Shudra. Second, he opened the door of education for all irrespective of caste and creed. He taught everybody irrespective of caste and creed. Many Chandalas like Prakriti became preacher preaching even Brahmins. Third, he did away with any iota of complexes of superiority or inferiority. In his Sangha there were lowliest born (Chandala), Vaishyas, Kshatriyas and Brahmins too. All became Bhikshu and Baudh. He pointed out as rivers from different regions or countries when fell in the ocean they lose their identity and become one, likewise people from different castes, creeds and nationality when join Sangha they become one. Fourth, he gave the lesson to be self reliant; to search for one's own salvation; to be enlightened- **atta deepo bhava**. Fifth, he taught to get relieved of superstitions and not to rely on anybody without self verification. He clarified not to believe in anything because it has been said by a highly placed or revered persons (including Tathagata Buddha himself) or is written in some holy book or is in practice since long. Believe only if it appeals to your conscience, reason and intelligence. Sixth, Buddha put emphasis on the purity of mind, love and compassion towards all, get rid of enmity act for betterment of others. Seventh, he taught to sacrifice self interest, act for welfare of others and not indulge in any kind of Himsa. His Manavadhama- be good, do good found full application and thereby, flourished well during the Mauryan regime. The Mauryans were neither Brahmins claiming representing sacerdotal power claiming superiority as God's men on the earth nor Kshatriyas claiming warriorship superiority over others. In traditional hierarchy they belonged to lowly fourth position and therefore they ruled on the basis of equality of all classes- no caste superior and no caste inferior by birth. The worth prevailed and nearly 140 years of the Mauryan rule dislodged the Brahmins superiority by mere birth. First, Chandra Gupta Maurya who is said to have adopted Jain Dharma and second by his grandson Ashoka, privileges based on birth were marginalised. Their rule is known as the golden age of the country and Ashoka has been acclaimed as the greatest ruler of the world. He was recognised as Ashoka, the Great. He ruled on the principle of Buddhist love and compassion believing in Dhammavijaya- neither oppression nor terror but rule of righteousness. The old brahmincal order of privilege gave way to equal treatment. Varna system was pushed into background. People of all castes were allowed to reside in the same vicinity. Sacrifical yagya were prohibited. But, Mauryan regime ended in conspiratorial way by an act regicide against the last Mauryan king Brihadrath committed by his own ambitious commander of the imperial army Pushyamitra, a Samvedi Brahmin of Sunga Gotra who became ruler by killing his own king during his review of a military parade organised by Pushyamitra himself.[23] He reestablished all lost rituals including the horse sacrificing or Ashwamedha Yagya. The culture of himsa was reinstated. Compassion was substituted by extreme pitilessness. Buddhist monks were targeted with royal declaration to pay a price of 100 gold pieces on the head of every Buddhist monk. The plight of Buddhists under Pushyamitra's reign can be perceived in narration of Dr. Harprasad Shastri: "The condition of the Buddhists under the imperial sway of the Sungas, orthodox and bigoted, can be more easily imagined than described. From Chinese authorities it is known that many Buddhists still do not pronounce the name of Pushyamitra without a curse."[24] Pushyamitra left no stone unturned for reestablishing superiority of birth ignoring worth. He got a Manusmriti composed by a scholarly Brahmin, Sumati Bhargava between 170B.C. and 150 B.C. deliberately called Manusmriti and declaring Brahmins as the supreme head of all castes the original script.[25] The foreign invaders and later rulers had to rule the country as smoothly as possible and for that purpose they had to depend upon the people who mattered. Muslim rulers did not like to touch the sensitive caste hierarchy issue and preferred to rule their Hindu subjects according to their traditional customs and usages. In order to make their rule smooth they chose Brahmins as advisers. Brahmins proved to be most accommodating. But warrior Kshatriyas continued their resistance and rivalry. So they were deprived of their position and were forced to exile from the capital centres. Thus, during Moghal period (in absence of Kshatriyas), Brahmins enjoyed unparalleled and unrivalled supremacy. To quote Max Weber:

"The invasion and domination of foreign conquerors benefited the power monopoly of Brahmins. The foreign conquerors divested the most important competitors of Brahmins of all power it conceived them to be politically dangerous. ...The power of Brahmins on the other hand grew during the time of the conquerors. After a period of fanatical iconoclasm and Islamic propaganda, the conqueror resigned himself to accept the continued existence of Hindu culture. Indeed, priestly power under foreign domination always serves as a refuge for the conquered and as a tool of domestication for foreign overlords."[26]

To quote Max Weber again:

"The Islamic conquest smashed the politico-military power of the Kshatriyas but sustained the Brahmans as an instrument of social control. The pretensions of the Brahmins in classical literature and law books were then stereotyped."[27]

Thus, the Moghal empire period strengthened the caste system rather weakening it. It was done so by leaving the matters in hands of Brahmins and of caste councils acting under them.

The Britishers followed the same policy of ruling the country according to the age-old Hindu customs and traditions and appointing the Brahmins as their advisers. Brahmins picked the opportunities, quickly imbibed the Western education and becoming partners in administration of the country. During early decades of the British rule Brahmins consolidated and enhanced social supremacy on the basis of their high positions in the administration. Later they began to develop individualism and sense of democracy on the basis Western education and put resistance to the British rule. Britishers started the policy of, **"Divide et Impera"** i.e. divide and rule. Caste played vital role in refusal to deploy cartridge made of beef and pork fat. Sepoy refused to do so for the fear of losing caste. With a view to divide Hindus many British administrators like Ibbetson, Nesfield and Risley developed anthropometric interests. Caste-based census were conducted in 1881, 1891 and 1901. It strengthened caste consciousness. In 1921, a critical statement of a Census Superintendent of Punjab pointed out: "Our land records and official documents have added iron bonds to the old rigidity of caste ...[the]Government's passion for labels and pigeon-holes has led to a crystallisation of caste system, which except among the aristocratic castes was really very fluid under indigenous rule."

Situation of casteism remained the same as earlier. Brahmins opposition to the education of lower caste remained prominent feature the Indian social life. In 1858, Bombay Government announced that "that all schools maintained at the sole cost of government shall be open to all classes of its subjects without distinction." But hard reality of casteist opposition and consequent government helplessness peeps through the Report of the Department of Public Instruction "the opposition of the higher castes to the admission of [Untouchables] boys to a public school was often so strong that, even with the best will in the world, the Department could do very little in the matter."[28] Even the leaders/social reformers and the government policy-makers "stood clearly for educating the upper classes, believing that education would filter downwards.[29] Not only the upper caste Indians were interested in keeping lower classes deprived of education for their selfish interest, the high British officers were also averse to educating the lower classes and mass education policy was a pretension. Dhananjay Keer very succinctly points out that Lord Ellenborough, President of the Board of Control in a striking note of caution to the Chairman of the Court of Directors, observed: "Education and civilisation may descend from the highest to the inferior classes, and so communicated may impart new vigour to the community, but they will never ascend from the lower classes to those above them; they can only, if imparted solely to the lower classes, lead to general convulsion of which foreigners would be the first victims."[30]

The treatment with outcaste students in the schools was most unbearably contemptuous. Two incidents, one relating to the reaction of caste students on admission of an outcaste able student and other the Brahmin teacher, are presented as sample of the affairs. Rev. Murray Mitchell narrated a moving story of admission of an outcaste boy into the lowest English class on the basis of his sufficient acquaintance with vernacular. In his own words:

"In a few minutes there came a deputation of Brahman boys, their dark eyes sparkling, and every gesture betokening emotion. 'We are going to leave the school; there are Mahars in it.' 'One Mahar, I think.' 'Yes; one is as bad as ten.' Am I to drive the poor boy away?' 'We do not know; only we go, if he remains. You need not touch him unless you like; you clever boys are near the top of the class, and the poor Mahar boy is at the foot. He is sitting on a different bench from you.' 'Yes, but there is matting on the floor, and it transmits pollution. We Brahmans are now all polluted and must wash away the defilement before we eat.' 'You wish me then to remove the matting!' We must not have been in the class'. 'Well at any rate, I cannot and will not put the boy out of the class.'

"I was puzzled. I did not wish to drive away the Brahmins; yet I could not in conscience dismiss the Mahar. 'Wait till tomorrow', I said, 'We are arranging classes, you know, and perhaps you deserve promotion'. So, rather sulkily, the Brahmins retired. The Mahar boy never came back. I suppose he found himself like a fish out of water; the high and the middle class, no doubt, stood firm; and I believe the teacher of that class did the same thing."[31] The Rev. Adam White found in his visit to a government school near Poona a Brahmin teacher Pantoji having a cane and some clods. When Rev. Adam White asked about clods kept there, the Brahmin teacher replied: "I use my cane in the case of caste boys. If I struck the Mahar pollution from the outcaste boy would come along with the stick and my whole body would be polluted. So when the Mahar boy is stupid, I just take a clod and let fly at him, and when I miss I take another."[32]

Many noble men, saints and reformers made efforts from time to time to reform the Brahmin bigotry, but sooner or later their impact faded away. It is true that Chaitanya Mahaprabhu, Ramanujacharya, Jnyandeo, Tukaram, Eknath, Maharshi Dayananda Saraswati, Swami Vivekananda, Raja Ram Mohan Roy, to name a few or some saints like Kabir, Raidas made efforts to reform the Hindu system. But they did not have long ranged impact due to the entrenched hierarchical caste structure to which they did not touch. The root of all evils remained untouched. They believed in changes but remained part and parcel of the system. Many saints criticised the evil of the caste system, prevalent social treachery through untouchability and they attracted followers and many sects developed, but social evils remained unmoved. The social of inhuman treatment was not due to outsiders but due to our own. It was in this backdrop that Swami Vivekananda ridiculed the claim of more powers from Britishers. He said: "None deserves liberty who is not ready to give liberty. Suppose the English give over to you all power. Why, the power that be, then, will hold the people down, and let them not have it. Slaves want power to make slaves."[33]

The historical march of the Hindu social structure shows march from original Vedic worth of only one class to division into three – Brahman, Rajanya and Vaishya according to the work tendency required for the social adjustment without inter se hierarch –to myth based creation of Chaturvarna with two artificial dimensions, the one hierarchical and other birth-based privileges and disprivileges and still towards a category of socially excluded class of fifth position- outcaste, antyaja, pachama, pariah, chandala and terming them despisingly as "walking carrion" or "walking corpses." On the basis of the accident of birth such people were declared untouchables and some where even unseeable, not permitted to come out during daytime or the common roads. Dalit class fell victim of birth-based prejudices. Dalits face unjust discrimination and inhuman treatment not because they cannot choose their caste but because such discrimination and inhuman treatment expresses prejudices.

Three Most Ignoble Hostilities of the Hindu Society

Generations have come, generations have gone, but story of the persecution of the Shudras has continued to go since the Brahminical appropriation of Hinduism, their claim of superiority over other varnas and establishing birth as the basis of social privileges for few and deprivation for many. Shambuka relates to Treta, Eklabya and Karna to Dwapar. The relevance of these deprivations lies in the fact that they have not remained the incidents of the past. They show the trailor of horror shows of the continuing phenomenon uptill now, though in a changed form and Rohith Vemula's tragic end is the obvious example in the present day Kaliyuga. The social mindset, mores, psychological bankruptcy of superiority-inferiority complex have stood with the same vigour.. These historical incidents of persecution and deprivation how merit has been casualty, fair competition has not been encouraged (rather has been discouraged) and talented persons have been persecuted for none of their fault but due to the accident of life of taking birth in a despised Varna /caste and how individual worth and initiatives have been killed. The net result being that Eklabyas are frightened to excel due to social persecution and Arjunas being assured of World Championship without challenge. The tradition of liberal education spread by Augustyas became dormant and the narrow status-quoist tradition of Dronacharyas and Bhishmas had been flourishing and are still flourishing.[34] We have refused to take lesson from our history of failures.[35] Modern Dronacharyas are not allotting research guides to Dalit students for years, are depriving lab facilities to research scholars of this community and are grooming upper castes favourites to excel in life.

Shambuka

Shambuka[36] is symptom of socially conceited mind of elites even in the era of the best administered Ramarajya. *Shambuka* was a Shudra pupil of liberal teacher seer Augustya. Recognising his talent he educated him and Shambuka excelled all the brilliant scholars of secluded education by Rishis who did not allow Shudras to study. His merit and excellent versality could not be tolerated by the protector of Dharma, as understood, adhered and propagated by them.[37] They hatched a conspiracy that the young son of a Rishi, named Kalmanish died of snake biting and snake was nobody else than Veda Itself who told him in dream that he had bitten the son of the Rishi because he was very much annoyed due to the unacceptable and prohibited deed of one Shudra. There are two versions. One is that the Rishi Kalmanish charged Rama that his son died because the King had committed some sin. Due to that the normal rule that son would not die before father was violated. Narada, the legendary sage roaming around the world, narrated that the cause of death of Rishi's son was the practice of penances by a Shudra and the boy would survive if that Shudra was killed. Rama went on tour searching that Shudra flying in his chariot and found the ascetic doing austerities. Shudra Shambuka, as part of his austerities, was keeping his head below and legs upside. On inquiry Shambuka answered, 'O, Rama, I was born of a Shudra combination and I am performing this rigorous penance in order to conquer the heaven with this body.'[38] Finding bad intention of Shambuka of trying to go heavens alive with body, Ram beheaded him. But, gave him salvation (Moksha). The second version is that Shambuka was well versed in Vedas and as pupil of Augustya had silenced all Brahmin Rishis in Shastrartha. Earlier Rishis commended his excellent knowledge and oratory. But coming to know his Varna, all Rishis became furious and Augustya escaped with him guessing dangerous intention of angered Rishis. In mean while, the very young son of Kalmanish Rishi died of snake biting and Rishis constructed the story of Veda biting the boy because Veda was very much perturbed by Shudra uttering Vedas and the boy could regain life if Shudra ascetic was killed.[39]

The story is so conscience pricking, irrational and unlike deed of virtuous and righteous Rama that some scholars like Purushottam Chandra Jain[40] and John Brokington[41] write that the story of Shambuka is of late origin" and it may be interpolation in Valmiki Ramayan. The unusual incident is such that it has posed problem for Hindu writers themselves. Bhavabhuti (Seventh Century) is uncomfortable with the story in his *Uttar Rama Charita*[42] while Kalidasa (Fourth Century) mentions Shambuka episode without any comment in his *Raghuvansam.*

On the other hand, Southern scholars depict the incidence of Shambuka beheading by Rama as an instance of injustice to Shambuka for his birth as Shudra. Dravidian movement found it as an attempt to reinstate apartheid varna system and E.V. Ramaswami used the incident to deny Rama's position as benevolent King.[43]

Some later authors try to justify that Shambuka beheading by Rama as he carried out his duty as King by punishing Shambuka and simultaneously protecting Shambuka, as a pious and devout sage, from persecution.[44]

A third view is expressed by Dr B.R. Ambedkar.[45] He points out that the incident of Shambuka demonstrates the unsustainability of the Varna system and extent to which its existence depended on the harsh punishment of those who sought to transgress it. So does Hari Shankar Prasad (a Ph.D. in Buddhism under Prof. J.W. de Jone of Australian National University). Citing Rajendra Prasad he observed:

"The puzzling question here is, R.P.[46] asks, "Why one fails to do a *Varnasharma* of his as we can see in the cases of Arjuna,

Yudhisthira, Duryodhana, Eklabya, and Shambuka? In this background, one is justified to say that the *Varnasharma* entails disutility of all moral teachings and formation of *Varnavyavastha* is a source of immoralities as we can see in the cases of *Eklabya, Karna and Shambuka*."[47]

Thus, Eklabya, Karna and Shambuka represent the fault line in *Swadharma*.[48] Swadharma is not only Varna-duty-centric (*Varnadharmika*) but also has inbuilt spontaneity (Sahaj) or naturalness (*Suabhavajala*[49]). That is message of Lord Krishna – *Guna Karma vibhashah*.[50] Shambuka story cannot be appreciated due to many obvious reasons. *First*, it is not based on rationality. God or any of his emissaries like Veda cannot think or do irrational. One thing is clear Vedas are next only to God – Judicious, Virtuous, justice loving. Had it been necessary for Veda to punish, He would have punished direct Shambuka and nobody else would have been preferred to be made via-media. *Second, if Rishis were virtuous why did they not put life in the body of the son of the Rishi with the power of their tapashya. Anyway, Shambooka beheading incident* defeats *swadharma* theory based on naturalness and *Gunakarma Vibhagashah*. As nobody listens Devapi, the son of a King, adopting priesthood, though his brother Shantanu remaining to Kshatriya fold or Vishwamitra, a Kshatriya having all virtues of a *Brahmarshi* being ever punished for breaking the *Varnasharma* (Kshatriyadharma) rule. Shambuka episode is nothing but a blot on Hinduism preaching omnipresence of God. It is nothing but hostile discrimination persecuting the incidence of birth in low caste. It is nothing but denial of virtuousness, righteousness and an attempt to excel in life by low caste and thereby a great national loss.

Eklabya

So is the story of Eklabya's gift of thumb to a completely underserving Guru who had never taught him archery. Eklabya was young prince of the Nishad (Bhila) Vyatraj Hiranyadhanus, the king of the outcastes in the kingdom of Magadha. He had keen interest in archery and approached with utmost desire to learn archery to Dronacharya, Kulguru of Hastinapur. He bluntly refused.[51] Balgangadhar Tilak, in Srimad Bhagvad Gita – Rahashya, 47 states he refused to train him because he did not belong to *Raj gharana*. Eklabya had resolute will to master archery. He made image of Dronacharya of clay and practiced self-training for many years treating that image as Guru. On the basis of self-acquired training, he became an archer of exceptional prowess. He excelled all the pupils of Dronacharya whom he had trained. It came to the surface when while going into forest with Guru Drona and other co-trainees, Arjuna saw a dog that was unable to bark due to an amasing construction of arrows in and all around his mouth. The construction was harmless to the dog, but prevented dog from barking. That was the height achievement of Eklabya in archery who did not like to be disturbed in practice by the barking of the dog. Drona was amased. But, looking into his promise given to Arjuna to make him the greatest archer of the world, Drona fell distressed. Coming to know that Eklabya had practiced before his statue, Drona asked Eklabya that he would have to prove true pupilship by paying **Gurudakshina** and as **Gurudakshina** he demanded right hand's thumb – the most valuable organ for archery. Eklabya cutoff the thumb and presented it to Drona. Whatever may be explanation, it was ungurulike.[52] The relationship between true guru and Shishya is that Shishya should be ready to pay everything to Guru, but Guru should also be ready not to accept anything (**Shishya Ko Aisa Chahiye Ki Guru Ko Sab Kuchh Deya; Guru Ko Aisa Chahiye Ki Shishya se Kuchh nahi Leya).** Not only this, Drona was not that sincere to Arjuna, as he did not teach Brahmashtra to Arjuna, though taught to his son-Ashwathama. Arjuna learned it from Indra. *Second*, it was beginning of two-fold damage to virtue/merit in India – Low born person horrified were discouraged to excel in some discipline according to their nature gifted genus and upper caste people believed in Guru's favouritism to keep/help them topped – no fair competition, no challenge![53]

Karna

The story of Karna is also example of Dronacharya and Parasuram's narrow-mindedness in imparting education and training. Karna became archer and a trained brave person on his own in spite of the refusal of Drona to teach him. He was second to none. That is reason why he was not allowed to take part in competition and when allowed in archery to throw *Shabdabhedi* arrow, a trick was played by Drona, though Bhisma Pitamah recognised as before the sound created by Dog, Karna had thrown his arrow on listening the sounds of Kraunch bird sitting on nearby tree and his arrow was found in her mouth.

He was not allowed to compete in Sawayambar of Draupadi. Karna had to get great humiliation of curse by Parshuram coming to know that he was not a Brahmin. Concealing his identity, Karna went to Parshuram[54] and acquired knowledge in Archery. One day Parshuram was sleeping keeping his head on the thigh (**Jangha**) of Karna. One big bee stung the thigh of Karna. With blood woozing from his wound Parshuram woke and seeing that Karna was unmoved and undisturbed in spite of the acute pain of bee stung, Parshuram got irritated. He asked who Karna was, as a Brahmin could not be that bearing and tolerant. Karna revealed his identity. Parshuram, became furious because had taken vow to teach only Brahmins, (he had taught archery to Bishma because he was son of Ganga). Purshuram cursed Karna to forget the all the knowledge required to weld the divine weapon *Brahmastra*.[55] But on appealing pleadings he limited the forgetfulness to when he needed most while fighting with an equal warrior, which led to the death of Karna.

All the above- Shambuka, Eklabya and Karna fell victim of the Hiduism appropriated by Brahminism whose cardinal principles emergd as follow:[56] (1) the graded inequality between the four varnas concentrated into entrenched castes; (2) complete disarmament of Shudras and untouchables; (3) complete prohibition of the education of Shudra and untouchables; (4) ban on the Shudras and untouchables on occupying places of power and authority; (5) ban on Shudras acquiring property; and (6) complete subjugation and servility of Shudras, untouchables and women.[57]

Cultural Discourse Between Dominant Castes and Dalit Perceptions

The accumulated impact of birth-based privilege and disprivilege has developed a divergent perception of Dalits.[58]

Table 2

Dominant Castes' Perception of Dalits	*Dalit Perception About Themselves*
Dirty-filthy fellows	Capable-But no opportunities
Thieves/Robbers	Hard-working
Cunning	Honest
Lazy-Kamchor	Assertive

(Contd.)

(Contd. Table)

Useless- Good for nothing	Straight forward/ less cunning
Glutton- Petu, khau	Culturally talented
Loose morals	Sensitive Emotional
Dishonest	Self- sacrificing
Quarrelsome-Disunity	Sagacious-good judgment
Ungrateful	Collective

Thus, an untouchable child is born with all disadvantages, disgrace, humiliation, discrimination, persecution and ill treatment to which the three chosen object of the present book are concerned who came in the society with worth- talent, intelligence and hard-working culture.

References

1. Julius Stone, Social Dimension of Law and Justice, Universal Law Publishing Co., (2009), p. 139.
2. Julius Stone, Social Dimension of Law and Justice, Universal Law Publishing Co., New Delhi, 2009, pp. 112-113.
3. Sanjeev Verma, "A dead sadhu, a live issue" The Indian Express,7.11.2016, p. 8.
4. C.F. Andrews, "Mahatma Gandhi: His Life & Ideas" Jaico Publishing House, 2006, p. 111.
5. Ronald M. Dworkin, 'Law's Empire', p. 384.
6. *Ibid*, p. 395.
7. *Ibid*., p. 388.
8. Justice D. P. Singh, Morality of Law, EBC, Lucknow, 2012, p. 40.
9. *Ibid*., p. 41.
10. Ashwamedhika parva 99.42.
11. Harold A. Gould, The "Hindu Caste System" quoted from the judgment of Justice Kulpip Singh in Indra Sawhney v. Union of India,1992 SCC(L&S)1 at p. 175.
12. The Complete Works of Vivekananda, Mayavati Memorial Lectures Edition, Vol. IV (1948), p. 305.
13. Selections From Swami Vivekananda, Advaita Ashram, Mayavati, Humalaya, (1944), pp. 99-100.
14. Selections from Swami Vivekananda, Adwait Ashram, 1944.
15. Abraham Eraly, Gem in the Lotus: The Seeding of Indian Civilisation (Viking, 2000) p. 115.
16. Vanaparva180.23
17. Vanaparva 180.25

18. Vanaparva 180.26
19. Vanaparva 313.108
20. Vanaparva 318.89
21. Shukraniti I. 1.39.
22. Shukraniti I. 1.38 Anushasanaparva: Tryah purve shudramulah sarve karmakarah smritah.
23. Abraham Early, The First Spring : The Golden Age of India, Penguin Books, 2011, p. 217.
24. Harprasad Shastri, Buddhist Studies, Chapter XXXIV, p. 820.
25. As K.P. Jaiswal in his Tagore Law Lecture observes, .Manusmriti written by Svayambhu Manu during the Vedic period was changed in 2nd century B.C. by Sumati on the initiative of Pushyamitra.
26. Quoted from M.A. Bagulia, Social Class, Anmol Publications Pvt. Ltd., New-Delhi, 2007, p. 87.
27. Ibid. p. 88.
28. Quoted in Zelliot, Eleanor, 'Dr Ambedkar and the Mahar Movement.' Ph.D. dissertation,University of Pensylvania.
29. Dhananjay Keer, Mahatma Jotirao Phooley-Father of Indian Social Revolution, Bombay Popular Prakashan, second edition,1974, p. 52.
30. Report of the Director of Education for the year 1857-1858, pp.10-11.
31. Mitchell, the Rev. Murray, The Recollections of My Missioary Life pp. 314-315.
32. Report of the Director of Education for the year 1857-58, pp. 315-316.
33. Selections from Swami Vivekananda, Advaita Ashrama, Mayavati, Himalaya, 1994, p. 513.
34. Dr Lohia used to distinguish between self-centred Bashisthiya-mind and Augustya liberal mind preferring latter for liberal education for all without discrimination.
35. There is a experience based adage, "failures are the pillars of success".
36. The Story of Shambuka appears in Valmiki Ramayana, Book 7; Adhyatma Ramayana, Uttrakhang sargas, 73-76.
37. Bhagwan Singh, Apane Apane Ram (a novel).
38. There is another story of Trishanku who wished to go to Heaven alive and on his strong request Rishi Vishwamitra sent him upward with the force of Mantras. But Trishanku could not enter Heaven as according to mythical rule nobody can enter Heaven without death and Trishanku is hanging in air-Indra not allowing to enter Heaven and Vishwamitra not allowing to come down. If Shambuka was following the prohibited path of Trishanku on his own (not by derivative force from Vishwamitra) he could be

punished by Indra. Nobody hears that Vishwamitra was ever punished for violation of the religious rule or for that reason anybody else was bitten by Veda for that.

39. *Ibid.*
40. Purshottam Chandra Jain, Labour in Ancient India, p. 16.
41. http://www.amazon.com/Rama-Steadfast-Ramayan-Penguin - Classics/dp/014044744X.
42. David Shulman, "Bhavabhuti on cruelty and compassion" in Questioning. Ramayanas : A South Asian Tradition (ed.) by Paula Richman, University of California Press, 2001, ISBN 0-520-22074-9, pp. 49-82.
43. Counter Currents, "Periyar's movement (http://www.counter currents.org/dalit_periar 280603.htm" (June, 28, 2003).
44. Motiramji Sastri, Ramayan (in Gujrati) Ahmedabad, 1961.
45. B.R. Ambedkar, Annihilation of Caste with a Reply to Mahatma Gandhi (http : //wear.alra.net/mainpile 2.phh. Documents/77/) (1936).
46. Rajendra Prasad, Karma, Causation and Retributive Morality : Conceptual Essays in Ethics and Metaethics, Delhi, Indian Council of Philosophical Research, 1989.
47. Harishankar Prasad, The Centrality of Ethics in Buddhism - Exploratory Essays, Motilal Banarasidass Publishers Pvt. Ltd. Delhi (2007) ISBN : 978-81-208-3239-8, p. 138.
48. Motiramji Sastri, Ramayan (in Gujrati) Ahmedabad, 1961. B.R. Ambedkar, Annihilation of Caste with A Reply to Mahatma Gandhi (http : //wear.alra.net/mainpile 2.phh. Documents/77/) (1936).
49. Rajendra Prasad, Karma, Causation and Retributive Morality : Conceptual Essays in Ethics and Metaethics, Delhi, Indian Council of Philosophical Research, 1989.
50. " Though another religion may be easy of observance, and one's own Action according to the four-class arrangement may be viguna (that is faulty), yet it is more proper; when a person is performing his own inherently natural duty (that is, duty which has been ordained for him according to the four-class-arrangement), based on natural inherent qualities) he does not thereby incur any sin.
51. Eklavya : A Powerful Archer and Charioteer, Retrieved 19 Nov. 2013; http:/.Vedabase.net/sb/4/14/44/en
52. The befitting answer would have been to make Eklabya of day and give the thumb of that clay statute.
53. By arranging the cutting of thumb-through reminding Drona of his words to make Arjuna best Archer, Arjuna demeaned himself. Eklabya gained sublimity. Arjuna forgot that the best way to become best is not others to drag down but to rise himself to reach

the height. Had he practiced more and more he could achieve as he had proved in aiming the eye of bird in training period and matsyabhedan at the time the Swayambar of Draupadi. But chose short cut inappreciable way and Guru Drona instead arousing confidence in Arjuna became instrumental with permanent blot on him.

56. What Congress and Gandhi Have Done For Untouchables, para 47, Dr Babasaheb Ambedkar Writings and Speeches, Volume 9, Maharashtra Government Publication. Website dedicated to the story of Karna
57. *ibid.*
58. Prakash, Louis, Political Sociology of Dalit Assertion, Gyan Publishing House, New Delhi, 2003 10.79

PART-II

DR AMBEDKAR AND HIS ACHIEVEMENTS

Columbia University (USA) conferred the Honorary Degree of LL.D. in its Bi-Centenial Celebration Special Convocation held in New York - 1952

Pt. Nehru's First Cabinet: Dr Ambedkar, Minister of Law, First From the Right.

3

A Brief Sketch of the Thorny Early Days Experiences of Dr Ambedkar

Dr Ambedkar was born of mother Bhimabai and father Ramji Sakpal. He was fourteenth issue of his parent. He was born in an untouchable Mahar family with British Army tradition. His grandfather Maloji Sakpal had joined British Army and retired as Havaldar. His father Ramji Sakpal was the Headmaster at the Army School in Mhow Cantoment near Indore. The date of birth in the primary school at Dapoli in Ratnagiri district of Maharashtra shows April 14, 1891. The exact date of birth is not clear. As per his version itself he was born at midnight amidst stars thought to be inauspicious.[1] Since, an astrologer had predicted the death of his mother very soon he was hated by his brothers and sisters. But he was blue eye boy of his mother. Since as an infant he was bonny and playful his mother poured affection on him due to his loveliness as well as the fact of his being the youngest one. It is common saying that the youngest issue is most darling to parent. The proud mother Bhimabai named him after her. After two years of the birth of Dr Ambedkar his father Ramji Sakpal retired from Military service on monthly pension of Rs 50. He left Mhow and settled along his family at his ancestoral village Dapoli. In 1896, Dr Ambedkar was admitted to the primary school at Dapoli. But very soon he was shifted to Satara where his father managed to secure a job in the military office. In school register his surname was as Ambavadekar basing on ancestoral village. It was changed as Ambedkar by a school teacher at Satara whose name was also Ambedkar and who liked him most. But his experience at school was not happy at all. His first name Bhimrao was also subject of humiliation by his classmates, peon and others. He was subjected to discrimination everywhere. Speaking of his disgraceful and disgusted experience at school Dr Ambedkar himself recalled:

"I knew that in the school I could not sit in the midst of my classmates according to my rank. I used to sit in corner by myself. I knew that in the school I was to have a separate piece of gunny cloth for myself to squat on in the classroom and the servant employed to clean the school would not touch the gunny cloth used by me. I was required to carry the gunny cloth home in the evening and bring it back the next day. While at the school I knew that children of the touchable classes, when they felt thirsty, could go out to the water tap, open it and quench the thirst. All they needed was the permission of the teacher. But my position was different. I could not touch the tap and unless it is opened by a touchable person, it was not possible for me to quench my thirst. In my case, the permission of the teacher was not enough. The presence of the school peon was necessary, for he was the only person whom the class teacher could ask to open the tap for me."[2] One can easily imagine the child psychology on inhumanly discriminatory treatment experienced during the school hours in its premises. No wonder Dr Ambedkar got broken. He did "hamal" work (act as coolie) for a day at Satara station. Coming to know his aunt (his father' sister) who was looking after him after the death of his mother at his age of six years only, was upset but in words of Dr Ambedkar himself," My aunt terribly felt humiliated over my conduct, but she loved me so much that she had no heart to punish me."[3] Added to fuel of school unhappy experience came the fire the treatment of his step mother. There is a Chinese adage that, 'even a step mother of China clay is dangerous.'[4] There is also a colloquial saying, 'the son of another wife of husband is more despicable even than his wife itself. Disgusted Dr Ambedkar planned to go to Bombay for getting some job in mill.' But having no money he could not. To accomplish his plan he planned to remove the purse of his aunt during night which she always kept tucked at the waist. He repeatedly failed thrice. On his success on fourth night, to his utter surprise and despair, he found only half an anna in it. Had he been successful in getting what would have occurred in his life it can only be guessed.

Despairs make the man resolute. There is an Urdu couplet," So much distresses made the living easy, (**Mushkilen Etani "Parin Ki Jeena Asan Ho Gaya).**So happened with Dr Ambedkar. He resolved: I must give up my truant habits, that I must study hard and get through my examinations, so that I could start earning my livelihood and thus become independent of my father." The providence always helps the resolute and courageous persons **(Himmte Marade Madade Khuda).** Dr Ambedkar's devotion, attentiveness and diligence were noticed by his teachers who advised his father to extend full support so may his son's extraordinary and exceptional devotion bring something extraordinary. His father did his best to provide for book requirements and other necessities even by borrowing from his daughters.

Dr Ambedkar inherited certain virtues from his family traditions. Like progeny of Military personnel forefathers he was brave - brave son of brave father - from the very beginning. With the family tradition of reading Ramayana and Geeta and enchanting 'Abhanga' of the great Saints and couplets of Saint Kabir and his mother's instruction to address the strangers with respect made him to full of humility- Vinayasheel.

In spite of the humility Dr Ambedkar could not receive return in the same coin from the society in which he had to live. He was put between Scylla of dire poverty compelling to attend classes wearing bare loincloth and charibdis of getting no water to drink. In school for Maratha lady peon even his satchel was untouchable. The ill treatment at school was diluted by the family atmosphere of devotion to great saint-poets like Moropant, Mukteshwar and Tukaram and reciting of Ramayana and Mahabharata. The family atmosphere developed Dr Ambedkar's keen interest in religious and theological discussions. After morning Puja (worship of deities) everyday his father would Dr Ambedkar: "Bhiva (a name given by his mother out of extreme love and affection in the place Bhima), you are going to learn a lot. You are going to be a great and learned man. You are going to get great fame and make the name of your family shine in the world."[5] He learned proficiency in English by his father who had been a teacher in the Army school.

There is proverbial saying, "extremity of pain becomes cure- **Dard Ka Had Se Gujar Jana Dava Hota Hai**." In the Indian caste-ridden society, no barber would cut hair of Mahars and no washerman would clean their clothes. Partly due to the curse of untouchability and partly due to financial inability to pay for such services, Dr Ambedkar and his brothers and sisters became self reliant. His sister used to cut their hair and clean their clothes.

Dr Ambedkar had faced many burnt of belonging to the untouchable community. He had very pinching experience of station master at Masur after knowing the caste of him and sons of his sister need of a cart to go to his father's place at Goregaon approaching the night, none of the cart men agreeing to lent cart out of fear of suffering pollution and one agreeing on double fare on condition that he would not drive, finding no water to take meal and remaining without food with hunger burning stomach throughout the night. In his own words, "I was a boy of nine when it happened. But it left an indelible impression on my mind. I could not forget how the attitude of the station master changed when he discovered that we were Mahars. I could not forget how we were denied even drinking water because we were untouchables."[6]

With bad experience at the local school his father shifted with family to Bombay where in better school and enlightened teachers, Dr Ambedkar felt relieved of facing frequent humiliation. But treatment from the classmates did not change. One day on being asked by his class teacher to solve an example on blackboard while he rose to go the blackboard his classmates protested that his proximity to the blackboard would pollute their tiffins kept behind the blackboard. To quote his biographer Janak Singh, "Some of boys rushed to remove their tiffin boxes before Ambedkar could reach there. The clanging sound of the metallic tiffin-boxes pierced Ambedkar's heart and although the incident was over soon, it left the lasting wound on his mind, which could not be healed even when he was hailed as a great leader."[7]

There is limit of everything. On the extremely deep-rooted prejudicial expression of a teacher that Dr Ambedkar was an untouchable, therefore, he was wasting his time in school education as it would lead him nowhere, though always polite and deferential to teachers, he reacted, "mind your business". Sanskrit teachers did not allow him and his brother to sit in their class as in their view untouchables could not learn Shastras. Dr Ambedkar and his brother had no option but choose Persian as the second language.

In graduation at Elphinstone College, Bombay he had the distinction of being first untouchable to reach the portal of that great institution. Dr Ambedkar's dedication to academic pursuits had deeply impressed his Persian and English teachers-Mr. Irani and Professor Muller. But, the fact of his being untouchable did not spare of his humiliation of not being served tea or water in the college canteen.

In general, untouchables met with hostile discrimination in villages. Observant Dr Ambedkar discovered there was clear division into the Touchables and Untouchables. The former lived inside the village and the latter outside the village. The former could live in north, east and western directions but the latter could live only in the south of the village. Dr Ambedkar was shocked to learn that it was offence for untouchables to live in vicinity of Touchables or in directions other than south; or acquisition of wealth- land, cattles and house with tiled-roof; or wearing of clean clothes, shoes, wrist watch and gold ornaments; sitting on chairs, riding on horse and palaquin. Not only this, somewhere wages to untouchables were given in kind of Gobaraha-corn contained in dung of bullocks used for crushing wheat crops.

What to say of experiencing hostility from caste persons, as student or teacher or even peon, the experience of Dr Ambedkar in service after gaining higher education-M.A., Ph.D., was not different. As bond of scholarship required he joined as Military Secretary to the Maharaja Sayajirao Gaekwad of Baroda. He experienced very bad and disgustful treatment- no drinking water was available to him in office, subordinates maintained distance from him, and even peon threw files and paper on his desk from a distance. As Dr Ambedkar later recalled, "As a man in the Accountant General's office at Baroda, papers had to be flung at me instead of handed to me, and carpet had to be rolled back lest the higher castes stood on the same material as I stood on". Not only this no one was willing to give accommodation including non-Hindus to him. He took shelter in a Parsi Inn telling to be a Hindu. On instigation of caste–Hindus even a group of Parsis (which did not suffer the vice of casteism) wielding lathis descended on the Inn and queried who he was. On reply that he was a Hindu, they shouted: "You arrant knave, you are despicable Untouchable we know." He was ordered to vacate the room immediately. Neither any Hindu nor any Muslim agreed to give him room to stay. Even Dewan's instruction was of no avail and he expressed his helplessness to help him in any way. In such a hostile situation Dr Ambedkar was left with no option but to resign and return back to Bombay. After serving only for three months (August, 21 to November) he left the job and returned to Bombay.

His well wisher Keluskar informed the Maharaja about the inhumanly treatment meted to Dr Ambedkar at Baroda and also made efforts to solve the accommodation problem by requesting a Professor at Baroda to accommodate Dr Ambedkar in his flat. He agreed to accommodate as a paying guest. But due to vehement opposition of the Professor's wife, a note of refusal was served on Dr Ambedkar on his arrival at the station itself. Disgusted Dr Ambekar returned from Baroda to Bombay.

The curse of the caste did not spare him in Bombay too. Whereever he tried for job, he was straightway rejected because of his caste. For job givers caste mattered most and not the merit and worth. Not only this, while trying to find means to make a living for his growing family, he started the job of a private tuition. He tried as an accountant and established an investment consulting business. But his caste came in the way. Coming to know that he was an untouchable client stopped coming to him. One can easily guess the state of the mind of a person treated very courteously abroad but treated most treacherously in his own country. He was compelled by circumstances to do some odd works.

After the distress of one year, he heard of a vacancy for the post a professor at Sydenham College of Commerce and Economics in Bombay. Having the bad experiences of rejection everywhere because of his caste, he did not leave it to chance and got in touch with his earlier acquaintances at London seeking recommendation letter. As a result caste did not come in his, wasy merit prevailed and he was appointed as Professor of Political Economics in the Sydenham College of Commerce and Economics, Bombay. Good days came. He drew the salary of Rs 450 per month. He was very popular teacher among the students. But, the caste mindset incurability continued among the teachers. He was treated as Pariah by his colleague Hindu Professors who did not allow him to drink water from the water pot (Jug) kept in the Professors' common room.

The school days experiences- both as a student and a teacher after having foreign degrees with distinction, of deprivation of minimum human dignity, deprivation, discrimination and prejudiced hostile cruel treatment did not bring in him depression or inferiority of any kind, rather they sharpened his mind to know why such treatment? He also begun to think that he was not alone who was facing the music of the caste-ridden hierarchical society. The whole of his community brethren were facing the same experiences. The conscience-pricking inflictions made him resolute and firm to root out the evil causes and fight for emancipation of the untouchables. For this he chose the right path of education.

References

1. This the view was expressed by Dr Ambedkar during a talk on October 28,1954 on the eve of his Diamond Jubilee celebrations held at Purandare's Stadium in Naigon.
2. Ambedkar's Writings and Speeches published by by Maharashtra Government,1990).
3. *Ibid.*
4. Quoted from Justice M.N. Vekatachaliah, A TRIBUTE to Justice K. Ramaswamy, Ceaseless and Relentless Journey, E.B.C., Lucknow, 2008, p. XI .
5. Quoted from Janak Singh, 'Dr B.R. Ambedkar- The Messiah of Downtrodden' Kalpaz Publications, 2010, p. 32.
6. *Ibid.* p. 38.
7. *Ibid.* pp. 38-39.

4

Academic Achievements, Writings and Posts held by Dr Ambedkar

Adversities did not detract Dr Ambedkar from the path of learning. His resolute conviction, urge for learning, hard labour, mission to do something special, got supportive recognition. Amidst intolerable humiliations from the caste students, narrow-minded teachers and even peons undaunted Ambedkar concentrated on study like aiming of the eye of bird by Arjuna or his vow - neither to bow nor run away (*Na Dainyam Na Cha Palayanam*). His father gave full support and finding it difficult to support the education of his two sons withdrew the elder son from college. His elder brother too began to contribute towards the study of Dr Ambedkar. He passed his Matriculation Examination from prestigious Elinphinstone High School in 1907. It created a history as no untouchable had ever completed Matriculation from that prestigious institution. His score was 282 out of 750. Though the marks were not very impressive, but it was a great achievement for the untouchable community which celebrated this occasion with great enthusiasm. His Matriculation success brought him in touch with many good persons and their company. He was honoured under the Presidentship of Mr S.K. Bole, a well known social reformer and another social reformer, Marathi writer of repute and teacher in Wilson High School, Mr Krishanji Arjun Keluskar attended it. The latter's meeting with Ambedkar proved to be a boon for him. Mr Kesulkar being impressed by him lent books and presented a copy of Life of Gautam Buddha authored by him which immensely impressed Dr Ambedkar in his later life. In graduation, after completing Intermediate anyhow, Dr Ambedkar again faced financial crunch and his father expressed his inability to support further study. In time of financial lurch, Mr. Keluskar came forward met Sayaji Gaekwad of Baroda, apprised him of adverse situation in which Dr Ambedkar was put. Benevolent king after being satisfied on interview as to the genuineness of Dr Ambedkar's need immediately sanctioned Rs 25 per month for him.

Dr Ambedkar completed his B.A. in 1912 with English, Politics, Economics and Persian. After graduation Dr Ambedkar joined a job in the state of Baroda, but very soon had to return to Bombay to look after his ailing father who did not survive and left for heavenly abode on Feb. 2, 1913 leaving Dr Ambedkar and his family in grief. He was in a fix what to do when even the support of father was gone. The night of grief ended with new rays of hopes.

On information and advice of his well wisher Mr Keluskar, Dr Ambedkar met Sayaji Rao Gaekwad of Baroda who informed about his proposal to send few students to New York for higher studies. He participated in interview for that purpose. He was selected and scholarship was awarded to him. In 1913, he went to New York as a Gaekwad scholar and joined the famous Columbia University. In U.S.A Dr Ambedkar found altogether different social atmosphere and breathed in the fresh air of equality. At Columbia he opted for Political Science, Moral Philosophy, Anthropology and Economics as subjects of his study. He had very congenial academic atmosphere there and was very much influenced by great scholarly teacher like Professor Edwin R.A. Seligman. Dr Ambedkar was so much impressed by the knowledge and impressive teaching of Prof. Seligan that he tried to attend all classes taught by him on the campus. He completed his M.A. degree in 1915. He was awarded the degree of Master of Arts on June 2, 1915 for his thesis on "Ancient Indian Commerce".

Next year in 1916 he submitted his thesis "National Dividend for India: A Historic and Analytical Study" for the award of Ph.D. degree which was accepted and awarded by the Columbia University. Later it was published under title 'The Evolution of Provincial Finance in British India.' It was a scholarly piece of publication. It was found to be indispensable for Indian Legislators that they used it as a reference book.[1]

Since he was awarded Ph.D. Degree before the stipulated time, Dr Ambedkar went to the London School of Economics and Gray's Inn in U.K. but had to return to Baroda on call from Dewan of the state and as per terms of the bond for scholarship joined a promising job. As the social ostracism by caste Hindus prevailed, he could not continue the job. But, determinant Dr Ambedkar did not become nervous and decided to pursue his studies which he had left at the London School of Economics and Gray's Inn. On the basis of some money saved by him as a Professor of Political Economy in Sydenham College and financial assistance from Chhatrapati Sahuji Maharaj of Kolhapur state and his friend Naval Bathena he sailed for London. In the case of inability to purchase books, he devoted maximum time in the library. He got D.Sc. in Economics from the London School of Economics on the thesis "Problem of the Rupee". He also received Bar-at-Law from Gray's Inn in 1922. While his stay in Europe, in 1923 he also studied Economics for sometime at the University of Bonn, Germany.

Writings of Dr B.R. Ambedkar

Dr Ambedkar was a prolific writer. His writings cover a wide range of areas of public concern- social problems, finance, formation of states, minorities, federal problem, religion etc. Some of his well known writings are given below.Though all writings have distinct marks, some of them are very useful for the exposure of embedded problems of the Hindu hierarchical and graded social structures, therefore, socially important books have been given a little of elaboration.

Castes in India (1917)

Originally it was a paper presented at an Anthropology Seminar organised by Dr A.A Goldenweizer Columbia University on 9th May 1916. Dr Ambedkar subsequently published it in 'Indian Antiquity' Vol. XLI (May 1917). Dr Ambedkar made clear that, 'caste in India means an artificial chopping off of the population into fixed and definite units, each one prevented from fusing into another through custom of endogamy. He discussed how superposition of endogamy on exogamy created caste and how the problem of surplus man (widower) and surplus woman (widow) was solved by custom of Sati, enforced widowhood and child marriage. In this work Dr Ambedkar concluded that endogamy is the only characteristic of caste and caste is an Enclosed Class. He narrated how the Hindu society composed of different classes – Brahmin, the priestly class, the Kshatiyas, the military class, the Vaishya, the merchant class, and, Shudra, the artisan or the menial class, with possibility of promotion and change of class on worth lost the open door character of the class system was converted into self-enclosed units called castes. That is to say, some closed the door: others found closed against them. Dr Ambedkar's indomitable conclusions are: (1) in spite of composite make-up of the Hindu population , there is deep cultural unity ; (2) that caste is a parceling bits of a larger cultural unit; (3) that there was one caste to start with; and 4) that classes have become Castes through imitation and excommunication.

(2) Small Holdings in India and their Remedies (1917).

(3) The Problem of the Rupee (1923).
In addition to narrating the problem of Rupees, Dr Ambedkar suggested the change in the Indian currency every 10 years so as to end the menace of hoarding of rupees and checking inflation.

(4) The Evolution of the Provincial Finance in British India (1925).

(5) Annihilation of Caste (1938).

Annihilation of Caste is a publication of his undelivered Address prepared for Presidential speech before the annual Conferene of **Jat- Pat- Todak Manal,** Lahore to be held in the month of April 1936. Coming to know the content of the speech the organisers cancelled the Conference. It was so well written with full of logic, evidences and convincing reasons that even the so called liberal Hindus could not swallow. The book swears to speak truth as truth with Lord Buddha's words- "Know Truth as Truth and Untruth as Untruth." His thesis, as Dhananjay Keer observes, "was logic on fire, pinching and pungent, piercing and fiery, provocative and explosive. It was to the minds of the caste Hindu leaders what silver nitrate is to a gangrene," It was so important that a big personality, no less than Mahatma Gandhi joined the issue and published review of the book in the "Harijan" dated July 11, and July 18, 1936. Mahatma Gandhi's review has two significant dimensions. The first dimension is the unconditional recognition of Dr Ambedkar's eminent position as indisputable scholar. He observed: "The committee appears to have deprived the public of an opportunity of listening to the original views of a man, who has carved out for himself a unique position in society. Whatever label he wears in future, Dr Ambedkar is not the man to allow himself to be forgotten. The second dimension of his review is his unsuccessful attempt to satisfy Dr Ambedkar about the interpretation of Hindu scriptures. In this book Dr Ambedkar exposes that caste is the root cause of all social evils: it has ruined the Hindus; its root Varnavyavastha has degraded the masses by denying them opportunity to acquire knowledge and therefore, the Hindu society can be relieved of all evils only by annihilation of caste and restructuring it on the principles of Liberty, Equality and Fraternity.

(6) Federation versus Freedom (1939).
(7) Mr. Gandhi and the Emancipation of the Untouchables (1943).
(8) Ranade, Gandhi and Jinnah (1943).
(9) Thoughts on Pakistan (1945).
(10) What Congress and Gandhi Have Done to Untouchables (1945).
(11) Communal Deadlock and a Way to solve it (1945).
(12) Who Were Shudras? (1946).
(13) Pakistan or Partition of India (1948).
(14) States and Minorities (1947).
(15) History of Currency and Banking (1947).
(16) The Untouchables (1948).
(17) Maharashtra as a Linguistic State (1948).
(18) Rise and Fall of Hindu Women (1948).
(19) Gospel of Buddhism (1952).
(20) Thoughts on Linguistic States (1955).

The work is the original contribution of Dr Ambedkar about the problems of the reorganisation of the Indian States. His suggestions to bifurcate or trifurcate certain existing state territories at that time had real significance. Sooner or later his suggestions became reality in the case of U.P., Bihar, Madhya Pradesh etc.

(21) The Buddha and His Dhamma (1957).
(22) Some books in pipe-line- Dr Ambedkar was a prolific writer on many challenging issues, more particularly in relation to the Hindu religious beliefs. He could not complete and publish books on Riddle of Rama and Krishna; Riddle of Hinduism; Riddle of Women etc.

In addition to the books, Dr Ambedkar contributed articles on many burning issues of the common concern. Some of his articles are mentioned below:

(1) Caste in India: Their Mechanism, Genesis and Development (1917).
(2) Independent Labour Party-Constitution and Rules (1939).
(3) What Ails the World Today (1943).
(4) Labour and Parliamentary Democracy (1943).
(5) Buddha and Future of His Religion (1951).
(6) Future of Parliamentary Democracy (1951).
(7) Essential Condition of President for the Successful Working of Democracy (1951).
(8) Linguistic States: Need for Checks and Balances (1954).
(9) My Personal Philosophy (1956).

Administrative and Political Journey of Dr Ambedkar

Dr Ambedkar had multifaceted personality and held different positions ranging from academia- to political- to religious status. An account of posts held by him between 1917 and 1956 is given below:

Table 3
Reference

S. No.	*Positions*	*Year*
	Military Secretary, Baroda State	1917
	Professor of Political Economy	1918
	Member of Legislative Council,	1926
	Province of Bombay	1928
	Member, Simon Commission, Bombay	1930
	Representative, Round Table Conference, London	1932
	Member Constitution Committee for India (Constituted by British Government)	1935
	Principal Law College, Bombay	1937
	Member of Legislative Assembly, Province of Bombay	1942
	Labour Minister, British Cabinet, India	1946
	Member Constituent Assembly of India	1947
	Law Minister, Nehru Cabinet (after Independence)	1947
	Chairman, Constitution of India Drafting Committee	1950

S. No.	*Positions*	*Year*
	Representative, World Buddhist Conference,	1952
	Member, Rajya Sabha (as Representative of Bombay)	1954
	Representative, World Buddhist Conference, Rangoon Representative, World Buddhist Conference, Kathmandu	1956

1. Kuber, W.N., B. R. Ambedkar, Publication Division, Government of India, 1978, p. 15.

5

Makers of Dr B. R. Ambedkar

Dr Ambedkar grew a tall Banyan tree giving sheltering shadow to the depressed, suppressed, persecuted, disprivileged, humiliated and compelled to lead the life of indignity. He continued his struggle for giving dignified life to the women and working classes. He struggled throughout his life for humanism, nationalism, patriotism and missionary zeal to work for the national cause by creative reconciliation to serve the cause of all segments of the society through drafting the most comprehensive social document (The Constitution of India) with splendid compromises. As the tiny seed is sown by a gardener, is watered and looked after it by him and one day it becomes a big /mighty tree, likewise Dr Ambedkar's life was shaped by many human-hearted loving and inspiring persons.

It is said that a child learns the first lesson of citizenship in the laps of the mother and care of the father. In spite of his misfortune to be born in Mahar caste, Dr Ambedkar was fortunate enough to have loving religious minded mother-Bhimabai and caring father like Ramji Sakpal. From loving mother he learnt the first lesson of humility to respect others and used to call the postman 'Mamaji' out of respect. Though firm he avoided rudeness in his behaviour. Humility gave return in good coins. His teachers, especially abroad loved, helped and inspired him in the enterprise of learning more and more. What his father had done special to him was sowing the seed of distinction in him. When his mother got angry with him due to his notorious activities and intend to slap him, his father would admonish her saying, "Bhiva's (the name used by his mother out of too much affection) ears and stomach are like our god Ganapati's. How fortunate he is can be seen from the lines on his palms. You should be happy that he is your son. He is going to be a great and famous man. You should be tolerant of his mischiefs which are like Lord Krishna's when he was a boy. You have no business to be harsh to him." His father extended his full care and encouraged him to reach the Himalayan height of name and fame extending his blessing after everyday family prayer. He used to shower blessings: "Bhiva, you are going to learn a lot. You are going to be a great and learned man. You are going to get great fame and make the name of your family shine in the world." In spite of financial crunch he arranged for learning of Dr Ambedkar. His young mind may not develop a sense of inferiority complex due to the indignity at the hands of caste Hindu classmates, teachers and even peons in the school/ college, his father made all efforts to divert his mind towards sublimity of enchanting Ramayana, Mahabharata and Abhangas of great Saints. His father also changed his school from his native village to Satara and then to Bombay.

Dr.Ambekar, after the death of his mother, when he was six years old, was put under the guardianship of his paternal aunt, the sister of his father. Despite her disability she made every effort so may the boy under her care should not feel that his mother was not there to take care of him lovingly. She poured all her affection on him and ignored even his unapprovable acts which hurt her. Dr Ambedkar himself has narrated his experiences with her. When meeting too much humiliations of discriminatory conducts at the hands of his schoolmates as well as teachers he had developed aversion for study and decided to leave it and had worked as a coolie at Satara railway station, on knowing that she became very sad. Her state of mind has been painted by Dr Ambedkar in these words, "My aunt (he later recalled) terribly felt humiliated over my conduct, but she loved me so much that she had no heart to punish me."[1]

There is a saying, "there is always a woman behind the success of a man." Dr Ambedkar had married twice- once in due course of life and the other out of the necessity of survival. Both were most caring leaving him completely free to pursue his ambitious plan of acquiring knowledge and high degrees and completing his books on different but challenging issue. He was married Rami, later renamed as Ramabai, the daughter of her then deceased father Bhiku Walangkar, a porter. The marriage took place when Dr Ambedkar was seventeen and she was nine years old. The marriage was solemnised in the open shed of a fish market of Byculla Market, Bombay, when all the shops had been closed. There was utter poverty in the family. Ramabai was also a child of nine years old. But she never claimed her marital rights and took all the responsibilities to run the family leaving Dr Ambedkar fully free to pursue his studies in the country and abroad. Within limited financial arrangements she pulled on the cart of family, when necessary by selling her ornaments. Behind the successful completion of Dr Ambedkar's studies her contribution cannot be ignored. She lived in utter poverty, lost her two sons who left her due to the lack of proper medical treatment was completely broken after the death of the younger son and herself died in 1935 after long illness, but never murumurred with any grudge.

Dr Ambedkar had bet his health in completion of drafting the Constitution and by 1948 he had invited diabetes, gout, arthritis and blood pressure. He was under treatment by Dr Malvankar. Doctor had advised him the company of a caring and good cook. At this juncture of the necessity of care Dr Sharda Kabir came in his contact in the Bombay Nursing Home itself where Dr Ambedkar was under treatment of Doctor Malvankar and Dr Sharda Kabir was also doctor serving in Nursing Home under Doctor Malvankar. The other factor bringing Dr Sharda Kabir near Dr Ambedkar was Dr Kabir's friendship with the daughters of Professor Rau who happened to be the old friend of Dr Ambedkar. At Professor Rau's house, Ambedkar and Dr Kabir were introduced to each other. She was overwhelmed by meeting Dr.Ambedkar. She was attracted because, "his outstanding ability to rise above all his peers despite the crippling tag of his caste was what made him adornable."[2] More than often meetings either at the residence of Dr Rau or at the Dispensary developed intimacy. She offered her services as nurse for few months at Dr Ambedkar's bungalow at Delhi. Conscious of his reputation as a man of character and unsullied morals, Dr.Ambedkar did not agree to keep a woman with him short of marrying her. She happily agreed to. His well-wishers were pressing him to remarry someone in the interest of his deteriorating health. Her family members happily supported because they were impressed by, "Dr Ambedkar's enormous reputation as a leader of the Untochables and as Minister in the Nehru's Cabinet, everybody thought that it was a great opportunity for her to become a Central Minister's wife." Dr Ambedkar was 54 and Dr Kabir was 37 years old. They married on April 15, 1948. Dr Kabir became Savita Ambedkar after her marriage. She was necessity of the ailing Dr Ambedkar. She was great support to Dr Ambedkar.

But for her careful nursing, it would not have been possible for Dr Ambedkar to accomplish the ambitious writings especially Buddha and His Dhamma. How she look after him is clear from her book on Life with Dr Ambedkar. She says, "Every morning after she had given him a hot water bath like a child and helped him dress up by handing him over whatever suit shirt or tie he wanted, he would look at the mirror repeatedly to satisfy himself about his apparel and looks. He would start his breakfast with porridge, follow it up with some cornflakes and the eggs to his taste. He would everything to be served hot and oven-fresh. She had specially got a hot plate placed near the dining table so that whatever he wanted was served hot. After the breakfast she would almost daily accompany him up to porch of their Bungalow, open the door of the car for him to be seated comfortably and drive out, waving back to her until the car had reached the outer gate. .... She was insignificant compared with Ambedkar. But following her marriage she remained with him like a shadow."[66] Ramabai helped Dr Ambedkar to climb at academic peak by her Tapasya. Savita Ambedkar helped him to live and work successfully by nursing him both as an able doctor-cum-nurse and as a good companion caring of food and everything to suit his health.

Role of the Teachers

The humility in conduct and sincerity in learning impressed very his liberal mined Brahmin teacher at the school who gave his name - Ambedkar to earlier Bhimarao Amvedvekar. His teachers of Persian sand English at the Elphinstone College were very much impressed by his dedication to academic pursuits and supported him with books which he needed to study. It is said where there is will there is way. While pursuing his study in Columbia University, Dr Ambedkar came across a very knowledgeable and impressive teacher as well as affectionate guide Professor Edwin R.A. Seligan. Professor Seligan inspired Dr Ambedkar to be self searching and reliant. On query of Dr Ambedkar what method of research should he follow, Professor Seligan him to go on studying earnestly so that could evolve his own method.[3] This was saying like Buddha - be yourself enlightened **(Uppa Deepo Bhava)**. Dr Ambedkar found the path and started devoting more and more time in library with ceaseless pursuit of knowledge. So much so, Dr Ambedkar was immensely helped by Propfessor R.A. Seligman in his joining to London School of Economics and Political Science for the degree of M.Sc.(Economics) and D.Sc. (Economics) and Gray's Inn for the degree of the Bar-at-Law. Professor Seligan had written recommendation letters to Professor Edward Cannan and Professor Sydney Webb which read, "Will you permit me to introduce one of my graduate students, Mr. Bhim Rao Ramji Ambedkar? Ambedkar came to us on a State Scholarship from Baroda and has been with us for three years. He is now spending a year in London to finish up his dissertation, on the financial history of India. He is an excellent student and nice fellow, moderate, broad and able, and I know that you will be glad to be of service to him in the prosecution of his researches."

Edward Cannan, Professor of Political Economy at the University of London was named by Dr Ambedkar as referee in his application for the post of Professor at Sydenham College of Commerce and Economics, Bombay. When College sought his opinion, he wrote to the Principal of the College, "I don't know anything about Ambedkar except that he came to do a thesis and attacked it and me in a way which showed he had quite extraordinary practical ability. I rather wonder if he is a pure Indian; his character is rather Scotch-American" This brief tributary recommendation made his appointment sure and he got appointment as Professor on the handsome salary of Rs 450 per month.

The other Professor who widely shaped Dr Ambedkar was Professor John Dewey, his Professor of moral philosophy at Columbia University, New York. Professor Dewey himself was a great pragmatic humanist. Dr Ambedkar learned from him eclective pragmatism to retain from social heritage only that much which is helpful and beneficial for the future generation. He says, "as society becomes more enlightened it realises that it is responsible not to conserve and transmit the whole of its existing achievements, but only such as made for a better future society." Professor Dewey's philosophical influence helped Dr Ambedkar in developing a kind of dynamism and humanism. It is akin to Heraclutes 'philosophy- everything is in flux, you cannot enter twice in the same water of the river. Dr Ambedkar' dynamism recognises that," there is nothing fixed, nothing eternal, nothing sanatan: "that everything is changing, that change is the law of life for individuals as well as for society." He developed dynamism under influence of his teacher Professor Dewey to humanism. Ambedkarian humanism is based on the principles of equality, liberty and fraternity.

Role of the Benevolent Non-Brahmin Princes

The makers of the destiny of Dr Ambedkar were some of the merit loving, generous, human faced and uninfluenced by the evils of the caste-ridden/stricken Indian society, royal Princes. In the list of such great men the name of Sayaji Rao Gaekwad of Baroda Sate comes to the forefront. The generous king he helped Dr Ambedkar in many ways and added glory to his life. First, he granted a scholarship of Rs 25 per month for pursuing his study in graduation at a time when his had expressed his inability to support for further studies. Second, he granted Baroda State scholarship to pursue higher study in New York's famous University, University of Columbia. Third, when[4] without his knowledge the state officials were pressing the recovery of scholarship amount as he had failed to serve Baroda State for ten years stipulated in the bond, the generous king ordered the writing off that amount Fourth and the highest honour was accorded to Dr Ambedkar by Sayaji Rao Gaedwad of Baroda State when during their visit to England in connection with the Round Table Conference, he invited Dr Ambedkar at the dinner at the Hyde Park Hotel in London. The other invitee was Rai Bahadur Sir Annepu Patro. It was quite surprising as at dinner table there were only three persons-one Prince, other a Knight (Brahmin) and another a Mahar. New York Times noted that the dinner table set for three "was more a sign of an isolated miracle than a symptom of any material change as yet in India's 5000-year-old social system". The other Prince who helped Dr Ambedkar and his family in lurch was Chhatrapati Sahuji Maharaj of Kolhapur State. Firstly, highly impressed by his credentials Sahuji financed launching of fortnightly paper named, "Mook Nayak"- leader of the dumb. The paper attacked rampant inequality in the Hindu society. Second, Sahuji Maharaj extended financial help to Dr Ambedkar when he decided to England to complete his study at London School of Economics and Gray's Inn which he had left midway in view of call from Baroda State to return back. Third, when Dr Ambedkar was in

England his family was in dire need of money Sahuji sent monthly help to his family. Fourth, Sahuji arranged Conference of Untouchables in Kolhapur presided over by Dr Ambedkar. He himself attended the meeting and declared in prophetic vein, You have found your saviour in Ambedkar. I am confident that he will break your shackles. Not only that, a time will come when, so whispers my conscience, Ambedkar will shine as front rank leader of all India fame and appeal".[5] Dr Ambedkar felt very elevated when Sahuji Mahraj personally went to see him at humble abode in Bombay.

Impact of Path-Breaking Social Reformers

Jotiba Phule (1827-1890)

The problem which Dr Ambedkar was experiencing with was not new, but it was age-old one. It had been experienced by many great souls earlier who had criticised the evils of the Hinduism the frontal attack was done by Jotirao Phule. He was Maharashtrian, fought for the emancipation of the Untouchables. Dr Ambedkar as vociferous reader had read Phule with great interest. He was influenced greatly by Phule's undaunted and relentless move to fight for the cause of Untouchables reminding their heroic past and tale of their being robbed of their freedom, wealth and dignity by the cunning Brahmins who had faced fiercest resistence from the Mahar and Mangs. Jotirao Phule explained the etymological origin of the Mahar caste. Mahar originated as combination of Maha (great) and Ari (enemy). The power usurper Brahmins found Mahars as greatest enemy. Phule's ballad, "Priestcraft Exposed" made enormous emotional appeal:

Lawless men leagued together
They made Brahma their chief
They plundered and caused chaos

Beating the people and bringing them together to their knees
degrading them into slaves
See, these are the Shudras

The rest left over, a tiny number
Rose up and challenged Parashuram
They took care to remain united

Of their countrymen, their beloved brothers
Many were slain
The Shudras no longer cared for unity

The maha-ari attacked Parashuram
Many women became widows
Parashuram routed the maha-ari

In constant fighting he broke their spirit
He did not spare pregnant women
He killed the newborn children

The great enemies of the twice
Came to the end of their strength
Thrust down and defeated

Those that were left were punished severely
Abused as Mangs and maha-ari, great enemies
See, these are the kshatriyas of the olden days.[6]

Jotiba Phule initiated good deal of research on untouchables. There are certain points of long range importance (1) The Shudras were originally valiant Kshatriyas; (2) Education is root of progress and betterment in society; (3) For Shudras freedom from the indignities, deprivation of economic and social status inflicted on them by the graded inequality operator caste Hindus was more important than freedom from foreign rulers. Dr Ambedkar was greatly impressed by Jotiba Phule on all the points. Dr Ambedkar was a well read scholar. He devoted 15 years to study Vedas, Smritis and Mahabharata and wrote a most masterly book with evidences from those religious books and scriptures, namely, Who Were Shudras? He inscribed this scholarly book to the memory of Jotiba Fule. (the spelling used by Dr.Ambedkar)(1827-1890) describing him "The Greatest Shudra of modern India who made the lower classes of Hindus conscious of their slavery to the higher classes and who preached the gospel that for India social democracy was more vital than independence".

Dr Ambedkar answered the questions: Who were Shudras? and, how they came to be fourth Varna of the society?

The Shudras were one of the Aryan communities of solar race;

There was a time when the Aryan society recognised only three Varnas namely, Brahmins, Kshatryas and Vaishyas.

The Shudras did not form separate Varna. They ranked as part of Kshatriya Varna in Indo- Aryan society;

There was continuous feud between the Shudra kings and the Brahmins in which the Brahmins were subjected to many tyrannies and indignities;

As a result of hatred towards Shudras generated by their tyrannies and oppressions, Brahmins refused to perform the Upnayana of the Shudras.

Owing to the denial of Upnayand the Shudras who were Kshatriyas became socially degraded, fell below the rank of Vaishyas and thus came to form fourth Varna.

Education was on the top priority of Jotiba Phule. His famous view on the necessity of education for amelioration of untouchable and freedom from slavery runs:

For want of education intellect deteriorated,
For want of intellect morality decayed,
For want of morality progress stopped,
For want of progress wealth vanished,
For want of wealth Shudras perished,
All these sorrows sprang from illiteracy.[7]

Jotiba was very critical of Manusmriti which deprived Shudras of education. He declared:

"Follow me, falter not now,
Down with Manu's injunctions,
Education imparts you happiness,
Joti tells you with confidence."

Jotiba realised and was convinced that social slavery was worse than political slavery. He also pinpointed the root cause lying in the caste system which was solid, unbreakable and enduring. Due to the lack of education, Shudras had accepted the mental slavery for ages. It could be wiped out only "by throwing open the gates of knowledge to the lower classes by disseminating education among them." He was of considered view that "ignorance meant darkness and education meant light." He did not mind oppositions and obstacles and frankly told his father, who had been frightened by orthodox Hindus, that, "Even at the risk of life I shall not give up the cause." He became the first Indian to start a girl's school. The seed of the compulsory primary education of children up to 12 years was son by him.

Dr Ambedkar shared similar views and feelings. He asserted the significance of education: "Education is weapon of creation of mental and educational development, weapon of eradication of social slavery, of economic development, of political freedom". He was also convinced that, "The untouchables are deliberately being kept away by Brahmins and other castes. It was just because they drive the education system. They just tried to behave with untouchables as inferior." That is reason why Dr Ambedkar gave highest priority to education in his struggle for the liberation of Dalits from the age-old oppressive character of caste-ridden Indian society. He also made clear that "the people don't sustain in the struggle of life until they get educated. That they get caught in the clutches of social problems such as insult, suppression, and desecration". He found inseparable relationship between education and development in society. He observed, "If you want to develop the society then you need to spread up the education. Education eradicates the bias of people which results on to minimise the exploitation, domination, of those people who try to take the benefit of the so-called illiterate people. If the people get knowledge through education then they can face the problems created by the dominators. Education reforms opinion, it tries to remove the walls built among the people. The biggest gift that is given by the education is that it creates itself confidence among us which is considered as the first stage of our development."

Dr Ambedkar shared similar view on primary education as Jotiba had. He pointed out that the spread of primary education is the base of national development. He added one thing more that there should be legislative Act on the primary education. He made clear that those countries which bear the minimum Dalit illiterates don't sustain in the competition of life. He gave education a human right touch and pleaded that it is duty of the government to accelerate the process by providing education.

Dr Ambedkar shared with Jotiba the view on the ill impact of Manusmriti in depriving Untouchables not only of education but causing many miseries through subordination, economic deprivation and killing all initiatives in life. He went ahead and as protest and demonstration of genuine concern for the depressed people's amelioration, he burnt a copy of Manusmriti. As a well read and having the experience of the education abroad in developed countries like the United States and the United Kingdom Dr Ambedkar also injected the idea of human touch.

In education too Buddhist humanitarianism was aimed at. The educational institutions started by Dr Ambedkar were named after Buddha or Dr Ambedkar himself. He created Peoples Education Society, Bombay with a view to infuse his Educational philosophy (1) the search for truth, and (2) to practice humanitarian principles in one's own life. In 1945, he started Siddhartha College at Bombay under the auspices of Peoples Education Society. He established other colleges under the supervision of Neo-Buddhists at Aurangabad as Milind College and Ambedkar Colleges at Mahad and Nagpur. The objective of education aimed at enlightenment, "to strive, to seek and not to yield."[8]

For Dr Ambedkar Jotirao Phule was one of his mentors like Buddha and Kabir. In an interview with Dhananjaya Keer in 1954, he had expressed his plan to write a book on the life of Mahatma Phule[9] whom he hailed as one of the India's greatest social reformers. But in view of his deteriorating health was not very much sure about completion and Mr Keer later fulfilled his unfulfilled desire by publishing, "Mahatma Jotirao Phooley-Father of Indian Social Revolution" (1964).

Mahadeo Govind Ranade (1842-1901)

The other foremost social reformer like Jotiba Phule was Mahadeo Govind Ranade. Ranade was contemporary of Jotiba Phule. The former was born in 1827 and died in 1890. Latter was born in1842 and died in 1901. Ranade was a lawyer and a judge by profession. In addition he 'a first class economist, a first class historian, a first class educationist and a first class Divine. He possessed immense quality of learnedness, objectivity and sense of inquiry to brood over a matter. Above all, he had a great human soul. He had in depth knowledge of the degradation of the Hindu society. But he was optimist. He was firm believer that, 'the fallen shall rise'. He had deep concern with the Indian society. He made clear that-

"I profess implicit faith in two articles of my creed. This country of ours is the true land of promise. This race of ours is chosen race."[10]

In his dispassionate, cool and rational assessment he found that the real causes of downfall and degradation of the Hindu society lied in certain weaknesses. The removal of such weaknesses from the Hindu society was imperative for the better system. It called for duty- duty to reform Hindu society. He did everything he could to accomplish the mission of reform of the Hindu society. For Ranade moral stamina was more significant than the political freedom.[11] For him social democracy was more important for political stability. He candidly admitted that there were no rights in the Hindu society which could approve of on moral sense of human standard. As a matter of fact, "there were privileges and disability, privileges for a few and disabilities for a vast majority." He was for the rights of all. He warned his opponents who pleaded for solution through political freedom. In his prophetic words:

"You cannot be liberal by halves. You cannot be liberal in politics and conservative in religion. The heart and head must go together. You cannot cultivate your intellect, enrich your mind, enlarge the sphere of your political rights and privileges, and at the same time keep your hearts closed and cramped. It is an idle dream to expect men to remain enchained and enshackled in their own superstition and social evils, while they are struggling hard to win rights and privileges from their rulers. Before long these vain dreamers will find their dreams lost."[12]

Ranade wished to cleanse the old order which was formed on wrong social system, was unequal and completely undemocratic, too weighed in favour of the classes and against the masses, too class-conscious and too communally-minded. In a nutshell, Ranade was of firm view that a good political democracy can be established only on bed-rock of sound social democracy.

So was the view of Dr Anbedkar. Dr Ambedkar's well considered view was that 'without social reform true feeling of nationalism cannot be evolved'. He expressed the view that religion was essential for the national unity. But would not work so if engendered exploitation, injustice and inequality. Dr Ambedkar added two more dimensions to Ranade's plea of social reform. The first dimension was to add economic reform along with social reform. Ranade put emphasis on cleansing the old rotten Hindu social system Dr Ambedkar added second dimension to create a new order based on the principles of liberty, equality and fraternity. He pointed out "The caste system is responsible for the unnatural division of labour, the historical downfall of Hindus, their moral turpitude and their weakness. The religious mindedness of the Hindus should be changed into the new religion based on equality, liberty and fraternity."[13]

Even in London during the Round Table Conference he had raised mighty voice, "freedom is the birth right if all Indians and even the untouchables have the right to live and die honourably." While moving the motion of the adoption of the Constitution on 26th November, 1949 Dr Ambedkar made a very prophetic speech in the Constituent Assembly:

"On the January 26, 1950, we are going to enter into a life of contradictions. In politics we will have equality and in the social and the economic life we will have inequality. In politics we will be recognising the principle of one man one vote and one vote one value. In our social and economic life, we shall, by reason of put social and economic structure, continue to deny the principle of one man one value. How long shall we continue to live this life of contradictions? If continue to deny it for long, we will do so only by putting our political democracy in peril. Political democracy cannot last unless there lies at the base of it social democracy. What does social democracy mean? It means a way of life which recognises liberty, equality and fraternity as the principles of life. These principles of liberty, equality and fraternity are not to be treated as separate items in a trinity. They form a union of trinity in the sense that to divorce one from the other is to defeat the very purpose of democracy. Liberty cannot be divorced from equality, equality cannot be divorced from liberty. Nor can liberty and equality be divorced from fraternity. Without equality, liberty would produce the supremacy of few over many. Equality without liberty would kill individual initiative. Without fraternity, liberty and equality could not become a natural course of things. We must begin by acknowledging the fact that there is complete absence of two things in Indian society. One of these is equality. On the social plane, we have in India a society based on the principle of graded inequality which means elevation for some and degradation for others."

Phule and Ranade both had strongly pleaded for reform in inequality based Hindu society. The former had also experienced the resistance and reactions of the degrade society both during schooling and in the course of taking measures for schooling of girls and children of the untouchables. Since Ranade belonged to the upper class he had not to suffer indignation at the hands of casteists. Both sincerely believed in the need of social reform. Dr Ambedkar had experienced the ugliest form of caste discrimination, humiliation, indignation and deprivation. From Ranade he might have learnt people fell to rise. He might have taken lesson that to bear humiliation without being forsaken might bring dignified treatment in future or what P.B. Shelley exhorted, 'If winter comes, can spring be far behind?' He was ill treated at the hands of caste-Hindus in his own country, but was loved and received most warm welcome and dignified equal treatment outside the country. But he never forgot the treatment of upper caste people with his brethren. He made many appeals through peaceful Satyagraha for recognition of untouchables as human being like others. But he was greeted with lathis and stones, denied water to drink and was prohibited from temple entry. Realising no possibility of reform ensuring liberty, equality and fraternity in the stronghold of caste-ridden Hindu society, he took the strong decision – if religion could not change to give the position of honour to untouchables, they should change their religion. He enlightened untouchables, "Because of untouchability your merit is gone unrewarded; there is no appreciation of your mental and physical qualities. Because of it you are debarred from entering into the army, police department and navy. Untouchability is a curse that has ruined your worldly existence, honour and name". Dr Ambedkar gave befitting answer of the question what would be gains of the change of religion. He explained, "What will India gain by Swaraj? Just as Swaraj is necessary for India, so also is change of religion necessary for the untouchables. The underlying motive in both the movements is the desire for freedom."[14]

Dr Ambedkar also took lessons from many other social reformers. There were a number of social evils requiring reforms, that is to say, (1) Early marriage, (2) Remarriage of widows, (3) Liberty of country to go outside the country, (4) Women's right to property; and (5) Education of women. He took inspiration from different social reformers who were sponsoring the cause of eradication of such evils. Raja Ram Mohan Roy and Ishwar Chandra Vidyasagar were prominent among them.

Impact of Spiritual Guides

Dr Ambedkar was impressed by the noble preachings of many saints. But he was deeply impressed by two excellent preachers of equality and human values

– saint Kabir and Tathagata Buddha. Dr Ambedkar was brought up in religious family environment. His parents were Kabirpanthi. Religious songs were enchanted in his family and worship was a daily routine. Courage, candidness and undaunted love for truth practiced by Dr.Ambedkar, appears to be based on the teachings of Saint Kabir. The idea of the assertion of worth, not birth as determinant one's ability was preached by Kabir and Buddha. Kabir appreaciated good conduct. So did Buddha. Kabir said, 'do not hurt anybody because wherever you have a look, there is our dearest to the heart' (**Ghav kahi per na ghalo, jit dekho tit pran hamaro, Bijak, Sakhi 341).** Buddha taught ahimsa. Kabir taught to search truth evaluation of one's own **heart (sancha shabda ka hridya dekhu vichar),** earlier Buddha had taught in Kalamo episode "Do not believe because I am saint and revered. When it appeals to insightful intelligence only believe then". Dr Ambedkar was not aggreable to any proposal which did appeal his conscience and could not be proved by reasons. His famous work-Annihilation of Caste, was written with cover page quotation from Buddha, "Know truth as truth and untruth as untruth." What was unjustifiable by reasons was not acceptable to Dr Ambedkar. Ambedkar paid much importance to reason and cited on the cover page of the earlier referred book also the famous saying of Drummond:

"He that WILL NOT reason is a bigot
He that CANNOT reason is a fool
He that DARE NOT reason is a slave"[15]

Dr Ambedkar never shied of speaking his inner voice with firm conviction –be his challenge to unchallengeable personality of Mahatma Gandhi on the issue of handling age-old evil of casteism or influential, convincing and successful amendment to Objective Resolutions moved by an uncontrovertible personality of Pt. Jawahar Lal Nehru in the Constituent Assembly on the issues of national outlook appeal and real socialistic measures to ensure economic justice to the masses. Buddha's teaching was, "no caste, no inequality, none higher, none lower, all are equal." So taught Kabir- everybody has likewise blood, flesh and other essentials elements of body, the whole creation is created of the same drop, all are same- who can be said as Brahmin and can be said as Shudra?. Dr Ambedkar strived for the equality of all by the artificially created caste barriers. Buddha lived for others. He preached to work for the good and happiness of maximum number and to give the message of such Dhamma which is initially, in middle and in the end welfarist. Kabir preachers to know and remove the miseries of others **(Kabir soi peer hai, jo jane per peer).** Ambedkar lived, struggled and suffered for neglected, deprived and enslaved masses. He worked for emancipation of the disprivileged classes-Dalits, workers and women. Like Buddha and Kabir Dr Ambedkar believed in self-sacrifice for the protection of the rights of the others .It is common knowledge that Dr Ambedkar did not take any time in quitting the highly coveted post of Union Cabinet Ministership of Law when he was ditched by his cabinet brethren and the Hindu Code Bill fell in Parliament which meant to provide equality and dignity to disprivileged Hindu women. The spirit of Buddha's preaching that enmity does not end by enmity, it can end only by love is guiding force behind Dr Ambedkar's peaceful Satyagraha staged for right of Untouchables to drink water from Chowdar Tank, Mahad and entry of Untouchables in Kala Ram temple, Nasik. Such peaceful demonstrations were staged with a view to inaugurate an era of equality in our country.

References

1. Cited from Janak Singh, Dr B.R. Ambedkar p. 30.
2. *Ibid*. pp. 205-206.
3. Dr Savita Ambedkar, ' My Days with Dr Ambedkar.
4. Dr Savita Ambedkar, ' My Days with Dr Ambedkar.
5. Janak Singh, Dr Ambedkar, p. 48.
6. Jotirao Phuley, Priestcraft Exposed, Dhananjay Keer and Mahsle(eds.) pp. 46-47.See also Rosalind O' Hanlon, 'Phule and the Inversion of Brahman Myth' (in) Ishitha Banerjee and Dube(ed.)Caste in History, Oxford University Press,2008 pp. 172-180 at p.p. 172-173.
   Jotirao Phule's manuscript on Cultivator's Whipcord.
7. *Ibid* p. 65.
8. Preface to Dhanajay Keer, Mahatma Jotirao Phuley Bombay Popular Prakashan, l974, p. VII.
9. Address of Dr Ambedkar on the 10th birthday of Mahadev Govind Ranade held on the 18th January, 1943 in the Gokhale Memorial Hall under caption, "Ranade , Gandhi &Jinnah, Bombay, Thacker and Co. Ltd., 1943.
10. *Ibid.*
11. *Ibid.*
12. *Ibid.*
13. *Ibid.*
14. *Ibid.*
15. Cover page of the Annihilation of Caste.

6

False or Under- Worshipped God? I

The great men are always surrounded by controversies-may be genuine, may be quite in-genuine. Dr Ambedkar was a great man. To raise controversy against him could be easiest way to bring one in limelight. Many controversies appear to be prompted by such objectives. One of such controversies relates to Arun Shourie's, 'WORSHIPPING FALSE GODS- Ambedkar, and the facts which have been erased, A.S. Publications (1997). No doubt Arun Shourie is well known for his Editorship of *The Indian Express* and as commentator of political affairs. He has been awardee of many honours, viz. Padam Bhushan, the Magsaysay Award, The Dada Bhai Naroji Award, the Astor Award, the K.S. Hegde Award and the International Editor of the Year Award.[1] He has every right to say as he has freedom of speech and expression. But his writing is and must be subject to scrutiny on account of objectivity, rationality and overall factual evidences. Ideologies, ingrained premises and predilections need to be avoided. Arun Shourie bears certain ideologies. His ideology is definitely against reservation policy and thereby conceding preferential treatments to the depressed people. In the referred book itself at p. 638 (paperback edition Rupa & Co. Third impression, 2006), he comments, "Social justice" today is nothing but a cover for out-and-out casteist politics. After nine judge-bench decision of the apex court in **Indra Shawhney** v. **Union of India** (the famous **Mandal case**) he contributed a series of Articles and talked of not only folly, but disaster and ultimately authored another book, Falling Over Backwards: An Essay Against Reservation and Against

Judicial Populism, 2006.[2] Arun Shourie's book, False God may be exposition of like ideology in estimation a journalist following the election return. No wonder! he was prized as Union Minister of Disinvestment.

On surface reading it is clear that the book presents only half truth. He starts from March 9, 1924, and no justice can be done to the great man Dr Ambedkar by ignoring or blacking out Ambedkar in the making, struggling to quench the thirst of acquiring knowledge and more knowledge despite the brunt of caste prejudices and having distinction in M.A., Ph.D. at California University, D.Sc. (Economics) London School of Economics, U.K. and Bar-at-Law from Gray's Inn (England). Anyway, Arun Shourie's charge's gravamen against Dr Ambedkar is four-fold:

1. Dr Ambedkar opposed the freedom struggle;
2. He collaborated the British for material gain;
3. He only piloted the Draft Constitution and he can in no way be called the father of the Constitution;
4. His conversion to Buddhism was mere opportunism.

As to the first charge Arun Shourie states, "there is not one instance, not one single, solitary instance in which Ambedkar participated in any activity connected with the struggle to free the country."[3]

Dr Ambedkar struggled throughout his life for freedom, not only for himself, but for dumb, weak, meek, bewildered by persecution and perpetual humiliation at the hands of the caste persons and the power that be. If freedom has any meaning it means right to live with human dignity and immunity from indignation. Dr Ambedkar did his best to fight against Britishers. But his way was quite different from the status-quoist freedom fighters. Dr Ambedkar was fighting on two fronts- one against the Britishers and the other against upper caste/class hegemony depriving human status to Untouchables. Dr Ambedkar had no pretension. He was honestly candid enough to publically declare in the editorial column of the **Bahiskrit Bharat** on the 29th July 1927: "If Tilak had been born among the Untouchables, he would not have raised the slogan "Swaraj is my birth right", but he would have raised the slogan" Annihilation of Untouchbility is my birthright."[4]

How can anybody ignore the role of Dr, Ambedkar in struggle for the freedom in teeth of his participation in the All-Parties Conference in 1928 and1930? In the All Parties

Conference of 1930 his emphasis on "the need of Hindu-Muslim unity against the British Imperialism for uprooting it", speaks aloud of his role in the freedom struggle. In the home of the Britishers in the Round Table Conference on 20th November, 1930 Dr Ambedkar put challenge, "Has the British Government done anything to remove Untouchbility?" He pointed out that "the wrongs against the Untouchables have not been righted although 150 years of British rule have passed". Dr Ambedkar[5] without any inhibition declared: "We must have a government in which the men in power will give their undivided allegiance to the best interest of our country. We must have a government in which men in power, knowing where obedience will end and resistance will begin, will not be afraid to amend the social and economic code of life which the dictates of justice and expediency so urgently call for. This role the British Government will never be able to play. It is only a government which is of the people, for the people and by the people that will make this possible." Of course, Dr Ambedkar was very assertive in the Round Table Conference with mighty voice, "Freedom is the birthright of all Indians and even the Untouchables has the right to live and die honourably."

Dr Ambedkar lived for the country, not for himself. In his own words, "I know has not been understood properly in the country. It has often been misunderstood....I say whenever there has been a conflict between my personal interest and the interest of the country as a whole, I have always placed the claims of the country above my personal claims. I have never pursued the path of private gain....so far as the demands of the country are concerned, I have never lagged behind." Dr Ambedkar was staunch critic of British Imperialism and firm believer that only in Swaraj Constitution we can get the chance of getting the political power into our own hands and salvation of our people.

2. Dr Ambedkar collaborated with Britishers for the betterment of neglected, persecuted and humiliated for none of their fault but due to the accident of birth in Untouchable community, poor and workers, and not for himself. His association with Britishers served the nation in better way. He joined as a member in Viceroy Labour Executive Council on July 20th, 1942 and became instrumental in labour reforms like reduction in working hour, leave with pay and other relating to factories, mines and other social security measures whose beneficiaries were the poor workers. It was vision of Ambedkar

to bring employers and employees' representative together "for mutual settlement of differences in a spirit of cooperation and goodwill." His association with Britishers was for betterment of our people. He never mortgaged his loyalty. As soon as he was elected to the Legislative Assembly of Bengal he gave slogan of "one Bharat". Even when he was member of the Viceroy's Executive Council his fearless individuality was never compromised. He showed enough courage to shelter in his dwelling house the famous freedom fighter Congress leader Sri Achyut Patwardhan. In February, 1942 participating in the Spring Lecture series at Wagle Hall, Bombay Dr Ambedkar roared; "We will defend our land. Do not be under the false impression that Pakistan would be able to spread its Muslim empire over India. The Hindus will make it lick the dust. I confess I have my quarrel with caste Hindus over some points...but I take avow before you that I shall lay down my life in defence of her land."[6]

A great man, no less than Mahatma Gandhi, issued testimonial as to patriotism to Dr Ambedkar. After the Round Table Conferences, being hurt by our own countrymen, in his conversation to Mahatma Gandhi, Dr Ambedkar said; "Gandhiji, I have no homeland". The prompt response of Gandhiji was, "You have got a homeland and from the reports that have reached me of your work at the Round Table Conference, I know you are a patriot of sterling worth."[7]

Who could be regarded as more sincere patriotic than Dr Ambedkar who preached nationalism through one language saying, "Culture is conserved by language. Since Indians wish to unite and develop a common culture it is the bounden duty of all Indians to own up Hindi as their language." Pleading for unity of the nation, he said "Her unity is as ancient as Nature. Within this geographic unit and covering the whole of it there has been a cultural unity from time immemorial. This cultural unity has defied political and racial divisions. At any rate for the last hundred and fifty years all institutions- cultural, political, economic, legal and administrative have been working on a single, uniform spring of action. In any discussion... the fact cannot be lost sight of namely, that the starting point, if not the governing factor, is the fundamental unity of India."

Who could be more anxious about retention of our freedom than Dr Ambedkar? In his last speech in the Constituent Assembly his concern became obvious when he expressed his anxiety, "What perturbs me greatly is the fact that India has not only once before lost her independence but she lost it by the infidelity and treachery of her own people. When Sindh was invaded by Mohemmed-Bin-Kasim, military commanders of King Dahir accepted bribes from Kasim's agent and refused to fight for their king. It was Jaichand who invited Mohammed Ghori to invade India and to fight against Prithviraj...In 1857, when a large part of India had declared a war of Independence against the British, Sikhs watched the event as silent spectators." He put a question before the Assembly,[8] Will history repeat itself?" Our independence will be put in jeopardy a second time probably be lost forever. We must be determined to defend our independence till the last drop of our blood. "It goes without saying that Dr Ambedkar was calling spade a spade. In similar words Honorable Mr. Justice P.B. Sawant repeated the tragic tendency mind set of people during invasions. **Indra Sawhney v. Union of India,** learned judge pointed out that 'there was a message divided we are, come and rule'.[9]

3. As to the denial of the prominence of Dr Ambedkar in drafting of the Constitution the dispute is without any essence. To say that, "His job was really that of a rapporteur" is the most uncharitable and ungrateful statement overlooking the tremendous job done by Dr Ambedkar which made evens his not so admirer, to admire him. The admission of Jaspat Roy Kapoor, a prominent member of the Constituent Assembly that how he had started with prejudice against Dr Ambedkar and how he developed an admiration for the very useful work and the very patriotic work which he had done, speaks a volume of things.[10] He said, "I have always found him to bring upon the subject a very constructive approach. On many occasions here seemed to be a deadlock, he came forward with suggestions which resolved the dead-locks." Rapporteur simply reports what transpires during discussions - he neither effectively takes part in discussions, nor clears the queries from participants, nor defends the decisions taken. But Dr Ambedkar did all these. The most prominent member of the Constituent Assembly Pt. Jawahar Lal Nehru hailed Dr Ambedkar as, "an illustrious architect of our Constitution." The President, Constituent Assembly, Dr Rajendra Prasad, in his speech on November 26, 1949, spoke: "Sitting in the chair and watching the proceedings from day today, I have realised as nobody else could have, with what zeal and devotion the members of the Drafting Committee

and especially its Chairman, Dr Ambedkar, in spite of his indifferent health, have worked. (Cheers.) We could never make a decision, which was or could be even so right as when we put him on Drafting Committee and made him its Chairman. He has not only justified his selection but has added luster to the work he has done."[11]

Dr Ambedkar is genuinely termed as the "Father of the Constitution", or "the author of the Constitution". Such titles are given by the people as expression of honour and gratitude for the great work done by knowledgeable persons, as Gandhi was adorned as 'Mahatma'; Vallabhbhai Patel as 'Iron -Man'; Subhas Chandra Bose as 'Netaji, Chandra Sekhar as 'Azad', again Gandhi as 'Father of the Nation' and yet again Patel as 'Bismark of India' and so on so forth. They are not literally taken. Dr Ambedkar deserved such honour. Drafting of Constitution of a nation is not an easy work. For this job Sir Ivor Jennings was contemplated in some quarters. Dr Ambedkar was choice in his place. Can anybody say that the Constitutions of South Asian Countries drafted by Sir Ivor Jennings are better in anyway than our own Constitution? Would Sir Ivor Jennings have better grasp and understanding of the most complex and complicated problems of multi-cultured, multi languages, multi religious and over all the caste-ridden Indian society with ingrained inequality? What is over all image of our Constitution drafted under Chairmanship of Dr Ambedkar? It is held as the first and foremost social document; the most comprehensive document of splendid compromises. How was it possible? Undisputed credit goes to the wide ranged knowledge of the constitutional law of the United Kingdom, U.S.A., Common Wealth of Australia, Canada, Switzerland, Japan and other significant countries acquired and assimilated by Dr Ambedkar as M.A., Ph.D. in political science from a renowned institution no less than the University of Columbia and D.Sc. (Economics) from the London School of Economics. Certain preliminaries are to be noted. First, humility of Dr Ambedkar itself did not allow him to take credit of writing the Constitution single- handed. He acknowledged the contribution of all. But, the great tribute paid by Sri T.T. Krishnamachari, himself a member of the Constituent Assembly to Dr Ambedkar speaks of the real position. He said, "The House is perhaps aware that of the seven members nominated by you, one had resigned from the House and was replaced. One died and was not replaced. One was away in America and his place was not filled up and another person was engaged in state affairs and there was void to that extent. One or two people were far away from Delhi and perhaps reasons of health did not permit them to attend. So it happened ultimately that the burden of drafting the Constitution fell on Dr Ambedkar and I have no doubt that we are grateful to him for having achieved this task in a manner which is undoubtedly commendable". Tajamal Hussain states, "The credit of framing this Constitution goes to the Law Minister. He is a genius. He knows everything about all the Laws and Constitutions of the world, what he does not know are not worth knowing. He has worked very hard from beginning to the end in spite of his indifferent health. Due to his ceaseless labour this remarkable Constitution has been framed."

Second, the way in which Dr Ambedkar explained the choice of the Union of States in preference to Federation, British parliamentary system in preference to the American Presidential system, establishing Article 32 of the Constitution as 'the very soul and very heart' of the Constitution, to illustrate only a few and the way in which varying divergent shades of opinions in the Assembly were convinced to agree to a final decision are nothing but the original contribution of Dr Ambedkar to the making of the India's Constitution.

Third, the contribution of Dr Ambedkar is of such magnitude that he has been hailed as the law giver for the Indian posterity. And, therefore, he has been honoured as modern Manu. As Manu scripted Manusmriti which has governed Indian people since time immemorial likewise The Constitution of India authored by Dr Ambedkar will govern the future generation. Some jurisprudents like late justice V.R. Krishna Iyer regard Dr.Ambedkar taller than Manu. The obvious reason being Manusmriti as it exists (has been existing since long) has become symbol inequality whereas the present Constitution authored by Dr Ambedkar envisions equality, non-discrimination and dignity to all. To quote justice V.R. Krishna Iyer: "...a great profile will fill the bill of this historic person Baba Saheb Ambedkar, a Mahar taller than Manu, a rebel more committed Pragna, Samta and Karuna of homo sapiens, with no status divide and penury gap and larger than any of his contemporaries in the country.

...whose soulful ambition was universal social justice, rooted in the compassion of the Buddha, burning with the accumulated rage of the Unpeople of the earth and demanding a crimson world order and egalitarian ethos where class and caste shall not inflict barbarity on anyone in the human race. He made a difference to India and shook and shaped the nation to wipe out social exploitation out of the land."

H.J. Khandekar a Maharashtra Congressman explained, I call this Constitution the Mahar law because Dr Ambedkar is a Mahar and now when we inaugurate this Constitution on the 26th of January, 1950, we shall have the law of Manu replaced by the law of Mahar and I hope that unlike the law of Manu under which there was never a prosperity in the country, the Mahar law will make India virtually a paradise. Well sir, even the social, political and religious reformers in the country like Gautama Buddha, Ramanuj, Kabir, Sant Tukaram, Raja Ram Mohan Roy, Swami Dayanand Saraswati, Thakkar Bappa and last, but not the least, Mahatma Gandhi found it very difficult to get rid of the ghost of untouchability. They agitated in the country but they did not succeed. Now, Sir, we have embodied an Article 17 in this Constitution to remove untouchability and I am sure that untouchability will be removed."

4. The charge that Dr Ambedkar's 'conversion to Buddhism was mere opportunism' appears to be totally in ignorance of the compelling reasons, historical background, possibility to convert to Christianity, Islam, Sikhism too. Arun Shourie blames, "....Ambedkar's conversion to Buddhism was merely a political act: his Buddhism had nothing to do with the teaching and life of the Buddha-there is not the slightest trace of any inner-directed search in Ambedkar , there is not the slightest trace that even an effort has been made to overcome the bitterness or presumption." The teachings of Tathagata Buddha were running in the very vein of Dr Ambedkar. He was conceived in the womb of his mother who had seen a dream as the mother Gautama had seen at the time of her conception of the child. He was told about the dream by his mother which had everlasting effect on him from the very beginning. He was born in a family of Kabirpanthis and Abhangas of Saint Kabir are not far away from the teachings of Buddha. His mother taught in her laps to respect everybody He practised it and his humility continued even when his teachers discouraged him by saying that he was merely wasting his time in schooling because he was not going to gain anything due to his being an Untouchable, he simply retorted 'mind your business.' Is not this the teaching

of Buddha to tolerant? When Dr Ambedkar achieved the honour of being first Mahar to pass Matriculation Examination from prestigious Eliphinstone High School in 1907 he was honoured and one of persons present at the commemoration meeting was Krishanji Arjun Keluskar and being deeply impressed by Dr Ambedkar along with other books he presented his new book, Life of Gautama Buddha. This book was thoroughly studied by Dr Ambedkar and proved to bring a turning point in his life.

The teachings of Buddha were assimilated/ chewed and digested by Dr Ambedkar. Here it is to be noted that to accept and practised principles of some great man it is not necessary to join the religion preached by him. It is the famous declaration of Swami Vivekananda, "I am not, as you know, the follower of Buddhism, still I am a Baudh'. He was so impressed by Buddha that declared the greatest man of the world, who could be ready to sacrifice even his life for the sake of saving the life an ordinary goat from being sacrificed in Yagya. If without being the follower of Buddhism, Swami Vivekananda could declare Buddha as greatest Karmayogi why Dr Ambedkar could not practice the preaching of Buddha? He believed in preaching of Tathagat Buddha and not Buddhism prevalent which had been killed, as S. Radhakrishnan observes, by Brahminism with fraternal embrace.. He preached his own version as Neo-Bddhism.

There are instances in abundance which clarify the deep impact of Buddha on Dr Ambedkar. **First,** the greatest everlasting contribution of Buddha to posterity is what we say in modern terminology-scientific temper. In Kalamo episode Buddha taught, do not believe in what I am saying or it is written in holy book of highest reverence believe only in that which appeals to your conscience. Dr Ambedkar while addressing the agitators for drinking water from Chowder Tank said, "Remember that nothing valuable in this world is achieved except by efforts. Mind you, do not leap into fire because I tell you to do so. Do it if you are fully convinced of the justice of your cause." **Second,** Buddha taught to search one's own salvation, nobody else will help other person, strive yourself Tathgatas are only guide. Dr Ambedkar exhorted fellow Untouchables, "Learn to live in this world with self respect. You should always cherish some ambition to do something in this world. They alone rise who strive. All things are now possible because of your being able to participate in the politics and the legislatures of this country. You must abolish your slavery yourselves. Do not depend for the abolition upon God or a superman. Your salvation lies in political power and not in making pilgrimages and observances of fasts". **Third,** Buddha Trisharana is I Go in the shelter of Buddha,;I Go in the shelter of guild (Sangh), I Go in the shelter of Dharma.(**Buddham Saranam Gachchami; Sangham Saranam Gachchami; Dhammam Saranam Gachchami).** Lord Buddha's call was to be enlightened, join organisation and do good for others. Dr Ambedkar, in view of the modern requirement of liberation from age- old slavery, reorganised Trisharana and gave call saying, "My final words of advice to you is educate, agitate and organise, and have faith in yourself. **Fourth,** Buddha was champion of equality, preached equally all-from Brahmins to the most despised persons, women, bandit etc. Dr Ambedkar strived for liberty, equality and fraternity. **Fifth,** Buddha was most liberal preacher. Dr Ambedkar was most political liberal, self-restrained, adjustable. How adjusting, sensible and patriotic he was, is clear from his utterances on eve of famous Poona Pact. Dr Ambedkar said, "There was before me the duty which I owe as part of common humanity to save Gandhi from sure death." During his public speech in London Gandhi himself had appreciated the stand of Dr Ambedkar on the issue of Untouchables. He complimented Dr Ambedkar in the following words, "I have the highest regard for Dr Ambedkar. He has every right to be bitter. That he does not break our heads is an act of self-restraint on his part."[12] **Sixth,** Dr Ambedkar was very much impressed by Buddha's Prajna (understanding); Karuna (love) and Samata (equality). Justice V.R.Krishna Iyer rightly points out, "He gave up Hinduism with its harsh, hierarchic and horrendous caste system and became a Buddhist as compassion and equal value of everyone's life appealed to him as preached by the ancient Light of Asia, the Buddha the Enlightened one. In 1936 May at Bombay in the course of his speech Dr Ambedkar had made clear that his conversion was prompted only by spiritual feelings. He said,[13] "I have decided once and for all to give up this religion my religious conversion is not inspired by any material motive. There is hardly anything that I cannot achieve even while remaining an Untouchable. There is no other feeling other than that of spiritual feeling underlying my religious conversion."[14] Dr Ambedkar had explained his experience as being 'new born'. Inspired by the wave of conversion all over Maharashtra he said: "This conversion has given me enormous satisfaction and pleasure unimaginable. I feel as if I have been liberated from hell." He further explained motive behind conversion: "We are making efforts to reach manhood."

Who Could be Better Hindu than Dr Ambedkar?

Dr Ambedkar was and remained true Hindu minus owning the evils of the caste system and its treacherous impact on society snatching from untouchables the dignity of a human being. He pointed out, "The caste system is responsible for the unnatural division of labour, and the historical downfall of Hindu, their moral turpitude and their weakness." Is there two opinions about it? Has not the ill impact of the evil of caste system and consequent untouchability heavily costed our country?

In his most celebrated and classic book 'Discovery of India' highlighted the pathology of Hïndu society. He observed, "But the ultimate weakness and falling of the caste system and the Indian social were that they degraded as mass of human beings and gave them no opportunities to get out of that condition-educationally, culturally and economically."

So was the view of Gandhiji. In an article in the Harijan on February 11, 1933 he wrote, "Untouchability as at present practiced is the greatest blot on Hinduism. It is (with apologies to sanatanists) against the Shastras. It is against the fundamental principles of humanity; it is the dictates of reason that a man merely because of his birth should be forever unapproachable and unseeable...The tragedy is that millions of Hindus believe in this institution as if it is enjoined by the Hindu religion."

Gandhi always accepted and appreciated the worth of Dr Ambedkar. When April, 1936 scheduled Jat-Pat-Todak Mandal' annual Conference proposed to be presided over by Dr Ambedkar was cancelled because many prominent caste Hindu office bearer did not approved of Dr Ambedkar's draft speech, Gandhi expressed his considered view (in Harijan, July 11, 1936), "The committee appears to have deprived the public an opportunity of listening the original views of a man, who has carved out for himself a unique position in society. Whatever label he wears in future, Dr Ambedkar is not a man to allow him to be forgotten." Gandhiji was also candid enough to accept the reality of the situation. He said, "Dr Ambedkar is a challenge to Hinduism. Brought up as a Hindu, educated by a Hindu potentate, he has become so disgusted with the so-called Savarna Hindus for the treatment that he and his people have received at their hands that he proposes to leave not only them but the very religion that is his and their common heritage.... Dr Ambedkar found that the vast majority of Savarna Hindus had not only conducted themselves inhumanly against those of their fellow religionists, whom they classed as untouchable, but they had based their conduct on the authority of their scriptures, and when he began to search them he had found ample warrant for their believes in untouchability and all its implications. He has quoted chapter and verse in proof of his three-fold indictment-inhuman conduct itself, the unabashed justification for it on part of perpetrator, and the subsequent discovery that the justification was warranted by their scriptures." Gandhiji accepted that, "no Hindu who prizes his faith above life can afford to underrate the importance of this indictment." He also accepted that many sharers of Dr Ambedkar's strong views in spite of caste humiliation and indignation 'remain in the Hindu fold does not warrant for disregarding what Dr Ambedkar has to say. Gandhiji's clear opinion was clear on the point, 'the savarna have to correct their belief and their conduct.' He unequivocally declared that, 'caste has nothing to do with religion.' He asserted that, 'it is harmful both to spiritual and national growth.' Even justifying the utility of Varna for bread earning arrangement, he asserted, 'there is nothing in law of Varna to warrant a belief in Untouchbility'. The essence of Hinduism is contained in its enunciation of one and only God as truth and its bold acceptance of Ahimsa as the law of the human family). "Even when he resorted to fast unto death in Yaravada jail, Pune, as a real Hindu and well wisher of Hinduism Gandhiji had not forgotten his commitment to fight against the evil of Hinduism. Even his resort to fast unto death in Yervada jail, had two equally valued commitment -first the withdrawal of the system of separate electorate and second, the end of Untouchability by change of hearts of the caste Hindus. He told to a journalist explaining the real objective of his fast, "What I want. what I am living for, and what I should delight in dying for, is the eradication of Untouchability root and branch I want therefore, a living pact whose life giving effect should be felt not in the distant tomorrow but today, and, therefore, the pact should be shield by an all-India demonstration of 'touchables' and 'untouchables' meeting together, not by way of a theatrical show but in real brotherly embrace. It is in order to achieve this, the dream of my life for past fifty years, that I have entered the fiery gates." Gandhiji further warned against hasty decisions only with a view to save his life. He said:

"My life I count of no consequence. One hundred lives given for this noble cause would, in my opinion, be poor penance done by Hindus for the atrocious wrongs they have heaped upon helpless men and women of their own faith. I, therefore, would urge them not to swerve an inch from the path of strictest Justice. My fast I want to throw in the scales of justice, and if it wakes up caste Hindus from their slumber, and if they are roused to a sense of their duty, it will have served its purpose. Whereas, if out of blind affection for me, they would somehow or other come to a rough and ready agreement so as to secure the abrogation and then go off to sleep, they will commit a grievous blunder and will have made my life a misery. For a while the abrogation of separate electorates would result in my breaking the fast, it would be living death for me if the vital pact for which I am striving is not arrived at. It would simply mean that, as soon as I called off the fast, I would have to give notice of another in order to achieve the spirit of the vow to the fullest extent."

Gandhiji further said:

"In attacking Untouchability I have gone to the very root of the matter, and, therefore, it is an issue of transcendental value, far surprising Swaraj in terms of political constitution," Gandhiji declared "and I would say that such a constitution would be a dead weight if it was not backed by a moral basis, in the shape of the present hope engendered in the breasts of the downtrodden millions that weight is going to be lifted from their shoulders."

After the fast, undertaken in name of God, was broken in the presence of Gurudev Rabindranath Tagore and many others in a religious environment, he did not fail to reaffirm his commitments to untouchables whom he honourably addressed as Harijans. Gandhiji said:

"The sacrificial fire, once lit shall not be put out as long as there is the slightest trace of untouchability still left in Hinduism. If it is God's will that it does not end in my life, I have the confidence that there are thousands of earnest reformers who will lay down their lives in order to purify Hinduism of this awful curse."

The moot question is: How many Hindus bend their ways on Gandhian noble commitment? Has untouchability gone and become a thing of the past? Who betrayed Gandhiji-Dr Ambedkar knowingly that untouchables cause was compromised forever agreed to the abandonment of the separate electorate or caste Hindus who forgot every commitment and wishes of the Great Soul keeping alive the treacherous practice of Untouchability.

One thing is clear Dr Ambedkar's interpretation of religion (Really Dharma) was completely in conformity with Gandhian concept of one God and therefore, equality among His creations. In Gandhian language of Bhajan, **"Vaishanava Jana To Tene Kahiye Je Peer Parai Jane Re."** There is no place of inferiority or superiority or inequality in Gandhian religion. So was the commitment of Dr Ambedkar. As early as 1923 in the reformed legislative council of Bombay, a social reformer S.K. Bole pleaded that Untouchability was a stigma on the good name of India and step needed for its eradication. He said, "We resent the segregation policy of the South African colonies and therefore we must set our own house in order. It is in our interest and in the interest of the country that the depressed classes should be given better treatment." Dr Ambedkar pointed out that three factors are required for the uplift of an individual-: Sympathy, equality and liberty. But none of them was available for untouchables in Hinduism which had been reduced to multitude of commands and prohibitions.

Dr Ambedkar made all efforts to convince that Hindu society must be reorganised on the basis of religion accepting Liberty, Equality and Fraternity.

Before embracing Buddhism Dr Ambedkar had left long rope before caste Hindus to embrace his brethren wiping out semblances of ingrained inequality .But they did not bend their ways, ideology and treacherous inhumanly practices. Two decade earlier to embracing Buddhism in 1956, on 13 October, 1935 at Yeol Conference Dr Ambedkar had made public statement, "Unfortunately, I was born a Hindu, it was beyond my power to prevent that, but I solemnly assure you I will not die a Hindu."

On March18, 1956, Dr Ambedkar chronologically narrated his efforts to get respectability in the Hindu-fold and its failure all the times. He said," I started the movement in the year 1017 that we are nit Hindus and that if we had not been so we would not have been remained Untouchables and would have also been Pujaris in temples. It is because of this fact that I started the temple entry movement in the year 1925. But the main motivation for it was not that we wanted to worship gods. The movement was launched because we wanted to assert our right. If I am a Hindu, I should also have the liberty and right to worship and become Pujari in the temples. But it is not so. On March 19, 1927, I started the Mahad Tank Satyagraha in Ratnagiri district to asset the right of Untouchables to take water from the tank. But again, attempts were made to coerce us, drive us away."

What Dr Ambedkar did as to decision of conversion, anybody could have done the same in view not only of denigration, persecution, and humiliation but also not providing water and food while hungry only because of the caste. When he took water from Chowder Tank and drank it, a large crowd of caste Hindus brutally attacked the gathering of depressed people, injured them. But unprovoked Dr Ambedkar rushed to the scene and calmed his men ready to return them in the same coin and restored peace. On June 6, 1927, nine caste men, after trial, were awarded four month's rigorous imprisonment. The matter did not end there. Caste Hindu rubbed salt into the wounds of the depressed classes by purification of the Chowder Tank by mixture of cow-dung, cow-urine, curd and cow-milk as mentioned in Manusmriti. The news flared up widely to the discomfiture of the Depressed Classes. Indignant Dr Ambedkar had no option but to issue inflammatory but emotional statements, "Lost rights are never regained by begging and appeals to the conscience of the usurpers but by relentless struggle. Goats are used for sacrificial offerings but not lions." He declared, "The question whether we belong to the Hindu religion or not is to be decided by us once for all. The question is whether religion is meant for men or men for religion. The Depressed Classes would die for that religion which did not care for them." Dr Ambedkar wanted to go to the Tank only to prove that the Depressed Classes people were also human beings like others.

Denied of all possibility to be the part of Hinduism and suffering intolerably the tragic fate of birth as untouchable Dr Ambedkar searched the source of evil. He found it in Hindu scriptures and prominently in Manusmriti. In order to appreciate the decision of Dr Ambedkar to hit at the very root some background facts need special mention.....

Dr Ambedkar's in-depth study of Hindu scriptures for fifteen long years had enabled him to know ins and outs of all religious books. His bonfire of Manusmriti did not show that he had less respect for Manu Vaivashwat Manu or his original work. Whatever haunted him was the present form of Manusmriti pouring despises humiliation and treacherous treatments against the Untouchables. It had become symbol of approving ingrained inequality and deprivations; allowing privileges for few and disprivileging masses. The decision to bonfire Manusmriti was to hit back at the strongest basis of all social evils. In words of Dr Ambedkar himself:

"The bonfire of Manusmriti was quite intentional. It was very cautious and drastic step, but was taken with the view to forcing the attention of caste Hindus. At intervals drastic measures are necessary. If you do not knock at the door none opens it. It is not that all parts of the Manusmriti are condemnable, that it does not contain good principles and that Manu himself was opt a sociologist, was a mere fool. We made a bonfire of it because we view it as a symbol of injustice under which we have been crushed across the centuries. Because of the teachings of Manusmriti we have been ground down under despicable poverty and so made the dash staked all, took our lives in our hands and performed the deed. At the root of the Hindu social system laid Dharma as prescribed in the Manusmriti. Such being the case, I do not think that it is possible to abolish inequality in the Hindu society unless the existing foundation of Smriti-religion is removed and a better one is laid in its place. I, however, despair of the Hindu society being able to reconstruct itself on a better foundation."

Can it be said that bonfire of Manusmriti was with a view to show any disrespect to it? Of course not! It was due to utter misuse of that pious book for personal end of certain classes and degradation of masses in the name of that. It was done on belief that caste Hindu may come forward and do something positive in direction of equality and dignity of masses so that the original respect for the Manusmriti may be restored. Every writer of repute says that the original Manusmriti has been infiltrated with many objectionable evil practices. Justice Rama Jois points out that, "Manusmriti is the collection of rules following not only from Vedas, Upanishadas, but also from epics and customs, some of whom are violative of Vedas." Justice Ramajois suggests: "Let us not reject the entire Manu Smriti as a whole. Let us reject such of the provisions in Manu Smriti which lead to unhappiness of a few or those which incite public resentment and retain and follow the invaluable provisions which are collected and reproduced in this book." But this is not answer to Dr Ambedkar's objections. Who will do it? Has Hindu intelligentsia or liberal religionists ever done so as to delineate the acceptable and unacceptable part of Manusmriti and directed to follow the former and discord the latter? If not how can anybody expect untouchables to draw such finer distinction for worshipping Manusmriti and continue to bear excesses, torture, persecution, denigration, humiliation and deprivation- social, economic and cultural? Buddha made efforts to reform Hinduism on the line of equality. It was a reaction against Brahmanism even while retaining much of its faith. Even this much reform was not tolerated by forces standing for Brahmanism. And, as Dr Sarvapalli Radhakrishnan views, "Brahmanism killed Buddhism with a fraternal embrace." Thus, Manusmriti was reduced in and infused in Brahmanism. Manuism and Braminism had become one and the same.

In the above backdrop Dr Ambedkar was not against Vaivashwat Manu. He regarded him a learned and great sociological jurist. He was against Manuism; against its being used to justify all sorts of evil practices to denigrate, humiliate and persecute the untouchable masses. He was real follower of Manu, " where ever women are worshipped, gods enjoy living there **(Yatra naryastu pujyante ramante tatra Devata**);" or there is chance of promotion and demotion in Varna according to one's own deeds i.e. a Shudra could go upward and become Brahmin and Brahmin could stoop down to Shudra according to his conduct. Manu preached worth as determinant of higher status, not birth. Who made mockery of Manu's real preachings?-Dr Ambedkar or Manuvadis themselves? Dr Ambedkar was against that Manusmriti which had been deformed by the vested interests that be. **Firstly**, may be by the Rishi who was entrusted the job of communicating his preaching to the common people. The original 58 Shlokas were told by Manu himself. Rest was entrusted to Bhriguji. **Secodly**, most possibly objectionable and mischievously inequality enforcing provisions might have been inserted during the regime Pushyamita Shunga, as many learned scholars believe. Whatever could be ways and means, one thing was clear that the existing form of Manusmriti could not be, is not be and will not be ever justified on touchstone of reason, liberty, equality and fraternity as accepted norms of the civilised society. The conscientious revolt of Dr Ambedkar was against this Manusmriti.

Dr Ambedkar was not against Brahmins. He was definitely against Brahmanism- an evil incarnate. Scriptures are told to support Brahmanism, which constructed casteism, which in turn encouraged superiority and inferiority complexes in society. The cult of Brahmanism has entangled not only the whole system of the Hindu society but has also badly affected even the equality adhering religions like Christianity, Islam and Sikhism. Dr Ambedkar clearly visualised it and defined Brahmanism as follow:

"By Brahmanism," he stated I do not mean the power, privilege and interest of the Brahmins as a community. That is not the sense in which I am using the word. By Brahmins I mean the negation of the spirit of liberty, equality and fraternity. In that sense it is rampant in all classes and is not confined to Brahmins alone though they have been its originators. The effect of Brahmanism were not confined only to social rights such as inter-dining and inter-marrying. It denied them also the civic rights. So omniscient is Brahmanism that it even affects the field of economic opportunities."

Dr Ambedkar could very well visualise the all embracing ill impact of the evil of Brahmanism that in his own Province Maharashtra, Mahar were not having equal terms inter-dining and inter- marrying with Chamars. Dr Ambedkar was against this cult of Brahmanism. It was a vicious circle. Scriptures were utilised to guard Brahmins with privileged status. Uncontrolled power made them wanton enabling them to enslave others by their cleverness. Brahmins lost hold of virtues and searched all possible ways to secure their livelihood on pretentious premises. By declaring others degraded they acquired special position in society. They secured their economic position by allowing everything permissible to them without any blot on them and ousting many people from doing anything outside menial works forced by them on such people. It goes without saying that Brihaspati became Guru of Devatas and Shukracharya became Guru of Rakshasas and ready to do anything for their flourishing. But nobody ever raised any objection against Shukracharya. Dr exposed multitudinous flexibility in livelihood for Brahmins arranged by them. He narrated: "A Brahmin can be a priest to Vishnu- the God of Love. He can be a priest to Shankar- the God of Destruction. He can be a priest at Buddha Gaya worshipping Buddha- the greatest teacher of mankind who taught the noblest doctrine of Love. He can also be priest to

Kali, the Goddess, who must have daily sacrifice of an animal to satisfy her thirst for blood; he will be priest of the temple of Rama- the Kshatriya God! He will also be a priest of the temple of Parashuram, the god who took Avatar to destroy Kshatriyas! He can be a priest to Bramha, the creator of the world. He can be a priest to a Priest to Pir whose God will not brook the claim of Bramha to share his spiritual domination over the world!"

Dr Ambedkar was against such Brahmanism- everything secured for the self proclaimed privileged class which could earn by whatever means they could, irrespective of its being reserved for some other class, but not untouchables who could do only menial and degrading jobs. What Dr Ambedkar opposed was this seclusion and deprivation of untouchables. Untouchables were left with no option in life but to weep on the tragic incident of their birth with no hope of liberation.

Dr Ambedkar had learnt a lot. He could distinguish between the ability and good points of Brahmins and ugly faces of Brahmanism, as had been done by Swami Vivekananda. To be Brahmin is always a good thing. But who is a real Bramin? If we put our real faith in scriptures, a real Brahmin is one who has worth. Mahabharata speaks so. In his response to Yaksha asking who is a real Brahmin, Yudhisthra said, "learning makes a real Brahmin." Tathgata Buddha preached that nobody becomes Brahmin by birth. One becomes Brahmin by conduct. Uninfilterated Manusmriti itself recognised – everybody is Shudra by birth, he becomes Brahmin by Sanskaras (**Janmana jayate Shudra, sankarat dwijyuchyate**) or promotion and demotion is possible depending on good or bad conduct. On this touchstone of worth, not birth makes a real Brahmin who could be a better/ real Brahmin than M.A.; Ph.D.; D.Sc.; Bar-at-Law with burning heart for social justice, Dr B.R. Ambedkar? Wittingly or unwittingly he is deservedly adorned as Baba Saheb Dr Bhima Rao Ambedkar.

In such surroundings of indignation, as Dr Presler observes, "Dr Ambedkar was now painfully conscious that his efforts to obtain liberty, equality and fraternity for Depressed Classes while within Hinduism, failed to meet his expectations, there was one last recourse that might be tried: to change his and their religion."

Dr Ambedkar explained the reasons for his preference to Buddhism. In May 1956, broadcasting from the British Broadcasting Corporation on topic, "Why I like Buddhism and how it is useful to the world in its present circumstances, " he said, "I prefer Buddhism because it gives three principles in combination which no other religion does. Buddhism teaches Prajna (understanding as against superstition and supernaturalism), Karuna (love) and Samata (equality). This is what a man needs for a good and happy life. Neither god nor soul can save society". Dr Ambedkar compared and contrasted Hinduism and Buddhism. He explained, "By discarding my ancient religion which stood for inequality and oppression today I am reborn. I have no faith in the philosophy of incarnation; and it is wrong and mischievous to say that Buddha was an incarnation of Vishnu. I am no more a devotee of any Hindu god or goddess. I will not perform Shradha. I will strictly follow the eight-fold path of Buddha. Buddhism is a true religion and I lead a life guided by the three principles of knowledge, right path and compassion. Hinduism believes in God. Buddhism has no God. Hinduism believes in soul. According to Buddhism there is no soul. Hinduism believes in Chaturvarnya. Buddhism has no place for the caste system." Religion for him meant Dharma-a way of life in which there is the mission of otherness, love for all equal opportunity to develop one's nature gifted talent without any hindrance and discrimination. As justice V.R. Krishna Iyer views, Dr Ambedkar shook the conscience of Hindus, when he explained the real connotation of religion. He said:

"I tell you, religion is for man and not man for religion. If you want to organise, consolidate and be successful in this world change your religion. The religion that does not recognise you as human being, or give you water to drink, or allow you enter the temples is not worthy to be called religion. The religion that forbids you to receive education and comes in the way of your material advancement is not worthy of appellation 'religion'. The religion that does not teach its followers to show humanity in dealing with its co-religionists is nothing but a display of force. The religion that asks its adherents to suffer the touch of animals but not the touch of human beings is not religion by a mockery. That religion, which precludes some classes from education, forbids them to accumulate wealth and to bear arms, is not religion but a mockery. The religion that compels the ignorant to be ignorant and the poor to be poor is not religion but a visitation.[15]

Dr Ambedkar reminded of the famous saying of Lord Buddha, "Hunger is the greatest disease, and no preaching could be by a person when afflicted with hunger." Dr Ambedkar made his followers realise that they suffered not only of hunger but numerous other disabilities too. He announced that Hindu religion neither appealed to his conscience nor his self- respect. He very emphatically said, "Religion is for the man and not man for religion" and exhorted them by saying" To get human treatment, convert yourselves. Convert for securing equality. Convert for getting liberty. Convert so that your domestic life may be happy."And, therefore, in 1935, Mahar Parishad unanimously endorsed Dr Ambedkar's decision and resolved to declare. "Good-Bye to Hindu Religion."

Once Dr Ambedkar declared his resolve to convert, but without definite resolve to convert to which religion, not only he and his followers had many options but many prominent functionaries of prominent religions like Christianity, Islam and Sikhism started contacting him with lucrative and attractive proposals. But, Hindus never came with definite proposal that they would treat him and his followers on equal footing. In spite of that Dr Ambedkar had soft corner for Hindu religion. He weighed comparative merit of joining one religion or the other. He found that the conditions of his men would not be substantially better in Christianity and Islam. Conversion to Christianity or Islam would have denationalized Depressed Classes. On 24th July 1936 *The Times of India* published Dr Ambedkar's view, "Conversion to Islam or Christianity will denationalise the Depressed Classes. If they go over to Islam, the number of Muslims will be double and danger of Muslim domination also becomes real. If they go over to Christianity, the numerical strength of the Christians becomes five to six crores. It will help to strength to the hold of Britain on the country." From the Hindus point of view among Christianity, Islam or Sikhism, he expressed the opinion that Sikhism would be the best. Because doing so Depressed Classes would remain within in the Hindu culture. He said if they embrace Sikhism, they will not harm the destiny of the country, but they will help the destiny of the country. They will not be denationalised. On the contrary, they will be a help in the political advancement of the country.

Who could be more nationalist or lover of the culture of the country than Dr Ambedkar? His inclination towards Sikhism was due to his entrenched nationalistic outlook and hidden love for Hindu culture. But two considerations dissuaded him from embracing Sikhism. First, the benefit of conversion to Sikhism would have been limited to Punjab and untouchables would actually lose political privileges in other provinces. Second, after his meeting with Sikh leaders he realised that the position of Untouchables would be of second grade Sikhs there.

Dr Ambedkar's choice fell on Buddhism. There was always a struggle in his mind- to remain or not to remain in Hindu-fold. On March 18, 1956, he took clear and final stand, and explained, "So long as the Shastras of the Hindus exist and the Shankracharya is in saddle, they cannot emancipate anybody and their talk to emancipate us is nothing but sham. The religion that I am going to give to the Depressed Classes is Buddhism. Everybody should be happy over it. There is no conflict of soul, God or even Gods in it. There is in this religion universal brotherhood, justice, equality and fraternity. All our problems will end only if we embrace Buddhism. Even amongst the depressed classes today, some sections do not have marital relations with each other. The Hindu religion is responsible for all these ills. I tried to stop it, but sad to say, some of our own people opposed me on this point. Unless we embrace Buddhism, caste struggle in our ranks and the middle classes will not come to an end."[16]

Dr Ambedkar had obvious choice of Buddhism as vehicle of emancipation to achieve justice. There is no other religion equal to Buddhism. It is Buddhism which talks of kindness, "As the mother protects her only child even at the risk of her own life; even so let one cultivate boundless thoughts of loving –kindness towards all beings." On the other hand no chance of such grace, even in dream, could be in Hinduism. Incorrigibility of Hinduism was realised even by Gandhiji, what to say of Dr Ambedkar. While resorting to fast unto death in Yervada prison, Gandhiji wrote to an associate who had remonstrated with him that his decision to fast was contrary to reason and dharma, Gandhiji wrote, "My step has not been dictated by reason; it was inspired by my inner voice. My reason, however, told me: Hundred of persons like you probably have to die to remove the blot of Untouchability." Is not it clear admission of the incorrigibility of the evil of Untouchability under Hinduism? How is it different from Dr Ambedkar' views who unequivocally exposed: "There have been many Mahatmas in India whose sole object was to remove Untouchability and to elevate and absorb the Depressed Classes, but every one of them has failed in his mission.

Mahatmas have come Mahatmas have gone, but the Untouchables have remained as Untouchables." Chaitanya Mahaprabhu, Jnyandeo, Sant Tukaram, Tirruvalluvar, Ramkrishna Paramahansa, Raja Ram Mohan Roy, Rabindranath Tagore, Maharshi Dayananda and a host of others fought against the evil of casteism rampant in Hinduism, but could not eradicate it. Would it have been wise on the part of Dr Ambedkar to rely on mere assurance that Hindu social reformers would eradicate casteism, wipe out Untouchbility from Hinduism and make untouchable on par with other caste –Hindus? Experience had made Dr Ambedkar wise enough to throw out any such gestation.

By embracing Buddhism he remained under the Hindu culture. Who could be more respectful to Gandhiji than Dr Ambedkar? On October 13, 1956 at a press conference Dr Ambedkar explained one of his reasons for embracing Buddhism He said, "I had once told Mahatma Gandhi that though I differed with him on the issue of Untouchability, when the time comes I will choose only the least harmful way for the country. And this is the greatest benefit I am conferring on the country by embracing Buddhism. I have taken care that my conversion will not harm the tradition of the culture and history of this land." He told *"I have changed the compartment not the train"*.

Buddhism is not different from Hinduism. It is said to be Hindu religion minus Brahmanism. Swami Vivekananda delivered a lecture on 26th September, 1893 under caption "Buddhism, The Fulfillment of Hinduism". Vivekananda was sworn Hindu Vedantist. He started, "I am not a Buddhist as you have heard, and yet I am." Swamiji said, "Shakya Muni came not to destroy, but he was fulfillment, the logical conclusion, the logical development of the religion of the Hindus". Swamiji suggested proper rapprochement between the Brahmanism and the Buddhism- the former represents intellect the latter the largeness of the heart. He concluded, "Let us then join the wonderful intellect of the Brahmin with the heart, the noble soul, the wonderful humanising power of the Great Master." Swami Vivekanada preached, practiced and envisioned equality. So strived, Dr Ambedkar for equality, liberty and fraternity. Was Dr Ambedkar not a real Hindu minus evil of Untouchability prevalent in Hinduism or true followings of Hinduism-Brahmanism?

Dr Ambedkar was spiritually Samyak Sambuddha. He got rare spiritual gain. According to the Hindu scriptural saying when good deeds (**punya**) of many lives accumulate only then the name God (Rama) comes on the lips a dying person. It is rarest of the rare occasion (**Janam Janam Muni Jatan Karahin, Ant Ram Kahi Awat Nahin-Tulasidas**) "Dr Ambedkar had completed his most auspicious spiritual work, "Buddha and His Dhamma" before he took his last breath. On December 5, 1956, Dr Ambedkar detained his secretary till late night. At 11.35 he asked him to place on his besides table the typescript of the Preface and Introduction to the Buddha and His Dhamma. While having the glance over them he took his last breath and early in the morning of 14th April, 1956 he was found by his wife Savita Ambedkar to have left for the heavenly abode. Dr Upendra Baxi gives tribute, "In his finitude, he recombined his emancipation from Hinduism with scholarly solitude in the hour of his dying." The mortal remains of Dr Ambedkar were consigned to the flames on December7, 1956, when the eight-day celebrations of the 2500th Buddha Jayanti ended in Sanchi.

5. There has been accusation against Dr Ambedkar of contradictions and disowning the Constitution which he had drafted. His words have been misconceived and misinterpreted. The accusation is that in the House he had said, "Now, Sir, we have inherited a tradition. People always keep on saying to me: Oh, you are maker of the Constitution. My answer is I was a hack. What I was a hack. What I was asked to do, I did much against my will." On another occasion again being accused that he was responsible for all ills because he had drafted the Constitution he retorted, "Sir my friends tell me that I have made the Constitution. But I am quite prepared to say that I shall be the first person to burn it out, I do not want it. It does not suit anybody." When repeatedly provoked as if he had committed some wrong by drafting the Constitution, he came out with his heart finding Constitution in action quite different from what for it was framed. Language of answer is note worthy. The first reaction began with calling out the inherited tradition of the people to blame others. It expresses his disapproval of tendency to accuse. The second reaction starts with, 'Sir, my friends tell me that I have made the Constitution'. It expresses again passing of blemish on him. For the appropriate answer of this unlike Ambedkarian outburst his real concern has to be searched. The immediate answer of Dr Ambedkar can only be

appreciated in light of the actual implementation of the so well drafted Constitution. The Constitution is implemented by the men at the helm of affair. To this his reaction was that, "we built a temple for a god to come in and reside, but before the god could be installed if the dèvil had taken possession of it, what else could we do except destroy the temple? We did not intend that it should be occupied by the Asuras. We intended it to be occupied by Devas". Devas and Asuras are symbolic expressions to express two sets of governance-The government of laws acting within the norms set by constitutionalism and intendment of the Constitution, and other the government of men going astray ignoring constitutional aspirations. It can be appreciated well keeping in view the suggestions of Mahatma Gandhi in 1948 that, (1) The Congress should be dissolved as had been the Party of the freedom struggle and in power it could meet with disrepute, and,(2) he suggested Congress members not to be power- drunk. On 25th November 1949 Dr Ambedkar made clear,"....however good a Constitution may be, it is sure to turnout bad Constitution. May be it turn out to be good if those who are called to work it happen to be a good lot. The working of the Constitution does not depend wholly upon the nature of the Constitution. The Constitution can provide only the organs of State such as Legislature, the Executive and the Judiciary. The factors on which the working of these organs of State depends are the people and the political parties they will set up as their instruments to carry out their wishes and their policies. Who can say how the People of India and their parties will behave? Will they uphold constitutional methods of achieving their purposes or will they prefer revolutionary methods, however a good Constitution may be? It is, therefore, futile to pass any judgment without reference to the part which the people and their parties are likely to play." Dr Ambedkar also warned of contradictions between political democracy and social democracy. He said, "How long shall we continue to live in this life of contradictions? How long shall we continue to deny equality in our social and economic life? If we continue to deny it for long, we will do so only by putting our political democracy in peril. We must remove this contradiction at the earliest possible moment or else those who suffer from inequality will blow up the structure of political democracy which this Assembly has so laboriously built up." Was the Constitution functioning well on stipulated line at the time Dr Ambedkar made the earlier referred remarks? Definitely not! Dr Ambedkar, as Union Law Minister had very diligently prepared Hindu Code Bill on the initiative of the Union Cabinet. The Bill was introduced in the Constituent Assembly (which was also working as Parliament) April 11, 1947. But could not be passed even within four years. After the adoption of the Constitution, he was again entrusted the job of getting the Bill presented for deliberations. The Bill contained mainly four items- abolition of the doctrine of the right by birth; right of property to women; right to have share by daughters from parent's property and provision for divorce. Due to the vehement opposition from orthodox Hindus both from within and outside House, the Prime Minister (though reluctantly, because he had been keenly interested in reform of Hindu law) asked Dr Ambedkar to drop the Bill. The statement of Dr Ambedkar and Pt. Nehru's response are worth noting. Embarrassed Dr Ambedkar resigned on 27th September, 1951 from the coveted post of Law Minister, Union Cabinet. In his resignation letter, Dr Ambedkar made clear his suffocation on non-performance of the government on the line of the constitutional commitment. He said, "Although I was not satisfied with the government's foreign policy and the treatment meted out to Backward Classes and the Scheduled Castes, I was continuing in the government because of the Hindu Code Bill, which was the greatest social reform measure undertaken by the Legislature in the country. No law passed by the Indian Legislature in the past or likely to be passed in the near future, can be compared to it in point of its significance. To leave inequality between class and class, sex and sex, which is the soul of the Hindu Society untouched and go on to passing legislation relating to economic problem is to make a farce of our Constitution and to build a pace on a dung heap." He further made clear that, "I must be true to myself and that I can be only by going out." Equally important is the reply of Pt. Nehru which confirms Dr Ambedkar's anxiety. Pt. Nehru said, "I quite understand your great disappointment at the fact that the Hindu Code could not be passed in this session, that even the Marriage and Divorce part of it had ultimately to be postponed I know very well how hard you have labored at it and how keenly you have felt about it. Although I have not been intimately connected with this Bill, I have been convinced of its necessity and I was anxious that it should be passed.. I tried my utmost, but the fates and the rules of Parliament were against us. It seemed clear to me that nothing that we could do could get it through during this session. Personally I shall not give up this fight because I think it is intimately connected with any progress on any front that we desire to make." Commenting on Pt. Nehru's state of mind at that time, The Times of India dated 29th September, 1951 quoted Johnson's famous remark on Goldsmith-

"He wrote like an Angel and spoke like poor Paul."[17]

Dr Ambedkar himself lamented the tragic end of the Bill after four years moribund pending in Constituent Assembly and Provisional Parliament in the following words:

"It was killed and buried, unwept and unsung after four clauses were passed."[18] It was very radical and revolutionary towards equalisation of gender. Dr Ambedkar clarified in his resignation speech: "The Hindu Code Bill was the greatest social reform measure undertaken by the Legislature in the country. No law passed by the Indian in the past or likely to passed in the future, can be compared to it in point of significance. To leave inequality between class and class, sex and sex, which is the soul of Hindu Society untouched and to go on passing legislation relating to economic problems is to make a farce of our Constitution and to build a palace on a dung heap".[19]

The hope of liberation and equality of Hindu women was also sealed. How jubilant and hopeful they had become in 1951 is clear from the large demonstration of excited women around the Parliament House on September 17, 1951- the day on which long awaited Hindu Code Bill was supposed to be discussed. Acharya Kriplani frankly admitted that reluctance on his part to support Hindu Code Bill provoked his wife to give him curtain lectures. The bill was hailed by many as long-awaited piece of social reform relieving women from bondage. The Hindu Code Bill was dropped on pretension of the lack of time as precedence was to be given to other bills. Dr Ambedkar made clear in long resignation letter: "I am sure the truncated Bill was dropped because other and more powerful members of the Cabinet wanted precedence for their Bills. I am unable to understand how the Benaras and Aligarh University Bills, how the Press Bill could have been precedence over the Hindu Code even in its attenuated form? It is not that there was no law on the statute book to govern the Aligarh University or the Benaras University. It is not that these universities would have gone to wrack and ruin if the Bills had not been passed in this session. It is not that the Press Bill was urgent. There is already law on the Statute book and the Bill could have waited. I got the impression that the Prime Minister although sincere, had not earnestness and determination required to get the Hindu Code Bill through."

The other matter which haunted Dr, Ambedkar's mind was the neglect of the Backward Classes and the Scheduled Classes. He unequivocally made clear: (1) "I was very sorry that the Constitution did not embody any safeguards for the Backward Classes. It was left to be done by the Executive Government on the basis of the recommendations of the Commission to be appointed by the President. More than a year has elapsed since we passed the Constitution. But the government has not even thought of appointing the Commission", and (2) "The provisions made in the Constitution for safeguarding the position of the Scheduled Castes were not to my satisfaction. However, I accepted them for what they were worth, hoping that government will show some determination to make them effective. What is position of the Scheduled Castes today? So far I see, it is the same as before. The same old tyranny, the same old oppression, the same old discrimination which existed before, existing now and perhaps in worst form. I have been wondering whether there is any parallel in the world to the condition of the Scheduled Castes in India. I cannot find any." Giving the detail of his concern and governmental neglect of the Scheduled Castes, he concluded, "You can, therefore, well imagine what pain it has caused me to see that the cause of the Scheduled Castes has been relegated to the limbo of nothing."

What a grand compliment and hint at national loss was presented by the Times of India? It read: "Bereft of the crown of Manu, Dr Ambedkar nonetheless leaves the government with a considerable record of achievement behind him. The cabinet is not overburdened with talent, and the department of this discerning scholar and industrious student of public affairs cannot but dim its limited luster. Political memories, it is true, are short but in shielding the old prejudices Dr Ambedkar showed himself capable of rising to the height of new responsibilities and occasion. India can ill afford to lose the service of this able politician and it would be little short of tragedy, personal and national, if Dr Ambedkar were to relinquish the national stage and relapse into communal politics. A formidable ally, Dr Ambedkar is also a foreman worthy of one's steel'. The last few years have seen him harnessing his outstanding abilities to constructive purposes and both the country and his community stand to gain if he continues in that path."

Can anybody still raise fingers at his outburst mentioned earlier? Did not Dr Ambedkar resign the cabinet post for the sake of the rights of women, the Scheduled Castes and the Backward Classes?

Dr Ambedkar has been hailed as modern Manu. Had the Hindu Code Bill been passed, he would have fully been justified as modern Manu –radically metamorphosed Manu, enforcing equality in the place of inequality, desegregation in the place of segregation, love and charity in the place of arrogance and discrimination. A few months before the ill fate of the Hindu Code Bill, Justice P.B. Gajendragadkar, a noted Bombay High Court Judge (at that time) and famous jurist scholar of Sanskrit, addressing the students of the Karnataka University on "Hindu Code Bill" observed:

"If Dr Ambedkar gives up Hindu Code, his achievement would go down in history as piece of poetic justice indeed. Destiny, however, seemed unwilling to concede to the Law Minister of full laurels of a modern Manu."

Was not Dr Ambedkar's act of quitting the union ministry a grand cause like Buddha voluntarily undertaking PRAVARJYA- to leave Shakya kingdom to relieve himself from participating in war with Koliya Ganarajya, as he was of firm view that war could not provide any solution, instead it might sow the seed of another war and he also did not like the social boycott his family and confiscation of their lands in case of his refusal to participate in war as the rule of Sangha demanded. Buddha's was the lone voice in the meeting of Sangha called by the commander of army (Senapati) who commanded the majority support for and those who were opposed to it were in minority and dared not to speak out. Buddha's was the lone, but firm voice to denounce war between Sakyas and Koliya on the issue of the distribution of the water of Rohini River for irrigation. To leave the kingdom for peace was not an ordinary decision. So was the decision of Dr Ambedkar to quit the union cabinet. Buddha's sacrifice had singular effect. The war proposal was vehemently opposed after departure of Buddha with laudable flag of brotherhood five persons from each side of Shakyas and Koliyas sat side by side and solved the problem peacefully. Dr Ambedkar's sacrifice also did not go in waste. An eleven-member the First Backward Classes Commission was appointed by the President on 29.1. 1953 within a period of one year four months and two days of the resignation of Dr Ambedkar from union cabinet on 27.9.1951. It was followed by enactment of Untouchability Offences Act, 1955 and four Acts relating to Hindu law concerning marriage, adoption, guardianship and succession i.e. quadrificaion of Hindu Code Bill. Like Buddha Dr Ambedkar became free to fight for the evils of Hinduism loaded with treacherous inequality of Brahmanism. He travelled as a free bird throughout the country and nearby Buddhist countries in search of liberty, equality and fraternity for the emancipation of depressed classes.

References

1. Inside page of Arun Shourie, Worshipping False Gods, Rupa & Co., 1997.
2. Arun Shourie's, Falling over Backwards: An Essay Against Reservation and Judicial Populism, 2006.
3. Arun Shourie, Worshipping False Gods.
4. Dhananjay Keer, Dr. Baba Saheb Ambedkar: Life and Mission, Bombay, Popular Prakashan, 1954, p. 81.
5. Dhananjay keer, Dr. Baba Sahed Ambedkar, supra.
6. *Ibid*. p. 166.
7. *Ibid*. p. 167.
8. Last Speech of Dr Ambedkar in the Contituent Assembly of India.
9. Indra Shawhney v. Union of India 1992 Supp. (3) SCC 217.
10. *Ibid.*
11. Speech of Dr Rajendra Prasad, President, Constituent Assembly, on November 26, 1949 in the Constituent Assembly.
12. B.R. Ambedkar, What Mr. Gandhi and Congress Have Done to Untouchables?, Bombay, Thacker and Company, Ltd.,1945 p.7.
13. V.R.Krishna Iyer, Explosive Ambedkar's Vision: A Value Revolution in Society and State (in) his book, "A Judge's Miscellany" B.R. Publishing Corporation, Delhi 2001, pp.71-95 at p.73.
14. *Ibid.*
15. Social Justice and Undone Vast, pp. 11-13.
16. Nanak Chand Rattu, Last Few Years of Dr Ambedkar, p. 73.
17. Dhananjay Keer, Dr Ambedkar: Life and Mission, Bombay, 1961, p. 396.
18. The Times of India, 29th September, 1951.
19. *Ibid.*

7

False or Under Worshipped God ? - II

Dr Ambedkar: Victim of Historical Neglect and Denial of His Due

Dr Ambedkar was a great genius in many respects. His genius did not find due opportunity to provide full benefit to the society. His ability as scholar of political science found opportunity as Chairman, Drafting Committee of the Constituent Assembly and world is witness with what legal acumen, political understanding, socio-economic comprehension to tackle the problems facing the country, he accomplished the job of drafting the Constitution so as to attract the compliments from the noted constitutional law scholar Granville Austin as 'first and foremost a social document'... 'the majority of India's constitutional provisions are either directly arrived at furthering the aim of social revolution or attempt to foster this revolution by establishing conditions necessary for its achievement.' But same could not be true of other spheres.

1. Dr Ambedkar was a scholar of repute in economics. He was the first Indian to have the distinction of D.Sc. from the London School of Economics on "The Problems of Rupees: Its Origin and Solution" which very ably exposed the factors responsible for Rupee fall. In 1923, in this book along with other things, Dr Ambedkar had made suggestions regarding de-circulation of currency every 10 years so as to tackle the problem of the hoarding of black money. Welcoming the act demonetisation of Rs 1000 and Rs 500 November 2016, Prakash Ambedkar rightly laments, "The great economic insight remained under wraps as thesis or volumes of books on the

shelf. In the last six decades, very little has been talked or studied about Ambedkar's economic works."[1] His use as a minister other than the Ministry of Law about which his assessment was that, "Law Ministry administratively was of no importance. It gave no opportunity for heaping the policy of the government. We used to call it an empty soap box only good for lawyers to play with", would have been more beneficial to the country. When the Economic Committee was formed, being primarily a student of Economics and Finance he was expecting his appointment on the Committee, but he was left out. Later he was included on protest. Planning would have been most appropriate department for him. But, before creation of the department, he left the government. His thought on the enhancement of the economy of the nation through industrialisation and agricultural industry could not find opportunity to be explored. Reserve Bank of India was established on the idea of Dr Ambedkar submitted to the Hilton Young Commission. He was instrumental in establishment of the Finance Commission of India. He had many imaginative ideas which could have helped the country immensely. Some of them have been implemented recently, that is to say, free economy with stable rupee. He advocated birth control rate to develop the Indian economy. The non-effective implementation is posing great problem before the country.

2. In 1997, after the elapse of forty-six years of the inauguration of our republic based on Dr Ambedkar written Constitution, a legal luminary of the world fame Dr Upendra Baxi started his oration by a "testimonial to a lack, an absence" and lamented that "the Indian Social Science landscape has disarticulated Baba Saheb Ambedkar by studious silence".[2] This truthful articulation of historical neglect can be looked through factual evidences:

In spite of the collective applaud of Dr Ambedkar by the Constituent Assembly, Dr Ambedkar's portrait could not be installed in the Central Hall of the Parliament before 1967 and that too on the petition presented by the Republican Party of India presented to the then Prime Minister Shri Lal Bahadur Shastri in October1964 to the effect that, 'a portrait of Baba Saheb Ambedkar,' the father of the Indian Constitution' must be given a place in the Central Hall of Parliament.[3] That Hall was already adorned with the portraits of national leaders and founding fathers." In 1967, in response to the referred petition,

Dr Ambedkar's portrait was installed with distinction in the courtyard of Parliament. But the portrait was installed on the cost borne by the public, mostly from Maharashtra.[4] It is another matter that the rare honour was given to Dr Ambedkar by installation of his portrait in the courtyard of the Parliament with the lofty words of Dr Radhakrishnan, the President of India: "The people of India will ever remain grateful to Dr Ambedkar for devoting all his time and talents in the framing of a worthy Constitution. India can never forget such a great son. The Smritis or the laws written by Manu have no relevance today. There is no doubt that in past all the laws of the Hindus and India were made by the Hindu Rishis and all of them Brahmin by birth. But Dr Ambedkar has proved by his wisdom and intellect that great Rishis like him can take birth in any community. Dr Ambedkar was not only an eminent constitutional law expert, he had also mastery over the Hindu philosophy and Hindu social laws. We have rightly honoured him by installing his statue in the compound of Parliament House."[5]

3. The highest civilian honour, Bharat Ratna was awarded to Dr Ambedkar not earlier than 1990, even though twenty-one distinguished national figures and founding fathers had been adorned with it. He was honoured by equality and social justice enforcer Prime Minister Mr V.P. Singh, the eleventh P.M. of the country. It is another matter that he was honoured along with another non-violent satyagrahi, the African Gandhi, Nelson Mandela.

4. Dr Ambedkar remained unnoticed in academic circle. Though in 1916 itself he had read a paper on 'Castes in India: Their Mechanism, Genesis and Development' at an Anthropology Seminar which was published in 1917 in the Indian Antiquity, yet the notable sociologists writing on caste system in India even after more than a decade did not refer Dr Ambedkar. Christophe Jaffrelot in his book, "Dr Ambedkar and Untouchability: Fighting the Indian Caste System", points out :

"Ambedkar began investigating the origins of the caste system more than a decade before Govind Sadashiv Ghurye- the first Indian anthropologist to do so, whose Caste and Race in India was published in 1932.Yet his contribution to Indian sociology was overlooked for many years, Oliver Herrenschmidt emphasises as a prelude to his own effort to redress this imbalance. The founding fathers of the Indian anthropology, such as M.N. Srinivas and Louis Dumont and most of their heirs, have ignored Ambedkar, even though he anticipated many of their arguments."[6]

5. The tendency to ignore Dr Ambedkar prompted Dr Upendra Baxi to comment, this complete disregard by the academia of Ambedkar poses a critical question concerning the modes of production of knowledge through the formal educational and research systems in India. How is it that these knowledge systems have produced a near total annihilation of the very author of Annihilation of Caste System?[7] Dr Baxi further comments, "the community of knowledge and communities of power in India are united in their marginalisation of Baba Saheb. Neither politics nor knowledge discovers in him a vision towards which India may move."[8]

By 1997 it was realized that there was paucity of literature on Dr Ambedkar. There was wealth of literature on Gandhi, Nehru, Rajendra Prasad and Patel. Even the research bodies like the Indian Council of Social Science Research, the Indian Council of Historical Research, the Indian Council of Philosophical Research and the University Grants Commission did not pay much attention in this regard. Chritophe Jafferlot in his book, "Dr Ambedkar and Untouchability: Fight the Indian Caste System" pointed out that no University in India had come forward to associate with to the publication of the collected works of Dr Ambedkar in spite of millions of rupees reserved by the central government for the project.[9] Similar feeling was shared by Suresh Mane who in his article, "Constitution and Dr Ambedkar's Vision for Social Change," comments:

"The communities of knowledge and communities of power, in their united silent conspiracy have tried their best to marginalise Babasaheb, yet his presence is felt whenever the Rule or Constitution is in jeopardy."[10]

6. Some noticeable change is found in the post first decade twenty- first century. May be so due to the rising political and electoral significance of Dr Ambedkar in view of the social justice orientation started by Prime Minister V.P. Singh, emergence of Kanshi Ram and Mayawati on political horizon and general world- wide consciousness towards marginalised groups of the people and hope of the electoral prospect of political parties lying in propagation of Dr Ambedkar as their political icon. Speaking on the occasion of Ambedkar Memorial Lecture in Ambedkar University, Delhi in 2013 Dr Upendra Baxi noticed, "There has been ferment in Ambedkar studies, especially since

the publication of Maharashtra Government of his collected works and the birth centenary celebrations that followed. The University Grants Commission has endowed Universities, Chairs, and centres for social inclusion, and the Indian Council of Social Sciences Research not lagged far behind in assisting special research and seminars in Ambedkarite thought. Independent scholars in Universities have to their credit some fine studies on Ambedkar's thought and action. And, judges and law persons have accorded Dr Ambedkar his due through their daily constitutional work as well as on the Golden and sixty years of Indian constitutionalism."[11] Still progress is not in the right direction. Dr Baxi feels that his earlier version expressed in **Ambedkar oration** is still true, "the murmur of anonymous persecutors' still haunts his thought and action; so do the[12] persistent Brahminical ' schizoid-paranoid' thought formations."

One may not agree with all what Arundhati Roy discusses in, *"The Doctor and The Saint"*, but there is much truth in her comment that, "History has been unkind to Ambedkar. First, it contained him, and then it glorified him. It has made him India's leader of untouchabilities, the king of ghetto. It has hidden away his writings. It has stipped away the radical intellect and the searing insolance."[13]

7. The greatest damage done to Dr Ambedkar is that he has not been allowed to acquire the secular, humanist and justice orientation which is long due to him. His followers have constricted his image to a Messiah of Dalits. And, his opponent orthodox caste-Hindus have done the same raising accusing fingers as obstacle in the liberation movement. There is ample scope for researches to view his contributions in right perspective as treasure for posterity.

At present nobody is remembering or honouring Dr Ambedkar in the right perspective. Although Arun P. Mukherji in his writing, 'B.R. Ambedkar, John Dewey, and Meaning of Democracy' argues that, 'Despite seven decades of marginalisation by India's political and intellectual elite, B.R. Ambedkar is now a major presence in the pantheon of Indian heroes. His statutes now dot almost every Indian town and city, erected by the Dalit followers, for whom he is Babasaheb, the revered father,'[14] the reverence is not genuine. First, as the learned writer himself points out statutes are erected by his followers by which he means Dalit communities. Dr Ambedkar wrote the Constitution, the basic law of the land, for all and coming posterity. Reverence must come from all sections of the Indian society. Second, Dr Ambedkar was from the core of heart a Buddhist and as such did not like hero-worship of any kind. He believed in real following of principles, he stood for. The real reverence of Dr Ambedkar would be to educate, organise and agitate for right cause, leave petty gains and work for the general welfare of the people. The present day political scenario reveals that Dalits are most disunited- scattered in almost all political parties. Not only this most of them gain political stature in some Dalit base party and leave for their own better future prospect in some other rising political party and began to salute the rising sun. They have no hesitation in leaving in lurch their own brethren being humiliated, persecuted and denied human dignity and security to life. Thirdly, the installation of statutes of Dr Ambedkar is not taken kindly by intolerant fundamentalists. In U.P. Chief Minister Mayawati installed not less than 15,000 statutes of Dr Ambedkar. To quote Jaffrelot, "More than a few of the new public statutes there and in other states have been profaned by garlands of shoes. This insult, higher castes putting their feet on the top of Ambedkar, is based on an ancient symbolism. Rama's younger brother, ruling in his stead while his elder brother is exiled in the forest, wears Rama's sandals on his head as sign of his subjection to the rightful king. Such insults to Ambedkar have caused riots all over India."[15] Fourthly, there is a race among the political parties to capture all possible platforms associated with Babasaheb Ambedkar. Besides, birthday and Mahaparinivana day many more occasions have been invented. One of such occasions being 26th November, the day on which our Constitution was 'enacted, adopted and given to ourselves' by the Constituent Assembly and had been celebrated as Law Day since 1979. The year 2016 was chosen by the Union Government to be celebrated as the Constitution Day with a view to main focus on Dr Ambedkar as architect of the Constitution. A very proud researcher and learned Professor came out with some comment and suggestion. The comment was that 'the Supreme Court ordained Law Day was converted into an executive ordered Constitution Day' and the suggestion was:"Parliament would better celebrate Ambedkar by declaring war on unconstitutional evils like Untouchability."[16]

8. The virtual neglect of Dr Ambedkar's academic worth has been a serious concern for many merit loving scholars. Delivering the Ambedkar Memorial Lecture in 1979 (on 24-25,

1979) at Madras University on, "Political Justice, Legislative Reservation for Scheduled Castes and Social Change", Dr Upendra Baxi lamented:

"There are many major and minor ironies surrounding Babasaheb's life and work. The nation is indeed so bankrupt in deference that in his life-time only one university in India recognised him as a true scholar and honoured itself by conferring on Ambedkar as D.Lit. degree, but that too happened after the Columbia University had thus honored itself." The Columbia University conferred honorary degree of LL.D. on Dr Ambedkar on June 5, 1952 at its 198th Convocation.The citation hailed Dr Ambedkar "as a framer of the Constitution, Member of Cabinet and of the Council of States, one of India's leading citizens, a great social reformer and a valiant upholder of human rights." Subsequently the Osmania University honoured him with D.Lit. on January 12, 1953 in recognition of his eminent position and his scholarly achievements. Dr Baxi rightly comments, "The Indian Nation despite its proud boasts about its being the ancient home of learning, has yet to learn to understand, let alone appreciate, men of learning who men of action are also. "This comment is most appropriate, when Dr Ambedkar was honored by Columbia University with LL.D., he received only one congratulatory message and that was from Dr Radhakrishnan, Vice President of India, saying; "I am very pleased to see in the papers that the Columbia University is conferring on you the honorary degree of Doctor of Laws. My warmest congratulations." To it, Dr Ambedkar replied: "I am very glad to say that there are at least some in India who are prepared to appreciate the honour that is being done to me."[17]

There are many Ambedkars and not only one. In order to do justice with Dr Ambedkar all need proper articulation and exploration. Dr Upendra Baxi narrates as many as seven (1) Ambedkars[18] a young student who bore the full brunt of the practices of Untouchbility; (2) the student scholar; (3) a militant editor and journalist; (4) a pre-Gandhian using innovative tradition of protest in the form of satyahgraha against the caste evils; (5 & 6) Gandhisised- Poona pact and the Constitution-making; and seventh, a renegade Hindu embracing Buddhism. Only the combination of all will present the real vision of Dr Ambedkar's emancipation as justice for Atisudras.

9. No serious attempt has been made to appreciate Dr Ambekar's original contribution on the juriprudential side. Dr Ambedkar has propounded the theory akin to Socrates with apposite modification having the analogy of state with Hindu system. He obeyed the norms. He tried to upgrade untouchables by wearing **yagyopavit** amidst enchanting of mantras by Brahmins. He tried to change the system through exposing the lawlessness of the Hindu graded degrading society. In hope of change in the discriminatory and inhuman law of Hindu system for nearly a decade he remained under dilemma to remain or not remain in Hindu fold and finding no hope of change allowing equality and freedom to their men, he declared leaving of Hinduism. As Socrates was not in favour of blind following of unjust law so was Dr Ambedkar. Dr Ambedkar made improvement upon Socrates by adding the element Satyagraha against the bad laws and if incorrigible then to leave governance by embracing some other set of norms to govern. Dr Upendra Baxi fondly calls Dr Ambedkar, 'an Aristotle of the Atisudras'.[19] Equality has intimate relation with justice. Though Aristotle appeared to justify the institution of slavery on account of natural law ideology to be both beneficial and just and thereby inequality prevalent in society. But his view on equality was complex. He stressed the inequalities of men as much as their equalities. In his later life he also appeared to mend his view on slavery when the ill and inhuman treatment with slaves was brought to his notice. He accepted that it is easy to see that those who hold the opposite view are also in a way correct. There were some meeting point between Aristotle and Dr Ambedkar. Aristotle did not subscribe to the Platonic division of society as ruler, auxiliary and artisan and justice, "to mind one's own business and not to be meddlesome". Dr Ambedkar discarded division based on Varnashrama system providing graded inequality and not allowing doing anything other than strictly prescribed for the particular class. Aristotle pleaded that all beings, in so far they are political animals, possess the same nature. They are on this level, all equal. Dr Baxi finds comparability between Aristotle and Dr Ambedkar. He says: "if Aristotle is to be considered a careful thinker, and a complex philosopher, Baba Saheb may be rightly termed as Aristotle of Atisudras. He (Dr Ambedkar) invented a pyramid of hierarchical inequality and made every untouchable, at least normatively, into a citizen from a subject. Equally revolutionary were his ideas of representation, efficiency, education, and social solidarity among the subalterns."

10. Treatment of the untouchable leaders, for whose cause Dr Ambedkar was fighting tooth and nail against the mighty hands of the proponents of the graded Indian society was so ungrateful that Dr Ambedkar might have been reminded of the famous lines of the British great poet William Shakespeare:

Blow blow thou winter wind,
Thou are not so unkind,
As man's ingratitude:

First, Aminchand, Dr Ambedkar's follower deserting him became President, Harijan League, Delhi, an organisation floated by the Congress, met Dr Ambedkar on pre-death day. He narrated how they were rewarded by Dr Ambedkar's criticism of Congress. He said: "Sir, the more you abuse and speak ill of the Congress Party, the more we are benefited, cared and looked after. So much so that we need not run after anybody even for minor gains. These come to us in plenty without our asking. With your blessings, we are thriving and flourishing in all walks of life."[20]

How Dr Ambedkar might have felt, one can very well visualize, when he said:

"All right goaded by your conscience, go your own way, enjoy the benefit you derive from Ambedkar- baiting from the Congress Party and the Hindus. But do not also forget to be grateful to your benefactors, the bread-givers. Behave like a dog, who while relishing the left over thrown to him from a distance never forgets the kindness of his master and would wag his tail in gratitude."

After departure of Aminchand Dr Ambedkar commented:

"Just see, to what level these people have gone down. There is nothing like a sense of human dignity and self-respect left in them except feeding their stomachs with the morsels of food thrown before them and to praise and sing the songs of the ruling party. But for these blacklegs, who are bartering the rights and interests of the community for their petty gains, we would have won the battle for our political emancipation long ago."[21]

Is the present day political scenario of Scheduled Castes representatives anyway better than what worried Dr Ambedkar? Are not they selling their souls away for sordid boons? Have not they become absorber of neo-brahminism? How many M.Ps. or M.L.As. belonging to the Scheduled Castes have got agitated on brutal attacks on Scheduled Castes (Una incident)? Have not they forgotten the real objectives of Dr Ambedkar's call to, "educate, organised and agitate?" Are not they getting educated only to promote their selfish interest- taking the benefit of belonging to a class and completely forgetting that class? Are not they completely disorganized and divided into many, many camps? Is there their united voice for which Dr Ambedkar was aspiring? Are not they tamed completely forgetting their roars as followers of Shri Kansiram or even Km. Mayawati and the leaders of BAMSEF? Have not Dalits as such forgetting the cherished belief of Dr Ambedkar: United we stand, divided us fall?

Second, in the first Parliamentary election Dr Ambedkar contested the reserved seat from Bombay north. He was the candidate of the Scheduled Caste Federation supported by Socialist Party. He lost the election by securing 1,23,576 votes. The winner was the Congress candidate Kajrolkar who secured 1, 37,950 votes. Kajrolkar had been Assistant with Dr Ambedkar in the Federation. Again in 1954 by-election of the House of the People, he contested from Bhandara. But he stood third and the Congress candidate won the election. In reality he could not get the full support of his own people who were inclined more to the Congress.

Third, during last day, the sorrowful state of Dr Ambedkar was caused by betraying of his hopes by the educated untouchables, who were not working for their brethren and enjoying the fruits of his achievements for themselves. In the evening of his life he was very much worried. On July 29, 1956 after massage of his leg Rattu (typist-cum personal assistant) humbly enquired: "Sir, why do you look so sad, worried and distressed these days, and even weep at times." Dr Ambedkar snubbed him and asked to go do his typing work. Next day while massaging his legs Rattu again posed the same question: "Sir, why do you look so sad and depressed, and even weep, at times. Excuse me, Sir, for asking this question, but pray kindly let me know what is eating you up?" Dr Ambedkar was very much moved by the words coming from a personal attendant putting service for years without any remuneration. Dr Ambedkar after expressing his worry about his unfulfilled life mission in teeth of his ill health, said:

"Whatever I have been able to achieve is being enjoyed by the educated few, who, with their deceitful performance, have proved to be a worthless lot, with no sympathy for their downtrodden brethren. They have belied my expectations; they live only for themselves and their personal gains. Not even one of them is prepared to do any social work. They are only treading the path of their ruination."[22]

Heartbroken Dr Ambedkar after wiping his eyes said at last to Nanak Chand:

Tell my people, Nanak Chand, that whatever I have been able to achieve for them, I have done it single-handed, passing through crushing miseries and endless troubles, in midst of abuses hurled at me from all sides, more so from the Hindu press, fighting with my opponents, all my life, as with a handful of my own people who deceived me for their selfish ends. But I will continue to serve the country and my downtrodden people till my end. With great difficulty, I have brought the caravan where it stands today. Let the caravan march on and further on, despite the hurdles, pitfalls and difficulties that may occur in its way. They must rise to the occasion, if they want to live an honourable and respectable life. If my people, my lieutenants are not able to take the caravan ahead, they should leave where it stands today, but must not under any circumstance, allow the caravan to lag behind. This is my message, probably my last message given in all seriousness, which I am sure will not go unheeded. Go and tell them. Go and tell them. Go and tell them" (Dr Ambedkar sighed in a guttural voice).[23]

11. The country failed to visualise Dr Ambedkar's prophetic visions of futuristic impact. Some of them have happened in the course of time and some other which have not been corrected are still headache for the country.

First, Dr Ambedkar' reading of communal Muslim mind proved to be true. He had forecasted that the formation of Pakistan could not be avoided. He had also made prophetic announcement that, "It will be the greatest folly to suppose that if Pakistan is buried for the moment, it will never raise its head again. I am sure burying Pakistan is not the same thing as burying the ghost of Pakistan."[24]

Second, Dr Ambedkar was in favour of one language of a province; (1) He had expressed his views on reorganisation of states and suggested trifurcation of U.P. keeping in view the population of areas with possible Capitals at Meerut, Kanpur and Allahabad. U.P. was divided into U.P. and Uttaranchal in 2000, vide Uttar Pradesh Reorganization Act,2000 with struggle left open for more state; in 2006 Uttranchal was renamed as Uttrakhand. (2). He had proposed bifurcation of Bihar with possible capitals at Patna and Ranchi. It came to be true in 2000 when Jharkhand was created carving out the territory of Bihar wide the Bihar Reorganisation Act, 2000. Ranchi became the capital of the newly constituted Jharkhand and Patna remaining the Capital as such; (3) He had also suggested the division of Madhya Pradesh into North and South Madhya Pradesh. In 2000, M .P. was bifurcated and Chhattisgarh was created with Raipur as its capital carving out the territory from M.P. Thus all the three-U.P., Bihar and M.P. had to be bifurcated in 2000, after the elapse of 45 years of Dr Ambedkar's suggestions given in 1955 i.e. one year before the enactment of the State Reorganisation Act, 1956;

Third, Dr Ambedkar had suggested with very convincing arguments the quadrificaion of Maharashtra-1. Maharashtra city state (Bombay), 2.West Maharashtra, 3. Central Maharashtra and 4. East Maharashtra. Had Bombay been kept separate many problems raised, from time to time, could have been averted.[25]

Fourth, Dr Ambedkar was dead against adoption of Article 370. He had categorically said to Sheikh Abdullah: "You wish India should protect your border, she should make roads in your area, she should supply you food grains and Kashmir should get equal status as India. But Government of India should have only limited powers and Indian people should have no rights in Kashmir. To give consent to this proposal, would be a treacherous thing against the interests of India and I, as the Law Minister of India will never do it."[26]

Dr Ambedkar could not check the passing of Article 370 providing special status to J&K., but he did not participate in passing it. It was done by Patel on Pt. Nehru's initiative Dr Ambedkar did not answer questions put during discussion on it. The bill was not introduced by Dr Ambedkar but N. Gopalaswami Iyenger. He narrated the special reasons of introducing special provision to take care of the exceptional affair existing in J & K and also gave reply to the questions.[27]

The threatening tone of Sheikh Abdullah in J & K Constituent Assembly can be seen in his statement:

"I will like to make it clear that any suggestion of altering arbitrarily the basis of our relationship with India would not only constitute the breach of the spirit and the letter of the Constitution, but it may invite serious consequences for a harmonious association of our state with India."[28]

Dr Ambedkar refused to be associated with Article 370 in any way. The result is obvious. The country is facing the music of the ill impact of Article 370 even today.

12. Dr Ambedkar's brilliance as a jurist of first water has never been probed, studied and appreciated.

First, Dr Ambedkar was the first Indian thinker who raised the problematic of "lawless law." He was naturalist who visualised and declared norms governing people to lack the quality of law worthy to regulate the human behaviour in the society. The norms positively created lose the sanctity of law responding obedience, if they are too inhuman, iniquitous and conscience pricking. The eternal law is the law of humanity encouraging equal treatment of all ensuring dignity to the members of the society. Even in the underdeveloped stage of the civic society lacking crystallisation of enforceable norms, Sophocles observed in his tragic play Antigone:

"Not of today or yesterday they are,
But eternal (none can date their birth)
Not I would fear the wrath of any man
(And grave God's vengeance) for defying these."[29]

Ulysses and Dante, brought the message of legendry hell for the human beings. Thus, "the hell was not beneath or beyond earth, but on it; it was a hell created on earth by men for other men." Dr Ambedkar viewed the position in Indian Hindu society and found that the scriptures are the creation of upper caste Hindus and their followers have created hell for untouchables on the earth by enacting and applying iniquitous and oppressive laws. The anarchic position is totally unacceptable on the standards of the civilised society.

Dr Ambedkar call vis-à-vis anarchic, aggressive, exclusionary and oppressive Hindu law prevalent from time immemorial to the present day exposes the lack of the element of acceptably enforceable norms. The norms excluding untouchables from the normal amenities of life were completely based on deep-rooted prejudices, economic exploitations and aggression. At least one study on the point is available before us which presents Dr Ambedkar's the exposure of Hindu society as totally antagonistic to the civilised world. Dr Upendra Baxi points out:

"Drawing scorchingly from the 'secred' 'law-texts, of Manu, Yagyavalkya, Narada and Vishnu, Ambedkar presents the full horrors of the 'classical' Hindu law and jurisprudence. Not merely did it deny 'equality before law' as a priciple to the untouchables, thus erecting permanent edifice of legitimated subalternity over them down the ages; it inscribed, furthermore, George Bataille terms as 'heterogenity'; that is, the extra territorialisation of the whole communities of human beings and their castigation as being outside the pale of humanity."[30]

The social exclusion of untouchable class from the Hindu-fold and degrading them as 'Antyaj', 'outcaste', 'not seeable', 'not touchable' etc. is the act of forced heterogineitisation and, therefore, "Ambedkar's characterisation of the Hindu law as a code of lawless is, by itself, a heterological practice."[31]

The oppressiveness of Hindu law has been very well exposed by Dr Ambedkar in the terms of the 'unmitigated bloody mindedness' and 'barbarism'. To quote Dr Baxi again:

"The very act of enunciation of these punishments suggests the plentitude of law as an act of terror. In characterising these laws as "lawless laws", Ambedkar may appear anarchronistically to subject the 'classical' Hindu jurisprudence to contemporary standards of liberal jurisprudence. But an alternative study is surely open. Ambedkar may be seen as narrating "the tradition of the oppressed" which teaches us (in the striking words of Walter Benjamin) that "the 'state of emergency' in which we i.e. the oppressed live is not an exception but the rule." Or, put another way, the rule of law always coexists with a reign of terror ala Benjamin. Ambedkar here educates us into thinking that the "cultural treasure" called Hinduism has an origin which cannot be contemplated "without horror." As Benjamin says: "There is no document of civilisation which is at the same time not a document of barbarism. If the tradition of Hindu law is a mark of civilised jurisprudence, it is also at the same time a testament to barbarism."[32]

In "Annihilation of Castes," Dr Ambedkar has very well exposed the barbarity preached by Manusmriti. It not only prohibited education to 'Sudras', but prescribed barbarous punishment: "If they were to enchant Vedas, their tounge be cut off, if they were to hear them molten lead would be poured into their ears".

Dr Ambedkar's exposure of Hindu law lawlessness prevalent in the 'sacred' is more creditable than radical naturalist Radbruch, the German positivist denouncing positivism and embracing naturalism experiencing the horror of Nazi Germany during 1930s Dr Ambedkar is pre- Radbruch. He dealt with the lawlessness of ancient scriptural law forming the ancient civilisation. Radbruch dealt with statutory lawlessness of Nazi-German rule of Adolf Hitler. Immediately after the close of the Second-World- War, he published, 'Statutory Lawlessness and

Supra-Statutory Law'.[33] Radbruch said that duly enacted statutes of Nazi regime lacked the very nature of law and therefore they were lawless. In his view justice has to be given primacy over legal certainty. He explained, "Where justice is not even aimed at, where equality- the core of justice- is deliberately disavowed in the enactment of a positive law, then the law is not simply 'false law', it has no claim at all to legal status."[34] Thus, Radbruch denied the positive law the nature of law (i) if its contradiction with justice reached 'intolerable level' (it may be termed conveniently the 'intolerability formula',[35] and (2) such enactment 'deliberately disavowed, equality- the core of justice (conveniently termed as 'disavowal formula).[36] R. Alexy puts Radbruch formula concisely to mean: "appropriately enacted and socially effective norms lose their legal character or their legal validity when they are extremely unjust," or 'law producing extreme injustice is no law'.[37] Radbruch's lawless law concept has doubly significance for the grave injustice done to the Indian masses by the structural commandments which lack total certainty, are full of contradictions and have no statutory sanctity. They are written by different learned person of a particular class to serve the interests of that class by exclusion and denigration of certain classes. Mahabharata itself admitted the differences among Vedas, Smritis and opinions of the Munis and suggested to follow the path set by virtuous men (**Maha Janoyena Gatah Sah Pantha.**). And, therefore, if they contradict the norm of justice, equality and humanity they are not law/ norm at all. The iniquitous, inhuman, unjust, treacherous, allowing discrimination with hostility laws are lawless. Dr Ambedkar's exposure of the element of lawlessness in Hindu scriptures is matchless. To quote Dr Upendra Baxi:

"And, what distinguishes him from radical naturalist thinkers like Gustav Radbruch (who made Aschuwitz the metaphor for a radical rethinking of political and legal theory) is that Ambedkar interrogates the organised millennial lawlessness structured through the 'sacred' law of an ancient civilisation. The daring of this enterprise is simply unmatched in cotemporary times."[38]

In his most celebrated book, "What Gandhi and Congress Have Done to the Untouchables, "Dr Ambedkar exposed the absurdity and lawlessness of scriptural laws denying even human existence of untouchables and relegating them to the status of crow, frogs and so on. He argues that the untouchables have been denied their title deed to humanity and have been condemned as 'merely living'. The superiority and inferiority is in built in the Hindu way of thinking. For them birth is all in all and worth has no meaning for them. Dr Ambedkar made clear that, ' with the aristocracy the notion that a Brahmin cannot be other the Brahmin and a man born as Pariah cannot be other than a Pariah, is not idle talk, is a living and operative faith.."[39]

Dr Upendra Baxi summarises[40] different types of lawlessness of law prevalent in Hindu society which have been exposed by Dr Ambedkar:

First, the norms which prescribe and perpetuate the condition of 'living death' of Atisudras, or the 'wretched of mankind' or the 'worst of humans'. Dharmasastras and Arthasastra traditions of living Hindu law perpetuate the violent social exclusion. It is continuing even after the constitutional guarantee of equal treatment.

Second, Dharma providing critical morality to sanctify adharmic and hostile discrimination against untouchables. Dr Ambedkar, "emphatically suggests that Chaturvarna did not originate with Manu, and indeed flays forms of degenerate Manu installation of the category of 'those are outside Chaturvarna,' a feat of Adharmic interpolation that fortifies, and fructifies, an encyclopaedic variety of forms of 'lawless law.'

Third, the Ambedkarite lawless law exemplifies many unspeakable acts of casteism separating wells for untouchables to draw water, denial of right to wear good garments and discrimination reservation in educational institutions, employment and legislatures.

Fourth, the lawlessness may operate without breaking the law. The grave injustice and persecution may operate by denial of work, taking of cattle across caste-men's field, indifferent or anti-untouchable attitude of police, misuse of ministerial discretion against untouchables and over and above the helplessness of administration to punish the organised mass against untouchables.

13. The original contribution of Dr Ambedkar to the jurisprudential study of jural relations in view of emerging scenario of justice for the common men and new look to right-duty correlativity in perspective of the long ranged social oppression of certain groups calling for inter- generational justice or justice across generations has not been properly probed into. Dr Ambedkar is quite innovative. He has his own reformulation

right-duty correlativity-much ahead the Hohfeldian analysis of jural relations, Dr Ambedkar has made it three dimensional-individuals or group of individuals, society and the state. Dr Upendra Baxi is the first jurist who has drawn our attention towards Dr Ambedkar's genius and innovative interpretation of right of the oppressed people. Dr Baxi points out:

"Departing fundamentally from the liberal paradigm of rights and justice Ambedkar sought to accomplish two unusual results. First, his theory of rights was addressed more to civil society than to the State: rights do not appear as constraints and limits on the power of the State. Rather, they emerge as legal entitlements costing corresponding obligations on the members of civil society: 112 rights, atypically in Ambedkar's thought legitimate an interventionist State, even in the dominant colonial formation."[41]

Dr Baxi shows how Dr Ambedkar has transformed Hohfeld's analysis of right in new perspective. He says:

"In Hohfeldian terms, Ambedkar's essential juristic strategy was to innovate jural relations: the depressed classes had a right, and the State a duty to eradicate obdurate discriminatory practices in civil society and the State had the power and the members of civil society were under liability to have their 'cultural' practices redefined. In other words, State has a power coupled with duty to which the rights of the depressed classes are corresponded.[42]

Dr Ambedkar's innovation finds expression in four ways:

First, the constitutional provisions enshrined in Articles 17 and 23 are so formulated by Dr Ambedkar in the Fundamental Rights chapter "which create offences and that the rights themselves are limitations on the power of civil society rather than that of the State".[43]

Second, as Dr Baxi makes clear, Dr Ambedkar converts the very nature of rights as negative liberties putting restriction on state power into positive liberties requiring affirmative state actions to protect the liberty of untouchables. The impact being that: "The majority communities 'rights' to cultural and religious freedom stand fully curtailed, normatively by the enunciation of the right of social equality of the depressed classes. The juristic phrases pregnant with possibilities of history-such as "equality before law", "equal protection of the law" and the "rule of law" transform themselves from being shields against State power to swords of sovereignty."[44]

Third, Dr Ambedkar was prophetic to interpret 'rights' in the form of 'basic needs'. Dr Baxi very succinctly formulates it: "The basic human needs of **Atisudras** were both material and non-material. The latter comprise a variety of needs for dignity and fraternity of respect for the **Atisudra's** right to be human; the former include a whole set of material needs such as access to basic needs for example, immunity from bodily and psychic aggression, access to public facilities, access to resources such as drinking water and access to participation in govern employment.[45]

Dr Ambedkar's concept of right as collective right or as basic needs is analogous to natural law thinkers. He does not offer any theoretical framework. The obvious reasons being: "Partly, he treats the needs as self-evident and their redressal also morally natural. Partly, he appeals to millennia old practices of denial of humanity to the **atisudras** as jusnaturalist ground, as it were, for basic entitlement." Dr Baxi rightly comments: "both nature and (Hindu) history furnish unproblematic grounds justifying conversion of needs in to rights."[46]

Somebody may agree or not agree with Dr Ambedkar's positive rights' enforceability, but it has presented food for future thoughts. As to the nature of preferential treatment/ affirmative action provisions, two interpretations have come into light. The first dismisses them as mere enabling provisions. The other, which is in consonance with Dr Ambedkar's point of view, pleads that such provisions involve the rights of the Depressed Classes and caste corresponding duty on the State to implement and give effect to them. Justice Pandian observed in **Indra Shawhney vs. Union of India (Mandal Case)**[47] that "the power conferred on the State under Article 16(4) is one coupled with a duty and, therefore, the State has to exercise that power for the benefit of all those namely, backward class for whom it is intended."[48] Justice K. Ramaswamy appreciated Dr Ambedkar's interpretation in sociological and constitutional angulations in **State of Karnataka vs. Appa Balu Ingle**[49] while interpreting Article 17 and the Protection of Civil Rights Act. Said the learned judge:

"The Act is not a penal law simpliciter but bears behind it monstrous untouchability relentlessly practised for centuries dehumanising the Dalits, Constitution's animation to have it eradicated and to assimilate 1/5 of the Nation's population in the mainstream of national life. .....it would be imperative to broach the problem not merely from the perspectives of criminal jurisprudence, but more also from sociological and constitutional angulations."[50]

Justice Ramaswamy approvingly quotes from M. P. Jain's Indian Constitutional Law:

"Article 17 read with Article 15(2) protects an individual from discriminatory conduct not only on part of the State but even on the part of the private persons in certain situations. The Supreme Court has stated that whenever any fundamental right like Article 17 is violated by a private individual, it is the Constitutional obligation of the State to take necessary steps to interdict such violation and ensure observance of the fundamental right by the private individual who is victim of transgression. The State is under constitutional obligation to see that there is no violation of the fundamental rights of such person."[51]

K. Ramaswamy J. further clarified:

"The thrust of Article 17 and the Act (U.O.A./P.C.R.A.) is to liberate the society from blind and ritualistic adherence and traditional beliefs which lost all legal or moral base. It seeks to establish a new ideal for society-equality to the Dalits, on a par with general public, absence of disabilities, restrictions or prohibitions on grounds of caste or religion, availability of opportunities and a sense of being a participant in the mainstream of national life."[52]

Fifth, the most innovative vision of Dr Ambedkar's address is to new forms and grammars of Indian demosprudence. It was quite new idea yet unknown to the political thinkers and the jurists. Dr Ambedkar's position has been exemplified by Dr Upendra Baxi:

" ... Ambedkar invented demosprudence even before the term was invented; he was too good a lawyer not to know the distinction between the two. He knew the need for development of jurisprudence in India-that is principle which will if not govern at least aid the conduct of governance and in general to (here to use a Foucaldian expression) the 'immense criticisability of things.'[53]

Ambedkar the activist social reformer practised demosprudence when he converted some basic needs into rights but as a constitution-maker he was careful not to convert all such needs into rights, as we can see from the chapter concerning directive principles; likewise in crafting representative democracy for a free India he deliberately refrained from sculpting principles and practice of referendum."[54]

The vision of Ambedkar as social activist showed his inclination towards conversion of needs into rights and direct democracy, but as framer of the Constitution he had to concede necessary adjustments. This dichotomy has very well been presented by Dr Baxi in the following passage:

"The tension between institutions of representative governance and looked at closely, direct democracy is nearly reflected in Ambedkar the constitution maker and Ambedkar the social activist. At the same moment, it is also his message that we eternally combat the abuse of governance discretion-that is for each new type of jurisprudence we erect a new demosprudence. Demosprudence is the new jurisprudence. This is the principal message of Dr.Ambedkar's life work."[55]

References

1. The Indian Express, 12.11.2016 p. 2, under caption 'Ambedkar said currency should be replaced every 10 yrs': Prakash.
2. Dr Uperdra Baxi, "Emancipation as Justice:Babasaheb Ambedkar's Legacy and Vision (in) V.T. Patil, Studies in Ambedkar, Devika Publications, Delhi, 1995.
3. Upendra Baxi, Dr. Ambedkar Memorial Lecture 1978 on, "Political Justice, Legislative Reservation for Scheduled Castes and Social Change, delivered at Madras University on 24-25 January 1979
4. *Ibid.*
5. President Radhakrishnan's speech at the time of installation of statue of Dr B R Ambedkar in the courtyard of Parliament in 1967.
6. Jaffrelot, Christophe, Dr Ambedkar and Untouchability: Fighting the Indian Caste System, New York: Columbia University Press, 2005, p. 31.
7. Upendra Baxi, Emanation As Justice: Babasaheb Ambedkar's Legacy and Vision (in) V.T. Patil, "Studies in Ambedkar" Devika Publications, Delhi, 1995, p. 16.
8. *Ibid.* p. 16.
9. Jaffrelot, supra p. 144.
10. Mane, Suresh, " Constitution and Dr Ambedkar's Vision for Social Change", (in) Mohammad Shabbir, edited, "Ambedkar on Law, Constitution and Social Justice", 'Rawat Publications, Jaipur, 2005.
11. Upendra Baxi, Ambedkar Memorial Lecture 2013 under title, '

"Restoring 'Title Deeds to Humanity': Lawless Law, Living Death, and the Insurgent Reason of Babasaheb Ambedkar" delivered under the auspices of Ambedkar University, Delhi.

12. *Ibid.*
13. Roy, Arundhati: "The Doctor and the Saint "(in) B.R. Ambedkar, Annihilation of Caste: The Annodated Critical Edition, New Delhi: Narayan, 2014.
14. Arun P. Mukherjee, John Dewey, B. R. Ambedkar and the Meaning of Democracy, New York University, Toronto.
15. Jaffrelot, Supra.
16. Upendra Baxi, Constitution Day After, 3.12.2016, The Indian Express, p. 10.
17. Dr Upendra Baxi, Dr Ambedkar Memorial Lectures- 1978 on "Political Justice, Legislative Reservation for Scheduled Castes and Social Change", University of Madras, Nalanda Art Printers, Madras.
18. Upendra Baxi, "Emancipation As Justice: Babasaheb Ambedkar's Legacy and Vision" (in) V.T. Patil, 'Studies in Ambedkar', Devika Publications, Delhi, 1995, pp. 17-22.
19. Upendra Baxi Ambedkar Memorial Lecture 2013 on "Restoring the 'Title Deeds to Humanity': Lawless Law, Living Death, and the Insurgent Reason of Babasaheb Ambedkar" organised by Ambedkar University, Delhi.
20. Quoted from Janak Singh, "Dr B.R. Ambedkar: Messiah of the Downtrodden, Kalpaz Publications,2010. p. 340 .
21. Quoted from Janak Singh, supra, p. 341.
22. *Ibid.*
23. Ibid. See also Rattu, "The Last Few Years of Dr Ambedkar,"Amrit Publications, 1997, p. 111.
24. Dr Ambedkar, "Pakistan or Partition of India", 1948.
25. Dr Ambedkar, 'Linguistic States'.
26. D.D. Basu, Commentary on the Constitution, Vol. 10.
27. *Ibid.*
28. *Ibid.*
29. Sophocles, Antigone.
30. Upendra Baxi, Emancipation As Justice, supra, p. 32.
31. *Ibid.*
32. *Ibid.*
33. Radbruch, Statutory Lawlessness and Supra-Statutory Law,1946
34. *Ibid.*
35. *Ibid.*
36. *Ibid*
37. *Ibid.*
38. Upendra Baxi, Emancipation As Justice, supra, f.n.18, p. 33.

39. Dr Ambedkar, What Congress and Gandhi Have Done to the Untouchables? (1945).
40. Ambedkar Memorial Lecture 2013 on "Restoring 'The Title Deeds to Humanity':Lawless Law, Living Death, and the Insurgent Reason of Babasaheb" delivered under the auspices of Ambedkar University, Delhi.
41. Upendra Baxi, Emancipation As Justice, supra, f.n. 18, p. 33.
42. *Ibid*. p. 34.
43. *Ibid.*
44. *Ibid.*
45. *Ibid.*
46. *Ibid.*
47. 1992 SCC (L.&S) Suppl. 1.
48. *Ibid.*
49. (1991) Suppl SCC 469
50. *Ibid.*
51. *Ibid.*
52. *Ibid.*
53. Upendra Baxi, Ambedkar Memorial Lecture 2013 on "Restoring 'Title Deeds to Humanity': Lawless Law, Living Death, and the Insurgent Reason of Dr Ambedkar", delivered under the auspices of Ambedkar University, Delhi.
54. *Ibid.*
55. *Ibid.*

8

Rocky Determination of Annihilation of Caste and Ensuring Participation of Untouchables in Governance of the Country

Solution of the problem of Untouchability

M.K. Gandhi
(Oct. 2, 1869 - Jan 30, 1948)
(Change in the mind-set of Upper Caste Hindus)

Dr B.R. Ambedkar
(April 14, 1891 - Dec. 06, 1956)
(Annihilation of Caste and Nothing Short of that)

Dr Ambedkar's determination to annihilate the caste was rocky. He viewed that short of political participation in the governance of the country emanation of the untouchables would always remain a distant dream.

Dr Ambedkar was firm, resolute and unstirred in any situation from his well considered rational decisions searching pragmatic solution. He was as embodiment of humility as Tathagat Buddha was and also as resolute in conviction as

Tathagata was. The story of Buddha- Alwak Yaksha dialogue shows Buddha's resolute stand. Tathagata was staying at Alwi in the house of Alwaka Yaksha. The story runs:

Alwaka Yaksha: "Shramana! Go Out".

Tathagata Buddha: "Very Good Awoos." And, went outside.

Alwaka Yaksha: "Shramana! Go Inside."

Tathagata Buddha: "Very Good Awoos!" And, went inside.

Alwaka Yaksha (second time) " Shramana! Go Out."

Tathagata Buddha: "Very Good Awoos!" Telling it went outside.

Alwaka Yaksha (third times): "Shramana! Go Outside."

Tathagata Buddha: "Very Good Awoos!" Telling it went outside.

Alwaka Yaksha (fourth time): Shramana Go Out.

Tathagata Buddha: "Awoos! I will not go outside. Do whatever you like."

Alwaka Yaksha: Shramana! "I will put question, If you fail to answer then I will disturb your mind or pierce your heat or catching your leg will throw across Ganges."

Tathagata Buddha: "Awoos! I do not perceive any person among Shramanas and Brahamanas including God, Mar (kamadev) and Brahma and world of gods-human beings who can disturb my mind or pierce my heart or throw across Ganges catching my legs. Still, ask what you wish to ask."

Tathagata answered all his questions very aptly. Alwak Yaksha surrendered and accepted the superiority of Buddha and expressed desire to accept Buddha as his Teacher.

Dr Ambedkar showed same blending of humility and firmness. In the very beginning when one of his teachers humiliatingly discouraged him by saying that he was wasting his time in vain, as he would gain nothing from study due to his being an untouchable, without being rude Dr Ambedkar retorted: "Mind your business." Where ever he felt that he was right he did not mind who his adversary was. To challenge Mahatma Gandhi on issue of the evils of Hinduism was a work of extraordinary courage and conviction and pursue it persistently was more than courage and conviction. It was resolute and unstirred conscientious well read and argued expression having no easy answer to be retorted.

Dr Ambedkar was also as resolute as Mahatma Gandhi was. He had a bundle of bitter experiences like Mahatma Gandhi's one. On this point he was true Gandhian with much more resoluteness. To elaborate and make it more clear. Mahatma Gandhi had gone to South Africa on call of Indian traders there. He was journeying by train from Durban to Pretoria in connection with the case of the Indian trader Dadabhai. When he reached the station Martzburg, he experienced the first brunt of colour prejudice. He was having the first class ticket with him. But, the white co-passenger in the compartment could not tolerate/ swallow the presence non-English man in that compartment. On his complaint, in spite of first class ticket with Gandhiji and showing that to the officer on duty, his luggage was unceremoniously thrown out on platform and he was forced to land on the platform of that insignificant station. The night was bitterly cold and the waiting room was unlit. He spent night with biting cold and apprehensions. Before this colour prejudiced inhumanly treatment, Gandhiji's nature had been pathologically shy and retiring. Now a new Gandhi was born in him. In that "wind-swept room of Moritzburg railway station he smarted under the insult inflicted on him. The iron entered his soul." This incident prompted him to stay in South Africa and "would sow the seeds of his fight for national self-respect." He determined that he would "reason, he would plead, he would plead to the better judgment and latent humanity of the ruling race, he would resist, but would never be a willing victim of racial arrogance. It was not so much a question of redeeming his own self- respects as that his community, his country, even humanity." Dr Ambedkar had experienced countless caste-prejudices- not only discriminatory, humiliating and arrogant behaviour of class fellows, teacher and even peons but also had to lose the job at Baroda and luggage was thrown on road in dead night from the house a Parsi, could not get services at many places. So much so could not get water to take meal and remained empty stomach for twenty-four hour while going to his father's place along with his brother and could not get a drop of water for two days while returning after arguing the Chowdar tank case in Bombay as he could not cross the over-flooded river in the way and was compelled to wait the river coming down crossable by car. Such incidents made Dr Ambedkar steel hearted man with resolute commitment to relieve not only himself from the upper caste bondage but the whole lot of weak, meek, dumb and bewildered masses of Untouchable. As South African thorny experience prompted Gandhi to resort non-violent Satyagraha, so chose Dr Ambedkar to stage peaceful Satyagraha for minimum recognition of Untouchables as human beings with equal right of entry in temple and drink the water from the tank.

In certain respects Dr Ambedkar's Satyagraha was more creditable than Gandhian one. Mahatma Gandhi had brave iron-man like Sardar Vallabhbhai Patel and many more to make his Satyagraha successful. Dr Ambedkar was to manage the show himself. Gandhiji had to stage Satyagraha against foreign rulers who had heart to say like General Smutt that he had no heart to face because he was so respectful to all and without offensive words. The success of Gandhi's Satyagraha was due to two obvious reasons; first, it was against foreign rulers. It had the solid support and approval of the nation, and second, Britishers, to be fair to them, did not inhere that much intense prejudice to the Indians as caste-people of India inhere against the Untouchables. Furthermore, the Britishers knew that their days were counted. Their rule was being thrown by one country after the other- United States, Canada, Australia and so on. Dr Ambedkar had to stage Satyagraha against our own Savarna Indians who had no heart to appreciate the peaceful Satyagraha for simple right of drinking water from tank, and to have Darshan of gods in temples like others. Their prejudices were more deep-rooted. They had neither heart nor tolerance and could brutally attack unarmed peace loving Untouchables taking rest during the night in some Pandal and spare none-even the old, women and children. Resentment and reactionary violence are natural. Wherever and whenever, injustice and excesses cross the limit, the victim people come to retaliate and try to meet violence through violent measures. So was going to happen at Mahad. After the incident of indiscriminate beating of untouchables at the hands of Savarnas, 100 lathi-wielding untouchables appeared on the scene with determination to retaliate. Dr Ambedkar getting inkling of aggravating situation rushed from rest house to the scene and calmed them down and restored peace. Had Dr Ambedkar not acted cool-headed and prudently and averted the situation, Mahad would have witnessed bloodshed on bigger scale. This exemplary self restraint on parts of Dalits under Dr Ambedkar's leadership was very much appreciated by Mahatma Gandhi. He also disapproved use of the seer brute force on the part of orthodox upper caste people without reason. Mahatma Gandhi supported the cause of untouchables sponsored by Dr Ambedkar without any reservation. In Young India, he published an Article on April 28, 1927 which read:

Dr Ambedkar, was [right] fully justified in putting to the test the resolution of the Bombay Legislative Council and Mahad Municipality by advising the so-called Untouchables to go to the tank to quench their thirst."

Mahatma Gandhi also exhorted "every Hindu opposed to Untouchability" to publicly defend the courageous Dalit of Mahad "even at the risk of getting his head broken."[1]

Dr Ambedkar and Mahatma Gandhi both loved Untouchables, accepted their miserable status in society only due to the accident of birth, shared the view that there was no rational basis of touchable and untouchable psychic mania and also wished that the evil of Untouchability must go. However, they differ in the ways of handling the issue. The basic and inherent social background of the two continued to control their response differently till the end. Dr Ambedkar was born Untouchable. Mahatma Gandhi was born in a Vaishanava Bania family and opted the cause of untouchables as a good and generous person. Dr Ambedkar had experienced the brunt of being an untouchable again and again. Mahatma Gandhi had no such bitter experiences of hostile discrimination he had only heard and seen what was happening in society. As Marc Gallanter views, "if Gandhi personified the evangelical approach, the secular approach was personified by the most gifted and wide-ranging spokesman to appear among the untouchables, Dr Bhimarao Ramji Ambedkar." Dr Ambedkar was educated in the best educational institutions of the world- Columbia (U.S.A.) and London School of Economics (U.K.). Mahatma Gandhi, except Bar-at-Law (which Dr Ambedkar also possessed), was mostly educated in India. Dr Ambedkar had privilege of studying with scholar of repute Professor Edwin R.A. Selligman and Professor John Dewey, the pragmatic humanist, whose philosophy was that: "as the society becomes more enlightened, it realises that it is responsible not to conserve and transmit the whole of its existing achievements, but only such as made for a better future society". Mahatma Gandhi was, more or less, traditionist. Dr Ambedkar was modernist and remained learner throughout the life and writing was his hobby. What is said of Arnold Toynbee is hundred per cent true of Dr Ambedkar. When a lady inquired from Arnold J. Toynbee why had he spent 37 years of precious time in completing 12 Vols. (1934-1961), book on "A Study of History", his one word answer was "CURIOSITY". So was the case of Dr Ambedkar. He spent 15 years time to study Hindu scriptures to make him understand and be able to say against them. Many of his works remained in pipe-line. Mahatma Gandhi was busy otherwise in national activities and social reforms. He spent 14 years of his beginning career in South Africa fighting with the discriminatory treatment and excesses committed by Britishers on the Indian traders there. In India too he was too busy to spent time for works other than the national movement. On the issue of Untouchability, Dr Ambedkar was more armed with irrefutable arguments, convincing reasons and evidentiary support. Mahatma Gandhi thought that Untouchability was anarchistic. Dr Ambedkar viewed it as an evil. Mahatma Gandhi thought it a religious matter to be tackled religiously by way of penance. On this point Gandhiji was nearer to Vivekananda who gave the simile of cobra of Bengali saying. When cobra sucks his poison back the victim of its biting is revived. Similarly, Brahmins who have bitten the system must withdraw their poisonous effect. Dr Ambedkar was more practical on this point. He pointed out that Untouchability had taken the form of economic system and therefore, is worst than slavery. He explained:

"The system of Untouchability is a gold mine to the Hindus. In it the 240 millions of Hindus have 60 millions of untouchables to serve as their retinue to enable the Hindus to maintain pomp and ceremony and to cultivate a feeling of pride and dignity befitting a master class, which cannot be fostered and sustained unless there is beneath it a servile class to look down upon. In it the 240 of Hindus have 60 millions of Untouchables to be used as forced labourers...In it the 240 millions of Hindus have 60 millions of Untouchables to do the dirty work of scavengers and sweepers which the Hindu is debarred by his religion to do and which must be done by non-Hindus who could be no other than Untouchables. In it the 240 millions of Hindus have 60 millions of Untouchables who can be kept to lower jobs ...In it the 240 of Hindus have the 60 millions of Untouchables who can be used as shock-absorbers in slums and dead-weights in booms, for in slums it is the Untouchable who is fired first and the Hindu is fired last and in booms the Hindu is employed first and the Untouchable is employed last."[2]

Dr Ambedkar was resolute and had very clear understanding of the inbuilt unequal structure of the caste-ridden Hindu society. He wished to annihilate the caste-system and give equal human status to his untouchable brethren. Mahatma Gandhi too wished to grant human dignity to the untouchables. Their objective was similar. Their sincerity was similar. Both disapproved Manusmriti. Mahatma Gandhi writes in his 'Autobiography- My Experiments with Truth': "The story of creation and similar things in it did not impress me very much, but on the contrary made me incline somewhat towards atheism."[3] On the point of need of the society both were complementary to each other. But the understanding and way to solve the social problem differ. Mahatma Gandhi was reformist. Dr Ambedkar was a radical revolutionary. Mahatma Gandhi was traditionist. Dr Ambedkar was modernist. Mahatma Gandhi as hard-core-religionist believed in Hindu Varnasharma system as conducive for social working- division of work. Dr Ambedkar found it the mother of all social evils-dividing society into touchables and untouchables, privileging some and deprivileging masses of minimum right to livelihood, human dignity and equality. Mahatma Gandhi believed in reform through change of heart of the caste Hindus and undergoing penance for committing wrong to untouchables on caste prejudices. Dr Ambedkar was of firm view that history of Hinduism has completely belied such hopes- Mahatmas have come and gone, but casteism goes on forever. Thus, only annihilation of caste and rooting it out, raising the status of untouchables through economic uplift, securing liberty, equality and fraternity can solve this age old problem. Mahatma Gandhi designed to solve the problems of untouchable within the Hindu-fold treating them part and parcel of Hinduism. Dr Ambedkar radically differed on the point. He had made clear in 1928 before the Simon Commission itself, "The problem of the untouchables should not be attached with the Hindus in general. The untouchables are exclusively exploited and depressed from the social point of view. They have been forced since centuries to suffer and remain as exploited, depressed, oppressed members of the Hindu society. This is why the doors of the educational institutions have been shut to them. Though human beings, they live beastly life and wander like nomad." Since Gandhi believed in the merit of Chaturvarna as workable social arrangement, he projected to promote untouchables from Antyaja or outcaste to the category of Shudras i.e. fourth and the lowest of the varnavyavastha with right to worship on equal footing with others and drink waters from public tanks on equal footing. Dr Ambedkar found cure worst than disease. To him nothing short of power sharing in governance of the country, their social amelioration and economic security could do. These are the reasons and certain utterances expressed in writings of Dr.Ambedkar, some interaction between Dr Ambedkar and Mahatma Gandhi following the **Jat-Pat Todak Mandal's** episode which give the impression that both were at dagger's drawn and at irreconcilable stage.

The reality is not so. Both were honest, sincere and committed to their inhered tradition and way of life. They spoke from heart their own views with flexibility to appropriate adjustment in order to achieve objective. In national interest and the interest of the untouchables themselves, a middle course-Buddhist Majjima Marga, was, is and will always be needed. Dr Ambedkar was a firm believer in Buddhist philosophy he would always be ready to rapproachment. Thomas Pantham appears to be nearer to truth when he notes: "Despite basic differences between and serious conflicts over, their respective political, social and religious philosophies and practical political strategies, both shared a genuine and deep commitment to the eradication of Untouchability."[4] He also supports his conclusion from the observation of Eleanor Zelliot, a noted scholar on Dalit movement in India that Article 17 of the Constitution, "stands as a triumph- for Congress, for Gandhi, for Ambedkar, and for India-however imperfectly the idea of complete equality and justice"[5] Extremism will bring out no solution.

From the core of heart both wished abolition of Untouchability- Dr Ambedkar's was overt act, Mahatma Gandhi's was covert act through his volunteers in the Constituent Assembly. But for the unconditional support of the latter, it would not have been possible to pass Article 17 with near unanimous voice.

Some of acts and utterances of Mahatma Gandhi and correspondence between Dr Ambedkar and Mahtma Gandhi reveal how both of them were concerned with the liberation of the country and the untouchables. At the age of 12, Gandhi found no wrong in touch of Uka, a family cleaner of latrines. In1898, Mahatma Gandhi had nearly pushed his wife Kasturba out of their house in Durban, South Africa on her refusal to clean the pot used by Dalit born Christian guest. So was the case when some untouchable family was admitted to Ahmedabad

Ashram in 1915. In May 1907, he wrote an Article in Indian Opinion speaking of "the wicked superstitions about Untouchability" and the way in which "in India some of us oppress the bhangis and force them to ... speak in obsequious language."[6] In South Africa, when the Indian Satyagrahis in jail refused to take meal touched by Dalits and refused to sleep with them, Gandhiji rebuked. He interpreted Britishers' discrimination with Indians what they had earned by practicing Untouchability in India.[7] In April 1918, writing preface to a book of poems authored by a Gujarati poet Padhiar depicting cruel treatment of Dalits, Gandhiji asked for reading out the poems "to men and women in their millions, in the same way that works like the Bhagwat are read out to them in every square."[8] In November 1920 amidst non-cooperation movement, through an article in 'Young India' he said, "we shall be unfit to gain swaraj so long as we keep in bondage a fifth of the population."[9] In 1920 on his policy of admitting untouchables in colleges and non recognition to those refusing admitting them, orthodox Hindus threatened to withdraw support from freedom movement led by Mahatma Gandhi. Mahatma Gandhi responded in Navajivan (December 5, 1920): The advice I receive from one and all that if I do not exclude the Antyajas from the national schools, the movement for Swaraj will end in smoke. If I have been a little of the Vaishanava in me, "God will also vouchsafe me the strength to reject the swaraj which may be won by abandoning the Antyajas."[10] Mahatma Gandhi, in so many words, clarified, "When I ask you to purify your hearts of "Untouchability, I ask you nothing less than this –that you should believe in the fundamental unity and equality of man. Invite you all to forget that there are any distinctions of high and low among the children of one and the same God."[11] In1921, addressing a Conference of Suppressed Classes in Ahmedabad, Mahatma Gandhi said:"How long can the Ramayana ... in which one who is regarded nowadays as an"untouchable" took Rama across the Ganga in his boat, countenance the idea of any human beings being untouchable on the ground that they are polluted souls?"[12] In 1922, finding it very difficult to convince all caste persons to complete desegregation, in places of strong prejudices, Congress Working Committee resolved to set up separate schools and separate wells for untouchables out of its fund. In 1925, Mahatma Gandhi started emancipator move. In Kerala at Vaikkam there was total ban on untouchables to move through roads surrounding the Shiva temple. Gandhi ji joined Satyagraha for untouchables right to move on roads surrounding the temple. The Satyagraha was launched by local untouchables with blessings of Periyar E. V. Ramaswamy Naikar and Sree Narayan Guru. Gandhiji talked to trustees and priests of the temple at the residence of Indanthuruthi Nambudiri on March 10, 1925. The orthodox Nambudiri could not understand reasons and was adamant on his preconceived notion that untouchables were reaping reward for their Karma. He ruled out any scope for reason, as that was a religious matter. He ruled out any agreement on referendum or arbitration by reputed pundits. At least, he showed inclination to obey the order of Maharaja to the effect of throwing open the roads.[13] A dialogue between Gandhi and Nambudiri Trustee is very instructive and shows the Gandhian way of persuasion.

Gandhiji: Is it fair to exclude a whole section of Hindus, because of their supposed lower birth, from the public roads which can be used by non-Hindus, by criminals and bad characters, and even by dogs and cattle?

Nambudiri Trustee: But how it is helped?

They are reaping the reward of their karma

Gandhiji: No doubt they are suffering for their karma by being born as untouchables. But why must you add to the punishment? Are they worse than even criminals and beasts?

On Mahatma Gandhi's initiative Maharaja of Travancore ordered that the roads from three sides of the Vaikkam temple be opened to all.[14]

All the above happened before any contact between Gandhi and Dr Ambedkar could be established. Dr Ambedkar hailed the role of Mahatma Gandhi. In1925, at a Depressed Classes Conference at Belgaum, appreciating the anti-Untouchability work of Gandhiji Dr Ambedkar said:

"Before Mahatma Gandhi, no politician in this country maintained that it is necessary to remove social injustice here in order to do away with tension and conflict, and that every Indian should consider it his sacred duty to do so ...However, if we look closely, one finds there is slight disharmony ... for he does not insist on the removal of Untouchability as much as he insists on the propagation of Khaddar or Hindu- Muslim unity. If he had he would have made the removal of Untouchability a condition of voting in the party. Well, be that as it may, when one is spurned by everyone, even the sympathy shown by Mahatma Gandhi is of no little importance."[15]

Thomas Pantham guesses influence of Mahatma Gandhi on Dr Ambedkar's Mahad Satyagraha for right to drink water from Chowdar tank as others. Mahad Conference was addressed by Dr Ambedkar in consonance with the Gandhian values of a Satyagrahi. Thus, on March 19, 1927, Dr Ambedkar addressed the untouchable Satyagrahis:

"No lasting progress can be achieved unless we put ourselves through a three-fold process of purification. We must improve the general tone of our demeanor, re-tone our pronunciations and revitalise our thoughts.[16] I, therefore ask you now to take a vow from this moment to renounce eating carrion ... Make an unflinching resolve not to eat the throw out crumbs. We will attain self-elevation only if we learn self-help, regain our self-respect, and gain self-knowledge."[17]

Again, on March 25, 1927 Dr Ambedkar launched Satyagraha and gave brilliant Presidential speech (in a pavilion featuring Gandhi' photo). He said:

"The Hindu community is set in the steel-frame of caste system in which one caste is lower than another in social gradation involving particular privileges, rights, inhibitions, and disabilities with regard to each caste. This system has created vested interests which depend upon maintaining the inequalities resulting from the system...[18]

The caste must be abolished if the Hindu society is to be reconstructed on the basis of equality, it goes without saying:

"If we achieve success in our movement to unite all the Hindus in a single caste as we shall have rendered the greatest service to the Indian nation in general and to the Hindu community in the particular."[19]

The above observation as to the evils of the Hindu caste-system may be compared with some of the observations of Mahatma Gandhi. "God", said, Mahatma Gandhi, "did not create with the badge of superiority or inferiority; no scripture which labels a human being as inferior or untouchable because of his or her birth can command our allegiance; it is a denial of God and truth which is God." Or, "I would not belong to the Hindu faith if I thought the caste was the basis of Hinduism."[20] Mahatma Gandhi could not imagine religious scripture like Ramayana would support untouchability. He pointed out: "How can Ramayana... in which one who is regarded nowadays as an ' untouchable' took Rama across the Ganges in his boat, countenance the idea of any human beings being 'untouchable' on the ground that they are polluted souls."[21]

Mahatma Gandhi did not know where about of Dr Ambedkar prior to his meeting with him in 1931. After meeting him Mahatma Gandhi told his secretary, "I did not know that he was a Harijan. I thought he was some Brahman who took deep interest in Harijans and therefore talked intemperately."[22] Before meeting Dr Ambedkar "Congressmen including Gandhiji did not have high regard for the political capacities of untouchables."[23] Mahatma Gandhi –Dr Ambedkar discussions reveal that Gandhi ji came to know many factual things through Dr Ambedkar, appreciated his concern for untouchables and both loved and honoured each other. If 1930s witnessed Gandhisation of Dr Ambedkar, it also witnessed Ambedkarisation of Mahatma Gandhi. In spite of some disagreement on approach to tackle the issues they learnt from each other and tried to mend to some extent. In their discussion on September 22, 1932 Gandhiji made clear, "without eradication of Untouchability root and branch the honour of Hinduism cannot be saved. That can only happen when untouchables are treated on par with caste Hindus in every respect". On October 17, 1932 Dr Ambedkar did not talk on the issue of Untouchability, but something of vital national interest.[24] Dr Ambedkar said:"I have come here for this. I want to request you to give up civil disobedience and to join the Round Table Conference. People like Iqbal who are enemies of the country will come to the fore front. We have to work any sort of Constitution. Hence though I am a small man, I request you to come." Dr Ambedkar talked of temple entry and common- dinner's futility in view violent opposition from caste Hindus and made clear that he only wanted that social and economic hardships of untouchables should end. He also told of oppression and injustice to untouchables unable to get house to live in. He apprised him of himself being insulted by Vaje's (In-charge, Servant of India) servant in his presence. Mahatma Gandhi's response was: "I understand your point of view, and I shall keep it in mind and shall see what can be done."[25] In their discussion on February 4, 1933, Dr.Ambedkar raised issue of temple entry of untouchables whether they would be allowed entry into the sanctum sanctorum, place flowers on the idol or offer oblations in tray? Mahatma Gandhi's reply was: "temple entry is meant for puja, if anything."[26] The discussion was thread bare:

"Dr Ambedkar: The Hindu mind does not work in a rational way. They have no objection to the untouchables touching them on the railway and other public places. Why do they object to it in the case of temples?[27]

Mahatma Gandhi: We are well caught on this point. I take up question of temple entry first of all because these people want to cling to Untouchability in the temples. Many sanatanist Hindus say that they would admit Harijans in schools and public places but not in temples. I ask them to grant the Harijans equal status before God. It will raise their status."[28] The candid admission of Gandhiji to be as harsh as truth and measuring himself with that standard is worth noting. He realised that he must exclaim with Sudras:

Where is there a wretch
So wicked and loathsome as I?
I have forsaken my Maker,
So faithless have I been.[29]

As to the issue of Untouchability as curse for all-untouchables, caste-Hindus and the nation itself, there was complete agreement between Mahatma Gandhi and Dr Ambedkar. As to no scriptural sanction for Untouchability, there was complete agreement between them. As to the basis of Untouchability being deep-rooted prejudices, there was complete agreement between the two. As to curability there was sharp difference of opinion between Mahatma Gandhi and Dr Ambedkar. Mahatma Gandhi thought the sinners must undergo penance and come forward to award equal treatment to untouchables. Dr Ambedkar thought it distant dream and never will come to be true. The root cause of Untouchability-caste must be annihilated. On this matter of the difference in angle of thinking, they agreed to disagree. In his letter to Dr Ambedkar from Sevagram dated August 6, 1944 (which was in response to Dr Ambedkar's letter received on July 31, 11944) Mahatma Gandhi wrote on the two issues referred therein-the Hndu-Muslim question and Untouchability that:

".. I know to my cost that you and I hold different views on this very important question. And I know, too, that on broad politics of the country we see things from different angles. I would love to find a meeting ground between us on both the questions. I know your great ability and would love to own you as a colleague and co-worker. But I must admit my failure to come nearer to you. If you can show me a way to a common meeting ground between us I would like to see it. Meanwhile, I must reconcile myself to the present unfortunate difference."[30]

Barring the difference in the angle of tackling the issue of Untouchability, ultimately there was no difference of opinion between Mahatma Gandhi and Dr Ambedkar as to the non-political programmes to eradicate caste-based discrimination like inter-dining and inter-marriage, etc. Mahatma Gandhi's ideology may conveniently be divided in to pre-1935 and post-1935 -period. In the former he had been feeling that even in fight against Untouchability, he need be looked like the protector of untouchables and the caste-Hindus as well. He did not realise the urgency of anti-Untouchability programmes on wider scale, as Dr Ambedkar was pressing. The reasons were obvious. First, Mahatma Gandhi, as Bhikhu Parekh notes was, "involved in several battles, that against Untouchability being only one of them, and political exigencies inevitably dictated their order of priority." Second, as Rajmohan Gandhi viewed, "He [Gandhi] would have united orthodox rank of opposition if he had commenced with an attack on caste. He chose to zero in on evil [Untouchability] none could defend." Very informative and authentic evidence coming from the horse's mouth supports Rajmohan Gandhi's assertion revealed by a person, no less than, Pt. Jawahar Lal Nehru, after eight years of Mahatma Gandhi's talking to an European journalist Tibor Mende:

"I asked [Gandhi] repeatedly: why don't you hit out at the caste system directly? He said, 'I am undermining it completely by tackling Untouchability'... [Gandhiji's] genius lay in finding the weakest point of the enemy, the breaking of his front."[31]

Mahatma Gandhi's side is also revealing. Dr Ambedkar, following the Poona Pact after recognising "so much in common" between himself and Mahatma Gandhi, put a suggestion "If you devoted yourself entirely to the welfare of the Depressed Classes, you would become our hero". Similar was the accent of Mahatma Gandhi's friend Charlie (Deenbandhu Andrews) who called him by the first name "Mohan". Recalling Mahatma Gandhi's repeated utterances that 'with Untouchability,' Indians were "not fit" for Swaraj, asked him not to try "to serve two masters" (Swaraj and anti Untouchability) and focus only on Untouchability. Mahatma Gandhi gave reason behind non-acceptance of his advice:

"My dear Charlie: My life is one invisible whole. It is not built after the compartmental system. Satyagraha, civil resistance, Untouchability, [and] Hindu-Muslim unity...are indivisible parts of a whole.

You will find at one time in my life an emphasis on one thing, at the time on [an] other. But that is just like a pianoist now emphasising one note and now [an] other. But they are all related to one another.

It is utterly impossible for me to say: 'I have no nothing to do with civil disobedience or Swaraj" Not only so ....Full and final removal of Untouchability...is utterly impossible without Swaraj...Love. Mhan"[32]. The apprehension of Rajmohan Gandhi, mentioned earlier was not without substance. The post Poona Pact hostility of caste-Hindus against Mahatma Gandhi for fighting the cause of Untouchability and ignoring the inherent status of Untouchability and inequality in the caste-system or Varnashramadharma witnessed violent protest during Mahatma Gandh's Harijan Tour. One incident of bomb throwing took place in July 1934, 'at what was mistakenly taken to be the car in which Gandhiji was travelling in Pune.'[33] Mahatma Gandhi also faced other bitter reactions from orthodox Hindus. Mahatma Gandhi had experienced many more aggressive and quite unbecoming protest from orthodox Hindus on even innocuous reforms like allowing of untouchables in public schools on par with others or their temple entry. Thus, Mahatma Gandhi's avoidance of direct hitting of caste was prudent step so as not to reach to the breaking point with no chance of come back.

Mahatma Gandhi, however, after 1935, was seen as a radically liberal egalitarian on the issues of caste and Varna. This change was partly due to the well reasoned and vehement criticism of caste and Varna thrown publicly by Dr Ambedkar. Earlier Mahatma Gandhi had admitted, in 1927, that prevalent understanding and practice of varnashrama, "is a monstrous parody of the original" and needed demolition.[34] He had also made adjustment for Sanatanists who were not against the removal of Untouchability, but were very much touchy about the inter-caste dinner and marriages. Thus, making clear that, "restriction on inter-caste dining and inter-caste marriage is no part of Hindu religion", but left it voluntary and not compulsory.[35] In 1935, in response to the open letter from a former Bombay High Court judge Sir Govinrao Madgaonkar Mahatma Gandhi wrote in Harijan, dated 16 November 1935:

" Varnashrama of the Shastras is today non-existent in practice. The present caste system is the very antithesis of Varnashrama. The sooner public opinion abolishes it the better.

In varnashrama there was and should be no prohibition of intermarriage or inter-dining....Though there is in varnashrama no prohibition against intermarriage and inter-dining, there can be no compulsion. It must be left to the unfettered choice of the individual as to where he or she will marry or dine."[36]

In spite of accepting non-prohibition of inter-caste dining and inter-caste marriage, he avoided compulsion and preferred to leave on the unfettered choice on individual. In Dr Ambedkar-Mahatma Gandhi open discussion on caste and varna, at least, two positive things came out; (1) after narration of his view point in the issues, Mahatma Gandhi observed:

"Such being my faith, I have always respectfully differed from those distinguished countrymen, Dr Ambedkar among them, who have held that Untouchability will not go without the destruction of varnashramadharma...At the present moment, it is the 'untouchable', the outcaste, with whom all the Hindu reformers, whether they believe in varnashrama or not, have agreed to deal. The opposition to Untouchability is common to both. Therefore, the present joint fight is restricted to removal of Untouchability, and, I would invite Dr Ambedkar and those who think with him to throw themselves, heart and soul, into the campaign against the monster of Untouchability. It is highly likely that at the end of it we shall all find that there is nothing to fight against in varnashrama. If however, varnashrama even then looks an ugly thing, the whole of Hindu society will fight it."

The other positive aspect of Mahatma Gandhi's rejoinder was that he admitted that savarna Hindus have to correct their belief and their conduct' in light of Ambedkar's criticism and both reformers and orthodox Hindus would gain by reading Ambedkar. He also accepted that the caste-system is, "harmful to spiritual and national growth." In response Dr Ambedkar appreciated Gandhi's candid admission that caste is harmful to spiritual and national growth.

1. The yet another important aspect of the Gandhi-Ambedkar exchange of view was the heart touching reaction of Gandhiji. On Dr Ambedkar's firm conviction that the teachings of Tathagat Buddha have long established that varna cannot be rationally defended as it was opposed to democracy as well as root cause caste- structure; in order to survive on equal footing the Hindu society had to be restructured a casteless society based on the trinity of liberty, equality and fraternity and finding

no visible change in the attitude of the caste Hindus, he had no option but to quit Hinduism and embrace some equality based religion, the reaction of Mahatma Gandhi was introspective. He said; **"If you repudiate us and go away I think that we only deserved it."**[37] He asked Hindus to atone their sin by giving equal status to them everywhere "If...any Harijan wants to give up Hinduism, he should be entirely free to do so...The course before savarna is ... on the one hand not to interfere with Harijans wishing to leave the Hindu fold...and, on the other hand, to insist on full justice being done to Harijans in every walk of life...The greatest hardship felt by thousand of Harijans is want of pure water for drinking and domestic use, denial of access to public schools and other institutions, constant pinpricks in villages and, last, but not least, denial of access to temples for worship...If they as a mass give up Hinduism, they will do so because of these common disabilities which brand them as lepers of Hindu society."[38]

The meeting of heart of the two great leaders and pouring hearts through words can be seen in reference to the much debated Poona Pact. When dialogue progressed Mahatma Gandhi desired a dialogue with Dr Ambedkar the meeting took place in jail premises on 22-23 September 1932.Thomas Pantham observes:

"The mutual respect and concern shown in their conversation was as remarkable and, arguably, as consequential as was their hard bargaining on terms of their agreement. Ambedkar began by saying: **'Mahatmaji, you must come to our rescue."**[39]

Gandhi, at one point during their discussion, said to Ambedkar:

"You have a perfect right to demand cent per cent security by statutory safeguards, but from my fiery bed I beg of you not to insist upon that right. I am here today to ask for a reprieve for my caste Hindu brethren. Thank God their conscience has been aroused...I entreat you...not to deprive Hinduism of the last chance to make a voluntary expiation for its sinful past. Give me the chance of working among the caste Hindus."[40]

Dr Ambedkar, at Mumbai Conference called to ratify the Poona Pact after giving to Gandhi 'a large part of the credit' for amicable solution of the dispute, said:"I must confess that I was surprised, immensely surprised when I met him that there was so much in common between him and me."[41]

As to the issue of the representation of untouchables in legislatures Dr Ambedkar's view was that untouchables would gain more dignified and assertive position through separate electorate. Experience had made him to realise that there was no chance of political gains for untouchables in Hindu-fold. They would be dwindled and lost. So by 1928, he began to assert politically their identity distinct from the common Hindu-fold. His first step in that direction was the submission of a charter of demand as the President, Bahiskrit Hitkarini Sabha before the Indian Statutory Commission, popularly known as Simon Commission. His demands included reserved seats for untouchables in legislative bodies, special educational concessions, and recruitment to the government posts. The demands found positive response in the Report of the Commission by way of substantial acceptance. Since Commission had been hailed by vehement opposition by leaders of both Hindu and Muslim communities and Report was declared unacceptable, the British Government decided to call a Round Table Conference inviting delegates from all major parties as well as the prominent interest groups. Dr Ambedkar was invited along with other leader of untouchable like Dewan Bahadur R. Srinivasan. Dr Ambedkar joined hand with other minority communities and demanded separate electorate for the scheduled Castes like other minorities. Mahatma Gandhi, who did not participate in the first Round Table Conference due to detention, joined the Second Round Table Conference and opposed separate electorate for untouchables tooth and nail treating it as, 'vivisection of the nation.' Mahatma Gandhi was opposed to the separate electorate as such. But, he grudgingly accepted it for Muslims, Christians, Sikhs and Anglo-Indians. But, he could not swallow separate electorate for untouchables and termed it as, 'the unkindest cut of all' with a vow to resist it with his life. Ultimately, the British Government announced Communal Award and made clear that Award could not be altered without the consent of the affected groups i.e., without the consent of Dr Ambedkar as the representative of the Depressed Classes. Mahatma Gandhi started Satyagraha of fast unto death in Yervada prison, Pune. He was opposed only to separate electorate and was ready to give reservational concessions. Dr Ambedkar bowed and agreed to relinquish the separate electorate in lieu of a system of reserved seats to be elected from "joint" or general electorate. On September 24, 1932 Poona Pact was signed between

Poona Pact

Depressed Classes and Congress leaders. Give and take worked-Mahatma Gandhi was happy that the separate electorate had gone and Depressed Classes had joined hands with common Hindu-fold in the process of joint electorate and Dr Ambedkar (though reluctantly) was satisfied with the gain of some more (a little less than twice) seats reserved for Depressed Classes. Earlier under Communal Award 78 separately elected members had to represent the Depressed Classes. Under Poona Pact the number was raised to 148. In 1937, the untouchables got as many as 151 seats.

The Poona Pact was ratified by both sides at respective conference in jubilant and cooperative way. On 25 September, 1932 Poona Pact was ratified at a public meeting of the leaders of the caste Hindus and Depressed Classes leaders at Bombay. The joint meeting was presided over by Pt. Madan Mohan Malaviya. The resolution pre-endorsed by Mahatma Gandhi and passed at Mumbai conference read:

"This conference resolves that henceforth, among Hindus no one shall be regarded as an untouchable by reason of his birth and those who have been so regarded hitherto will have the same rights as the other Hindus in regard to the use of public wells public roads and other public institutions. This right shall have statutory recognition at the first opportunity and shall be one of the earliest acts of swaraj Parliament, if it shall not have received such recognition before that time."[42]

After his release from prison Gandhiji issued a press statement which goes on:

"The settlement arrived at is, so far as I can see, a generous gesture on all sides. It is a meeting of hearts, and my Hindu gratitude is due to Dr Ambedkar, Rao Bahadur Srinivasan and their party on the one hand and Rao Bahadur Rajah on the other. They could have taken up an uncompromising and defiant attitude by way of punishment to the so-called caste Hindus for the sins of generations. If they had done so, I atleast could not have resented their attitude and my death would have been but a trifling price exacted for the tortures that the outcastes of Hinduism have been going through for unknown generations. But they chose the noblest path and have thus shown that they have followed the precept of forgiveness enjoined by all religions. Let me hope that caste Hindu will prove themselves worthy of this forgiveness and carry out to the letter and spirit every clause of the settlement with all its implications."[43]

In his speech at Mumbai Conference Dr Ambedkar gave "a large part of the credit" for successful compromise to Mahatma Gandhi and also pointed out much of common between the two.[44]

There was clear view of Gandhiji to ameliorate the conditions of untouchables in two ways; first, granting equality among Hindus and ending Untouchability, and second, providing reservational benefit to them through statutory measures. Much of debate becomes inconsequential in view of this broader and long ranging perspective. Much of heat, confusion and hostility between the two great men has been contributed by extremists on both sides. Some of reputed foreign scholars have added fuel to the fire of avoidable controversy. For Gandhi, the two equal values laid behind his Yeravada prison satyagraha-abandonment of separate electorate for Hindu unity and caste Hindu atonement for injustices done by them to untouchables. He liked first more but not the second less. For him no one could be abandoned at the cost of the other.

Dr Ambedkar's argumentative assertion had singular effect on Mahatma Gandhi's later day's ideology and he tried to correct himself with more radical approach to the caste reform. The earlier hard and fast justification of varna based occupation and earning the bread was met with flexibility. He left his the iron-law hereditary profession in respect on untouchables. In December 1947, Mahatma Gandhi made clear that a 'Bhangi' should not be forced to clean laboratories today and if he can become a barrister, he should not be prevented from doing so. He encouraged and practiced inter-dining in his house and Ashramas. By the evening of his life he would attend and bless only those weddings, of which one of the parties was a Harijan. On Dr.Ambedkar's marriage with a Saraswat Brahmin girl he concurred with Sardar Patel that " if he (Gandhiji) had been alive would have blessed it."[45] Dr Ambedkar regretfully said "We did not understand him". On it the great scholar socialist leader Madhu Limaye said: "It was Ambedkar's greatness that he saw the nobility of Gandhi's soul and buried the old hatchet."[46] Dr Ambedkar paid highest complement to Gandhi on September 6,1954 when he said : "all of us knew that the Dalits were the nearest and dearest to him."

On 6 September 1954 Dr Ambedkar while speaking in Rajya Sabha on the Report of the Commissioner for Scheduled Castes and Tribes for 1953, proposed[47]:

" ... the abolition of the salt tax was done in the memory of Gandhi. I respect him and suggest to you that you levy the tax and create a Trust Fund in the name of Gandhi— Gandhi Trust Fund for the development or settlement untouchables. After all, the untouchables, according to all of us, were the nearest and dearest to him and there is no reason why Gandhi may not bless this project from Heaven, namely, levying the tax and using it for the development of the wasteland and settling the scheduled castes on this wasteland...".

But, a great scholar and authority on Indian competing equalities as Marc Galanter guessing too much of political gain preference behind Yeravda prison fast remarked, "Ironically, this fast is often referred to as Gandhi's fast against Untouchability".[48] Likewise, Eleanor Zelliot, a scholar of repute on Indian social problem, in her article entitled, "Gandhi and Ambedkar: A Study in Leadership,"[49] finds slighting of Dr Ambedkar by chanting ' Mahatma Gandhi Ki Jai on the occasion of passing Article 17, abolishing Untouchability on 29 November 1948. (In nature of things it was not unusual. Dr Ambedkar was the chief architect of the Constitution including Article 17, no doubt but he was first among the equals carrying one vote on division on certain issues. Article 17 was passed overwhelmingly. Which invisible force guided almost all the members who mattered most? It was the invisible wish of Gandhiji working as guiding force in the Constituent Assembly, so long as he was alive and even after his death on January 30, 1930. How there can be anything objectionable, if the honourable members paid homage to the great soul after ten months of his leaving for the heavenly abode, on a cause for which he had fought for since the childhood. The role of Gandhiji instanteously and sponteously was appreciated by Dr Ambedkar himself, after the five years the death of Mahatma Gandhi, as has been discussed earlier. Again writings of some of the communist leaders put too much motive behind Gandhi's efforts relating to anti- touchability. E.M.S. Namboodripad found more an aspect of political tactics in Gandhi's in constructive work for Harijans. He points out:

"Gandhi's interest in Harijan cause and activities... should be considered as nothing but an effort on his part to disengage the Congress from the situation in which it had been placed following its break with the government. It was an effort to find out points of contact with the British, to pursue the negotiations on constitutional reform started and temporarily broken at the Second Round Table Conference, and to recognise the Congress with a view to enabling it to meet this new situation".[50]

E.M.S. Namboodripad also painted Gandhiji as, "astute political leader of a class – the bourgeoisie, in whose class interests he always acted."[51]

The journalist of the same ideology, Arundhati Roy wrote in 2014 an introduction to the new edition of Dr Ambedkar's, "Annihilation of Caste" (1936).[52]The caption of the Introduction is, " Doctor and Saint." She revived the old the historic debate between Dr Ambedkar and Mahatma Gandhi with some selective presentation and certain concealments. What Rajmohan Gandhi concludes of her approach is to 'barricade battles to be unending' and "to substitute Ambedkar as India's chief hero."[53]

Not only this, many scholars who are interested in the continued ideological battle between the two great actors against Untouchability use to quote more than often Dr Ambedkar's reaction against Gandhi's Yarvada prison fast which came out in pre- Pact period that is to say, "he (Gandhi) has staked his very life in order to deprive them (untouchables) of the little they have got" or " his determination to fast unto death is worthy of a far better cause," but thanks giving from Dr Ambedkar and Mahatma Gandhi after the Pact is just overlooked. Again the reactions following 1937 poll in which out of 171 seats only 73 true and independent representatives could be chosen and 78 went in the account of Congress, are cited that is to say, Congress made through Poona Pact, "a handsome profit of its political transaction." Yet, at another occasion the most celebrated book on, "What Gandhi and Congress Have Done for Untouchables" is cited to ignore the Gandhi's contribution in anti-Untouchability move. It also came out when election outcome in Bombay had gone massively in favour of Congress with the support even from the untouchables.

Time has proved the fallibility of both- the statutory abolition of Untouchability (could be caste) cannot help fully unless public consciousness extends supportive hands and public consciousness may not spontaneously support reformative measures. Most times laws foster or create public opinion. In national interest the proper co-operation of the two should be welcome. So requires the spirit of the Constitution. A very valuable hint has been given by Eleanor Zelliot:

"[However,] despite Ambedkar's criticism of Gandhi and Gandhi's unwillingness to include such men as Ambedkar in the structure of his reform schemes, there were indications that each was conscious of the other's necessary place in any final solution of the problem of untouchability. [Thus], the paths of Gandhi and Ambedkar, while they often diverged, ultimately converged, forcing on the Indian conscience the problem of untouchability as an issue of national concern. [...]"[54]

The most wonderful effect and success of the like mindedness on the issue of the abolition of untouchability is the quite new dimension added to Article 17 of the Constitution.The most noticeable significance of Article17 abolishing Untouchability and declaring its practice in any form punishable by law is that as other fundamental rights it is not guaranteed against the state only. Article 17 along with Article 23 is addressed against the whole society. Speaking of the referred Articles Dr Upendra Baxi very insightfully writes: "The Constitutional articulation is remarkable in that it, in a chapter on fundamental rights, creates specific offences and that the rights themselves are limitations on the power of civil society rather than that of the state."

It is too difficult and unattractive to praise any good work in right perspective. It is easier and attractive to present anything in wrong perspective to discredit some person. It so happened with Mahatma Gandhi with all sincerity he coined a respectable word for untouchables- Harijan, he changed the name of his publication and started the magazine in the name of Harijan. The expression 'Harijan' very simply means, the men of Hari (God). It is always said- **Nirbal ke Bal Ram** (god is helper or strength of those who are weak. Even Tulsidas has prayed Lord Rama and Sita whom the most helpless persons are dearest. *(Gira, arath jal- bichi sam Kahiat bhinna na bhinna, bandaun sitaram pada, jinhi parampriya khinna) or* "knowing the bhakta of Hari the love accelerated, with tearing eyes brows became stand still" **(Harijan jani priti ati badi, sajal nayan pulkawali thadi).** But, some people started spreading rumour that 'Harijan' is derogatory as it meant, according to them, the children of God communicative of the children whose parentage is unknown. On that count untouchables began to hate the word Harijan, resolved not to give positive credit to Mahatma Gandhi and tried to discredit him by boycotting the use of 'Harijan'. In Bombay Legislative Assembly where one bill defining scheduled castes as 'Harijans' was fiercely opposed by Bhaura Gaikwad who sought an amendment to drop the expression 'Harijan'.

He protested: "If all the touchable classes were the people of God, were the touchable classes assume to belong to monsters?"[55] The amendment failed. But the move did communicate the feelings of resentment and resentment was without any substance. Likewise the poetic expression of Professor J. Mangiah that Untouchables were all right Gandhi turned them into malcontents:

Untouchables our folks are good,
Till Gandhi told them they were Gods
Content they were to faith they stood
To Congress lessons now each nods.[56]

Even Jag Jivan Ram was critical of the Congress organisation- Harijan Sewak Sangh, calling it erroneous in conception, faulty in emphasis, and halting in execution.[57]

Experience is the best teacher and socio-legal experience gives the lesson that both. Dr Ambedkar and Gandhi represent complementary moves to eradicate Untouchability. Dr Ambedkar was visible mind continuously working for that Gandhiji was invisible force behind that move without coming into picture.In spite of Dr Ambedkar's bitter criticism of Mahatma Gandhi and Congress on the issue of the emancipation of untouchables, Mahatma Gandhi never allowed himself to become bitter and continued his tirade against Untouchability. When Independence was very near, on June 14, 1947, Mahatma Gandhi asked Congress men to frontally address Untouchability and caste injustice and also the question of Adivasis. He said: "And what about 'untouchables'? If you say that "untouchables" are nothing, the Adivasis are nothing, then you are not going to survive yourselves. But if you do away with the distinction of savarna and avarna, if you treat Shudras, the untouchables and the Adivasis as equals then something good will have come out of a bad thing [partition]."

Everything happens due to certain causes- relationship between cause and effect cannot be ruled out. The untouchables, now the Scheduled Castes (and also the Scheduled Tribes) enjoy the benefit of abolition of Untouchability, prohibition of beggar, reservation in Lok Sabha and Legislative Assemblies of the states (now in Gram Panchyats and Munipalities), services under the union and the states and also in educational institutions with many other safeguards under the Constitution. Much of the credit for all these goes to Dr B.R. Ambedkar. Sequence lies like this:

* Had he not represented before and given charter of demands for untouchables as an entity distinct from general Hindus before the Idian Statutory Commission (Simon Commission), he would not have been invited as representative of the Depressed Classes by the British Government to participate in the Round Table Conferences held in England and the issue of untouchables with such gravity would not have attracted the people at large both inside and outside the country.

** Had he not represented Depressed Classes with full vigour and logicity, the separate electorate for the Depressed Classes would not have been announced by British government, had the British government not done so, the importance of Dr Ambedkar in the eye of Mahatma Gandhi and leading Congressmen would have not touched the Himalayan height necessitating the compromise of statutory safeguards with more reservational seats in the legislature and commitment of the caste-Hindus to grant equal treatment with untouchables at public places including their entry into temples.

*** Had Dr Ambedkar not persistently raised the illogicity and unjustness behind the practice of Untouchability and inbuilt evil of the caste-system in scholarly way with reason and proof and announced his decision to convert to some other religion, the pressure on Caste-Hindu would not have been build up so as to mend their attitude towards untouchables with accommodative spirit.

**** Had Dr Ambedkar not been inside the Constituent Assembly, the issue of S.Cs. and S.Ts. would not have been taken up treating it as minority and had it not been taken as one of minorities the position of S.Cs and S.Ts. would not have been taken so seriously. Starting from reservation for all minorities the claim of all other minorities was denounced and reservation and safeguards only for S.Cs. and S.Ts. was announced.

But all these would not have found the constitutional sanctity, as they are, had Dr Ambedkar not found the opportunity to participate in the Constitution-making process. Had the Congress members, who were in overwhelming majority in the Constituent Assembly not extended their full cooperative hands it would not have been possible the smooth sailing on the issues of safeguards provided to the Scheduled Castes etc. On this juncture the cooperative enterprise became most pressing between the two giants of the Indian socio-political horizon.

Barring the too political compulsion of Dr Ambedkar as a political leader heading a political party, struggling for its survival and image at election (which required exposure of opposite strong political party) necessitating frontal attack, Dr Ambedkar had immense regard for Mahatma Gandhi from the core of heart. Mahatma Gandhi, as astute elder politico-religious (chastenised) man and enamoured by the scholarship and reasoned argument of Dr Ambedkar, had extreme love and affection for him. The broad national minded Gandhiji always searched the opportunities for Dr Ambedkar to play constructive nation building role utilising his talent, intelligence and diligence with immense capacity and sense of responsibility to work hard to accomplish the entrusted job. He could do it very secretly and nicely with the help of his trusted Lieutenant for whom his words were like the word of God (Sardar Vallabha Bhai Patel).. A detail account of such blessings will be presented in the concluding chapter of the part II dealing with Dr.Ambedkar. Here it would be sufficient to hint that (1) in the induction of Dr Ambedkar in the Constituent Assembly as representative chosen from Bombay legislature (after having lost his membership from Bengal due to its forming the part of East Pakistan after partition), (2) his induction as Law Minister in Nehru Cabinet, and (3) his choice as Chairman, Drafting Committee of the Constituent Assembly, Mahatma Gandhi's will prevailed through the good offices of Sardar Vallabhbhai Patel on which Dr Ambedkar himself expressed surprise and he was doubly surprised on his choices as Chairman, Drafting Committee, Constituent Assembly. The unseen hands of Gandhiji transformed Dr Ambedkar from staunch protector of the rights of untouchables into world renowned maker of the Constitution of the country inhabited by one-sixth population of the world- a maker of the Constitution- first and foremost a social document with splendid compromises. The other visible cooperation of invisible Mahatma Gandhi was the unconditional support of Congressmen who were representing the wishes of Gandhiji on all issues including the abolition of Untouchability and different safeguards to the Scheduled Castes and Scheduled Tribes. As clarified by Nehru, though not present as member, Bapu had played greater role in the making of the Constitution. Dr Ambedkar himself had expressed his gratitude to the unprecedented cooperation of the Congress through discussion inside the House and on party forum outside the Assembly (cited in the last chapter). Dr Ambedkar's prime object was to emancipate the untouchables and with a view to accomplish this objective he could shake hand with anybody. When his opponents began to criticise him for joining the union cabinet shaking hands with Congress, he answered showing flexibility in vision (without losing autonomy) to accomplish the goal. He said:

"The fact is, I am like a stone. Wherever I may be, in whatever company I may find myself, I would never lose my separate identity. If anybody asks for cooperation I would gladly give it for worthy cause. I cooperated with the Congress government for four years with all my might. But I never merged myself with the Congress. I would gladly help and cooperate with those who are sincere in their words and deeds for the interests of the Scheduled Castes. But I would never help those who are sweet tongued and whose intentions and deeds are contrary to the interests of our people."

No wonder this had singular effect attracting cooperation of almost all prominent members of the Constituent Assembly. The matter of reservation started on August 8, 1947 with the idea of providing its benefit to all the minorities in cabinet, services and the legislatures. But by November 23, 1948 the sub-committee of the Advisory Committee on Minorities began to realise that, "the reservation of seats for religious communities, .. did lead to a certain degree of separatism and was to that extent contrary to the conception of a democratic state." Consequently, a number of members gave notice for resolutions seeking to recommend the Constituent Assembly that there should be no reservation of seats in the legislatures for any community in India. One member Shri V.I. Munniswami Pillai gave notice of an amendment seeking to exclude the Scheduled Castes from it. Ultimately, on May 11, 1949 Advisory Committee passed resolution with overwhelming majority to deny any reservational benefit to the minorities. But keeping in view the peculiar position of the Scheduled Castes it realised the necessity of reservation for ten years as decided earlier. Thus, Shri Pillai amendment was passed with one dissenting voice. The finally passed resolution read:

"That the system of reservation for minorities other than Scheduled Castes in Legislatures be abolished."

The Advisory Committee also agreed unanimously to include in the list of the Scheduled Castes four classes of East Punjab, namely, Mazhabis, Ramdasis, Kabirpanthis and

Sikligars who suffered from the same disabilities as other members of the Scheduled Castes so that they would get benefit of representation given to the Scheduled Castes.

References

1. Mahatma Gandhi, Complete Works of Mahatma Gandhi, Vol. 33, p. 268.
2. B.R. Ambedkar, What Congress and Gandhi Have Done to the Untouchables?, Dr.Babasaheb Ambedkar's Writings and Speeches, Vol. 9, Education Department, Government of Maharashra, 1945, 1991, p. 196.
3. M.K. Gandhi, An Autobiography or The Story of My Experiments With Truth, Navjivan Publishing House, Ahmedabad, 2013 (First published in 1927.
4. Thomas Panthom, Against Untouchability. The Discourse of Gandhi and Ambedkar (in) Gopal Guru edited, Humiliation-Claims and Context, Oxford University Press, p. 179.
5. *Ibid.*, citing Zelliot, 1986, 1988, p. 194
6. M.K.Gandhi, Complete Works of Mahatma Gandhi 100 Vols., New Delhi:Publication Division, Vol. 7 p.470
7. *Ibid* Vol. 9, p. 181.
8. *Ibid* Vol. 14, pp. 344-345.
9. *Ibid*. Vol. 19, p. 20.
10. *Ibid*. Vol. 19, p. 73.
11. *Ibid* Vol. 57, p. 147.
12. *Ibid*.
13. A dialogue between Gandhi and Nambudiri Trustee is very instructive and shows the Gandhian way of persuasion.
    Gandhiji: Is it fair to exclude a whole section of Hindus, because of their supposed lower birth, from the public roads which can be used by non-Hindus, by criminals and bad characters, and even by dogs and cattle?
    Nambudiri Trustee: But how it is helped? They are reaping the reward of their karma
    Gandhiji: No doubt they are suffering for their karma by being born as untouchables. But why must you add to the punishment? Are they worse than even criminals and beasts?
    Nambudiri Trustee: They must be so, for otherwise God would not condemn them to be born Untouchables.
    G: But God may punish them. Who are we human beings to take the place of God and add to their punishment?
    N: We are instruments. God uses us as His instruments in order to impose on them the punishment that their karma has earned for them.

G: But supposing the Avarnas outside Varnas, i. e., Untouchables, said that they were instruments in the hands of God in order to impose afflictions on you? What would you do?

N. Then Government would stand between them and us and prevent them from doing. Goodmen would do so. Mahatmaji we beseech you to prevent Avarnas from depriving us of our old privileges.

On refusal of priests even to concede to Arbitration, Gandhiji persuasively sought state intervention and on his initiative Maharaja of Travancore ordered that the roads from three sides of the Vaikkam temple be opened to all. Quoted from Eleanor Zelliot, "Gandhi and Ambedkar- A Study in Leadership" (in) Ishita Banerjee-Dube (edited) Caste in History, Oxford University Press, 2008, pp. 197- 209 at p. 198.

14. *Ibid.*
15. Charles F. Andrews, Mahatama Gandhi: His Life and Ideas, Jaico Publications, 2006. See Also Gopal Guru, edited, Humiliation-Claims and Context, Oxford University Press, p. 179.
16. Thomas Panthom, Against Untouchability. The Discourse of Gandhi and Ambedkar (in) Gopal Guru edited, Humiliation-Claims and Context, Oxford University Press, p. 179.
17. Dhananjay Keer, 1991, p. 71.
18. *Ibid.*
19. GoM 1982:14-16. Cited from Thomas Pantham, Against Untouchability- The Discussion of Gandhi and Ambedkar (in) Gopal Guru edited Humiliation-Claims and Context, Oxford University Press, 2009, p. 188.
20. Quoted from Charles F. Andrews, Mahatma Gandhi-His Life and Ideas, Jaico Publishing House, 2006, p. 120.
21. *Ibid*. pp. 113-114.
22. Quoted from Eleanor Zelliot, " Dr Ambedkar and Mahar Movement", Ph.D. dissertation , University of Pennsylvania, 1969, p. 178.
23. *Ibid*.
24. M.K. Gandhi, Collected Works of Gandhi, Vol. 57: 5 September, 1932-15 November 1932.
25. *Ibid*.
26. *Ibid*. Appendix 59:13 January 1933- 9 March 1933.
27. *Ibid.*
28. *Ibid.*
29. M.K. Gandhi, Introduction to an Autobiography or The Story of My Experiments With Truth, Nav Jivan Publishing House-Ahmedabad, p. xv.

30. *Ibid.* and Mahadevbhaini Diary, Vol. VIII, pp. 117-122.
31. Raj Mohan Gandhi, Independence and Social Justice- The Ambedkar- Gandhi Debate, Economic and Political Weekly, April 11, 2015 (Vol. L, no. 15), p. 35 at p. 42.
32. M K Gandhi, Complete Works , Vol. 55, pp. 196-169.
33. Quoted from Thomas Pantham, Against Untouchability- Discourses of Gandhi and Ambedkar (in) Gopal Guru edited, 'Humiliation-Claims and Context, Oxford University Press, 2009 p. 179 at p. 195.
34. M.K. Gandhui, Complete Works, Vol. 35, p. 2.
35. M.K. Gandhi, Complete Works, Vol. 57, pp. 388-389.
36. *Ibid.* Vol. 68, pp. 151-152.
37. *Ibid.* Vol. 53, p. 499.
38. *Ibid.* Vol. 68, pp. 315-316.
39. Thomas Pantham, Against Untouchability, supra, p. 193.
40. Pyarelal 1932, pp. 70-71 , Quoted from,Thomas Pantham, Against Untouchability, supra, p. 193.
41. *Ibid.* p. 188., Cited by Thomas Pantham, supra at p. 194.
42. M. K. Gandhi, Complete Works, supra Vol. 57, p. 118.
43. *Ibid.* Vol. 57, pp. 123-125.
44. Pyarelal, 1932, p. 188, as quoted earlier.
45. Sardar Patel's Correspondence (Ed.) Durga Das, Vol. 11, p. 327.
46. Pyarelal to Dr Hardev Sharma of the NMML. See also Madhu Limaye, Manu, Gandhi and Ambedkar and Other Essays, Gyan Publishing House, Delhi, 2008. p. 29.
47. Rajya Sabha Debates, 6 September 1954, column. 1472.
48. Marc Galanter, Competing Equalities- Law and Backward Classes in India, Oxford University Press 1984, p. 33.
49. Eleanor Zelliot, "Gandhi and Ambedkar : A Study in Leadership" (in) M. J. Mahar edited, The Untouchables in Contemporary India, New Delhi 1972, pp. 69-112.
50. E.M.S. Namboodripad,The Mahatma and The Ism,1958 p. 62, quoted from Upendra Baxi, Ambedkar Memorial Lecture 1978 on "Political Justice, Legislative Reservation for Scheduled Castes and Social Change", Delivered at Madras University on 24-25, January 1979.
51. *Ibid.*
52. Arundhati Roy," The Doctor and The Saint" (in) B.R. Ambedkar, Annihilation of Caste: The Annodated Critical Edition, New Delhi, Narayan.)
53. Raj Mohan Gandhi,"Independence and Social Justice, Economic and Political Weekly, April 11, 2015 p. 35.
54. Zelliot appears to depart and make amend on her earlier views expressed in 1972 article, Gandhi and Ambedkar: A study in

Leadership (in) Ishita Banerjee-Dube (ed.) Caste in History, Oxf. Univ. Press. 2008, 2010, pp. 197-209 at p. 209.

55. On issue of the use of the expression "Harijan", Dr Ambedkar was not touchy. He was practical. Dr Ambedkar made clear that the use of the term "Harijan", "has not elevated them in the eyes of the Hindus- The new name has become completely identified with the subject matter of the old. Everybody knows that Harijans are simply no other than the old untouchables. The new name [therefore] provides no excape to the Untouchables from the curse of untouchability." Dr Baba Saheb Ambedkar : Writing and Speeches - Untouchables or the children of India's Ghetto and other Essays on Untouchables and Untouchability : Social, Political and Religious, Education Department, Government of Maharashtra, 1999, Vol. 5, p. 363.
56. As quoted in Zelliot's Article, supra, f.no. 54, p. 206.
57. *Ibid.*

9

Critical Appraisal of Baba Saheb: Eminence, Statesmanship and Nation Building

[*14th of the April is celebrated as "Ambedkar Jayanti" every year. It is the birthday of Dr B.R. Ambedkar, the great icon on the Indian politico-legal horizon. Birth days come and go. Everybody celebrates his birthday in his own way. Dalits remember him as their messiah, liberator from subservience and guide to achieve human dignity the resolve of educate, organise and agitate.*

Dr Ambedkar, Chairman Drafting Committee and Other Members

Dr Ambedkar presenting a copy of the Constitution to the President, Dr Rajendra Prasad

[Different political parties organise the celebration with great pomp and show visualising the vote attracting prospect of down-trodden people. The former have genuine faith in his ideology though having some political compromises hither and thither and latter keeping the electoral expediency. One good sign in this regard is that even those who did not subscribe to Dr Ambedkar's ideology or once talked of, "False Worshipping God" have begun to commend his contribution in nation building. But, nobody pays the real tribute which that great ambassador of the humanity deserves].

The writers think, and have firm faith and the study in the book reveals that Dr Ambedkar and his contribution in the nation building have not been properly highlighted and evaluated. Neither Ambedkarites nor his critics have done justice to the great scholarly nationalist and the great nation builder. Ambedkarites detract from the path of right thinking due to their hyprobolic expressions falling prey of the evils Dr Ambedkar fought for throughout his life.[1] The opponent chooses few astrey expressions which give impression of a reactionary against social evil without positive and constructive programmes to eradicate them and think beyond trivialities. Dr Ambedkar was very learned person with virtue of moderation, reconciliation and over all humanism. Thus, in one way the adjective **Babasaheb** may appear completely unsuitable to his philosophical thinking of human being i.e. complete absence of hero-worship, Bhakti-cult and complex of superiority preached by Manuwadis. However from another angle,the prefix attached to Dr B.R. Ambedkar- Baba Saheb may have convincing connotations to those for whom he was in no way less important than priest or Baba sermonising to do something significant for the common men. The honour of Bharat-Ratna is also very negligible tribute to his immense and unparalleled contribution in nation building and anxiety for the future of India. There are many recipients[2] of that award and it was conferred on Dr Ambedkar at a very belated time i.e. 1990, after forty years of the working of the Constitution.[3] The antagonist completely fail to read, understand and appreciate what Dr Ambedkar was. They pick up some utterances occasionally made and strong criticism of Hindu caste-ridden society. Though, there are many ifs and buts and many surfaced differences between Dr Ambedkar and Gandhiji, thanks to the large-heartedness of the great-man Gandhiji who, within his utmost priority to get Independence, appreciated the learned presentation of Dr Ambedkar, his feelings and willingness to wipe out caste-ridden evils from the Indian society and a great constitutional law expert with vision of the future of India.

The adjectives used about Dr Ambedkar in this book are well thought, expressing the originality of his personality and overall outlook towards life and pride in what Dr Ambedkar was. Thus, Doctor (Dr) is expressive of well read, learned and self acquired worth of Dr Ambedkar. He completed his graduation from the well reputed and famous Elphinston College, Bombay. He acquired M.A., Ph.D. and LL.D. from Columbia University, U.S.A.; D.Sc. from the world renowned London School of Economics, U.K.; D.Sc. from Bonn University, Germany and Bar-at-Law from Gray's Inn. In addition he was conferred many *honoris causa* degrees. Bhimrao indicates his extreme respect for women in general and his mother in particular. Bhimabai was his mother and he gave her a pride place in his name. Ramjirao was his pride father. The place of father's name in his name is expression of perpetuating the name of his father with glory - a worthy father of a worthy son. Ambedkar shows his extreme love and respect for the village wherefrom he came. So everything is original with natural love and affection and constant story of climbing on the Himalayan height of glory with one mantra of success-acquisition of knowledge.

The Life and noble deeds of Ambedkar fully justify the epithet, 'a man becomes perfect by experience'. He reached the Constituent Assembly with a perfectly moderated, visionary and nationalistic positive thinking. He reached there at 55 years of age with full of maturity and love for all with moderate compromising approach. The famous Geeta is said to have come out of Lord Krishna's mouth which became world unequalled treasure of knowledge and that is accumulated, revised, modified by experience of Lord Krishna's 78 years vision of life and the world. The teachings of Tathagat Buddha came after 45 years experiences of life and self-realisation. So was with Dr Ambedkar who was born in 1891 and started his contribution to the Constituent Assembly in 1946 and as a Chairman, Drafting Committee since August 30, 1947. One who comes to know about his role in drafting of the Constitution, answering questions during debates, firmness, deep knowledge satisfying the members of the different shades in the Constituent Assembly, amenability to reasons, persuasion and compromistic reconciliatory approach will not believe that he was the same persecuted at every step in life, agitating for the cause of untouchables, bitter critic of the Hindu caste-ridden society and cumulatively an angry young man and energetic man full of angers against social evil. Responsibility made him broad-visioned person with Indianness and national outlook striving for constructive nation-building.

II
Position of Eminence vis-à-vis other Eminent Persons

In-depth study and varied knowledge Ambedkar proved to be next to none. As a man of prominence and constructive role in nation-building with great futuristic vision he was next to none, except one. Their relations have not been assessed aptly by authors, speakers and think tanks except one. And, that one is the great socialist learned thinker Sri Madhu Limaye who in very small but scholarly book[4] containing five articles on Gandhi, Ambedkar and some others, has revealed a lot that how great Dr Ambedkar and that unequalled man were. The trinity of Nehru, Patel and Ambedkar had most everlasting contribution. Who was better in comparison to whom is not easy, wise and just decision. Nehru's nation building programme, Patel's national integration with firm, patriotic appeal and iron hand

and Ambedkar's assimilation of ideas, views of different shades, apt and accurate convincing reply, giving the Constitution with Granville Austin compliments 'a work of splendid compromise' and genuine concern and anxiety to defend the independence till the last drop of blood are incomparable, par excellent and never ending contribution to the Independent India.

The man who was unparalleled, without participating in the Constituent Assembly, was Bapu - the great soul, Gandhi. He loved all and was respected by all. He could err and occasionally misjudge the situation. Somebody could disagree with him, criticise him but nobody could doubt his sincerity in future of India and greatest contribution in bringing independence. That was reason why his was the last word and everybody paid due respect from the core of his heart.

The above was true with respect to the relationship of Dr Ambedkar and Bapu too. Dr Ambedkar was well-read, his analysis of Hindu scriptures was appreciated by Bapu, his outlook on social problem was more accurate than Bapu, his approach to the unsuccessfulness of social justice without annihilation of caste was, is and shall remain a hard reality, he openly criticised by posing question. : what Congress and Gandhi have done for untouchables, his occasional denial that Gandhi had done nothing for him etc. have been the expression of Dr Ambedkar's anxiety to provide justice to the dumb, despised, and persecuted Dalit poor masses. He had enough expectations from a towering personality and sympathiser with untouchables and depressed people like Bapu. Not finding response in that degree he was critical to Bapu. But, he never lost faith in Bapu and his respect for him was never lessened. He was critical of Gandhiji, of course. Some of the acts of Gandhiji also did not appear defensible that is to say, (1) Gandhiji's censor of the then Central Provinces Prime Minister Dr Kher for his inclusion of one Untouchable in his cabinet, and (2) Gandhiji's silence on the episode of the rape of 14 years Untouchable girl, Bachuma by three Muslims-S.P., Sub Inspector of Education Department and a lawyer and the Mohemmedan minister-in- charge decided to set them free in spite of rejection of their application against convictions by the High Court and Governor General in Council. Dr Ambedkar felt that Gandhiji's silence was keeping in his view of maintaining Hindu-Muslim unity and it led Dr Ambedkar to comment: "Does this not show that Mr Gandhi's sympathies for the Untouchables are limited by his politics?" But, on personal level he had immense regard for Gandhiji and his indispensable role in the country's liberation. Poona Pact is the obvious example. Dr Ambedkar valued the life of Bapu much more important than the protection of the interest of depressed people through communal award. The nation needed Gandhiji. Dr Ambedkar bowed and led Bapu to break his unto the death fast against the communal award. It was the highest evaluation of the life of Bapu and greatest respect paid by Ambedkar to Bapu. Bapu returned it in good coin due to his great love of Ambedkar for his wide knowledge and ability to handle the ticklish and complex constitutional issues. But, what he did for Ambedkar was hidden without becoming public.

To make it more clear Dr Ambedkar himself was surprised at finding his place in the Drafting Committee, his being chosen as its Chairman and his induction in Nehru cabinet as Law Minister. To quote him: "I came into the Constituent Assembly with no greater aspiration than to safeguard the interests of the Scheduled Castes. I had not the remotest idea that I would be called upon to undertake most responsible function. I was, therefore, surprised when the Assembly elected me to the Drafting Committee. I was more than surprised when the Drafting Committee elected me to be Chairman."[5] He was surprised to the greater extent when he was offered the office of the Law Minister in the national government led by Pt. J.L. Nehru who had graciously written letter to Dr Ambedkar making offer to join as a Cabinet Minister and that too Law Minister of the Union Government. All these were happening in spite of the hard reality expressed and recognised by Dr Ambedkar that he was in opposite camp and had bitterly criticised Congress calling it a burning house and discouraged and condemned the association of the untouchables with Congress which could not be trusted to undertake a radical programmes of social and economic reconstruction without which the untouchables could never succeed in improving their lot.

The unexpected favour done to Dr Ambedkar by the three most important figures of that time - Dr Rajendra Prasad, Sardar Vallabhbhai Patel and Pt. Jawahar Lal Nehru were matter of only speculation by Dr Ambedkar. When he had lost membership of the Constituent Assembly due to partition of the Bengal from where he had been chosen, Dr Rajendra Prasad and Sardar Vallabhbhai Patel considering his worth and utility in the great job of shaping the reports of various committees, discussion and original draft of Sir B.N. Rau in form Draft Constitution ensured his entry from Bombay and Patel got him elected as the Chairman of the Drafting Committee. But, the million dollar question is why? Behind all these unexpected happenings there was some invisible force whose words or mere indication of desire were carried on by his trusted soldiers during the independence movement and thereafter. Some indications, hints and evidences show the role of hidden spirit which had great appreciation for learning and worth of Dr Ambedkar.

First, moving the Objective Resolution in the Constituent Assembly on 12 December, 1946 Nehru revealed the role of Mahatma Gandhi without participation in proceedings of the Constituent Assembly: "There is another person who is absent here and must be in the minds of us today - the great leader of our people, the Father of our Nation - who has been the architect of his Assembly and all that has gone before it and possibly of much that will follow

.... his great spirit hovers over this place and blesses our understanding."[6]

Second, Sri B. Shiva Rao, one of the members of the Constituent Assembly and author of the five volume Framing of India's Constitution has revealed how he had submitted a list of prominent members[7] who were not members of Congress Party, but were men of special knowledge and distinction, to Mahatma Gandhi. Dr Ambedkar's name was one of such persons. Mahatma Gandhi realised the contribution to be made by independent scholarly and experienced persons. He passed on that list to J.L. Nehru and Sardar Vallabhbhai Patel for making necessary arrangements for their entry in the Constituent Assembly who dutifully obeyed and all such persons became members of the Constituent Assembly. The list included names of Dr Ambedkar, Sri Alladi Krisnaswami Ayyar, Shyama Prasad Mukkerji, H.N. Kunzru, N.G. Ayyangar, K. Santhanam, M.R. Jayakar, Sachchidanand Sinha, K.M. Munshi (an estranged Congressman) and B. Shiva Rao etc. Dr Ambedkar had lost membership of the Constituent Assembly due to partition and part of Bengal gone to the then East Pakistan. Dr Rajendra Prasad[8] and Sardar Vallabhbhai Patel[9] (both wrote letter to Mr. B.G. Kher, the then Prime Minister of Bombay to elect Dr Ambedkar immediately as the Constituent Assembly might not be deprived of his valuable services and Dr Ambedkar got elected from Bombay.

Thirdly, when Constituent Assembly started proper functioning, the need of a Chairman of Drafting Committee was realised. Pt. Nehru and Sarojini Naidu were anxious about the search of the Chairman of the Drafting Committee. They approached Mahatma Gandhi. One suggestion was to request Sir Ivor Jennings, who had authored many Constitutions of the South Asian countries, to draft the Indian Constitution. Mahatma Gandhi instantly said, there is a very learned and legally qualified person like Ambedkar with you. Why not to try him by giving an opportunity to draft the new Constitution?[10] The will of Bapu was mandate for Sardar Vallabhbhai Patel whose offer was accepted by Dr Ambedkar. Dr Ambedkar agreed to co-operate by the framing of Constitution.[11] And, Dr Ambedkar was unanimously chosen as Chairman, Drafting Committee to his pleasant surprise.

Fourthly, in induction of Dr Ambedkar into Nehru Cabinet in 1947, again Gandhiji is said to have prevailed over hesitant Nehru. Rajgopalachari's story reveals: "Nehru had frankly told Gandhiji that he would not have Dr Ambedkar in his cabinet, because he was a blockade in the Freedom struggle. Gandhiji told Nehru that freedom has come to India and not to Nehru and therefore, Dr Ambedkar's talent and capacity should be utilised for building up modern India.[12] Nehru was, thus, left with no alternative except inducting Dr Ambedkar as Law Minister in his Cabinet. Gandhiji is said to have been approached by Babu Jagjivan Ram after consultation with Sardar Vallabhbhai Patel for the above purpose.[13]

The occasional outburst of Dr Ambedkar on the evil of caste ridden Indian society were based on his priority - his priority was annihilation of caste which was only way to ensure social justice. In Gandhi's priority independence of the country was at top. He never approved caste riddenness but he knew that at that time to touch that issue could adversely affect the cause of liberation from the British clutches. He had a series of dialogues through writings but ultimately abandoned it and closed his reply to Ambedkar with these words, *"At the end of the Chapter, I hope that we shall all find ourselves in the same camp." Humility and open mind were Gandhi's loveable qualities."* Even his letter to Shrada alias Laxmi Kabir on 8th Feb. 1948 expresses the frustration with performance of Congress.

Gandhiji was also not satisfied with the affairs of post-independence period. Few months prior to his death Gandhiji had expressed the view that Congress should dissolved because it had been a party of freedom struggle and would come to disrepute as a ruling party. He had also warned - "do not be power drunk." The relation between Mahatma Gandhi and Dr Ambedkar has been very well summed up by Madhu Limaye: "There was undoubtedly a sharp difference of outlook between Mahatma Gandhi and Dr Ambedkar. But an objective evaluation of their roles cannot but lead to the conclusion that both were working towards the same goal, of course, in their own different way."[14] Gandhiji was a universal leader of suffering humanity. His impact on Nelson Mandela and end of apartheid in South Africa and on Martin Luther King, Jr. and his role in peaceful non-violent agitation leading to enactment of the Civil Rights Act, 1964 cannot be overlooked. To quote Madhu Limaye, "Mahatma Gandhi was not a sectional leader. He was a universal benefactor, especially of the poor and lowly. His was a message of love, of mutual adjustment and conflict resolution. B.R. Ambedkar, though he called himself only a champion of the Scheduled Castes, was a worshipper of knowledge.[15] He knew the ultimate key to power is knowledge." This knowledge worship and its fruits led due recognition by the nation builders and Dr Ambedkar found an opportunity and utilised to the best of his ability for the welfare of all. His respect for Bapu was immense. Reminded by Sardar Patel on his second marriage with a Brahmin girl, popularly known later as Savita Ambedkar, that "if Bapu had been alive today, he would have given you his blessings on your marriage."[16] Dr Ambedkar heartily concurred, "I agree that Bapu, if had been alive, would have blessed, the marriage."[17] Dr Ambedkar also expressed sincere view before Gandhian Pyarelal that Bapu was not alive to give his blessings and regretfully admitted: "We did not understand him."[18] Pyarelal reacted to somebody that "it was greatness of Dr Ambedkar that he saw the nobility of Gandhi's soul and buried the old hatchet."[19] All's well that ends well. In 1954, Dr Ambedkar paid the highest compliment to Bapu by saying that "all of us, – including Ambedkar himself - knew that the Dalits were the nearest and dearest to him."[20] On this issue the sincere advice of Madhu Limaye is most desirable, healthy and worthy to be accepted by all SCs, STs and OBCs men and women, "beware of the fake Ambedkarites. Embrace the real Ambedkar, a conscience keeper of Gandhi."[21]

III
Dr Ambedkar's Humility and Enlightened Outlook

A really educated person becomes enlightened and full of humility.[22] His vanity vanishes and for good and appreciable works he gives credit to others. So did Dr Ambedkar. For successful accomplishment of the drafting of the India's Constitution he gave credit to different persons and bodies.

First, Dr Ambedkar said, "The credit that is given to me does not really belong to me. It belongs partly to Sir B.N. Rau, the constitutional advisor to the Constituent Assembly who prepared a rough draft of the Constitution for the consideration of the Drafting Committee."[23]

Secondly, a part of credit was conceded by him to all the members of the Drafting Committee who sat continuously for 141 days and "without whose ingenuity to devise new formulae and capacity to tolerate and to accommodate different points of view, the task of framing the Constitution could not have come to a successful conclusion."[24]

Thirdly, he put on record the greater share of credit to the Chief Draftsman of the Constitution, Mr. S.N. Mukherji.[25] His ability contributed to put the most intricate proposal in the simplest and clearest legal form and saved the Drafting Committee from further delay.

Fourthly, he gave all credit for the smooth sailing of the Draft Constitution in the Assembly to the Congress Party. It shows Dr Ambedkar's expression based on experience in the Constituent Assembly with that party whom he had called earlier as 'burning house', conservative and unable to render good to down-trodden. He candidly accepted that the constructive and co-operative presence of "Congress party had brought into the proceedings a sense of order and discipline." The presence of the Congress Party had immensely helped the Drafting Committee to pilot the Constitution in right perspective.[26]

Lastly, it was the extreme humility of Dr Ambedkar to express his gratitude to the Drafting Committee to unanimously elect him as Chairman of the Committee in spite of the fact that more learned experts of the Constitutional law were present and available. He specifically mentioned the name Sir Alladi Krishnaswami Ayyar. To quote Dr Ambedkar, "I was therefore greatly surprised when the Assembly elected me to the Drafting Committee. I was more surprised when the Drafting Committee elected me to be its Chairman. There were in Drafting Committee, men, bigger, better and more competent than myself such as my friend Sir Alladi Krishnaswami Ayyar.[27] I am grateful to the Constituent Assembly and the Drafting Committee for reposing too much trust and confidence and for having chosen me as their instrument and given me the opportunity, of serving the country."[28]

IV
Patient Hearer and Accurate Replier with Convincing Reasons and Unparalleled Legal Acumen

The originality and special importance of Dr Ambedkar did not lie in the fact that the final draft of the Constitution is the expression of his original ideas. Of course it was not. The importance and significance lies in the fact how Drafting Committee under his chairmanship assimilated the ideas expressed in first draft prepared by Sir B.N. Rau, the Constitutional Advisor to the Constituent Assembly, after having world-wide tour and interactions with statesmen and hon'ble justices of different English speaking countries, view expressed in Objective Resolutions, debate there on and different versions of different members, understand them and incorporate them in the final draft. The significance lies in his art of scholarly persuasion, satisfying members debating on different issues and being persuaded by good and convincing arguments. His answers were so full of reasons and well researched facts and law that other members of the Assembly had to accept or persuade him to change his version.[29] At many places Dr Ambedkar had to surrender his views in order to achieve consensus. The result being that most cited authority on the Indian Constitution, Granville Austin commends the Indian Constitution based on decision-making by consensus i.e. making the Constitution by unanimity or near unanimity. One of the members of the Constituent Assembly, Thakurdas Bhargava said, "I am really very glad that we have been able to prepare such a splendid constitution with unanimity."[30] G. Austin concludes his scholarly book with words, "Equipped with the basic qualifications, attitudes, and experience for creating and working a democratic constitution, Indians did not default their tryst with destiny."[31]

The simplicity, naturalness and scholarly answer of Dr Ambedkar to the biggest charge of delay - a case of Nero fiddling while Rome was burning, is worth learning. Apart from pointing out the appointment of Drafting Committee on 29th August, starting work from next day, continuously seating for 141 days, dealing with actually moved 2473 amendments out of 76358 tabled before House, Dr Ambedkar gave a comparative study of the time consumed in preparation of the Constitutions of the different countries along with length of the Constitution. It can be presented in a tabular form.[32]

The Constitutions of U.S.A., Canada, Australia, South Africa are smaller than ours.[33] Secondly, they were passed as moved. But our Constituent Assembly had to deal with 2473 amendments.[34] That was reason why Dr Rajendra Prasad in his address on Nov. 26, 1949 asserted that, "the details of which were given by the honourable Dr B.R. Ambedkar yesterday, we have no reason to be worry for the time spent."[35] The Drafting Committee had also made improvements upon the original draft presented to the Assembly by the Constitutional Advisor Sir B.N. Rau. Sir Rau had submitted 243 Articles and 13 schedules. Dr Ambedkar's draft contained 395 Articles (originally 396 finally 395) and 8 schedules.

Table 4

Country	*Time taken in framing the Constitution*			*Length of the Constitution*
	Start	*Completion*	*Total time*	
U.S.A.	May 25th, 1787	Sept. 17, 1787	4 months	7 Articles First four Divided in sections, total 21 sections
Canada	10th October, 1864	March, 1867	2 yrs. 5 months	147 sections
Common-wealth of Australia	March 1891	Became law on 9th July, 1900	9 (Nine) years	128 sections
South Africa	Oct. 1908	20th Sept. 1909	1 year	153 sections
Constitution of India	9th July, 1946	26th Nov., 1949	2 yrs. 11 months 17 days	Arts 395 + 8 Schedules

Dr Ambedkar very scholarly refuted the charge of one of the members Mr Naziruddin who termed Drafting Committee as drifting committee. He took it as a compliment while making a difference between drift without mastery and drift with mastery, he told, "to be in search of something better is not the same as drifting."[36] He also admitted fruitfulness of the presence of many rebels. Instead of yesmanship, they contributed towards alive discussion being more important than the mere mechanical work of passing the Constitution.

Through out the discussion legal acumen of Dr Ambedkar peeps through. He was firm but amenable to reasons and corrected himself. He was of view that 'republic' in preamble be replaced by 'State'. But, conceded to categorical opposition of Sir Alladi Krishna Swami Ayyar.[37] Not only this, he defended that and also allayed certain apprehensions that India's association with the commonwealth would in some way detract from the sovereignty of the people. To quote him, "Every independent country must have some kind of a treaty with some other countries, and there was no reason to suppose that a sovereign country becomes less sovereign just because it had made a treaty with another country." Dr Ambedkar ruled out the substitution of expressions "We on behalf of the people of India from whom is derived all power and authority of independent India"[38] in the place of, "We the people of India" as proposed by Mrs. Purnima Banerji and supported by Mahavir Tyagi and J.B. Kiplani." Dr Ambedkar found no justification for change as 'we the people of India' "could convey no other meaning than that the Constitution emanating from the people and "the sovereignty to make this Constitution is vested in them." It was Dr Ambedkar who put some question mark on Objective Resolution. He placed emphasis on remedy as rights had no meaning in absence of remedy. He pleaded for socialism. He also pleaded for 'fraternity' to be added in the preamble and it was accepted.[39]

Dr Ambedkar persuasively preferred the adoption of the 'Union' in the place of 'Federation' because our federation was not formed as a result of any agreement among the autonomous states like U.S.A. The state has no right to secede. To quote Dr Ambedkar "the federation is a union because it is indestructible."[40] The expression "union" substituted the expression 'federation' used in the original draft of Sir B.N. Rau. Dr Ambedkar also persuasively prevailed on the issue of parliamentary democracy providing more responsibility through collective responsibility than Presidential system which ensures stability. Defending emergency provisions Dr Ambedkar explained flexibility of our federation in the form of convertible federation. During normal times completely federal, but during emergency acting as a unitary government. Taking lesson from history of unamendability in U.S.A. and Australian Constitution allowing very a few amendments the former 27 and later 8 only and warning of the main architect of American Constitution Jefferson, "We may consider each generation as a distinct nation, with a right, by the will of the majority, to bind themselves, but to none bind the succeeding generation more than the inhabitants of another country", provided for flexible amending procedure under the Constitution.[41]

Dr Ambedkar accepted the retention of the expression "backward in clause (3) of draft Article 10 (now clause 4 Article 16). He pointed out that unless you use some such qualifying phrase as "backward" the exception made in favour of reservation will ultimately eat up the rule altogether." He also made clear that a backward community is a community which is backward in the opinion of the government.[42]

Accumulated knowledge, moderation and way of presentation had made Dr Ambedkar a moving encyclopedia with magic effect. In incident of Constituent Assembly debate on Objective Resolution moved by Nehru is quite amusing, surprising and making Dr Ambedkar what he later became. When discussion reopened in 16th December 1946, the Assembly had become tense due to amendment moved by Dr M.R. Jayakar. Dr Rajendra Prasad, the President exclaimed, "if Dr Jayakar's argument was correct, Pandit ji resolution was out of order". He unexpectedly invited Dr Ambedkar, out of turn, on 17th December, 1946. Dr Dhananjay Keer writes, "Everybody thought that Dr Ambedkar by playing such dangerous role would go with the mover of the amendment to rise against the will and the objections of the Congress bosses who were the nation's most powerful leaders, was to meet one's waterloo. The Congress members were ready with their hands raised to cripple their avowed enemy and throw him down". Dr Ambedkar was surprised as there were 20 or 22 speakers ahead of him and his turn would have come next day. He told that he had come without preparation. He began with his extempore speech which was par excellent and was greeted with loud cheers and applause.

Apart from brilliant speech his appeal to the majority party to act with great statesmanship, "even to make a concession to the prejudice of people who are not prepared to march together" so that they come willingly to join was marvelous which ultimately resulted in the Assembly converted into MICROCOSM-IN ACTION. His speech was so impressive that the honourable members had to change their mind about Dr Ambedkar and it changed the political career of Dr Ambedkar himself. To quote, an eye-witness Mr M.V. Gadgil, "His speech was so statesman like, so devoid of bitterness and so earnestly challenging that the whole Assembly listened to it in rapt silence. The speech was greeted with tremendous ovation and he was so smothered with congratulations in the lobby".

He earned the respect of all and that might have one of the reasons why Dr Rajendra Prasad wanted to have him in the Constituent Assembly at any cost and wrote letter to B.G. Kher, the then Prime Minister of Bombay who got him elected.

V
Dr Ambedkar: A Patriotic Indian with Futuristic Vision of a Statesman

Dr Ambedkar as a true Indian with humanist and social cohesion touch was very anxious about the fate of the country after the Independence and threat put by animosities of caste and creed. He was not sure of the role of diverse parties with opposing political ideologies. His sincere desire was "to defend our Independence with last drop of our blood."[43] He observed in his speech in the Constituent Assembly on 25th Nov. 1949:

"Will Indians place the country above their creed or they will place creed above country? I do not know. But this much is certain that if the parties place creed above country, our independence will be put in jeopardy a second time and probably be lost forever. This eventuality we must all resolutely guard against. We must be determined to defend our independence with the last drop of our blood."

For achieving the noble idea of independence and nation building, Dr Ambedkar suggested certain 'dos' and 'don'ts'.[44]

Dr Ambedkar was a great patriot. Even his critics could not resist their words of appreciation. Commending the highly admirable work done by Dr Ambedkar, Sri Jaspal Roy Kapoor observed: "I have developed an admiration and also affection

Table 5

Sr. No.	*Dos*	*Don'ts*
1.	Hold fast the constitutional methods of achieving our socio-economic objectives.	Abandon bloody methods of revolution like Civil disobedience Non-co-operation and Satyagraha.
2.	Never to surrender liberty before any body. Liberty necessary for democracy and it must be self-reliant.	Completely avoid Bhakti cult and hero worship, as they are surest road to degradation and to eventual Dictatorship.
3.	Ensure political democracy to be based on social democracy. Ensure union of the trinity of Liberty, equality and fraternity.	Refrain from indulging in contradictory i.e. thinking one without others.

for Dr Ambedkar for the very useful work and very patriotic work, which he has done. His very first speech in this Assembly had dispelled all my doubts and fears in relation to him and today I can say that I consider him to be one of the best patriots of this country."[45] Another member Shri Syamnandan Sahaya joined the spirit of admiration and said, "the great architect of our great Constitution. Dr Ambedkar, Sir, deserves the gratitude not only of this Assembly but of this nation."[46]

Dr Ambedkar was a great statesman. He was not a politician at all. He joined Nehru cabinet with ambition of noble cause to serve the dumb, depressed, voiceless, crushed, persecuted and deprived masses being becoming part of the governance of the country – to serve from within the government. The moment he thought he could not serve properly the cause of depressed, women etc. he quit the Law Ministership is 1951 on feeling his ministership irrelevant on the issue of Hindu Code Bill and ultimately it could not be passed at that time. It goes without saying that a politician thinks of next election. A statesman thinks of next generation. A statesman has vision of future. He is prophetic in planning for future.

1. Firstly, the Drafting Committee had to work within the parameter of Objective Resolutions. The prophetic and visionary Ambedkar forcefully expressed his disappointment on absence of remedies. Mere mention of right without remedy or redress would serve no meaningful purpose. He also pointed out that, "even the usual formula that no man's life, liberty and property shall be taken without the due process of law finds no place in the Resolution. He also argued that doing justice, socially, economically and politically without adoption of socialist economy/nationalisation of industries would carry no meaning.

Preamble enshrined the noble objectives given in the Objective Resolution and Dr Ambedkar was successful in adding fraternity in the Preamble as without that equality and justice would have become ineffective. His visionary lament found place during the very first year experience of the Constitution when The Constitution Ist Amendment, 1951 amended Article 19(5) and Article 305 by adding monopoly; second decade of the functioning of the Constitution when the Congress Government pressed nationalisation of Banks and during third decade when by the Constitution 42nd Amendment Act, 1976 Preamble was amended and "secular and socialist" were added in it.

Secondly, Dr Ambedkar's draft contained "an elaborate clause designed to establish state socialism in important fields of economic life by the law of the Constitution itself, so that the implementation of the plan would not be left to the will of the Legislature." But he had to bow before preponderance of member's opinion to provide directive principles merely non-justiciable status. The benefit of it was taken by the caste members in Courts in *Champakam Dorairajan v. State of Madras*[47] and Article 46 was held to play a second fiddle to the fundamental right enshrined in Article 29(2). While speaking on the Constitution First Amendment Act, inserting clause (4) Article 15, Dr Ambedkar lamented that Article 37 of the Directive Principles has been made but a ridicule. The significance of the Directive Principles began to be realised by the start of the second decade of the functioning of the Constitution. Equal importance was attached to both – Fundamental Rights and Directive Principle by great constitutional law expert G. Austin who declared both to form the conscience of the Constitution. In 1971 the Constitution was amended to give precedence/ priority to Directive Principles enshrined in clauses (b) and (c) of Article 39 over Articles 14, 19 and 31 and the Supreme Court itself treated both equal in Minerva Mills v. Union of India.[48]

Thirdly, as a member of the Flag Committee Dr Ambedkar play a vital role in getting accepted Ashoka Dharma Chakra at Sarnath as a national symbol on flag. It has a vital significance. Pt. Nehru very aptly explained the significance of Ashok Chakra: "We have associated with the flag of ours not only this emblem but in a sense the name of Ashoka, one of the most magnificent names not only in India's history but in world history."[49] Sir Sarvpalli Radhakrishnan pointed out that "the Ashoka's wheel represents to us the wheel of the law, the wheel Dharma."[50] Mohd. Saadullah explained that "the Chakra which is there in the Centre of the Flag symbolises motion, progress and advancement from aesthetic and other considerations also it suits the genius, tradition and culture of India."[51] Another member Shri Thirumala Rao pointed out "we have rightly selected the Chakra as our emblem, as the historic reminiscence of the period of Ashoka."[52] This Chakra, as Rhys David says, "is intended to send rolling the Royal chariot wheel of universal empire of truth and righteousness."[53]

Mrs. Sarojini Naidu clarifying what did wheel represent, made very brilliant explanation-, "It represents the Dharam Chakra of Ashoka the magnificent who sent his message of peace and brotherhood to all over the world. Did he not anticipate the modern ideal of fellowship, brotherhood and cooperation? Does not that wheel stands a symbol for every national interest and national activity? Does it not represent the Chakra of my illustrations and beloved leader, Mahatma Gandhi and the wheel of time that marches and marches and marches without hestation and halt? Does not represent the ray of the Sun? Does it not represent the eternity? Does it not represent the human mind? Who shall live under that flag without thinking of the common Indian? Who shall limit its functions? Who shall limit its inheritance? To whom does it belong? It belongs to India?

Fourthly, Dr Ambedkar paid more emphasis on remedy along with right. Speaking of the guaranteed right of enforcement of fundamental rights, Dr Ambedkar said: "If I was asked to name any particular article in this Constitution as the most important – an article without which this Constitution would be a nullity – I could not refer to any other article except this one. It is the very soul of the Constitution and the very heart of it."[54] These prophetic words of Dr Ambedkar have proved to be boon for those whose rights have been infringed. The Supreme Court has added more lusture to this remedy by giving slackness in *locus standi* and developing Public Interest Litigation process to make the enforcement of fundamental rights more meaningful.

Fifthly, Dr Ambedkar was very particular that the superintendence, direction and control of all elections should be vested in a non-party commission. We all know how an independent Election Commission is doing well as saviour of free and fair election.

Sixthly, the reconciliatory approach of Dr Ambedkar led to accept many propositions which did not like but was pressed by preponderance of the opinion of the Constituent Assembly members; (i) He had made clear that his own conviction was that reservations would be needed for a longer period and he quoted Burk's famous saying "large empires and small minds go ill together." But he conceded the final proposal of ten (10) years reservation for SCs and STs in the union and the State Legislatures. We all know that Dr Ambedkar was more correct. Before every ten years expiration the figure of 10 years is changed to another 10 years by addition. At present 10 years of Article 334, the Constitution has been substituted by 70 years and in the end of 2019 this figure would be raised to 80 years and so on; (ii) Dr Ambedkar did not like Article 31. He himself made clear during his speech during debate while The Constitution 4th Amendment Bill, 1955 was discussed: "Article 31 was an article for which we were not responsible. Even then, "we have made that article as elastic as we possibly could in the matter of compensation." That was outcome of three adamant approaches of Patel, Nehru and Pant. Dr Ambedkar made a prophetic statement: "there are in my judgement three cases or three paths that one might follow. The first path would be full compensation, the second, no compensation and the third, compensation as determined by law." We all know how problematic and controversial Article 31 had been in post-constitution period and how property right has been deleted from the Fundamental Rights and Article 300-A has been inserted which reads : "No person shall be deprived of his property save by authority of law." The controversy regarding compensation still continues and judicial intervention has not been able to stop it.

Seventhly, there is much truth in the statement of Syed Muhammad Sa'adullah, honourable member, the Constituent Assembly: "Drafting Committee was not a free agency. They had to work out a Constitution consistent with Objective Resolution passed by 308 members of the Constituent Assembly;" Drafting Committee was also to take into account views of Hon'ble members during discussions on different issues. It had also to honour prepondence of opinion of the members. But, the special contribution of Dr Ambedkar was how he digested the different shades of opinions, gave a workable and acceptable shape with a tinge firmness. The reality was summarised by the hon'ble member Frank Anthony: "I do not believe that anyone of us can really gauge the volume of work and the intensity of concentration that must have been involved in the production of this voluminous and by no means easy document. And while on occasions, I may have not agreed with Dr Ambedkar, it always gave me the very greatest pleasure to listen to his tremendous grasp not only of fundamentals but of details, of the clarity with which he invariably presented his case. It has been said that this Constitution has received a mixed reception. It is inevitable that its reception should have been mixed because, inevitably, it is a mixed Constitution. It is composite in character. It is a blend and proper blend between idealism on the one side and the realism on the other."[55]

Dr Pattabhi Sitaramayya, another prominent member of the Constituent Assembly said, "......What a steam-roller intellect he brought to bear upon this magnificent and tremendous task : irresistible, indomitable, unconquerable, leveling down tall palms and short poppies; whatever he felt to be right he stood by, regardless of consequences."[56]

VI
Dr Ambedkar: A Dreamer of Casteless Society with a Salt of Realism

Dr Ambedkar was of firm view that our Constitution "is strong enough to hold the country together both in peace time and in war time." Dr Ambedkar was of view that "castes are anti-national in the first place because they bring about separation in social life. They are anti-national also because they generate jealousy and anti-pathy between caste and caste." But he was hopeful like Bapu who believed in the change of heart.

Dr Ambedkar pointed out, "we must overcome all these difficulties of we wish to become a nation in reality. For fraternity can be fact only when there is a nation." Dr Subhash Kashyap while delivering Convocation Address at Dr Babasaheb Ambedkar Marathwada University, Aurangabad on 5th Feb. 2000 said, "Dr Ambedkar was a strong votary of uniform civil code. He was against reservations for Scheduled Castes in perpetuity. He did not want the Scheduled Caste status for some citizens becoming a permanent stigma on Indian Society. Above everything else, Babasaheb was for a casteless, classless, egalitarian society and a strong united India,"[57] and on 6th December 1956, Shri N.V. Gadgil said, ".......very recently I had some discussion with Dr Ambedkar, and he said to me, no more privileges to Scheduled Castes."[58]

All those who take plea against preferential treatment or reservation take shelter in some one observation of Dr Ambedkar wishing casteless society which was the one side of coin. It was idealistic side. They knowingly ignore realistic side of the coin of reservational justice and Dr Ambedkar's view about that.

The presence of Dr Ambedkar in the Constituent Assembly was quite helpful for providing safeguards to the depressed people. But, it is also reality that he had to concede and was not satisfied with safeguards provided under the Constitution. He said "the provisions made in the Constitution for safeguarding the position of the Scheduled Castes were not to my satisfaction."[59] The Scheme submitted by Dr Ambedkar with Note on Minorities and Fundamental rights included the following:[60]

1. All basic industries were to be owned by the State, to be run by it or by its public corporations.
2. Subsisting rights in basic and key industries and insurance were to be acquired by the State after payment of compensation in the form of debentures.
3. Agriculture was to be State industry – the land acquired by the State was to be divided into collective forms of standard size to be cultivated collectively.
4. The representatives of the minorities in the cabinet were to be elected by members of each community in the legislatures by single-transferable vote; the representatives of the majority community were to be elected by the whole House by single transferable vote.

5. The Scheduled Castes were to have the right to representation based on population in certain cases and in others with weightage.
6. At least representatives of the Scheduled Castes should be on every Public Service Commission and every committee constituted for making appointments.

This scheme was vehemently opposed by Dr K.M. Munshi who said: "Ambedkar submitted an exhaustive and elaborate Note on Minorities and Fundamental Rights as well as constitutional structure. If the scheme were accepted, the State would be a totalitarian apparatus run for the benefit of Scheduled Classes in which the majority would be politically reduced to the status of second class citizens."[61] The Ambedkar's Scheme could not be accepted.

The idealist side, referred earlier, cannot ignore the realistic side. Rather the talk of caste/classless society idealism can be thought of only if the realistic side becomes reality. The hard reality of Indian social structure is that it lacks equality. It is a graded and degraded society with entrenched hierarchical caste structure. Two great national leaders were struggling hard with sincere efforts to solve the problem. One was searching solution through idealistic appeal for change of heart. The other was exposing realistic problem having no solution in near future. Thus, Mahatma Gandhi was idealist making appeal to Hindu good senses. He thought that untouchability is the root cause of all evils and said: "To remove untouchability is a penance that Caste Hindus owe to Hinduism and to themselves. The purification required is not of 'untouchables' but of the so called superior castes. There is no vice that is special to the 'untouchables', not even dirt and insanitation. It is our arrogance which binds us, superior Hindus, to our blemishes and which magnifies those of our downtrodden brethren whom we have suppressed and whom we keep under suppression."[62] He went to the extent of saying, "I do not want to be reborn, but if I am reborn, I wish that I should be born as a Harijan, as an untouchable, so that I may lead a continuous struggle, life long struggle against the oppressions and indignities that have been heaped upon these classes of people."[63] His sincere belief was that Hindu will change their attitude and rigidity of the caste system would be removed. But that did not happen, nor is there any hope of its happening. The other leader was untouchable who had burnt of untouchability and had suffered indignation on that count. He was realistic. Dr Ambedkar was well versed in Hindu law, knew its niceties and ill effect deeply rooted in popular belief. He pointed out that untouchability is offshoot of caste system. Abolition of untouchability while leaving caste system to flourish could serve no purpose. Like a doctor he believed in right diagnosis. He argued, "The aim of abolition of untouchability alone without trying to abolish the inequalities inherent in the caste system is a rather low ...... aim (and) is a crime. Let us problem the evil to its very roots and not be satisfied with mere palliatives to assuage our pain. If disease is not rightly diagnosed, the remedy will be useless and the case may be delayed."[64]

Dr Ambedkar rightly pointed out that caste had sanctity of Shastras. He explained caste is not a physical object like a wall of bricks or a line of barbed wire which prevents Hindus from co-mingling which has, therefore, to be pulled down. Caste is a notion, it is a state of mind; destruction of caste does not, therefore, mean the destruction of a physical barriers. It is notional change.........

It must be recognised that Hindus observe caste not because they are inhuman or wrong headed. They observe caste because they are deeply religious."

Dr Ambedkar believed in holistic view. He was well aware of the fact that reservation and will not make Indian society a casteless society. Casteism and communalism is in the vein of the Indian society. Dr Ambedkar exposed many things. Firstly, Dr Ambedkar was apprehensive of Hindu majority communalism. He believed that Congress was using nationalism as a cloak for a free field for rank communalism. According to him the social psychology of the Hindu communal majority was dominated by the dogma which believed in graded inequality.[64] He pointed out that inequality embodied in Chaturvarna was an official doctrine. Furthermore, their caste system is a sword of political and administrative discrimination. Secondly, Dr Ambedkar took realist view of caste longivity. To quote him:

"Whatever view may be taken of caste as a national or social institution it is useless to ignore it, and so long as caste continues to be used as one of the distinguishing features of an individual's official and social identity, it cannot be claimed that a decennial enumeration helps to perpetuate an undesirable institution." On 25th November, 1949 in his last speech in the Constituent

Assembly he put emphasis on interrelationship between the political structure and social structure. Social structure pervades and influences political structure. Thirdly, Ambedkar believed in the dictum diamond cuts diamond. Making plea for representation of minority and depressed classes, he asserted that communalism must be his policy. To quote him : "I am not ashamed of it. I will say that India cannot proceed on the path of political progress without communalism. Without communalism there can be no self-government in India. That is the position I would assert without fear of challenge."[65]

Fourthly, Dr Ambedkar candidly exposed lack of two things in Indian society. The first is equality. On social plane Indian society is based on the principle of graded inequality which means "elevation of some and degradation for others. On economic plane it has people having immense wealth against many who live in abject poverty. Fifthly, Dr Ambedkar put a note of caution in view of contradictions. He said: "On 26th January 1950, we are going to enter into a life of contradictions. In politics we will have equality and in social and economic life we will have inequality. In politics we will be recognising the principles of one man, one vote, one value. In our social and economic life, we shall, by reason of our social and economic structure, continue to deny the principle of the man one value. How long shall we continue to live this life of contradictions?[66] How much shall we continue to deny equality in our social and economic life? If we continue to deny for long we will do so only by putting our political democracy in peril. We must remember this contradiction at the earliest possible moment for else those who suffer from inequality will blow up the structure of political democracy which this Assembly has so laboriously build up."[67]

Thus, Dr Ambedkar's casteless society means castelessness of the whole society and not denial of reservation to the depressed for the sake of castelessness and allowing of perpetuation of caste factor by upper class people adding salt to social injury. Secondly, vice of caste system can be removed only by annihilation of caste. Thirdly, so long as caste is source of deprivation and degradation for such deprived people reservation will continue.

VII
Contribution of Dr Ambedkar Recognised with a Sense of Gratitude and Lesson for Future

Dr Ambedkar lived for India, worked for India and sacrified his life for India. Though he was generous to express a sense of gratitude for contribution made by the members of the Drafting Committee, but due to lack of that much interest shown by the members of the Drafting Committee and more often absence the whole burden fell on Dr Ambedkar and the Secretary of the Drafting Committee. Dr Rajendra Prasad, President, Constituent Assembly was right when he expressed thanks to the Drafting Committee and its Chairman Dr Ambedkar. He said:

"Sitting in the Chair and watching the proceedings from day-to-day, I have realised as nobody else could have, with what zeal and devotion the members of the Drafting Committee and especially its Chairman, Dr Ambedkar, in spite of his indifferent health have worked. We could never make a decision which was or could be even so right as when we put him (Dr Ambedkar) on the Drafting Committee and made him its Chairman. He has not justified his selection but has added luster to the work, which he has done."[68]

Pt. Jawahar Lal Nehru expressed the view in Parliament that "there is no doubt that no one took greater care and trouble over Constitution making than Dr Ambedkar."[69] Sir Alladi Krishnaswami Ayyar, the learned Advocate and scholarly man on the Drafting Committee expressed his view: "I would be failing in my duty if I do not express my high appreciation of the skill and ability with which my friend the Honourable Dr Ambedkar has piloted this Constitution and his untiring work as the Chairman of the Drafting Committee."[70] Shri Jaspat Roy Kapoor commended him as one of the best patriots of the country. Shri M. Ananthasayanam Ayyangar, another member of the Constituent Assembly said, "The very person who came to doubt and criticise has ultimately taken charge of this Constitution and framed it. I congratulate him and I congratulate ourselves for the goodwill shown to him and the manner in which he has reciprocated it." Yet another member Shri Shyam Nandan Sahaya calling Dr Ambedkar the great architect of our great Constitution said that Dr Ambedkar "deserves the gratitude not only of this Assembly but of this nation."[71]

All the above praises showered on Dr Ambedkar. But, at what personal cost? In Janoon of giving his best to the nation he lost his health, developed diabetes and other serious illness and sacrified his life for the national cause. Otherwise, 65 years of the age is not too much for a life. He could live longer had he not developed many diseases due to the pressure of work put on him.

The authors are of view, firm view and conviction that Dr Ambedkar will shine like Dhruvatara on the Indian national sky. It was not enough that the hon'ble members of the Constituent Assembly and his fellow members in Drafting Committee or blessings of the father of the Nation showered on him. Dr Ambedkar has given alot for Indian nation, not only Indian nation but to whole of the humanity struggling with the issue of racial and caste problems and discriminatory culture inhered since long. Dr Ambedkar's life, work, achievement and overall earned goodwill of all is a great message to the humanity reminding humility of Tathagat Buddha and greatly practised Buddhist way of life of Ashoka, the great.

It is a message of prospect for those for whom he fought for throughout the life serving the great cause of equality, liberty and fraternity. If Dr Ambedkar could do or earlier Shambook and Eklabya could present unparalleled examples other depressed people can do so provided they practise the great message of Dr Ambedkar - educate, agitate and organise. Educate yourself, your children and distribute/spread the knowledge, the imperishable and ever increasing wealth (Saraswati Ke Dwarki Badi Apurab Baat, Jyon Kharache Tyon Tyon Bade, Bin Kharache Ghati Jaat). Agitate on wrong. Do not bear injustice and learn from injustice to strive for justice. Do not kill your conscience and where conscience prickingness comes agitate for good of all. Organisation gives strength, develops a sense of otherness and fraternity and fight for right cause. Adopt Ambedkar's message a new version of Buddha – Buddham Sharnam gachch – be enlightened/educated – Appdipo bhav; Dhammam Sharanam Gachch – follow the path of righteousness, be invictus on right points; Sangham Sharanam Gachch – unite for democratic cause and effective means to serve the people through right path of governance. Follow Dr Ambedkar – keep store of learning, book, may be constitution clinging with your heart and pointer of finger to go to the parliament by uniting and assert yourself in decision-making process of governance. Try to govern and not remain always be governed.

The great achievement or noble deed of framing the Constitution despite all odds – burnt of partition, raising heads of communalism, presence of 565 odd princely states and so on so forth, provides immense chance of retrospection to upper class people – think positively, constructively, recognise worth of even lowliest, be human, develop fraternity and repose faith based on evaluation of ability etc. Be Gandhi – large hearted, great soul, above pride and prejudice, do all thing for merit recognition, trust in worthiness, give opportunity to prove one's metal. Here the words of Shri Shyamanandan Sahaya, hon'ble member of Assembly from Bihar may prove prophetic for the upper strata of the society. He said: "This Constitution is unique in another respect. Mahatmaji's methods once again proved how with goodwill towards opponents, one could win over and conquer the worst of critics and we now see a practical example of a high ideal translated into action, namely, that the achievement of independence would go to the credit of Mahatmaji and its codification of one of the Mahatmaji's worst critics, viz. the great architect of our great constitution. Dr Ambedkar, Sir, deserves the gratitude not only of this Assembly but of this nation."[72]

The upper class of Indians can have introspection what have they done in past; how much India has lost without co-operation of talented depressed class people? On this point the views of Shri S. Nagappa, hon'ble member Constituent Assembly may prove to be eye opener and trend-setter for all. Shri Nagappa said:

"Well, Sir this has proved to what heights Dr Ambedkar, though he is a member of the Scheduled classes, if an opportunity was given, can rise. He has proved this by his efficiency and the able way in which he has drafted and piloted this Constitution."[73]

He further said:

"Now I think this stigma of inefficiency attached to the Scheduled classes will be washed away and will not be attached hereafter, only if opportunities are given", they will prove better than anybody else will."[74]

It is highly appreciated and introspection by all in retrospect is eye opener, as expressed in words of hon'ble Mr. Justice P.B. Sawant in his concurring decision in famous *Indra Sawhney v.*

Union of India.[75] After referring to contribution made by Vyasa, Valmiki and recently Dr Ambedkar to the Indian history, Justice Sawant said:

"These few instances demonstrate that intelligence, perception, character, scholarship and talent are not a monopoly of any section of the society. Given opportunity, those who are condemned to the lowliest station in life can rise to the loftiest status in society."[76]

The learned judge also threw light on retrospect —

"One can only guess how much this country has lost for want of opportunities to the vast majority all these centuries."[77]

VIII
Grand Compromistic Approach and Most Benefitting and Convincing Reply to Critics

What is written in the Constitution all of them are not necessarily the views of Dr Ambedkar. He differed on many counts. But ultimately drafted what was agreed upon by consensus or near consensus or majority on division of vote. He himself made clear: "No human made Constitution or document is perfect and it is trite saying that the actual always falls short of the ideal. Even though I am a member of the Drafting Committee, I have very great objection to many of the principles that have been embodied in this Constitution. It does not lie in my mouth to criticise individual provisions of the Draft Constitution, as I am, as much responsible as any other member of the Drafting Committee for the incorporation in our Constitution."[78] Answering to criticism of the Constitution Dr Ambedkar made clear that it did not deny other alternative on issues like parliamentary democracy or acquisition of private property or more restrictions on fundamental rights: "What I do say is that the principles embodied in the Constitution are the views of the present generation, or if you think to be an overstatement, I say that they are the views of the members of the Constituent Assembly. Why blame the Drafting Committee for embodying them in the Constitution."[79] Dr Ambedkar knew how to reconcile, make compromises and give honour to the majority views. On 2nd September, 1953 while speaking on Andhra Bill (1953), he made clear: "People always keep on saying to me – Oh, you are the maker of the Constitution. My answer is I was a hack. What I was asked to do, I did much against my will."[80]

Keeping in view the Indian circumstances, shock of partition, deciding single Constitution for both centre and state, need of unification, maintaining unity and integrity, experiences of other Constitutions etc. the bulkiness, copying different provisions with necessary modifications to suit Indian circumstances, minority problems of SCs, STs and most backwards areas, no clarity about the map of India due to princely states remaining outside indulged in bargaining, no better Constitution could have been framed than our Constitution. The Constitution gives guidelines. Its success depends on the people who administer the country on the basis of the constitutional mandate. There is much force and truth in speech of Shri B.M. Gupte. Shri Gupte said, "After all, a Constitution cannot be judged merely from its text or on paper.... So it is not, the Constitution that matters, nor the people who make it, but is the men who work the Constitution and the spirit in which they work it. Any Constitution may be good on paper, but its success depends upon the manner in which it is worked."[81]

The Constitution of India was framed by patriotic, well-intentioned statesmen thinking of India's future, but came to be implemented by power hungry, partisan, unpatriotic persons. That pained Dr Ambedkar. On 2nd Sept. 1953 Dr Ambedkar answered in Parliament (Rajya Sabha) the question of Shri M.S. Ranawat as to his defending the provision incorporated in the Constitution. He also answered charge of Dr K.N. Katju for having drafted the Constitution which was corrected by the Chairman as defended the Constitution because it was a majority decision. Dr Ambedkar had become disenchanted by performance to the persons at the helm of affair and answered: "Sir, my friends tell me that I have made the Constitution. But I am quite prepared to say that I shall be the first person to burn it out. I do not want it. It does not suit anybody."[82] Dr Ambedkar got an opportunity to explain on 19th March, 1955 during the Constitution (7th Amendment) Bill discussion when Dr Anoop Singh repeated and reminded about his above comment. Dr Ambedkar was too cautious of the sanctity of Constitution that he gave reason.

"We built a temple for a god to come in and reside, but before the god could be installed, if the devil had taken possession of it, what else could we do except destroy the temple? We did not intend that it should be occupied by ASURAS. We intend it to be occupied by the DEVAS. That is the reason why I said I would rather like to burn it."[83]

IX
Indianness and Prophetic Vision of Dr Ambedkar

It is true that Dr Ambedkar had strong objection to the constitution of a Constituent Assembly. But that was opposition to the Constituent Assembly proposed to be constituted on terms of the British Government and Cabinet Mission plan. The speech of Dr Ambedkar on 6th May, 1945 addressing the Annual Session of the All India Scheduled Castes Federation held in Bombay is clear enough that he did not like Constituent Assembly under British influence or Constitution framed by the Britishers and imposed on India as was done in the case Canada and Australia was completely unacceptable. To a question: who should frame a Constitution of India? The answer of Dr Ambedkar in view of New Dominion status was that the Constitution must be so made that it may not only command the obedience but also the respect of all. He made clear: "This can happen only if the Constitution is framed by Indians for Indians and with voluntary consent of Indians.[84] And, when he was convinced of this Indianness as dreamt by the Congress Party itself, he did not hesitate to join hands and contribute his best to the framing of the Constitution. Dr Ambedkar in his address in the Constituent Assembly had pointed out the reality to be faced in future. He warned if anything went wrong in future, the fault could not lie with the framers of the Constitution but with those charged with the sacred duty of enforcing its provisions. Speaking of realities to be faced he pointed out that problem of untouchability was not so simple. It is not only a system of unmitigated economic exploitation, but also a system of uncontrolled economic exploitation. That is, because there is no independent public opinion to condemn it and there is no impartial machinery of administration and restraint."

The constant problem of India has been and is the problem of meek, humble, dumb, persecuted, deprived masses. Justice V.R. Krishna Iyer once posed a question — whether India being free, are Indians free? He himself replied quoting Dr Ambedkar — "One must distinguish between the freedom of a country and the freedom of the people in the country....... Philosophically it may be possible to consider a nation as a unit but sociologically it cannot but be regarded as consisting of many classes and the freedom of the nation if it is to be a reality must vouchsafe the freedom of different classes comprised in it, particularly those who are treated as the servile classes." Dr Ambedkar had addressed the Constituent Assembly as to real problem to be faced and struggled when the Constitution comes in action. He said:

"We have in India a Society based on the principle of graded inequality which means elevation of some and degradation of others. On the economic plane, we have society in which there are some who have immense wealth as against many below abject poverty. On 26 January, 1950, we are going to enter into a life of contradictions. In politics, we will have equality and in social and economic life we will have inequality. In politics we will be organising the principle of one man one vote and one value. In our social and economic life, we shall, by reason of our social and economic structure continue to deny the principle of one man and one value. How long shall we continue to live life of contradictions?"[85]

This prophetic words of Dr Ambedkar expressed on 25.11.1949 are still hovering over our heads and looming large crying for solution if India has to survive. Dr Ambedkar was very sore of Hindu discrimination, inhuman treatment of untouchables and continued persecution. He had declared in 1937 that he had no control over where he could have born. He was born in Hindu community. But, he declared that he would not die as Hindu. He could have converted and greeted with high offers by Christians or Muslims. But he converted to Buddhism in his evening of the life. This in his own words: "I have changed the compartment, not the train." Thus, he remained in Hindu fold.

X
Concluding Remarks with Message of the Life of Dr Ambedkar

Dr Ambedkar's life is life of great struggle, but indomitable zeal and to develop more confidence, resolute will and urge to achieve height through learning and acquiring wide range knowledge. His prophetic vision of annihilation of caste is perpetual truth that Indian social cohesion and nation building can never be complete without establishing a casteless society and that cannot be a reality unless caste is abolished and annihilated. He was right when he said that had Lokmanya Tilak been born in untouchable community, his slogan would have been. "Abolition of caste/untouchability is our birth right" Freedom with humiliation does not carry any meaning. The following messages from Dr Ambedkar's life are most pressing and essential for meaningful national life in India.

1. The high aim of acquiring knowledge and proper education should be achieved at any cost. Ill treatments should not discourage, they should develop firmness to agitate, expose and strive for eradication of the evil.

2. Prove trust-worthiness. What responsibility you take, complete it with full vigour to the best of your ability and tirelessly. Make yourself proud, your community proud and your nation proud. Humility (sheel) must be ornament - neither suffer inferiority, nor develop vanity.

3. Develop self respect, scientific temper with a sense of inquiry and be never shy of pointing out defects and wrong irrespective of the fact from where is it coming. Ability of Dr Ambedkar to honest exposure of lack of remedy in Objective Resolution presented by Pt. J.L. Nehru in the Constituent Assembly changed his life and political career. To quote eye-witness Mr. N.V. Gadgil: "His speech was so statesmanlike, so devoid of bitterness and so earnestly challenging that the whole Assembly listened to it in rapt silence. The speech was greeted with tremendous ovation and he was smoothered with congratulations."[86] His open challenge on Hindu social evils to Bapu was a task of great, greater and greatest moral courage and Bapu — the great man and great soul, appreciated and was instrumental in bringing Dr Ambedkar to the Constituent Assembly, Drafting Committee and Nehruvian Cabinet. Honesty and ability paid and was returned in form of good coin.

4. The greatest message and lesson for the present India is the practised view of Dr Ambedkar and also Bapu to avoid hero-worship and Bhakti-cult which has made parties principleless, struggle for vote-catching statues and hero-worship. Dr Ambedkar completely discouraged such tendencies. On occasion of his Golden Jubilee celebration he said: "you have been celebrating my birthday for fifteen years. I have never attended them. I have always been opposed to them. You have celebrated my Golden Jubilee now; let that be enough. Let there be no more celebrations."[87]

The Ambedkarite honest expression from core of heart peeps in Bapu's reaction on erection of his statute in Mumbai in 1947. He said : "I must dissent emphatically from any proposal to spend any money on preparing statue of me, especially at a time when the people do not have enough food and clothing. In Bombay the beautiful insanitation reigns. There is so much overcrowding that poor people are packed like sordidness. Wise use of ten lakhs of rupees will consist in its being spent on some public utility. That would be the best statue."[88]

Will our present generation politicians learn some lessons from Ambedkar-Gandhi heart-appealing problem - solution statesmanship to worship the crying living gods starved of education, food and shelter? One should not forget that even sincere extravagance at the cost of weak, meak and bewildered is challangeable. One shayar has rightly said:

"Din men deep Jalane Kucch Nahi Hoga,
Rakh Mein Aag Lagane se Kuchch Nahi Hoga,
Ab Tujhe Milane Ko Mumtaj Kahan Shah Jahan,
Lash pe Taj Uthane Se Kuchch Nahi Hoga."

(No purpose would be served by kindling lamp during day; No purpose would be served by putting fire in ashes; Now there is no hope of getting Begum Mumtaj O Shahjahan!; No purpose would be served by constructing Taj on corpse).

5. Message of Dr Ambedkar's life, achievement and recognition of greatness by all sections of society irrespective of caste and creed is source of encouragement for downtrodden and inspiring introspection and calculate loss to Indian Society by depriving of opportunity to low-born persons for the upper classes. The depressed and backward, have to take lesson nothing is impossible in the world. If Dr Ambedkar, a Mahar could be nation treasure accepted by all people, why not other who enjoy better position than what untouchables of Dr Ambedkar's time were not able to enjoy — to take water from pond or enter into temple, ride on cart and so on so forth? Caste-people must remind themselves of historical damage done to the national cause by incidents of Shambook, Eklabya etc. It has doubly damaged the national cause — Low born got discouraged and dissuaded to earn name and fame by learning and noble deeds due to fear of punishment and upper caste people began to decay due to favouritism and lack of challenge. Vyasa, Valmiki and Ambedkar should be eye-opener and their source of introspection, correction and national outlook through

assimilation of all caste and creeds without inhibition or prohibition.

6. The problem of reservation, its continuance and its impact has to be objectively viewed. Only slogan mongering, wrong major premise that reservation bring sub-standard persons or reservation based on caste consideration would divide society and bring class-clash has to be viewed and answered with Dr Ambedkar is insight. Unless social equality and its breeding political and economic equality is ensured, fraternity become reality, veiled casteism ends, the problem of reservation will continue.

Those who talk of Dr Ambedkar's plea for casteless society or reservation as self-liquidating early process present not the whole truth but only selective presentation to suit their power perpetuation under the veiled casteism. Some observations are equally or even more weighty. Pointing out the inseparability of political and social culture, Dr Ambedkar observed:

"Why it is necessary that in the Indian Constitution, the communal scheme must find its place and why is the public services for the untouchables should be specified and should be assigned to them as their separate possession".[89] His answer lies in societal facts of the inherent antagonism between Hindu and untouchables, no trustworthiness of caste Hindus, dogmatic Hindu belief in graded inequality which is inimical to liberty and fraternity. He was also aware of deceptive ideology of caste Hindus- "They deceive the world by using nationalism as cloak for a free field for rank communism".[90] It is hard reality. Caste Hindus have created three types of reservations one for SCs and STs, one for OBCs and others for General Category (GC).[91] The net outcome is that much superior reserved category candidates are adjusted in reserved category and most ordinary careerist are given high berth in general category. Can such hard realities inspire the confidence among reserved category people that in case of reservation done away merit will be honoured or 100 per cent posts will be filled in by general category ousting meritious depressed people. The bogy of caste reservation should breed the vice of 100 per cent perpetuated reservation in favour of the upper caste. One should be cautious of danger what P.B. Sawant J. exposed in famous Mandal case, "What should further not be forgotten is that hither to for centuries, there have been cent per cent reservations in practice in all fields, in favour of the high caste and classes, to the total exclusion of others. It was a purely caste and classes based reservation.[92]

The view of Dr Ambedkar that irrespective of caste as a national or social institutions, it is useless to ignore it and "so long as caste continues to be used as one of the distinguishing features of an individual's official and social identity it cannot be claimed that a decennial enumeration helps to perpetuate the undesirable institution".

The message of Dr Ambedkar to the depressed people is clear never surrender the claim being by flowery deceptively attractive slogan of nationalism through casteless society by undoing reservation. And to upper privileged class people Dr Ambedkar's message is that come open mind, remove social inherently graded and degraded inequality, stop appointments even without minimum qualifications[93] and out of dead panel to savarnas[94] because depressed cannot be befooled if the hidden reservation, rather more injurious to the national cause, is continued. Otherwise leveling reality will take place. What Philadelphia Declaration of I.L.O. declared "poverty anywhere in the world is threat to the prosperity everywhere" or what Martin Luther King, Jr. said, "denial of liberty to any section will put threat to the liberty of all" or what Dr Ambedkar warned if continuing of social and economic equality's denial is not removed, "those who suffer from inequality will blow up the structure of political democracy which the Assembly has so laboriously built up" will become a reality.[95]

7. Everlasting message of Dr Ambedkar is to those who matter more in a democratic governance. Spencer has said- "For form the government let fools contest, what governs best is the best". So is the case with the Constitution. Few pages American Constitution drawn in Horse and buggy age is working well only with 27 amendments in 228 years, Australian Constitution is doing well with only 8 amendments in its 117 years functioning. We are crossing century with is less than seven decades with anarchic situation, corrupt instrumentality and decay or complete absence of political morality. Thus, Dr Ambedkar's message is guiding force. On November 25, 1949 while speaking in the Constituent Assembly he said:

"I feel however good a Constitution may be, it is sure to turn out bad Constitution. May be, it may turn out to be good if those who care called to work it happen to be a good lot. The working of the Constitution does not depend wholly upon the nature of the Constitution. The Constitution can provide only the organs of state such as Legislature, the Executive and the Judiciary. The factors, on which the working of these organs of the state depends, are the people and the political parties they will set up as their instruments to carry out their wishes and their policies. Who can say how the people of India and their parties will behave? Will they uphold Constitutional methods of achieving purposes or will they prefer revolutionary methods, however good a Constitutional may be."[96]

Will the political parties leave the path of betraying the confidence of people through rampant corruption, murder of the Constitutional morality, propriety and norms in the name of Constitutional machineries functioning? Will the people avoid hero-worship and Bhakti-cult and will move on with entrenched feeling that liberty lives in the heart of the people? There is no substitute of vigilant public opinion in a democracy with political equality based on socio-economic equality guarded by fraternity.

Up India, follow Ambedkar and make your presence felt in this world!

References

1. Some admirers of Dr Ambedkar call him Manu who gave Manava Dharam Shastra. Eleanor Zelliot, an academician described Dr Ambedkar as a 'Modern Manu'. Eleanor Zelliot, The Social and the Political Thought of B.R. Ambedkar (in) Thomas Pantham and Kenneth L. Dalton (eds.) Political Thought in Modern India, New Delhi, Sage Publications, 1968. Shri K.M. Jodhe, Honourable Member, Constituent Assembly, called him Modern Manu. Dr P.B. Gajendragadkar, though not, Ambedkarite but a former Chief Justice of India in his address at Aurangabad pointed out that several members of the Constituent Assembly and many country-men called him a 'Modern Manu'. He saw poetic justice in it, as Dr Ambedkar became the law giver of the 20th Century - the Modern Manu. Another member of the Constituent Assembly, Sh. S.M. Ghose also expressed the view that Dr Ambedkar has rightly been called Manu.

   The 'Manu' conferment may be due to extreme appreciation of Dr Ambedkar's work in drafting the Constitution. He may be said to have the learning of Manu and laying down law for the governance. But he would not have liked to be compared with Manu. Firstly, he himself had burnt a copy of Manu Smriti for the caste-ridden hierarchical stamp. Secondly, Manu Smriti is sacred book of Hindus, the Constitution is the basic law - Grundnorm for all castes, sects, creeds etc. Thirdly, Manu smriti is mainly the work of Brahmin Bhrigu. Manu had written only 58 Shlokas. Thereafter, he handed over to Bhrigu, his disciple who inducted Brahminical Superiority. Dr Ambedkar was author himself or defender of collective decisions of the Assembly. Fourthly, Manusmriti, encouraged discriminatory treatment in relation to different castes or Varnas, Constitution authored by Dr Ambedkar preaches non-discrimination. Fifthly, Manusmriti allows persecution of untouchables, the Constitution authored by Dr Ambedkar safeguards deprived people and punishes discriminator.

2. Before Dr Ambedkar, Bharat Ratna had been conferred on 45 persons
3. It was conferred on him posthumously in 1990 after 40 years of the inauguration of the Republic of India and thirty four years after his death and that too with emergence of depressed classes assertion on national scene.
4. Madhu Limaye, Gandhi v. Ambedkar-A Futile Controversy (in) Manu Gandhi, Ambedkar etc., Gyan Publishing House, 2009.
5. Dr Ambedkar's speech on Adoption of the Constitution on 25th, Nov., 1949 in the Constituent Assembly, C.A. Deb. Vol. XI, pp. 972-81; B. Shiva Rao, The Framing of India's Constitution- Select Document, Vol. 4, p. 937.
6. Nehru's Speech in Constituent Assembly on Dec.12, 1946.
7. G. Austin reveals this in his book that: "B. Shiva Rao informed the author that in June 1946 he presented Gandhi with a list of fifteen prominent Indians, his own name among them, whom he thought should be elected to the Assembly, Gandhi agreed with the idea and with the names and sent it on to Nehru and Patel who arranged that the persons be named as candidate." G. Austin: The Indian Constitution: Cornerstone of a Nation, Oxford Univ-Press 1966 (11th impression 2007), p.13.
8. On 30th June 1947, Dr Rajendra Prasad, President of the Constituent Assembly had written letter to B.G. Kher, the then Prime Minister of Bombay to elect Dr Ambedkar immediately. Dr Babasaheb Ambedkar; Writings and Speeches, Vol. 13, pp. 24-26.
9. Sardar Vallabhbhai Patel had talked to Mr. Kher and had written letter to him on July 1, 1947 requesting him to elect Dr Ambedkar, if possible, before 14th i.e. beginning of the next sitting of the Constituent Assembly. Sardar Patel's Correspondence, Vol. 5, p. 149.
10. It was Gandhi who is said to have suggested the name of Dr Ambedkar for the Drafting Committee. It so happened that Jawahar Lal Nehru and Smt. Sarojini Naidu went to Gandhi ji to

tell him that they are not finding a capable person to prepare the Draft Constitution for India, and they are thinking of inviting a Constitutional Expert like Ivor Jennings, who had prepared Constitutions of various countries. On hearing this, Gandhi ji instantly suggested the name of Dr Ambedkar and he relieved Nehru from a great worry." The Rajaji Story (1937-1972) Rajmohan Gandhi, p. 137.

11. The Rajaji Story, 1937-1972: Rajmohan Gandhi, p.137.
12. The Rajaji Story, 1937-1972: Rajmohan Gandhi, p.137.
13. Dekhi Suni Baten: Indrani Jag Jivan Ram, vol.II, p.15.
14. Madhu Limaye, Gandhi v. Ambedkar. A futile Controversy, Manu, Gandhi, Ambedkar etc., Gian Publishing House, 2009, p.11.
15. Madhu Limaye, who is more Relevant: Gandhi- Ambedkar or Kashiram and its llK? (in) Madhu Limaye, Manu, Gandhi and Ambedkar and other Essays, Gian Publishing House 29/6 Shakti nagar, Delhi-2008, p. 23.
16. Sardar Patel's Correspondence, Durga Das ed., Vol. 11, p. 327.
17. *Ibid.*
18. Pyarelal to Dr Hardev Sharma of the NMML. Quoted in Madhu Limaye.
19. *Ibid.*
20. Rajya Sabha Debates, 6 September, 1954 colmn 1472.
21. Madhu Limaye, Ambedkarism: Fake and Genuine (in) Madhu Limaye, supra 14 p. 20.
22. Dr Ambedkar's speech on Nov. 25, 1949 in the Constituent Assembly on Adoption of the Constitution, C.A. Debates, Vol. XI, pp. 972-81.
23. *Ibid.*
24. *Ibid.*
25. *Ibid.*
26. *Ibid.*
27. *Ibid.*
28. *Ibid.*
29. A single member of the Constituent Assembly Mr. Naziruddin had not appreciated the role of Dr Ambedkar as he thought Constitution was not original. But others recognized the role of Dr Ambedkar without any reservation (inhibition). He called Drafting Committee, to which Dr Ambedkar gave a befitting reply C.A.D, Vol. XI.
30. S. Ramakrishnan (ed.) The Makers of the Indian Constitution-Myth and Reality authored by Shesh Rao Chavan, Bharatiya Vidya Bhawan, 2000 pp. 115-116.
31. G. Austin, The Indian Constitution: Corner stone of a Nation(1966) p. 330.

32. C.A.D., vol. XI
33. C.A.D., vol. XI, pp. 972-81 at pp. 973-974.
34. *Ibid*
35. C.A.D., Vol. XI, p. 984-995 at pp. 973-989.
36. Supra f.n. 30.
37. B. Shiva Rao, The Framing of India's Constitution- A Study (1968)- (Second ed.), Universal Law Publishing Co. Pvt. Ltd. 2012 (reprint) p. 129.
38. *Ibid* pp. 129-130.
39. Dr Babasaheb Ambedkar; Writings and Speeches, vol.13, pp. 6-14.
40. C.A.Deb., Vol. VII, p. 48.
41. *Ibid.*
42. B. Shiva Rao, Supra f.n. 36 p. 200.
43. Dr Ambedkar's speech on 25th, Nov.1949 on Adoption of the, C.A. D. Vol. XI, pp. 972-81. See also Dr Babasaheb Ambedkar; Writings and Speeches, Vol.13, pp. 1206-1218.
44. *Ibid*
45. Supra f.n. 33 pp. 117-118.
46. Supra f.n. 33 pp. 119.
47. A.I.R. 1951 SC 226.
48. (1980) 2SCC 591 : A.I.R. 1980 SC 1789.
49. The Framing of Indian Constitution (B. Shiva Rao, 1968, 2007 Reprint) p. 502.
50. *Ibid.* p. 504, C.A.Deb., p. 745.
51. *Ibid.* pp. 505-506.
52. C.A.D. Book No. 1, Vol. -VII, p. 761 (vol.I).
53. C.A.D., Vol. VII, p. 953.
54. Dr Babasaheb Ambedkar; Writings and Speeches, Vol. 15, pp. 944-955.
55. *Ibid.* pp. 1201-1202.
56. *Ibid* pp. 1202-1204.
57. 41 Annual Convocation: Dr Babasaheb Ambedkar Marathawada University, Aurangabad, 5th Feb. 2000, pp. 2-3.
58. Supra f.n. 53, Vol. 15, p. 982.
59. Dr K.M. Munshi, Pilgrimage to Freedom, Bharatiya Vidya Bhavan, p. 202.
60. *Ibid.*
61. *Ibid.*
62. M.K. Gandhi, Untouchability (edited by Baratan Kumarappa), p. 3 (1964).
63. *Ibid.*
64. Quoted in M.L. Sahare, Dr Bhimrao Ambedkar: His Life and Work, 31(1988).

65. S. Ramakrishnan, Makers of Indian Constitution, Bhartiya vidya Bhavan, 2000, pp. 190-193 at p. 193.
66. *Ibid*, p. liv.
67. Speech of Dr Ambedkar on 25th January 1949 in the Constituent Assembly, C.A. Deb., Vol. XI, pp. 972-981.
68. S. Ramakrishnan, Supra, f. n. 30, p. iv.
69. Dr Rajendra Prasad, Speech on Nov. 26, 1949 in the Constituent Assembly, C.A.Deb., Vol. XI, pp. 972-981.
70. Cited from S. Ramakrishanan, Supra f.n. 30, p. 114.
71. *Ibid.*
72. *Ibid*, p. 119.
73. *Ibid.*
74. *Ibid*, p. 117.
75. *Ibid.*
76. Indria Sawhney v. Union of India (Mandal Case) 1992 Supp (3) SCC 217.
77. *Ibid.*
78. Dr Babasaheb Ambedkar : Writings, Speeches, Vol. 13, pp. 1174-75
79. *Ibid.*
80. S. Ramakrishnan, Supra f. n. 30, p. 123.
81. *Ibid*, p. 123.
82. *Ibid*, p. 181.
83. *Ibid*, p. 181.
84. *Ibid*, p. 40. The same was the view of Swaraj Party Resolution on White Paper and Communal Award, May 1934, Faizpur Congress Resolutions, Dec. 1946, Resolution in Provincial Assemblies, 1937 etc.
85. Dr Ambedkar's Speech in Constitution Assembly on 25th Nov. 1949 on Adoption of Constitution, C.A.D., Vol XI.
86. Quoted from S. Ramakrishnan, Supra f.n. 30, pp. 199-20.
87. *Ibid*, p. xiii.
88. *Ibid*
89. S. Ramakrishnan, Supra f.n. 30, p. 190. See also Dr Baba Saheb Ambedkar : Writings and Speeches, Vol. 9, pp. 423-425
90. Ibid, pp. 190-194. See also Dr Ambedkar, *Ibid*, Vol. 9, pp. 170, 172.
91. See Anirudh Prasad, The University Education Administration and Law, Deep and Deep Publications, New Delhi, 2000.
92. Indra Sawhney v. Union of India 1992 SCC (L & S) suppl. 1 at p. 211 (per P.B. Sawant, J.) = 1992 Supp (3) SCC 217.
93. There are many cases where the candidate without minimum qualifications are appointed in general category. In DDD. Gorakhpur University in 1998, a Ph.D. in Political Science was

appointed as a Reader in Law Department and Ph.D. in Linguistic (Arts) was appointed as Professor in Law Department. After a decade the former's appointments have been quashed by the Supreme Court approving decisions of the Chancellor and Hon'ble Allahabad High Court, the latter is still Professor of Law.

94. In 2010, a panel was drawn for appointment of the Vice-Chancellor in Hidayatullah National University of Law, Raipur, C.G. A Professor out of that panel joined and worked for two months. Thereafter he resigned on 07-02-2011 with a view to join some other University. The panel became dead. A fresh panel had to be prepared. Another academically unknown person out of the same panel was appointed as V.C. He joined on 31.03.2011. He is so powerful that inspite of repeated letters to the highest officers of that University at State and national level he continued and got the statute amended for further extension beyond 65 years of age. Where is merit? Are these hidden reservations less injurious to national education cause than reserved category person with, atleast minimum qualifications?
95. Cited by S. Ramakrishnan, Supra f.n. 30, p. iv.
96. C.A. Deb., Vol. XI.

PART – III

JUSTICE K. RAMASWAMY AND HIS CONTRIBUTION TO THE NATION

Release of Autobiography of Justice K Ramaswamy by K.G. Balakrishnan, The Chief Justice of India

10

Justice K. Ramaswamy: The Great Indian Sociological Jurist Judge

[The life of Justice Ramaswamy is a legend – a tale of rising from dust to summit giving message that a man from most humble beginnings can rise to pinnacle by hard work, industry and sincere devotion to duty. He is the first Supreme Court Judge to declare the Preamble as the basic feature of Constitution. He is a gentleman who synthesises the rare qualities of being learned and humble. His judgments exude concern for secular and just society with the trinity of equality, liberty and fraternity which has today become a prime need of the Indian state and society. He pleads to make the political democracy a success on the bed-rock of social democracy. Through creative interpretation and pulsating heart to do justice to the poor and downtrodden, Ramaswamy J. made all efforts to convert the Constitution into living organ from a mere document. His sincere commitment to duty, hard work, then and there judgment in open court, soon after the completion of arguments, record disposal of cases and writing judgments are real contribution to our judicial system and need to be observed for reducing mounting arrears and delay in justice delivery system.]

A word on law and sociological jurisprudential approach

Jurisprudence is the science[1] as well as the eye of law[2]. Sociological searching explanation of jurisprudence in general and constitutional and statutory in particular, serves greater social purpose than any other way of viewing the subject matter of Jurisprudence (law) - Analytical positivists view that law is consciously made - command of sovereign, historical school jurists view that law is not enacted (made consciously) but is found (evolved through practising customs), on the other hand Sociological jurists do not bother whether law is made or found, they view how law acts in society, what is purpose of law, how law serves the society in a functional way ? Sociological school thinks of the felt necessities of the life, living law and social engineering. In jurisprudential frame work justice Ramaswamy belongs to sociological Jurisprudence with a little tinge of functional and realist overtone. He has inclination towards Pound's social engineering, on social justice translation into reality he appears to be following the path set by great Indian Justices dealing labour issues – M.C. Chagla and P.B. Gajendragadkar, and judges dealing with social problems of hierarchical Indian society - K. Subba Rao and V.R. Krishna Iyer and O. Chinnappa Reddy. He has great appreciation of wind of change through international standards set by Universal Declaration of Human Rights, 1948; Covenant on Economic and Civil Rights, 1966, I.L.O. and conventions dealing rights of women. Sociological approach peeps through his decisions by moulding technicalities to subserve the law as purposive enterprise. The following study may reveal his sociological geniuses.

(i) A Social Justice and Engineering Orientation Judge

The call of diversity and representative complexion of judiciary is getting momentum throughout the world and therefore, our country cannot remain in isolation. The diversity is needed as only one set up trained judges belonging to one community may not express the diverse need and expectations of diverse group. The constitutional set up envision assimilation, participation and cooperation in governance of the country. "Injustice anywhere is a threat to everywhere as poverty anywhere is a threat to prosperity every where."[3]

The participation of all segments of the society serves great purpose, as judges are part and parcel of the society. As the great human being and social transformation loving Judge Earl Warren observed in one of his addresses, "Our Judges are not monks or scientist but participants in the living stream of our national life, steering the law between the dangers of rigidity on the one hand and formlessness on the other."[4] The felt necessities[5] of the time play vital role in shaping the judicial pronouncements. More so, the ever lasting guiding spirit in Marshallian declaration that, "It is the Constitution we are expanding which to endure for ages, and, consequently to be adapted to the various crises of human affairs."[6]

It is also hard reality that the training and upbringing of the Justice may solve the crises in human affairs and it may aggravate crises. Chief Justice Warren's unanimous pronouncement in ***Brown* v. *Board of Education***[7] to the effect that "separate can never be equal because education is the very foundation of good citizenship," "the schools are the gateway to education and any kind of separation" may affect their hearts and minds in a way unlikely ever to be undone is the excellent example of peaceful social transformation with the stroke of judicial pen. But earlier Taney C.J.'s denial of unfortunate Blacks right to citizenship and according them inferior status due to slavery body sacrosanct in ***Dred Scott* v. *Sanford***[8] and Justice Brown's majority opinion in ***Plessy* v. *Ferguson***[9] declaring "separate but equal" giving licence to states to racially segregate schools, public transport and political process are examples of the latter. The cumulative effect being such that Bodenheimer comments," "If the same court, in the famous *Dred Scott* decision, had recognised the strength of anti-slavery sentiments in many parts of the country instead of taking the extreme view that the institution of slavery was sacrosanct the Civil War might conceivably have been avoided."[10]

It is also important in Judicial pronouncement to incorporate the effect of the direction in which law moves. Law is to be stable but it cannot stand still. In U.S.A., the dissenting judge in *Plessy* case Harlan had guessed the wind of change and pleaded colour-blindness of the constitution. It gave food for future thought. But, it took nearly six decades to become the unanimous court decision in ***Brown* v. *Board of Education*.**[11] A similar messages was given by the dissenting opinion of Subba Rao J. in ***T. Devdasan* v. *Union of India***[12] treating Article 16(4) not an exception to Article 16(4) but a facet of equality which found full expression in the majority decision of 7 Judge Bench in ***State of Kerala* v. *N.M. Thomas***[13] but was not appreciated in subsequent cases and was ineffectuated on one pretext or the other. *Thomas* opinion found credence in nine-Judge Bench in ***Indra Sawhney* v. *Union of India*.**[14] But again the message of change was not appreciated by the Indian Judiciary and the enabling nature, no right-duty imposition and exception of equality have been hovering over again and again. Much water has flown under the bridges since *Champkam*[15] ruled Directive Principles as sub-servient to fundamental rights. At least one down to earth Judge read the message of changes in time and socio-economic justice dispensation.

The real cause of socio-economic dispensation, serving the poor, downtrodden, depressed and bewildered can be served in two ways - *first*, by large hearted, sympathetic whites or upper caste Indians like Harlan J.[16] or Earl Warren[17] Judges in U.S. and Koka Subba Rao[18] and Krishna Iyer justices in India[19], and *second,* by real experience of having burnt of stresses and stresses of backwardness and sufferings in life like Thurgood Marshall J.[20] in U.S. and K. Ramawamy J. in India.[21]

Social reservation implementation requires creatively socio-economic Justice envisioned under the Constitution. Given the opportunity the justices from the depressed classes may be able to read the constitution in light of the felt necessities of the time and pressing need of making equality the reality. The illustration of the immense contribution of K. Ramaswamy J. may throw a new light on constitutional interpretation with sociological glasses and objective enshrined in Articles 14, 15, 16, 38, 46 and 335.

(ii) Impeccable Integrity, hard work and creative Role of Model

The journey of K. Ramaswamy J. from dust to summit, contribution to constitutional law jurisprudence, appreciation and insight into ground and grass root reality of the Indian society etc. establish that given the opportunity, as Justice Iyer had been repeatedly arguing, there are some Dalits who can excel and prove to be better than many non-social group reservation persons who find berth on superior court benches on the basis of caste, acquaintances and better mooring.

K. Ramaswamy was born not only in a Schedule Caste family, he had to suffer ill treatment of his step mother, experience utter poverty and deprivation, had to work as an agricultural labourer on only eight annas for ton hours and continue study even though some time name was struck off school rolls due to non-payment of class fees and sit in class on kindness of Head Master. In spite of all odds his firmness and desire to study made him a first class student. He defied all odds and justified adage; "where there is will, there is way." He had to earn to learn and thus, was self-made.

He had experienced discrimination to which a Schedule Caste person is tied with from the cradle to the grave. But that did not deter him from achievements. From the very beginning he was self-respecting and on his sincere working ability he was appointed as Additional Public Prosecutor as youngest Law Officer with eight years standing at Bar and first Dalit Law Officer in the country. Within a very short time he established his credential as one of the best Prosecutors and maintained a difference between Prosecutor and persecutor on dictate of his conscience. He had established undoubted conduct, integrity and honesty and efficiency in discharge of his duties as Public Prosecutor, Government pleader and private practitioner to the full satisfaction of the entire Bar and the High Court Judges who had expressed their appreciation in their judgements.

It goes without saying that his work as Prosecutor and Government Pleader was of such remarkable marks that his appointment was commended by O. Chinnappa Reddy J., of the SCI who foresaw his successfulness as a judge in view of his experience as Public Prosecutor and Government Pleader added by hard work.[22] Sri P. Sriamulu had congratulated noting well deserved appointment in view of his hard work and sincerity marked as a good Advocate, different from others.[23]

His quality judgments made A.I.R. to report his judgments from very first day. Prior to that A.I.R. did not generally report the judgments of the newly appointed judges. The distinction of Ramaswamy J. was that he never reserved any case and as soon as the arguments were concluded dictated judgments in open Court.[24] His ground experience and knowledge about the poor agriculturists prompted him to write judgment preferring purposive interpretation. He appreciated the problem of poor agriculturists claiming payment of sugar cane product and dismissed the writ petition of the Punjab National Bank in ***Punjab National Bank* v. *Challapalli Sugars Ltd*.**[25] When the appeal was preferred by way of S.L.P. before a Division Bench, Justice O. Chinnappa Reddy, who was of one of the members of the bench, wrote a letter to Ramaswami J. to the effect that the judgment was very well written and the approach was excellent. He put confidence : "I am sure you will write

Table 6

Category *MAIN CASES*	*Larger Bench*	*Full Bench*	*Bench*	*Single*	*Total*
WP	SE	3	13	2017	2033
CC	–	–	–	113	113
AS	–	–	–	1166	1166
SA	–	–	–	8	8
CMA	–	–	2	21	23
CRP	SE	–	1	27	28
TRC	–	–	1	–	1
WA	–	–	9	–	9
CCCA	–	–	–	36	36
HC	–	–	43	–	43
ITC	–	–	4	–	4
Crl. Petns.	–	–	–	63	63
Crl. RC	–	–	–	1	1
Cont. Appeal	–	–	1	–	1
Total	–	**3**	**74**	**3452**	**3529**

many more such judgments.[26] His deep study was seen in his well reasoned decision in ***D.V.K. Prasadrao* v. *Govt. of A.P.***[27] upholding government's implied power to fix admission rates to theatres as reasonable restriction under Article 19(6). His stand was approved by the Apex court. His Judgment in ***Mohan Ranga Rao* v. *State of A.P.***[28] on doctrine of 'unjust enrichment' was approved by seven Judge Constitution Bench of the SCI on appeal to it. Justice Ramaswamy started *suo motu* public interest litigation relating to workers in clay mines not looked after properly by their employers and their bad health conditions and prostitute colony ransacked by police and providing appropriate relief at once.[29] His creative role in PIL was very much acclaimed by Justice P.N. Bhagwati of the SCI. Bhagwati J. expressed his gladness that Justice Ramaswami had started, "entertaining public interest litigation with a view to helping the poor to combat exploitation and injustice and realisation of their socio-economic entitlements and utilising the strategy of public interest litigation in a creative and imaginative fashion.[30]

(iii) Punctuality and Commitment to Work

The punctuality, quick disposal, sincerity towards duty of Justice K. Ramaswami, as a High Court Judge can be appreciated in view of the following figures during 1.1.1987 to 5.10.1989.

High Court of Andhra Pradesh : At Hyderabad
Statement showing the disposals of the Hon'ble Mr. Justice K. Ramaswamy during the period from 1.1.1987 to 31.12.1987.

Table 7

MISC. CASES					
WAMP	–	–	18	–	18
CMP	–	–	10	230	240
WPMP	1	–	44	1141	1186
Appln.	–	–	–	54	54
Crl. MP	–	–	3	32	35
Total	**1**	**–**	**75**	**1457**	**1533**

No. of Court working days = 210
No. of days present = 207

Source : Ceaseless and Relentless Journey, p. 80.

High Court of Andhra Pradesh : At Hyderabad

Statement showing the Disposals of the Hon'ble Mr. Justice K. Ramaswamy from 1.1.1988 to 31.12.1988.

Table 8

Category MAIN CASES	*Full Bench*	*Bench*	*Single*	*Total*
Writ Petitions	–	20	5721	5741
Contempt Cases	–	2	105	107
First Appeals	–	–	1674	1674
Second Appeals	–	–	9	9
Misc. I Appeals	–	–	5	5
Civil Rev. Petitions	–	–	54	54
Writ Appeals	–	11	2	13
SCLPs	–	10	–	10
CCCAs	–	–	63	63
Referred Cases	12	–	–	12
Total	**12**	**43**	**7633**	**7688**

Table 9

MAIN CASES	*Full Bench*	*Bench*	*Single*	*Total*
WAMP	–	57	3	60
CMP	–	9	342	351
WPMP	–	63	1644	1707
Applications	–	1	50	51
Crl. Misc. Petns.	–	5	2	7
Total	**–**	**135**	**2041**	**2176**

No. of Court working days = 208
No. of days present = 206
Source : Ceaseless and Relent Journey, p. 81.

High Court of Andhra Pradesh at Hyderbad

Statement showing the Disposals of the Hon'ble Mr. Justice K. Ramaswamy from 1.1.1989 to 5.10.1989.

At the time of the elevation of Justice Ramaswami to the Supreme Court, The Hindu newspaper had published "Ramaswamy's distinction" on October 5, 1989 thus :

Table 10

Category *MAIN CASES*	*Bench*	*Single*	*Total*
Writ Petitions	11	1546	1557
Contempt Cases	1	49	50
First Appeals	–.	2441	2441
Second Appeals	–	17	17
Misc. I Appeals	–	425	425
Civil Rev. Petitions	–	165	165
Writ Appeals	15	–	15
CCCAs	–	2	2
Total	**27**	**4645**	**4672**

No. of Court working days = 156
No. of days present = 152
Source : Ceaseless and Relentless Journey, p. 82.

"As judge of the High Court, he had the distinction of disposal of the highest number of cases. In 1988, he had disposed of 7688 Main Matters and 2176 Miscellaneous Matters, the highest figure in the country. From January to April, in this year, he had disposed of 2441 appeals and a total of 4672 and earned a distinction."[32]

Justice K. Ramaswamy's commitment to his work as the High Court Judge has been discussed earlier which shows how punctual and devoted to the work he was. He was present in 2007 for 207 out 210 days, in 1988 for 206 out of 208 days and during 1989 (before his joining the SCI) for 152 out of 156 days. He had delivered record number of judgments. Work was worship for K. Ramaswamy J. which is clear from his declining of Sikkim High Court Chief Justiceship. In 1989, before his elevation to the Supreme Court, K. Ramaswamy J. was offered the appointment as Chief Justice of Sikkim High Court which he declined for reasons, to be elaborated in his own words :

"In that High Court no cases were pending for disposal and I could not sit idle doing no work. On the other hand, I preferred to remain in the Andhra Pradesh High Court to be able to serve the State, contributing towards reduction of arrears in the High Court."[33]

He continued to sail on the same boat as the Judge of the Supreme Court of India. He topped the list of judgment writers. He had written 2227 judgments to his credit while the previous total of top position was of Chief Justice J. C. Shah. The computer network dated March 6, 1998 showed the following figure :

Judge Name	*Judgments*
K. Ramaswamy	2227
J.C. Shah	1783

In 1996, K. Ramaswami J. had delivered 610 judgments/ order apart from judgments written by other judges of Bench participated by him.

(iv) Sharp and Activist Judicial Actor

Justice K. Ramaswamy has been very intelligent and sharp judge to grasp even the complex issues. B. Sen points out how sharp Justice Ramaswamy was shortly after he had joined the SCI, Mr Sen appeared before the Bench of which K. Ramaswamy J. was a member along with Mr Justice Punchhi. The matter related to right to worship by a congregation in a Church to quote Mr Sen :

"It was a complex issue when a secular court was being called upon to decide in the context that the right to worship according to their conscience is guaranteed under the Constitution. Punchhi J. was a little puzzled and hesitant but K. Ramaswamy had got the point, which needed to be examined."[34]

M.N. Krishnaswami, a senior advocate of the SCI and twice Vice-President of the Supreme Court Bar Association appreciated Ramaswami J. for his camphor - like quickness in understanding the crux of the matter, humane and justice-oriented approach, of ability to the Juniors, equal mindedness, equanimity, firm faith in God and in Truth, courage of conviction and above all matchless honesty.[35]

On the basis of his performance K. Ramaswamy J. has been termed as activist Judicial actor. Judges may be restraintivist judicial actor or activist judicial actor. K. Ramaswamy J. belongs to the latter category of the judges. Dr Upendra Baxi observes that he is inaugural judicial actor, "who deployed Judicial activism for the depressed under classes of contemporary Indian, inaugurated new spheres of social action litigation."[36]

K. Ramaswamy has been a hard working and most committed judge to his judicial duties. Noting having no godfather at Bar to help him stand on his feet, Justice O. Chinnappa Reddy J. commended Ramaswamy J. that, 'he managed to survive and then to make good, all because of his hard work, his industry and his temperate wisdom"[37] whose wisdom made him radiate humility and warmth along with knowledge.

(v) Insightful Appreciation of Indian Socio-legal problems through a Sociological Jurist Glasses

K. Ramaswamy J. believes in social insight to appreciate and tackle legal problems of the Indian society. He appreciates Earl Ehrlich's difference between formal law and living law or Dean Roscoe Pound's distinction between law on the paper and law-in-action and prefers to interpret the formal or law on paper in light of the requirement of law in action with the help of social engineering principle. Like Holmes J. for him "law is not brooding omnipotence in the sky, but a flexible instrument of social order." This led him to put more and more emphasis on reformism enshrined in preamble and commitments under Article 38(1) "to strive to promote the welfare of the people by securing and protecting as effectively as it may a social order in which justice, social, economic and political shall inform all the institutions of the national life and under Article 38(2)" to strive to minimise the inequalities in income, and endeavour to eliminate inequalities in states, facilities and opportunities, not only amongst individuals but also amongst groups of people residing in different areas or engaged in different locations" and other provisions contained in the Directive Principles of State Policy and Articles 15(4) (5) and 16(4) (4A) (4B).

The grass root reality of Indian social life has prompted Justice K. Ramaswamy to take a stand different from other status quoist scholar judges. It can be very well appreciated by tackling of the following social problems.

(a) Social Reservation and Inapplicability of Reverse Discrimination Doctrine

Judiciary gives life to lifeless letters of the Statute. It fills the gap in law and social demands. But, that creativity depends and is related to the peculiar social phenomenon. K. Ramaswamy J.'s social insight into the peculiar Indian structure and specific constitutional provisions to safeguard the interests of poor, depressed and bewildered SCs/STs and SEBCs led him to denounce the American reverse discrimination doctrine in the Indian context. Though both in the United States of America and India the country has experienced the problem of racism and casteism so as to isolate certain population from the main stream of the national life. But, in U.S.A. this gap has been filled by creative interpretation of equality clause by Chief Justice Earl Warren in ***Brown v. Board of Education***[38] and subsequent executive orders during 1960s. In India preferential treatment in favour of SCs/STs and SEBCs. K. Ramaswamy J. finds, in this situation difference, the basis of non-importation of American doctrine of reverse discrimination. In India, more than often judiciary has placed emphasis on this doctrine to adversely affect the cause of preferential treatment envisioned in favour of depressed classes. Ramaswamy J. specifically citing the application of 'reverse discrimination' doctrine in ***Ajit Singh Januja v. State of Punjab***[39] by the three judge bench and then by five judge bench in ***Ajit Singh II v. State of Punjab***[40] presents a compare and contrast between the American and Indian legal position. He points out :

"The American Constitution does not contain an express provision of protective discrimination in favour of Afro-Americans, like their counterpart Dalits, Tribes and other OBCs, expressly in grafted in the Indian Constitution. As far as the American Constitution is concerned, from ***Brown v. Board of Education***[41] case of 1954 onwards, it was only a judge made law. Therefore, they introduced the principle of reverse discrimination. The seven-judge bench in ***Thomas case***[42] and nine-judge bench in **Mandal**[43] held that the rights of Dalits and the Tribes is part of the right to equality in Article 14, Article 16(1) and 16(4) "as an emphatic way of ensuring equality." So long as the constitutional provisions are operational and adequate representation in service under the State is not secured to Dalits, Advasis and OBCs, the question of reverse discrimination will never arise."[44]

Referring to ***R.K. Sabharwal v. State of Punjab***[45], how the social reservation group also compete for services under State both for general category and reserved category, Ramaswamy J. presented a practical note on the issue. He pointed out: "The question of reverse discrimination, therefore, does not arise, since it is a case of open competition on 'equal opportunity'." For reserved posts, no selection was ever made in excess of the prescribed quota - Except in class III and IV posts in Central Services, even so many years of operation of the Constitution, till date the target of filling the prescribed quota has not been achieved. Practising fraud on the

Constitution, Dalits and Adivasis are not being selected and general candidates usurp reserved posts while the executive turns a blind eye to it. The Theory of reverse discrimination, therefore, is dangerous and explosive, contrary to above constitutional scheme. It was a shot in the arms for the avowedly hostile elements out to subvert and distort the constitution."[46]

(b) Pragmatic Approach

In India mostly decisions are given on premise that merit is outcome of objective, impartial and merit based decisions of those who matter. The sociological fact, or more specifically its left wing, realist searchlight reveals otherwise. And, this has been appreciated/exposed by Justice Ramaswamy.

1. He pointed out in ***P.G.I. of Medical Education Research v. K.L. Narsimhan***[47] how selection on reserved seats are not done objectively, posts are left vacant and after three years are dereserved.[48]
2. He has pointed out how on caste-line some are discriminated even in Judiciary and promotion is deprived and how others are promoted ignoring their notoriously being corrupt on plea that they were due to retire in a short time and they could earn their pension and selection grade.[49]
3. He exposed mindset of some of Justices. "One Bharthari Prasad of Higher Judicial Service was of impeccable integrity, ranking high in equality dispensation of justice. On his transfer, his successor District Judge brought water from the Ganges and got the chair cleaned in the Court and he was later elevated to the High Court. When this news was published in the media, since Mr Prasad refused to speak falsehood by denying the news, he was made to retire compulsorily.

The wide jurisprudential knowledge enabled him to decide worker interest oriented cases asserting social justice through making law socially relevant and a tune to the needs of time. In ***Consumer Education and Research Centre v. Union of India***[50] the imprint of Harold J. Laski's A Grammar of Politics[51] is clearly visible. K. Ramaswamy J. observed ;

"Jurisprudence is the eye of law giving an insight into the environment of which it is the expression. It relates the law to the spirit of the time and makes it richer. Law is the ultimate aim of every civilised society, as a key system in a given era, to meet the needs and demands of its time."

In Chameli Singh v. State of U.P.[52]

The social conditions and the need of providing accommodations to Dalit was appreciated by K. Ramaswamy J. speaking for a three judge bench comprising of he himself and Faiaz Uddin and B.N. Kirpal JJ. The issue related to official lethargy after finalisation of the scheme for acquisition for housing to Dalit: could the urgency be diluted by the act of officials ? Ramaswamy J. gave very wide and dynamic meaning to right to live in light of the Universal Declaration of Human Rights, 1948. Right to life was interpreted to include the right of shelter, which in turn was explained, is not a mere protection of life and limb. Said, the learned judge, it is home where a person has "opportunities to grow physically, mentally, intellectually and spiritually. Right to shelter, therefore, includes adequate living space, safe and decent structure, clean and decent surroundings, sufficient light pure air and water, electricity, sanitation and other civil amenities like roads etc. so as to have easy access to his daily avocation."

K. Ramaswamy J. further elaborated :

"The right to shelter, therefore, does not mean a mere right to a roof over one's head but right to all the infrastructure necessary to enable them to live and develop as human being. Right to shelter when used as an essential requisite to the right to live, should be deemed to have been guaranteed as a fundamental right."[53]

Reading Directive Principles of State Policy and ensuing of socio-economic justice, he added duty on the part of State and ruled, "to bring the Dalits and Tribes into the mainstream of life providing these facilities and opportunities to them is the duty of the State as fundamental to their basic human and constitutional rights."[54]

In the above backdrop Ramaswamy J. said delay by itself accelerates urgency: Larger the delay greater be urgency. Reason being that,"so long as the unhygienic conditions and deplorable housing needs of Dalits, Tribes and poor are not solved or fulfilled, the urgency continues to subsist." He pointed out that "providing the sites to the Dalits, Tribes and poor itself is a national problem, and a Constitutional obligation."[55]

Such a decision can be pronounced by only a judge having human face, humane approach with pragmatic and sociological appreciation of the genuine problem of downtrodden and official neglect or lethargy or apathy causing delay in giving effect to state commitment to provide social, economic and educational service to the dalits.

In ***Muralidhar Dayadeo Kesekar v. Vishwa Nath Pandu Barde***[56] in the same vein, a division bench of K. Ramaswamy and B. L. Hansaria JJ. upheld the statutory restraint on sale of agricultural land allotted to SC/ST/BCs or the poor and the prior permission of competent authority for such alienation was declared constitutionally valid. An agreement to sale was declared void under Section 23 of the Contract Act, 1872. The Court exemplified the concept of distributive justice and declared that economic empowerment to tribals, Dalits and poor to be a facet of fundamental right under Article 21 and State Policy to allot agricultural hands to them aims to render socio-economic justice. The prohibition on alienation was held to effectuate the constitutional policy of economic empowerment under Articles 14, 21, 38, 39 and 46 read with the preamble to the Constitution. The Court put main emphasis on preamble envisaging removal of economic inequalities and relieve Dalits from all forms of Exploitation. Explaining the distributive justice, it was made clear that :

"Distributive justice accomplishes the proportional equality. The proportional rewards to the groups of the people would enable the groups of people to level up their income and economic status in proportion to their membership in the country's population."[57]

Speaking of economic empowerment through economic Justice to SCs/STs ensuring socio-economic democracy as part of political democracy envisaged under Article 46 of the Constitution, the Court observed, "Economic empowerment, is, therefore, a basic human right and a fundamental rights as part of right to live, equality and of dignity to the poor, weaker sections, Dalits and Tribes."[58]

(vi) A Humanist, Besides Noted Jurist

The appointment of K. Ramaswamy J. on the Supreme Court of India heralds a new era in judicial thinking in line of great sociological Jurist bring socio-legal revolution with creatively innovative outlook. He goes further defying elitist character. Speaking of "Judicial Process and Social Change" in the beginning of the 1980s O. Chinnappa Reddy J. had observed in one of this extra-judicial writings noting that "The juristic community of legislators, lawyers, judges and bureaucrats are drawn, essentially, from the elitist classes and those that are not so drawn very soon hasten to join the elitist class. The so-called juristic community as a whole is class oriented and when they talk or think of social change it is generally in a patronising and superior or abstract or suspicion or even insincere way. Hence the failure of the juristic community to propound and develop a legal ideology explaining the connection between law and social change; hence the failure of the law until now as an effective instrument of social change."[59] But Ramaswami J. has genuinely served the cause of social change through law with his humanist touch. He had risen from dust to doyen by dint of hard work. To quote Justice G. Bikshapathy, a senior Judge Andhra Pradesh High Court, "His way of life and quality as a human being, his judicious approach coupled with human touch to all the issues is to be imbibed by one and all. Every judgment rendered by him either in the High Court of Andhra Pradesh or the Supreme Court, always bore the golden imprints of humanity and compassion to the oppressed, depressed and weaker segments of the society."[60] It is true that his heart always pulsated to do justice to the poor and downtrodden.[61]

Ramaswamy J. established his reputation as an innovator of new precedents without at the same time, devaluing the precedent already operative.[62] The distinguishing contribution of Ramaswami J. can be found in different ways.

(vii) Inhered and ingrained sociological juristic outlook to render social justice

The inspirational dictum of Ramaswamy J. appears to be Claud Mulin's Quest of Justice which states, "It was the boast of Augustus that he found Rome of brick and left clay of marble. But how much nobler will be our sovereign's boast, when he shall have it so say that he found law truth and left cheap; found it a patrimony of the rich, left it the inheritance of the poor; found it two edged sword of craft and oppression, left it the staff of honesty and the shield of innocence." The real objective of our foremost social document aiming social revolution[63] through giving meaning to the conscience expressed in its Part III and IV can be translated into service to 'we the people of India' only if social engineering with judicial statesmanship is adhered to.

K. Ramaswamy J. has left no stone unturned to make the above constitutional reality with juristic insight developed by the study and acquired knowledge of great American and Indian progressive judges, American and Australian futuristic ideological revolutionary pronouncements and standards of human rights envisaged under international documents like The Universal Declaration of Human Rights (1948), the International Convention on Socio-Economic and Cultural Rights, 1966 and The Right to Development Convention.

K. Ramaswamy J. believes in reason-experience amalgamation and mutual correction. For him law is not only logic, nor experience, but logic and experience both in famous twentieth century sociological jurist Dean Roscoe Pound's words, "law is an experience developed by reason and reason tested by experience." For him like Pound Law is social engineering balancing the conflicting interests in society with minimum of waste and friction."

Among the Indian Juristic thinkers and great judges K. Ramaswamy has been immensely influenced by Justice P.B. Gajendragadkar and Justice K. Subba Rao (both hon'ble Chief-Justices of India). The former threw light on social function of law including providing social justice. In his famous book 'Law, Liberty and Social Justice' Justice Gajendragadkar approvingly had cited Cohen to mean law as, "a science of social adjustment. Its main object, being to establish socio-economic justice and remove the existing imbalance in the socio-economic structure." This inspirational messages peeps through Judgments of K. Ramaswamy J. Gajendragadkar J.'s message about social Justice to include both economic and Social justice, more particularly in view of Hindu social hierarchical structure has been guiding force. Likewise, the Koka Subba Rao's messages through ***Social Justice and Law***[64] explaining compound word social justice with adjective 'social' and noun 'justice' has served as path setter for K. Ramaswamy J. Subba Rao explained that social meant relating to society which is a group of men with common organisation and Justice meant the quality of being just and fair to all the individuals in the group. For him justice meant justice for all and not to favoured classes. For him, 'social justice is the balancing wheel between the haves and have-nots.[65] It is not aimed to pull down the advanced sections of the society, but only the upliftment of backward sections thereof without unduly and unreasonably affecting the interest of the former. It ensures balanced development for the confiscation without producing equalise poverty, but does land to social upliftment." The main way to ensure social justice through guarantee of political, economic and equal equalities was based on two principles:

(i) to give equal opportunity to every citizen of India to develop his own personality in the way he seeks to do, and
(ii) to give adventitious aids to the under-privileged to face boldly competition of life.

Justice Subba Rao's dissenting opinion in ***T. Devadasan v. Union of India***[66] treating Article 16(4) as not exception to Article 16(4) but a facet of enforcing equality and his view on demand of justice to provide adventitious aids to II or III class horses in comparison to class I in ***Chitralekha v. State of Mysore***[67] can be seen exercising effect on K. Ramaswami's decision on socio-economic issues. For K. Ramaswami J. social justice is a bond of social necessity which can be ensured only guaranteeing equality in result or reality. He has also been immensely impressed by Nehruvian pledge to create new order of socio-economic equality and fulfill the ambition of the greatest man of our generation (Gandhiji) "to wipe out every tear from every eye" and Dr B. R. Ambedkar's commitment to make political democracy a social democracy and ensure liberty, equality and fraternity as guiding principles of national life, had singular impact on Ramaswamy J.

(viii) A Constitutional Law Judge, Not CPC Judge

There are two types of judges on the Courts - CPC Judges and constitutional law judges. K. Ramaswamy J. belongs to the latter group of judges. The former believes in the strict interpretation rule based Littra Scripta and latter believe in Marshallian wording that judges should not forget that it is the Constitution which they are interpreting which has to endure for ages and meet the various crises of the national life. For K. Ramaswamy the constitution is not fastidious document but endures to serve successive generations. Ramaswamy J. explains the two abovc referred group of judges as follow :

CPC Judges[68]: While interpreting the law in Littra Scripta (CPC Judges) fold their sleeves, blame the draftsmen and bolic the hopes and faith of the peoples in the efficacy of law.

Constitutional Law Judges[69]: Stretch their arms, iron out the crease of law and put on flesh and blood to the dry bones of law and reach injustice wherever it is found. It may be conveniently referred to the American Supreme Court decisions in Dread Scott, Plessy and even the decisions during New Deal Period (1930s) and Indian decisions in ***A.K. Gopalan v. State of Madras***, (1950) compensation cases and Habeas Corpus, which fall in the category of C.P.C. judges. On the other hand American Supreme Court decision in ***Brown v. Board of Education***[70] and Indian Supreme Court decision in ***State of Kerala v. N.M. Thomas***[71], ***Maneka Gandhi v. Union of India***[72], ***Minerva Mills v. Union of India***[73] and ***Bandhu Mukhi Morcha v. Union of India***[74] can be put in the latter category. The same may be true of great revolutionary judgment of the Australian High Court in ***Mabo (2) v. Queensland***[75].

K. Ramaswamy J. has demonstrated and established himself as a constitutional law judge with imaginative and innovative interpretation of the Constitutional mandates. In ***Ravichandran Iyer v. Justice A.M. Bhattacharjee***,[76] treating the judicial office of essentially an office of public trust and innovating in-house-procedure[77] for correction of errant judges, he ruled that instead of earlier passive judicial role a judge while giving effect to the constitutional ideals has to play a creative role. Said, K. Ramaswamy J., "In the on-going complex of adjudicatory process, the role of the judge is not merely to interpret the law but also to lay new norms of law and to mould law to suit the changing social and economic scenario to make the ideals enshrined in the Constitution meaningful and a reality."[78] Depreciating the role of a judge as aloof umpire, Ramaswamy J. asserts that, "law is a reflex of the social conscience, expression of social will, the judicial process is to give effect to the social conscience, the social habits, the social norms and the social mores."[79]

The judgment of K. Ramaswamy J. dealing with gunpoint detention of an SC member from going to newly constructed pond in ***State of Karnataka v. Appa Balu Ingale***[80] that mens rea was not essential ingredient for constituting an offence rising out of practice of untouchability, is obvious example of a constitutional law judge appreciating ugly practice of untouchability inspite of Protection of Civil Rights Act, 1955 (renamed in 1976 for Untouchability Offence Act, 1955) and SCs/STs (Prevention of Atrocities) Act, 1989. The message of Ingale case was that "Judges should respond to human situation to combat social evils." It was also said that the court as the vehicle of transforming the nation's life, would respond to the nation's needs and add to interpret the law with pragmatism to further public welfare and to make the constitutional animation a reality." Dr Upendra Baxi a renowned Jurisprudent quoted with approval and appreciation the approach and perspective held in Appa Balu Ingale case in his article 'Potable Water a Fundamental Right to Dalits' published in the Hindu. K. Ramaswamy J.'s interpretation of the Fifth Schedule of the Constitution in ***Samatha v. State of A.P***[81]. is another example to give live meaning to the constitutional provision in light of the Universal Declaration of Human Rights, the International Covenant on Socio-Economic and Cultural Rights, 1966 and the Right to Development vis-a-vis Articles 14, 15, 16, 21, 23, 38 and 46 of the Constitution of India. The Supreme Court was dealing with the issue of Adivasis entitlement to the protection of land in Tribal areas of Andhra Pradesh. The Governor of A.P. had prohibited transfer of land in Scheduled Area from tribals to non-tribals. The Court upheld its validity by giving extended meaning to right to life under Article 21 to include the right to live with human dignity with minimum sustenance and shelter and right and duty of the State to formulate appropriate national development policy aiming constant improvement of the welfare of the entire population and of all individuals, "on the basis of their occupation, free and meaningful participation in development and in the fair distribution of the benefits resulting therefrom." Ramaswamy J. pointed out that human rights and fundamental rights are indivisible and interdependent. They require effective implementation so as to eradicate social injustice. He ruled that it is the duty of the State to preserve land in the Scheduled Areas for the socio-economic empowerment of Adivasis as part of their development. ***The Samantha case***[82] ruling reminds us of the 1992 pronouncement of the Australian apex Court in ***Mab-o (2) v. Queensland***[83] which had ruled that, "Merian people were entitled, as against the whole world to possession, occupation, use and enjoyment of the lands of the Murray Islands." Reacting on the Arun Shourie's[84] terming of Samantha Judgment as interpolation of the Constitution K Ramaswami J. says, "it is not an interpolation of the Constitution but an act of judicial statesmanship to prevent exploitation of Adivasis to preserve their socio-economic entitlements and tribal autonomy within the notified Scheduled area."[85] Comparing the Indian approach towards accrual of benefits to Adivasis and Australian counterpart, K. Ramaswami J. commented: "When the Australian Hight Court declared the autonomy of the tribals and their entitlement to retain the lands in the Tribal area, that government had accepted. But, unfortunately, in India, despite the Constitutional mandate of Schedule Five, every attempt is being made to overturn Samantha Judgment. It is said that the Attorney General of India, a human rights activist, went on record recommending to the Government of India to amend the Constitution to undo the benefits derived by the Adivasis from the judgment."[86]

(ix) Innovative Interpretation evolving New Fundamental Rights

K. Ramaswamy J. tried his best to interpret the Constitution as a social document of revolution and for that he gave new dimension to the right duty relationship, refused to maintain distinction between the significance of the fundamental rights and the directive principles of State policy on account enforceability and otherwise and gives message sharing Professor Amartya Sen (Nobel Laureate) that, 'education, health, human security and dignity are not social gains of economic reforms but are really economic gains of social reform. Mere economic growth without social justice will not mean development but would remain a Rootless, Ruthless, Voiceless, Jobless, and Futureless growth."[87] In ***Samantha v. State of A.P***[83] keeping in view the problem of displacement and deprivation of tribals in name of mines, dams, industries, wildlife sanctuaries, road, railways etc., Justice K. Ramaswamy observed:

"Since the executive is enjoined to protect the social, economic and educational interest of the tribals and when the State leases out the lands in the Schedule areas non-tribals for exploitation of mineral resources, it transmits the above correlative constitutional duties and obligations to those who undertake to exploit the natural resources and who would also improve social, economic and educational improvement of tribals."[89]

The creative and innovative judicial outlook of K. Ramaswamy J. is influenced by the South East Asian thinking that duty is more important and common welfare is preferable to hardcore westerner right oriented Lokian emphasis. His concern for common men, deprived, disprivileged has inspired him to give due credence and place to the directive principles of state policy. Expansive meaning to development oriented rights can be discerned from his decisions or the decisions of the benches of which he was honourable member. A few examples are presented here.

(a) Right to Education as Fundamental Right

As early as mid 1980s, as a A.P. High Court Judge, K. Ramaswamy J. ruled in ***Murali Krishna Public School case***[90] that education is a fundamental right and it is the duty of the State to have imparted to the Dalits and Adivasis. His decision was with a view to give effect to Article 46 of the Constitution which takes care to promote educational interest of weaker sections of the people, in particular, of the Scheduled Castes and Scheduled Tribes, so as to protect them from social injustice and all forms of discrimination. The issue related to the recognition of private educational institution established in Harijanwala locality of Dalits imparting free education to Dalits. The matter was dealt by Ramaswamy J. taking into account Articles 45, 46 and 15(4). The learned judge noted the essentiality of education to lay foundation of good citizenship noted the ground reality of Dalit Rikshaw pullers and the daily wage earners unable to comply the condition of recognition. He observed that "in view of Article 45 of the Constitution, it is the duty of the State to impart compulsory education to the children in the egalitarian socialist society with secularism as its goal." Ramaswamy J. insisted on the point that, "Right to education to the Dalits is a fundamental right and it is the mandatory duty of the State to provide adequate opportunities to advance their economic and educational interest by establishing schools." In the areas where no government school was available it was decided to be the duty of the State to establish schools in the area of Dalits.

This case demonstrates living law approach of Ramaswamy J. There was no government school in that area. The only school imparting education to Dalits was given temporary recognition and was asked for withdrawal on non-compliance of technical formalities. The judge himself had appointed an advocate of bar as commissioner to inquire into matter. The advocate on inquiry had reported that the School was situated in Harijanwala and mothers of children had informed about condition and at the time of 167 students with 4 teachers including Headmistress. Parents of children were rikshaw pullers or daily wage earners. No fee was charged and School was run on collecting donations from philanthropists. There were 13 conditions for application for recognition. Through data facts collected by the advocate commissioner Justice K. Ramaswamy came to know the situation. To insists upon fulfillment of condition would amount to say, "you Dalits are not entitled to a School since you can never comply with our conditions though you are in dire need of education and constitution gives you such a right."[91] With a view to providing meaningful interpretation Ramaswamy J. quoted Harold J. Laski, A. Grammar of Politics' to explain equality as providing adequate opportunity laid open to all. He also quoted ***Warren J. in Brown v. Board of Education***[92] declaring education as perhaps the most important function of the State and local government. He interpreted relevant provisions of the Constitution to say, "right to education to the Dalits is a fundamental right and it is mandatory duty of the State to provide adequate opportunities to advance their economic and educational interest by establishing schools."[93]

The learned judge noted dereliction on the part of the authorities, directed recognition to be granted to the School from L.K.G. to Class V and grant entire amounts as per rule within six weeks. The learned judge also directed to secure as expeditiously as possible adequate site for construction of a permanent school nearer to locality and also to provide necessary funds for its construction and other amenities.[94]

This case appreciates the living law concept. Legislature frames law but cannot foresee all eventualities. The effective part comes on subordinate legislation and executive has to take effective measures for implementation. It has to be realistic and pragmatic to the situation and as Ramaswamy J. said,"in appropriate case they should tailor their actions to relax them as to sub serve the purpose of the Constitution and the Act."[95] Dealing with the issue of capitation fee a Division Bench of the Supreme Court consisting of Kuldip Singh and R.M. Sahai JJ in ***Mohini Jain v. State of Karnataka***[96] declared the right to education at all level as fundamental right under Article 21. But that spirit was diluted by the subsequent larger bench decisions[97] and commercialisation triumphed over the basic right of education and it has now been limited to the children from six to fourteen years.[98]

(b) Social Justice As Fundamental Right

For the first time in ***Calcutta Electricity Supply Co. Ltd. v. Subhash Chandra Bose***[99], the apex Court ruled the right to social justice as a fundamental right. In dissenting judgment K. Ramaswamy J. placed reliance on the Universal Declaration of Human Rights, International Convention of Economic, Social and Cultural Rights, 1966 and ruled that in view of Articles 39(c) and 21 right to social and economic right is a fundamental right. K. Ramaswamy J. reiterated this concept delivering the unanimous judgment of a three judge Bench in ***Consumer Educational Research Centre v. Union of India.***[100] He pointed out that social justice is an integral part of justice in the generic sense. He explained justice is the genius, of his social justice is one of its species. Said, Ramaswamy J.:

"Social justice is a dynamic device to mitigate the sufferings of the poor, weak, Dalits, tribals and deprived sections of the society and to elevate them to the level of equality to live a life with dignity of person. Social justice is not a simple or single idea of a society but is a essential part of complex social change to relieve the poor etc. from hardships, penury to ward off distress and to make their life liveable for greater good of the society at large."

Ramaswamy J. read preamble and Article 38 of the Constitution, the supreme law and held that they envision social justice as its arch to ensure life to be meaningful and livable with human dignity.

It is to be noted that ***C.E.S.C. Limited v. Subash Chandra Bose***[101] was decided by a three judge bench on Nov. 15, 1991 and Ramaswamy J. was dissenter. Punchhi J. had written leading majority decision with which Ranganath Mishra C.J. had concurred. ***G.E.R.C. v. Union of India***[102] was decided by three judge bench on January 27, 1995. Justice Punchhi was member of both benches and A.M. Ahmadi C.J. had joined as next judge in the latter case. The dissenting view of Ramaswamy J. became unanimous view of the Court (including agreement of Punchhi J.). With social justice fundamental right dimension Article 21 was given a dynamic and expansive meaning. Said, Ramaswamy J.,"the jurisprudence of personhood or philosophy of the right to life envisaged under Article 21, enlarges its sweep to encompass human personality in its full blossom with invigorated health which is a wealth to the workmen to earn his livelihood, to sustain the dignity of person and to live a life with dignity and quality."[103]

(c) Right to Health and Medical Care as Fundamental Right

In ***Consumer Education and Research Centre v. Union of India***[104] the issue through a PIL was raised as to the right of a workman to health and medical care. K. Ramaswamy J. preferred a dynamic meaning of Article 21 in light of Articles 39, 41, 43, 38-A and ruled that these provisions make a workman's right to hygienic conditions in workplace and leisure as Fundamental rights. Article 47 was held to be one of the primary duties of the State to improve public health. Since asbestos is prone to lung cancer and allied ailments, it was held that the court can give directions in appropriate cases to state or its undertakings/instrumentalities, company or private employer to make the right meaningful and pay compensation to affected workmen. Allowing the writ petition, all the industries were directed :

(1) to maintain and keep maintaining the health record of every worker up to a minimum period of 40 years from the beginning of the employment or 15 years after retirement or cessation of the employment whichever is later; (2) the Membrane Filter test to detect asbestos fiber should be adopted by all the factories or establishments on a par with the Metalliferrous Mines Regulations, 1961 and Vienna Convention and rules issued there under; (3) all the factories whether covered by the Employees' State Insurance Act or Workmen's Compensation Act or otherwise are directed to compulsorily insure health coverage to every worker; (4) the Union and the State Governments are directed to review the standards of permissible exposure, limit value of fiber/cc in tune with the international standards reducing the permissible content as prayed in the writ petition referred to at the beginning. The review shall be continued after every 10 years and also as and when the ILO gives directions in this behalf consistent with its recommendations or any convention; (5) the Union and all the State Governments are directed to consider inclusion of such of those small-scale factory or factories or industries to protect health hazards of the workers engaged in the manufacture of asbestos or its ancillary products; (6) the appropriate Inspector of Factories in particular of the State of Gujarat, is directed to send all the workers, examined by the ESI hospital concerned, for re-examination by the National Institute of Occupational Health to detect whether all or any of them are suffering from the occupational health hazards, each such worker shall be entitled to compensation in a sum of rupees one lakh payable

by the factory or industry or establishment concerned within a period of three months from the date of certification by the National Institute of Occupational Health.[105]

(x) Interpretation of Law in Context of Social reality

Justice K. Ramaswamy's Judicial activism exposing social reality and thwarting of the causes of constitutionally envisioned beneficiaries by resorting foul means and caste certification through different channels-conversion, adoption and marriages, has been a matter of record. As a High Court Judge he exposed misuse of adoption process in ***A.S. Sailaja v. Principal, Kurnool Medical College***[106] . In that case a Brahmin girl after having failed in the entrance examination for admission into the M.B.B.S. course, appeared next year as an adopted daughter of a shepherd Backward class who was serving as a servant in her father's office who was a practising Advocate. She was denied admission under backward category and therefore, she filed petition. K. Ramaswamy J. accepting her adoption valid under the Hindu Adoption and Maintenance Act, was not agreeable to extend its benefit to social reservation on ground that she had not suffered the handicaps which a Backward Class person would be subjected to. She was neither socially backward nor educationally backward. In ***Bandi Srinivasa Rao v. Special officer***[107] he also tackled wisely the issue of the benefit of social reservation under S.C. category to a son born out of wedlock between Backward Class father and Dalit mother. Ramaswamy J. took a pragmatic approach i.e. if he had lived with Dalits and had experienced same handicaps as an untouchable and suffered social disabilities, he would be given benefit of S.C. candidate. But, if he was brought up as B. C. with his father with all advantages, he could not be given the benefit as S.C. candidate. But, the Division Bench directed Director of Medical Services to ascertain and decide about the social status of ***Sailaja***[108] by setting aside the decision of single Judge bench (Presided over by Ramaswamy J.). The Division Bench avoided giving verdict on the correctness the views taken by the single Judge, Ramaswamy. In one of his extra judicial writings, Ramaswamy J. commented, "I had a hearty laugh for their religious and relentless devotion to alternative remedy, the sense of Justice rendered by the learned Judges by shrinking their responsibility to decide the constitutionality and correctness of the Judgment rendered by a Single Judge and directing a medical man to sit over a law man, a High Court Judge[109]. The correct position was again set by K. Ramaswamy J. in the famous ***Valsamma Paul v. Cochin University***.[110] The learned judge gave a meaningful definition of social democracy as "a way of life which recognises liberty, equality and fraternity as the principle of life. They are not separate items in a trinity[111] but they form union of trinity . The learned Judge explained, "Without equality, liberty would produce the supremacy of few over the many. Equality without liberty would kill individual initiative. Without fraternity, liberty and equality could not become a natural course of things".[112] This observation of J. was obviously inspired by Dr Ambedkar's last but one day before speech (25.11.1949) in the constituent Assembly pointing out social democracy a *Sine qua non* for political democracy.[113] With a view to make all the constitutional schemes and concession serve the real cause of social democracy the learned Judge put emphasis on the real status of beneficiaries and not to allow mingling of upper caste in the category of disadvantaged so as to chew all the benefits meant for dalits. On the issue of transplantation of some higher caste people in socially deprived class through adoption or marriage, K.Ramaswamy J. put a big radar that in order to claim benefit, the claimant must have suffered stresses and strains of deprivation. He ruled that "the object of reservation is to remove these handicaps, disadvantages, sufferings and restrictions to which the member of the Dalits or Tribes or OBCs were subjected and was sought to bring them in the mainstream of the nation's life by providing them opportunities and facilities.[114] The decision of Ramaswamy J. was prompted with vision to give effect to secularism, and mobility of all castes for national integration ensuring inter-caste marriages or adoption from one caste to another. It may require allowing "enough lee ways for free mobility and integration of all sections of society as homogeneous group." However, they have to be interpreted in a way so as to reconcile the right of the individual and society's right, namely, "social justice[115]". In view of this social justice requirement the benefit of social reservation was denied to upper caste people transplanted to depressed class by way of marriage or adoption or claiming benefit of reservation on false caste certificate. The cause of downtrodden has been adversely affected by bogus caste certificates. The evil of procuring such certificates has been great concern as the undeserving persons for social reservations have snatched opportunity from genuinely deserving SCs/STs and OBCs. In

Kumari Madhuril Patil v. Tribal Development[115], K. Ramaswamy J. noted the ground reality "the admission wrongly gained or appointment wrongly obtained on the basis of false social status certificate necessarily has the effect of depriving the genuine Scheduled Castes or Scheduled Tribes or OBCs candidates as envisioned in the Constitution the benefit conferred on them by the constitution"[117]. The genuine candidates are losers. Not only this, the false fabrication, after gained entry resort dilatory tactics and put all hurdles in due inquiry by scrutiny committee. Since student may be minor, at the time of application for admission, "it is the parent or guardian who may play fraud claiming false status certificate".[118] In order to add utmost expedition and promptitude Ramaswamy J. issued 15 commandments regulating issue of social status certificate of SCs, STs and OBCs.

In ***Air India Statutory Corporation v. United Labour Union***[119], taking the inspiration from Mahatma Gandhi[120], K. Ramaswamy J. gave a dynamic interpretation saying that the concept of socialism needs interpretation in the backdrop of the socio-economic justice envisioned in the Constitution. The issue in the case was whether on the abolition of Contract Labour system in an establishment the employer was under duty to absorb the workmen. Rmaswamy J. said that Contract Labour (Regulation and Abolition) Act, 1970 did not intend to denude workers of their source of livelihood. It is a socio-economic welfare legislation. Asserting the fundamental right nature of right to livelihood, he said "right to socio-economic justice and empowerment are constitutional rights. Right to means of livelihood is also a constitutional right. Right to facilities and opportunities are only part of and means to right to development. Without employment or appointment, the workmen will be denuded of their means of livelihood and resultant right to life, leaving them is lurch since prior to abolition, they had the work and there by earned livelihood."[121]

Air India Statutory Corporation decision is remarkable from many angles. It gives functional meaning to equality in light of Social Justice. Ramaswamy J. explained that "the concept of social justice embeds equality to flavour and enliven the practical content of life. Social Justice and equality are complementary to each other so that both should maintain their vitality. Rule of law, therefore, is a potent instrument of social justice to bring about equality in result."[122]

Second, Keeping in view the Preamble, fundamental rights and directive principles, viz. Articles 14, 15, 21, 38, 39, 43-A,46 and fundamental duties, Article 51-A a shift in Judicial orientation was suggested from private law principles to public law interpretation harmoniously fusing the interest of the individual entrepreneur and the paramount interest of community.[123] Ramaswamy J. pointed out that distinction between public law and private law is getting obliterated. The appropriate government and 'control' was suggested to be interpreted in the changing commercial scenario broadly in keeping with the constitutional goals and perspectives. The learned Judge summarised 13 principles to view control.

The constitution of the Corporation or instrumentality or agency or corporation aggregate or Corporation sole is not of sole material relevant to decide whether it is by or under the control of the appropriate government under the Act.

If it is a statutory Corporation, it is an instrumentality or agency of the State. If it is a company owned wholly or partially by a share capital, floated from public exchequer, it gives indicia that it is controlled by or under the authority of the appropriate government.

In commercial activities carried on by a Corporation established by or under the control of the appropriate government having protection under Articles 14 and 19 [2], it is an instrumentality or agency of the State.

The State is a service Corporation. It acts through its instrumentalities, agencies or persons -natural or juridical.

The governing power, wherever located, must be subject to the fundamental constitutional limitations and abide by the principles laid in the Directive Principles.

The framework of service regulations made in the appropriate rules or regulations should be consistent with and subject to the same public law principles and limitations.

Though the instrumentality, agency or person conducts commercial activities according to business principles and are separately accountable under their appropriate bye-laws or Memorandum of Association, they become the arm of the government.

The existence of deep and pervasive State control depends upon the facts and circumstances in a given situation and in the alternate situation it is not the sole criterion to decide whether the agency or instrumentality or person is by or under the control of the appropriate Government.

Functions of an instrumentality, agency or person are of

public importance following public interest element.

The instrumentality, agency or person must have an element of authority or ability to effect the relations with its employees or public by virtue of power vested in it by law, Memorandum of Association or bye-laws or Articles of Association.

The instrumentality, agency or person renders an element of public service and is accountable to health and strength of the workers, men and women, adequate means of livelihood, the security for payment of living wages, reasonable conditions of work, decent standard of life and opportunity to enjoy full leisure and social and cultural activities to the workmen.

Every action of the public authority, agency or instrumentality or the person acting in public interest or any act that gives rise to public element should be guided by public interest in exercise of public power or action hedged with public element and is open to challenge. It must meet the test of reasonableness, fairness and justness.

If the exercise of the power is arbitrary, unjust and unfair, and public authority, instrumentality, agency or the person acting in public interest, though in the field of private law, is not free to prescribe any unconstitutional conditions or limitations in their actions.

The above control tests were evolved in view liberalised free economy, private and multinational entrepreneurship resulting into wider commercial production. The learned Judge made clear-Even some of the public corporations are thrown open to the private national and multinational investments. It is axiomatic, whether or not industry is controlled by government or public corporations or statutory form or administrative clutch or private agents, juristic persons, corporation whole or corporation sole, their constitution, control and working would also be subject to the same constitutional limitations given in the trinity, viz., Preamble, the Fundamental Rights and the Directive Principles. They throw open an element of public interest in its working. They share the burden and shoulder constitutional obligations to providc facilities and opportunities enjoined in the Directive Principles, the Preamble and the Fundamental Rights enshrined in the Constitution.

(xi) Preamble as Basic Structure and Secularism With Positive Connotation

In ***S. R. Bommai v. Union of India***[124] K. Ramaswamy J. was the first Judge to declare Preamble as basic feature of the Constitution. It was quoted with approval by the Lord Chief Justice of England in his speech on the occasion of Silver Jubilee celebration of the Supreme Court of India. It was also referred to and was commended by Justice V. R. Krishna Iyer in his book.[125]

After citing a number of authorities on secularism, K. Ramaswamy J. gave a fresh meaning in ***S. R. Bommai v. Union of India***[126] to secularism "to represent faiths born out of the exercise of rational faculties, to enable people to see the imperative requirements for human progress in all aspects and cultural and social advancement and indeed for human survival itself. "Secularism has many positive connotations so as to help liberation of mankind and liberation of human soul from bondage of ignorance, superstition, irrationality, injustice, fraud, hypocrisy, and oppressive exploitation[127]. He pointed out that secularism operates as a bridge to cross over from tradition to modernity.[128] For him secularism does not believe in harking back but believes on positive line in basic values of freedom, equality and fellowship and development. What India needs more is the increasing secularization of society and culture with a sense of tolerance.

Reiterating secularism as basic structure of the Constitution K. Ramaswamy J. in triology of cases upheld State efforts to separate secular activities from religious matters. In ***A. S. Nagayana Deekshitulu v. State of A.P.***[129] on March 19, 1996 a division bench of K. Ramaswamy and B. L. Hansaria JJ. upheld the constitutionality of A.P. Charitable and Hindu Religious Institutions and Endowments Act, 1987 abolishing the hereditary rights of Archaks and office-holders. Decision given by Ramaswamy J. expresses his sense of compassion for poor Archaks in small temples by upholding a social security scheme worth Rs 75 crores formulated under the said Act. With a view to uphold the constitutionality of the Act, Ramaswamy J. in his learned Judgment cited excerpts of slokas from different religious books, authorities on religious writings and ruled that Articles 25 and 26 protect only integral or essential part of religion. Non-integral or non essential parts of religion are secular in character and can be regulated by legislation. The learned Judge pointed out that while performance of religious service is integral part of religion, the priests or Archaks performing such service are not essential. Hansaria J.

supplemented. Again, in ***Bhuri Nath v. State of J&K***[130] speaking for the court consisting of K. Ramaswamy and G. B. Patnaik JJ., Justice Ramaswamy upheld the constitutionality of J & K. Shri Mata Vaishno Devi Shrine Act, 1988 which provided for better management, administration and governance of Shri Mata Vaishno Devi Shrine vesting funds etc. in Board. Governor of J & K was made ex-officio Chairman of the shrine Board and in the case Governor being a non-Hindu alternate arrangement was to be made by the Governor nominating an eminent person professing Hindu religion and qualified to be a member of the Board, as chairman of the Board. The issue raised before the Court related to the exercise of power by the Governor: could he exercise his power as Chairman on his own or on the advice of the Council of Ministers. Ramaswamy J. speaking for the Court ruled that Governor was to exercise his powers, as Chairman of the Shrine Board on his own and not on the advice of the Council of Ministers. That helped the development of the shrine free from political interference. As per P. P. Rao, Senior Advocate of the Supreme Court of India on visit of the Mata Vaishno Devi Shrine "he was happy to see the enormous development that had taken place since then (Judgment of the Court). The Board officials expressed their gratitude to the Supreme Court."[131]

The net effect of Justice Ramaswamy's Judgment in Vaishno Devi Shrine Case was noted by The Hindustan Times in its editorial dated 16th of January, 1997. It read: "Perhaps the most significant part of the Judgment is the emphasis on "secularising the matters of religion" that fell outside the rituals and other practices that formed an integral part of its belief system. The manner in which the clergy operated or were treated in terms of financial and other benefits was one part of it. Considering that many places of worship in the country belonging to different religions were in a poor state of upkeep because the clergy manning them had developed a vested interest running them as a monopoly, if not a zamindari, the Judgment should have the way for the better assertion of the rights of the worshippers at such places. The management of several Muslim Wakf properties is a case in point. What is important is that the secular viewpoint should find application across the board so that no religious community has the feeling of being singled out."[132]

The third case related to the constitutionality of The U. P. Kashi Vishwanath Temple Act, 1983. The constitutionality was challenged in ***Sri Adi Visheshwara of Kashi Vishwanath Temple v. State of U.P.***[133] A larger bench than the earlier two cases was constituted to hear this case. Judgment of the three Judge bench consisting K. Ramaswamy, K. Venkataswami and G. B. Patnaik, JJ. was also handed down by K. Ramaswamy, J.. Speaking for the unanimous court, the learned Judge reiterated secularism as basic feature of the Constitution. The impugned Act drew a distinction between religious and secular functions of the Temple. It entrusted to the Board only secular function of administration and management of the Temple and Temple fund which are not essential part of religion. There was only change in management from Pandas to Board. Therefore, it was held that the impugned Act did not interfere with freedom of conscience and right to profess, practice and propagate religion. The Board consisted of eminent persons. Reiterating the view of the Court taken in ***A. S. Narayana Deekshitulu case***[134], Ramaswamy J. said that qualified persons would be appointed as Archaka, periodic training and continuing education would improve and augment excellence. The learned Judge gave very alive meaning to law as social engineering and emphasised history and custom to be vehicle of progress. It was pointed out that it is a well-settled law that administration, management and governance of the religious institution or endowment are secular activities and state could regulate them by appropriate legislation.

(xii) Special Honour and Some Opinions about K. Ramaswamy as Judge

K. Ramaswamy J. hailed from Andhra Pradesh. He served A.P. Government as Public Prosecutor and Government pleader and A. P. High Court. He also served on the Supreme Court bench from 1989, in length as SCI Judge in line of Justice K. Subba Rao and Justice O. Chinnappa Reddy (who hailed from A.P.) so far as longer service is concerned (for eight years). He had many appreciations both as Government Pleader and as Judge of A.P.H.C. and the SCI.

Some Jurist Judges pioneer in the field of social cause and leading members of the A.P.H.C. Bar and Supreme Court have expressed opinions about K. Ramaswamy J. which are presented in brief here.

*"With your experience as Public Prosecutor and Government Pleader and your capacity for hard work, I am sure you will make a successful Judge".

O. Chinna Reddy J.(on resumption of H.C. Judgeship by K. Ramaswamy vide letter dated 29.9.1982)

**"Hard work and sincerity always marked you as a good Advocate different from others."

P. Sriramulu, retired Judge and member, Jaswant Singh Commission.

"I was very happy to read your Judgment in ***Punjab National Bank v. Challapalli Sugara Ltd. (WA No. 836 of 1982). The Judgment is very well written and, to my mind, the approach is excellent. I am sure you will write many more such Judgments."

O. Chinnappa (Retd) J. (one of the Judges approving stand of Ramaswamy J. in S.L.P.)

****"I am glad to find that you have started utilising the strategy of public interest Litigation in creative and imaginative fashion."

P. N. Bhagwati J. Judge Supreme Court of India (later C.J.I) in his letter dated 20.7.1984.

Hon'ble Shri Justice K. Ramaswamy's life is classic example of continuing struggle against the twin evils of social and economic inequality into which the Indian society was ameshed. His rise to the Supreme Court was neither an accident nor a routine occurrence happening to anyone aspiring for high prizes in the cause of Justice. He personifies the dictum of Chief Justice Hughes of the Supreme Court that 'life is only work, then more work and then more work."

Bar citation at the time of unveiling of Portrait of Ramaswamy J. on 3.2.1996 by Hon'ble A. M. Ahmadi, C.J.I.

1. "Portrait is placed in the Association Hall to serve as an inspiration to the youngsters of the present and future generations. He had set an illustrious example that there is no inspiration without prescription, that genius is nothing but infinite capacity for hard work and that industry and integrity pay without fail".

Speech of Shri Venkata Reddy, Senior Advocate, former Advocate General and Chairman, the portrait (of Ramaswamy J.) Committee at the time of unveiling ceremony of portrait.

2. "Example set by Mr. Ramaswamy and Justice Ramaswamy should serve as a beacon light for all the oppressed classes, who, we hope, will be inspired by his portrait in the High Court Bar Association and by dint of hard work will achieve what he had achieved".

Shri M. Panduranga Rao, senior Advocate, on the same occasion.

3. "Dispensing Justice with a single minded devotion to the truth, Dr Ramaswamy won wide spread acclaim for his speedy and forth right decision in pronouncing Judgments in thousands of cases pertaining to Civil, Criminal, Constitutional, Taxation and Company Law matters with remarkable competence, a rare skill that set him distinctly apart as a distinguished doyen of the Judiciary. Insight and an in depth understanding of the human psyche have helped to enrich his Juridical mastery, galvanising the machinery of law with judgments that often call for clever adaptation and interpretation of the canons to comply with the changing social scenario. Respectfully flexible in his interpretation of the law yet undeterred and firm in his Judgments. Ramaswamy is a living exposition of the maxim 'Work is Worship'. His privileged presence is a beacon light to today's generation, a path finder for tomorrow".

Part of citation presented to Ramaswamy J. on the occasion of the unveiling ceremony of his portrait.

4. "I look upon you as a noble gentleman who synthesises the rare qualities of being learned and human".

Justice H.R. Khanna, Pitamah of Judicial Fraternity, in his teller dated 17th September, 1998.

5. "All the members of the Bar remember you very often. By your camphor like quickness in understanding the crux of the matter, by your humane and Justice-oriented approach, by your affability of the juniors, by your equal mindedness, by your equanimity, by your firm faith in God and in truth, by your courage of conviction, and above all, by your total and matchless honesty, you have carved out a place in all our hearts".

Letter of M. N. Krishnaswami, Senior Advocate, SCI and twice the former Vice-President, the Supreme Court Bar Association dated Oct.12, 1998.

6. "Your decisions were balanced, you have tried to administer Justice tempered with mercy. Other things being equal, you have tried to lean towards the weak, the deprived and the handicapped to whom Justice has been denied".

Justice K. Bhaskaran, former C.J., A.P.H.C. in his letter dated July 9, 1997 written on the eve of the retirement of Ramaswamy J.

7. "Justice Ramaswamy is a Jurist, reformist and a symbol of honesty all rolled into one human soul. His life portrays the saga of a mass born against odds defying the same and achieving many things which very people born with silver spoon could achieve. He is standing example of the proof of the proverb.-where is a will there is a way.

"As the saying goes -Success serves the brave, fortune favours the brave. For Justice Ramaswamy success did not come for asking, he had to prove his metal by his dint of hard work.

"His contribution for the development of constitutional law of this country is well known, his Judgments, his interpretation of constitutional provisions had a human touch. Thus, they converted into a living organ from a mere document".

Justice Santosh Hegde, Speech on the occasion of the unveiling of portrait of Ramaswamy J.

8. "From the day he took oath as a High Court Judge of High Court of Andhra Pradesh, he took the challenge to administer Justice without fear or favour and always preferred to uphold the rugged truth of life as sole purpose of the administration of Justice than niceties of law".

Chief Justice Devinder Gupta, C.J., A.P.H.C. at the time of unveiling of Portrait ceremony.

9. "He is a Judge with impeccable integrity. In fact, this is one of the most important criteria for any Judge. The entire Bar all over the country liked him for his impeccable integrity, simplicity and a good human being."

Shri P.H. Parekh, President, Bar Association of the Supreme Court speaking on the same occasion.

10. "His Judicial pronouncements are progressive and inspired by intense humanism. The law reports bear ample testimony of His Lordship's burning passion for social justice and for his deep concern for the uplift of the victims of unjust socio-economic structures. He held several posts and whichever post he held, he held it with dignity and distinction."

Shri C. Padmanabha Reddy, speech on the same occasion.

11. "Justice Ramaswamy shares Professor Amartya Sen's view that education, health, human security and dignity are not social gains of economic reform but are really economic gains of social reform,mere economic growth without Social Justice will not mean development but would remain a Rootless, Ruthless, Voiceless, Jobless and futureless growth."

Justice M.L. Venkatachalaiah, former C.J.I., Chairman, NHRC, Chairman, National Commission to Review the working of the Constitution, Tribute (in) Ceaseless and Relentless Journey, 2008, p. XIV.

Other Distinctions

1. "As Judge of the High Court, he had the distinction of disposal of the highest number of cases. In 1988, he had disposed of 7688 main matters and 2176 miscellaneous matters, the highest figure in country. From January to April, in this year (1989), he had disposed of 2441 appeals and a total of 4672 and earned a distinction."

   The HINDU, "Ramaswamy's distinction", dated 5.10.1989
2. On his retirement from the SCI, 'The Geography' a magazine of international repute published from Washington, U.S.A. took exclusive interview of Ramaswamy J. and published his full-page photograph in the June,1997 issue of the magazine.

K. Ramaswamy J. is the second SCI. Judge whose unveiling of portrait ceremony was celebrated after Justice Koka Subba Rao.

His contribution in preparation of NHRC comments placing Dalit/Caste issue on agenda the Durban Conference (inspite of Government of India's contrary stand) and his balance, brilliant and historic address to the Durban Conference on, "Racism, Racial Discrimination, xenophobia and Related Intolerance" on 6th Sept, 2001 attracted many commendations including thunderous applause from all delegates. Mary Robinson, Chairperson of the U.N. Commission and Secretary General of the Durban Conference appreciated NHRC stand and stated, "The NHRC has taken a principled stand on the issue and I heartily congratulate them".[135s]

3. In 1993 at Manila Conference of World Jurists Organisation, Ramaswamy J. read two papers - one on the Abolition of Child Labour and another on the Independence of Judiciary. Along with paper of Justice Donalds of South Africa his papers were accepted as lead papers. His suggestions on Independence of Judiciary were accepted with grace of a resolution passed by the Conference to that effect.
4. Ramaswamy J. worked with distinction as member, NHRC.

5. "He did splendid job as chairman of advisory panel of National Commission to Review the Working of the Constitution and in words of its Chairman, "the Commission was grateful for the splendid road-map he laid down for the betterment of the conditions of the dalits and the under privileged".

Justice M. N. Venkatachaliah, Tribute, Ceaseless and Relentless Journey (2008) pp. XI - XVI at p. XI).

(xiii) Souring Tine of Discrimination

Justice Ramaswamy's life is message both for have-nots and haves, he has been 'an eminent Judge and a great human being whose life is a shining example of the virtues of truthfulness, austerity, grit, determination and high purpose.'[136] He had experienced all odds to break a man in his life journey, viz. becoming motherless at the age of eighteen months, step mother's ill treatment,[137] having being refused shelter in his own house while suffering from small pox, no money to deposit fee and working as child agricultural labourer to collect money for the purpose of study and so on. Success came to him because one golden thread that ran throughout his whole life-both public and private- was, 'a firm determination not to refer the crooked chord of convenience to the golden met-wand of rectitude.'[138]

The steely framework of body and mind to fly in the sky with firm determination made Ramaswamy J. maker of his own destiny. But, one factor was such that he was made to feel it throughout his life. He was born in a scheduled caste family about which he speaks in his memoir, "The status of Dalits from the cradle to the grave is linked and tied with the caste." Everything was not in order in his judicial career. Inspite of his impressive performance at bar and as Government Pleader he could not get due place in the eye of those who matter in judicial appointments, on the one pretext or the other, both as Judge, A.P. High Court and Judge, Supreme Court of India.

1. Resisted and Delayed Appointment as a H.C. Judge

K. Ramaswamy was most appreciated Public Prosecutor, Government Pleader and private practitioner. Some of Hon'ble Judges had recorded their appreciations in their judgments.[139] His fairness was appreciated. Justice A. Gangadhar Rao had complimented him saying that after O. Chinnappa Reddy he was the only Public Prosecutor who had courage to say that a prosecution had no case if he found that conviction was not sustainable.[140] On the other hand, he argued cases with so confidence and ability as all the cases were allowed in appeal against acquittals. When around 20 appeals had been allowed against acquittals and were converted into convictions with sentences imposed, one senior Counsel complimented K. Ramaswamy saying it was a "field day for the prosecution" as due to his ability acquittals were got converted into convictions.[141] His good self was conscientious pleader. Two remarkable utterances on blank cheque offer on insistence to get accused convicted show what sort of great man he was- he said he was Prosecutor and not a persecutor[142] and on assurance that no third person would know about the offer of payment, he would say that there was one person between the two and that was his conscience and God.[143] He had established reputation as an honest, hard working and able counsel. By all standards he deserved elevation as a Judge to the High Court. But he could not be elevated in due course.

1. When Chief Justice Sri Sambashiv Rao Garu initiated his name for elevation and consulted four of Senior Judges of the High Court (informal Collegiums at that time), they did not approve on whimsical ground that he was too young to be elevated.[144] He was 45. The reason was not convincing as 45

Table 12

Sl. No.	*Name of Incumbent*	*Date of birth*	*Date of appointment as H.C. Judge*	*Age*	*Date of elevation to SCI*	*Age*	*CJI*
1.	Sri Y. V. Chandrachud	12.7.1920	19.3.1961 (Bombay)	40 yrs,	28.8.1972	52	22.2.1978 to 11.7.1985
2.	Sri P.N. Bhagwati	21.12.1921	21.7.1960 (Gujarat)	38 yrs	July, 1973	51	12.7.1985 to 20.12.1986
3.	Sri R.S. Pathak	25.11.1924	1962 Allahabad	37 yrs	20.2.1978	53	21.12.1986 to 18.6.1989

(Contd.)

(Contd.Table 12)

Sl. No.	*Name of Incumbent*	*Date of birth*	*Date of appointment as H.C. Judge*	*Age*	*Date of elevation to SCI*	*Age*	*CJI*
4.	Sri S. Murtza Fazl Ali	20.12.1920	9.4.1958 J & K	37+	2.4.1975	55	---
5.	K. Ramaswamy	13.7.1932 (as per school certificate)	29.9.1982 A.P.	50+	16.10.1989	57+	---

year could not be too young age for elevation to the High Court, as many appointments had been done to the different High Courts in late thirties of age of the appointees and from 1, 2, 3 given below became CJI in due course.[145] The comparative details are given below.

In A.P. High Court itself one person was elevated as Judge who was younger to him.

2. Second time the High Court Chief Justice, who had succeeded the earlier C.J. violently turned down the suggestion of his elevation.[146]

3. On insistence of the Government of India through Chief Minister, High Court Chief Justice sent the reply that his case would be considered at the appropriate time.[147] And, when the Union Government insisted by pointing out one of earlier recommendees being younger to him, the Chief Justice High Court instead of recommending his name in the proper form, used the language as if he was not competent for appointment as a judge.

4. When K. Ramaswamy's case was processed along with others, the C.J.I. did not cleverly clear his name but ultimately agreed to his appointment.[148]

When his name reached to the President, Sri Neelam Sanjiva Reddy did not sign the warrant for six months which could be signed by his successor in the noble office of the President, Sri Giani Zail Singh.[148] He joined as Additional Judge, A.P. High Court on 29th September, 1982. Obviously his experience with the Chief Justice was not happy. He realised and felt from the core of heart that he was appointed at the instance of the executive in spite of the damaging remark of the Chief Justice of the High Court- whose remark was not well founded. In words of Ramaswamy J., "It would be obvious that the said comment (as to his incompetence) was motivated, prejudicial and contrary to the facts because I hail from the Dalit community and so I was presumed to be incompetent." His heart breaking expression can be seen in other context in his own words:

"When I have established transparency in my character, impeccable integrity and honesty and outstanding performance of my duty, as mentioned by the distinguished members of the Bar in the High Court as well as the Supreme Court on the respective dates of my elevation and retirement, characterising my being an incompetent person for appointment as a judge of the High Court reveals the mindset as being prejudicial against a Dalit who was discriminated against all the qualities mentioned by people who matter. Perhaps (there might have been) many more victims of this kind of discrimination in other High Court."[150]

It is another matter that he was confirmed as a permanent Judge within three months of his joining.[151]

2. Resisted and Delayed Appointment as a Judge of SCI

Again the story of resistance was repeated in the case of his elevation to the SCI. It appeared that his name was recommended by the Government of India in October, 1987. But the proposal was turned down by the then Chief Justice of India.[152]

Again in November, 1988 his name was considered for elevation to the SCI and at that time too, the Chief Justice of India turned it down.[153]

Third time, initially he was offered Chief Justiceship of Sikkim and on his declination to join that due to no work in that small Court, he was chosen for elevation to SCI. On 4th October, 1989 he received a phone call from Hon'ble CJI, E.S. Venkataramaiah to reach Delhi by the evening of 5th October, 1989.[154] He was sworn in as judge of the Supreme Court on 6th October, 1989.

Justice Ramaswamy could not be elevated to the Supreme Court in 1987 and in 1988 in spite of government's insistence due to lack of concurrence of the then Chief Justice of India, Hon'ble Mr. Justice R. S. Pathak. The resistance and delay was bound to call reaction, feeling and thinking about the incidences.

Justice Ramaswamy's feeling was that at third time it was at the behest of the executive that his name was proposed and the Hon'ble CJI was gracious enough to accept the proposal. In his estimation the new CJI was a different person from his predecessor "who did not want a Dalit would become the Chief Justice of India in the 20th Century and within 50 years of Independence."[155]

3. Discrimination in Assignment of Works as a Judge

The other discrimination experienced by Justice Ramaswamy was treatment of acting Chief Justice of Andhra Pradesh High Court with him for his candid writing of scholarly judgment in a judicious way. As an Additional Judge of A.P.H.C. his dutiful fairness was not appreciated. In a matter of denial of appointment to a person as a clerk on charge of his being associated with Naxalites and thereafter appointment done on direction of a single Judge bench, Ramaswamy J. was sitting in appeal along with Justice P.C. Reddy. Both agreed as to dismissal as remedy had already been given by appointing the candidate under the direction of single judge. They differ as to non-disclosure of materials collected on the back of the candidate. Reddy J. took view that there was no violation of the principle of natural justice.[156] Ramaswamy J. showed dissent with the view of Reddy J. on two grounds - one legitimate expectation of appointment on selection for appointment and the other requirement of the principle of natural justice.[157] Reddy J. wanted from Ramaswamy J. to withdraw dissent on merit. Even as an additional judge he stuck to his stand.[158] Reddy J. got annoyed and when he became Acting CJ he did not assign any judicial work worth reckoning. On humiliation of being ignored for assignment of important matters on unwanted and unjudiciously, Ramaswamy J. wrote many letters to him on ignoring his position and assigning worthwhile works even to his juniors but no change in attitude came out.[159] He wrote to his colleagues also pressing for full Court reference to discuss the issue. No judge came forward. On demand of decency, judicial decorum and his being a disciplinarian, he remained cool and did not divulge the matter of internal administration though seriously objectionable but took the matter to be noticed by colleagues "who showed little interest, either they did not like to incur the displeasure of the ACJ or because it happened to a Dalit judge and, more likely both."[160]

4. Victim of Media Mindset

He had also fallen victim of social mindset when the controversy of impeachment of Justice V. Ramaswamy, then Judge Supreme Court of India and earlier Chief Justice of Punjab and Haryana High Court was at the top of newspapers. One Indian magazine published for NRIs inserted photograph of K. Ramaswamy J. in the news relating to Justice V. Ramaswamy. It was done inspite of the fact that K. Ramaswamy had never been Chief Justice of Punjab and Haryana High Court of which corruption charge against V. Ramaswamy J. related. Not only this, K. Ramaswamy J. was one of the members of two Constitution Benches dealing with the corruption charge of V. Ramaswamy J.. For his predominant concerns with the dignity of the judiciary he did not sue that magazine for damages, in spite of his character, integrity, reputation and personal image tarnished (As also advised by many persons to file a suit for damages). But what did he feel is remarkable, "this is indicative of the mindset of the people that the poor are generally corrupt."[161]

In present day controversy of ***Collegiums v. NJAC*** the experience of K. Ramaswamy J. may throw some light on solution. It is common knowledge that 1980s has been not regarded in good taste for judicial appointments to the higher judiciary for impression that Law Ministers had been assertive. Perhaps Collegiums emerged during early 1990s in that background. But, it is also true that it was that period when for the first time apex court experienced the taste of the services of SCs, OBCs and Women. K. Ramaswamy J.'s query is most truth searching:

"Had I not been recommended by the Executive and ultimately appointed, would it not have amounted to a denial of opportunity to the poor to have their representative in the judiciary? Without representation to all sections of the society can the judiciary be called a representative institution or should it be termed as oligarchy, a monopoly of the dominant class? Does the nominee of the Executive betray the efficacy of the Judicial process or contribute to degenerate conduct or rectitude?"

(xiv) Everlasting Exemplary Contribution of Justice K. Ramaswamy

The life and achievement along with performance of Ramaswamy J. is message and example. His non-judicial life is tale of rising from dust to summit on practised motto- work, more work and more and more work by winning over hurdles in the life. His Autobiography reveals how as a young boy he had to bear the treacherous and torturous treatment of maternal aunt and his step mother, he was forced to live as a paying guest in his own house and ultimately made homeless with the option of reading in lamp post and living on pial (Dalan) of the house of some other person, he had to live without meal many a days, one meal in a day many a times, work as agricultural labourer on ten annas a day, cook for others and so on. But, he neither broke nor bent before all odds and adverse situations. He had to earn to learn and he did earn and learnt. One redeeming factor of his life was that his urge for learning, committed effort and brilliance was appreciated with possible help and encouragements by dedicated and kind hearted teacher like Malikarjun Rao and a great and humane teacher, good administrator and strong disciplinarian headmaster Sri K. Seetharama Swamy and others who helped him with books and moral support by allowing private classes held by them without tuition fee.

His judicial life shines with glory of a humane judge, speaking the language of social justice within the framework of Preamble, Fundamental rights and Directive Principles of State Policy imbibing international standard of viewing human rights and human justice.

Gandhian and Ambedkarite human touch and steely framework, firm and clear commitment to life will leave him long remembered with examplary solution of problems. It is common knowledge that judicial empire is breaking due to overcrowd of arrears, delay and sometimes lack of openness. All problems are interconnected- lack of quick disposal breeds piling of arrears, arrears cause delay and more delay. Non-disposal of cases and pronouncement of judgments at once after the completion of arguments cause delay, arrears and sometimes, suspicions. Judicial life of Ramaswamy J. may provide guidance to solve many a problems.

1. As a A.P. High Court Judge he did not allow adjournment as matter of routine. He allowed adjournment in exceptional cases when the Counsel was unwell or made candid request that he could not receive material instructions from the party and sought short accommodation for that purpose.[162]
2. He never reserved any case for judgment.[163]
3. As soon as the arguments were concluded, he dictated the judgment in open Court.[164]

4. He seldom went on leave and his presence on the Court was maximum i.e. 207 days out of 210 during the period from 1.1.1987 to 31.12.1987; 206 days out of 208 days during the period from 1.1.1988 to 31.12.1988 and 152 out of 156 days during the period from 1.1.1989 to 5.10.1989. He had record of disposal cases,[165] as The Hindu dated 5.10.1989 published, he disposed of 7688 main matters and 2176 miscellaneous matters in 1988.

As a vacation Judge in A.P. High Court he continued to sit up to 11 in the night with a view to finish the work. He did not retire from the Bench until he finished the work of the day.[166]

As the Judge of apex Court too, his way of handling the cases is exemplary.[167]

1. He adopted five principles to tackle the backlog of cases:
   (i) He disposed of posted cases and avoided granting needless adjournments[167];
   (ii) In S.L.P. cases, instead of granting leave, after the notice was served, the cases were heard and disposed of;[168]
   (iii) In order to avoid delay, after hearing for admission, in case of interference, short notice was directed to be served through Court as well as Dasti service by the Counsel so that service on respondent was effected at once;[169]
   (iv) As soon as notice was served and counter filed, without grant of leave and kept pending, cases were disposed of at the notice stage itself[170] and
   (v) Judgments were dictated then and there in the Court.[171]
2. On Mondays and Fridays a large number of cases were posted. From the date of his presiding over the Bench, he never rose without disposing all the listed cases.[172]
3. When necessary, he used to sit until 7.30 p.m. and cleared the board.[173]

K. Ramaswamy J.'s self imposed motto, mission and commitment was that-

"Justice is not only done, but manifestly seen to have been done and should be done expeditiously without needless protraction."[174]

(xv) Messages of Jusice Ramaswamy's Life and Judicial Aspirations

Message for unprivileged and hard pressed persons

"Bear sufferings with fortitude and muster inner strength to survive."

"Mission is to be discovered which has to be fulfilled in right earnestness with firm determination and clear visions, undeterred by hurdles and adversities in the way. The life is a continuous struggle for one's advancement".

"Virtue is its own reward. Brilliance is loved and encouraged".

"Life is education. Learning gives creativity, creativity leads to thinking, thinking provides knowledge, and knowledge makes the man great".

Messages for Judicial Concern

"Faith of people in a democracy governed by rule of law will be sustained by expeditious dispensation of Justice".

"The Constitution through its Preamble, Fundamental Rights and Directive Principles created a secular state based on the principle of equality and non-discrimination, striking a balance between the rights of the individuals and the duty and commitment of the State to establish an egalitarian social order."

"Pluralism is the keynote of Indian culture and religious tolerance is the bed-rock of Indian secularism".

"Political democracy can last long only if social democracy is ensured. Social democracy means, 'a way of life which recognises liberty, equality and fraternity as principles of life... they form union of trinity. Without equality, liberty would produce the supremacy of the few over many. Equality without liberty would kill individual initiative. Without fraternity, liberty and equality could not become a natural course of things".

Cf. Dr Ambedkar's closing speech on 25.11.1949 in the Constituent Assembly - "What we must do is not to be attained with mere political democracy; we must make our political democracy a social democracy as well. Political democracy cannot last unless there lies on the base of it a social democracy".

"The heart of judicial independence is judicial individualism. With a view to make the formal equality the equality in fact and real the role of the Judge is not merely to interpret the law but also to lay new norms of law and mould the law to suit the changing social and economic scenario so that the ideals enshrined in the Constitution become meaningful and reach the so far unreached and ensure that they enjoy the results in reality".

"Judges are participants of the living stream of national life, steering the law between the danger of rigidity on the one hand and formlessness on the other. - a judge must be a jurist endowed with a legislator's wisdom, historian's search for truth, prophet's vision, capacity to respond to the needs of the present, resilience to cope with the demands of the future and decide objectively constitutional issues, disengaging himself from every personal influence or predilection."

"The Judicial function of the Court.... Is to build up Judicial statesmanship and judicial review is for smooth social change under the rule of law with a continuity of the past to meet the dominant need and aspirations of the present."

References

1. Roscoe Pound, Jurisprudence, Vol. I. Etymologically and in its broadest sense Jurisprudence is the Science of law.
2. Harold J. Laski, A Grammer of Politics - "Jurisprudence is the eye of law".
3. Martin Luther King, Jr., Letter from Birmingham Jail, Albama, 16th April, 1963, Atlantic Monthly, Aug. 1963 (issue), p. 78.
4. I.L.O. Philadelphia Declaration, 1944.
5. Warren C.J., The Law and Future, 52, Fortune, 106 (Nov., 1955).
6. Felix Frankfurter J.
7. Marbury v. Madison, 2 L Ed. 60; 54.S. (1 Cranch) 137 (1803), Marshall C.J.
8. 347 U.S. 483 (1954). See also 349 U.S. 294 (1955).
9. 60 U.S. (19 How.) 393 (1857).
10. 163 U.S. 537 (1896).
11. Edgar Bodenheimer, Jurisprudence - The Philosophy and Method of the Law (1974) p. 372.
12. 347 U.S. 483 (1954).
13. A.I.R. 1964 S. C. 149.
14. A.I.R. 1976 S.C. 490 : (1976) 2 SCC 310.
15. 1992 Supp (3) SCC 217.
16. State of Madras v. Champkam Dovairajan A.I.R. 1951 S.C. 226.
17. Harlan J's humanist touch in Plessy v. Fergusan on the plea that American Constitution is colour blind and disallowing segregation policy in his historic dissent sowed the seed of change which became a tiny tree in Brown v. Board of Education.
18. Warren C.J. ruled 'Separate can never be equal' in Brown's case. He delivered unanimous decision after great imaginative persuasion be he was a great man with human touch. He had worked only for one day on the Supreme Court. His human touch was so kind and impressive that when a businessman inquired from the Negro watchman standing on the gate of the Court how did he feel of the new Chief Justice, the answer of the watchman

was "For the first time I have realised that I am also a human being." Such was the human element in Earl Warren.

19. Subba Rao J.'s dissent in T. Devadasan v. Union of India A.I.R. 1964 S.C. 149, his views in R. Chitralekha v. State of J. and K. and extra judicial writing Social Justice and Law show how large-hearted humanist he was.

20. Krishna Iyer has been well known judge speaking for poor, helpless and disprivileged. Prison reform, workers right and continuous endeavour to see dalits, backwards and women on superior courts had been mission of his life. He had written many letters to P.M., Union Law and Social Welfare ministers. His zeal and sincerity to see representative/reflective judiciary in his speech provoked some advocate to invoke contempt proceeding which could not be allowed by Advocate General on his following reply letter :
"The truth is that I am for Nayadis (humblest of Dalits) and their upliftmen in status and educational and public service opportunity, to such an extent that they may sit on the pedestal of high judicial office with no less distinction as those now on the Bench. They may land social lustre to the institution and no stigma to the Bench. Please call Dr Ambedkar's statement : "The Hindus wanted the vedas and they sent for Veda Vyas who was not a caste Hindu. The Hindu wanted an epic, and they sent for Valmiki who was an untouchable. The Hindus wanted a Constitution and they sent for me."

A. Krishnaswamy, "V.R. Krishna Iyer : A Living Legend," Universal Law Publishing Co. Pvt. Ltd., 2000.

Justice Iyer had also exposed H.C. Bar resolution against his inhered willingness to see dalits on superior courts to amount "that the High Court is so high and the Panchama proletarians so low that they can never be thought of for Judgeship and even to mention it as a possibility on equal terms is depreciation of the High Court."

For Krishna Iyer's human face and human justice see, Anirudh Prasad Chandra Sen, Pratap Singh, "Judicial Power and Judicial Review" EBC, Lucknow (2012).

21. Thurgood Marshall was son of a freed slave who hand worked as a dining car waiter, but had served Negores immensely as Counsel of National Association for the Advancement of Colored People (NAACP). His greatest success was the unanimous decision of Warren Court when as an advocate he convinced Chief Justice Warren to end School segregation in Brown v. Board Education 347 U.S. 483 (1954). He also served on S.C. Bench for nore than two decades (1967-1991).

22. For contribution of Thurgood Marshall and Ramaswamy J. see Anirudh Prasad and Chandra Sen Pratap Singh, Judicial Power and Judicial Review, EBC (2012) pp. 799-800.

23. *Ceaseless and Relentless Journey, EBC, 2009.* p. 60 (letter of O. Chinnappa Reddy J. dated Sept. 29, 1982).
24. *Ibid.* p. 61 (lettr of P. Sriamulu). His work was also appreciated by Chief Justice Obul Reddy openly and C. Krishna Reddy J. reposing his faith to guide the Court on correct lines; *Ibid.* p. 62.
25. *Ibid.* p. 64.
26. (1983) 2 APLJ 127.
27. Letter cited in Ceaseless and Relentless Journey, p. 68.
28. A.I.R. 1984 A.P. 75.
29. (1985) 2 APLJ 361.
30. Ceaseless and Relentless Journey (2012) pp. 74-75.
31. *Ibid.* pp. 75-76 (Letter of Justice P.N. Bhagwati dated 20.7.1984).
32. Ceaseless and Relentless Journey, p. 83.
33. Ceaseless and Relentless Journey (2008), p. 96.
34. B. Sen., Six Decades of Law, Politics and Diplomacy : Some Reminiscences and Reflections, Universal Law Publishing Co. Pvt. Ltd., p. 294.
35. Letter dated Oct. 12, 1998 quoted at p. 155 of Ceaseless and Relentless Journey (2008).
36. Upendra Baxi, "Explorations in the Geographies of [Injustice]" (in) S.K. Verma and K. Kusum (eds.), Fifty years of the Supreme Court of India : its Grasp and Reach (OUP, 2000) 156-209 at p. 176.
37. O. Chinnappa Reddy J., as Chief Guest on the occasion of Ramaswamy's Felicitation Committee, Hyderabad, Ceaseless and Relentless Journey (2008) p. 152.
38. 347 U.S. 483 (1954).
39. (1996) 2 SCC 715 (popularly termed as Ajit Singh I case).
40. (1999) 7 SCC 209.
41. 347 U.S. 483 (1954).
42. (1976) 2 SCC 310 = A.I.R. 1976 S.C. 490.
43. 1992 Supp. (3) SCC 217.
44. Ceaseless and Relentless Journey (2008), p. 226.
45. (1995) 2 SCC 745.
46. Ceaseless and Relentless Journey (2008), p. 22.
47. (1997) 6 SCC 283.
48. *Ibid* at p. 300. For further discussion see, Chapter 11C 11(5) of this book.
49. Ceaseless and Relentless Journey (2008), pp. 175-175.
50. A.I.R. 1995 S.C. 992.
51. Harold J. Laski, A Grammar of Politics, S. Chand and Co. Ltd.; Ram Nagar, New Delhi, first Indian Reprint, 1979 p. 577 (originally published by George Allen & Unwin Publishers Ltd. 1925, 1930, 1934, 1938 and 1967).

52. A.I.R. 1996 S.C. 1051.
53. *Ibid.*, p. 1053.
54. *Ibid.*, p. 1054.
55. *Ibid.*, p. 1057.
56. (1995) Supp. (2) SCC 549. (D/on 22.2.1995).
57. *Ibid.*, p. 550.
58. *Ibid.*
59. O. Chinnappa Reddy J., "Judicial Process and Social Change", (1981) 1 SCC J. 4.
60. Quoted from Ceaseless and Relentless Journey (2008), p. 257.
61. Chief Justice (of A.P. High Court) Devinder Gupta, *Ibid*, p. 256.
62. Views expressed by Shri C. Padmanabha Reddy on the occasion of portrait installation of Ramaswamy J. by Bar Association of A.P. High Court; *Ibid*, p. 261.
63. Granville Austin in his most celebrated and off quoted by our apex court, The Indian Constitution - Cornerstone of Nation (1966, Oxf. Univ. Press) stated the Indian Constitution is predominantly "a social document aimed at furthering the goals of social revolution or attempts to foster to revolution."
64. K. Subba Rao, Social Justice and Law, ICPS (1974), p. 251.
65. *Ibid*, p. 251.
66. A.I.R. 1964 S.C. 179.
67. A.I.R. 1964 S.C. 1823.
68. Ceaseless and Relentless Journey (2008) p.
69. *Ibid* p.
70. 78 L. Ed. 873 : 347 U.S. 483 (1954) and also 349 U.S. 294 (1955).
71. A.I.R. 1976 S.C.490 : (1976) 2 SCC 310.
72. A.I.R. 1978 S.C. 597 : (1978) 1 SCC 248.
73. (1980) 3 SCC 625.
74. (1984) 3 SCC 161 : A.I.R. 1984 S.C. 802.
75. (1992) 175 C.L.R. 1.
76. (1995) 5 SCC 457.
77. In-house procedure is a procedure short of impeach to deal with High Court and the Supreme Court Judges for bad conduct which does not reach the gravity of misbehaviour. It is self-regulatory procedure adopted by the judiciary itself. Since C.J.I. is the first among the judges, he should be approached and apprised with necessary material against the erring judge and be requested to deal with matter appropriately. The in-house procedure had its impact and a message from the Chief Justice of India and Justice A.M. Bhattacharjee and Justice Vijaya Bahuguna resigned.
78. *Ibid.*
79. K. Ramaswamy, Social Justice and Rule of Law (in) Journal of Law and Social Policy, H.N.L.U. Raipur, Vol. 2, 2002, July, 2008, pp. 1-63 at p. 23.

80. A.I.R. 1993 SC 1126 (discussed in detail elsewhere) ; (1991) Supp. 1 SCC 600.
81. (1997) 8 SCC 191.
82. (1997) 8 SCC 191.
83. (1992) 175 CLR 1.
84. Arun Shourie, "Courts and Their Judgments".
85. Fifth Schedule of the Constitution - Whether a Boon or a Bane for Adivasis (Chapt. XXXII in) Ceaseless and Relentless Journey, 2008, p. 244 at p. 252.
86. *Ibid.*
87. Justice M.N. Venkatachalaiah, A Tribute (in) Ceaseless and Relentless Journey (2008) pp. XI-XVI at p. XIV.
88. (1998) 8 SCC 191.
89. *Ibid.*
90. A.I.R. 1986 A.P. 204.
91. Murali Krishnan case, A.I.R. 1986 A.P. 204, pp. 204-205.
92. 347 U.S. 483 (1954).
93. M. Krishnan case, p. 208.
94. *Ibid.*, p. 209.
95. *Ibid.*
96. (1992) 3 SCC 66.
97. Unni Krishnan v. State of A.P. (1993) 1 SCC 645 (Five Judge Bench) and T.M.A. Pai Foundation v. State of Karnataka A.I.R. 2003 S.C. 355 (2003) 6 SCC 696 (Eleven Judge Bench).
98. Articles 21-A and 51-A (K) added by The Constitution (86th Amendment) Act 2002 (w.e.f. 1.4.2010) For critical evaluation see Justice K. Ramaswamy Social Justice and Rule of Law (in 2(2) Journal of Law and Social Policy, H.N.L.U. Raipur (2008) pp. 1-63 at pp. 36-39.
99. (1992) 1 SCC 441.
100. (1995) 3 SCC 42. Other judges on the Bench were A.M. Ahmadi C. J. and M.M. Punchhi J.
101. (1992) 1 SCC 441.
102. (1995) 3 SCC 42.
103. *Ibid*, p. 101.
104. (1995) 3 SCC 42.
105. *Ibid*, pp. 73-74 (para 31).
106. A.I.R. 1986 A.P.209
107. (1986) IAPLJ40.
108. A.S. Sailaja v. Principal, Kurnool Medical College, A.I.R.1986 A.P.209
109. Ceaseless and Relentless Journey (2008) p. 85.
110. (1996) 3 SCC 545. (K.Ramaswamy and Hansaria JJ.)
111. *Ibid.* 553.
112. *Ibid.*

113. "What we must do is not to be attained with mere political democracy; we must make out political democracy a social democracy as well. Political democracy cannot last unless there lies on the base of it a social democracy". B.R.Ambedkar.
114. (1996) 3SCC 545 at pp. 565-566.
115. *Ibid* p. 557 (para 14)
116. (1994) 6SCC 241
117. *Ibid* p. 254 (para)
118. *Ibid.*
119. (1997) 9SCC 377. The bench consisted of K. Ramaswamy, B.L. Hansaria and S.B.Majumdar JJ. K. Ramaswamy J. delivered the main decision to which Majumdar J. concurred. Thus it was unanimous pronouncement on the fate of labourers.
120. Ramaswamy J. extensively cited from Gandhi's book Socialism of My Concept explaining urge to end grinding pauperism, absence of starvation among masses, economic equality by abolishing the eternal conflict between capital and labour etc. *Ibid*, at p.427(para 51)
121. *Ibid*. pp. 432-435. (para 57-58).
122. *Ibid.* p. 419 (para 43).
123. *Ibid* pp. 400-402 (para 14-15).
124. (1994) 3SCC1 at p. 205 (para 248).
125. See, Ceaseless and Relentless Journey (2008) p. 164.
126. *Ibid.*
127. (1994) 3SCC1 at p. 164(para 179).
128. *Ibid.*
129. *Ibid.*
130. (1996) 9SCC548.
131. (1997)2SCC 745.
132. Views expressed by P.P. Rao on the occasion of the unveiling of the portrait of Ramaswamy J. under the auspices A.P.H.C. Bar Association. Ceaseless and Relentless Journey (2008) p. 259.
133. Editorial, The Hindustan Times 16.1.1997.
134. (1997)4SCC 606(d/on march 14, 1997).
135. Quoted from Ceaseless and Relentless Journey (2008) pp.237-243 at p. 241.
136. The good words from the pen of former C.J.I. Venkatachalaiah in Tribute to Ceaseless and Relentless Journey (2008) p. x 1.
137. About which Justice Venkachalaiah J. commented, 'Through a Chinese adage', 'a step mother even made of china clay is dangerous'; *Ibid.*
138. *Ibid*. p. xiii.
139. Ceaseless and Relentless Journey (2008). Justice O. Chinnappa Reddy (as he then was a A.P.H.C. Judge) had paid economiums

to K. Ramaswamy in the Judgment, *Ibid* p. 48. So have done some other judges.

140. *Ibid*. p. 41.
141. *Ibid.*
142. *Ibid*. p. 44.
143. *Ibid*. p. 45.
144. *Ibid*. p. 59.
145. Anirudh Prasad and Chandrasen Pratap Singh, Judicial Power and Judicial Review, Eastern Book Co. (2012).
146. Ceaseless and Relentless Journey, F.B.C. (2008) p. 59.
147. *Ibid.*
148. *Ibid*. p. 60.
149. *Ibid.*
150. Ceaseless and Relentless Journey (2008), p. 156.
151. *Ibid.*
152. *Ibid*. p. 95.
153. *Ibid.*
154. *Ibid*. p. 96.
155. *Ibid.*
156. Ceaseless and Relentless Journey (2008), p.93.
157. *Ibid.*
158. *Ibid.*
159. Please see letters of Ramaswamy J. addressed to Acting Chief Justice and brother and sister judges given on pages 89 to 93 of Ceaseless and Relentless Journey, 2008.
160. *Ibid*., p. 94.
161. Ceaseless and Relentless Journey (2008), p.157
162. Ceaseless and Relentless Journey (2008), p. 64.
163. *Ibid.*
164. *Ibid.*
165. *Ibid*., pp. 80-82.
166. *Ibid*., p. 102.
167. *Ibid.*
168. *Ibid.*
169. *Ibid.*
170. *Ibid.*
171. *Ibid.*
172. *Ibid.*
173. *Ibid.*
174. *Ibid.*

PART – IV

ROHITH VEMULA AND HIS MESSAGE

ROHITH VEMULA
(A Dalit Scholar who left for Heavenly abode at 27)

11

Rohith Vemula: The Unblossomed Genious

On 17th January 2016, a 27 year intellectually brilliant Dalit Ambedkarite Rohith Vemula was compelled by torturing circumstances to end his life in a room of the hostel of Hyderabad Central University. He was a meritorious student. He never used his caste status for reservation benefit. He was a brilliant student at college and cleared CSIR fellowship twice. He was Ph.D. research scholar in Life Science Department of HCU. But, the bright student was not allowed to pursue his research after he completed his one year Ph.D. (Science, Technology and Societal Studies) Course work in June 2015 because of one police investigation and two by the university authorities based on a complaint lodged by an ABVP President of the Central University of Hyderabad – N. Susheel Kumar who had made mountain of a mole hill. On August 3, 2015 Mr Kumar posted anti-Ambedkar Students Association post on Facebook inciting hatred against ASA. Coming to know 30 students of ASA demanded apology from ABVP student leader. The bone of contention flared up when Susheel Kumar asserting that he was forced by mob to write an apology and upload it on Facebook and was attacked in V.C. Office leading to his hospitalisation. This was not that serious matter to attract union ministers. The lies of Susheel Kumar came to surface when hospital report revealed that there was no blunt trauma. Dr Shivananda, Chief Executive Officer of Archana Hospital, Madinaguda, where Susheel Kumar was admitted on August 4, 2015 after the alleged assault, talking to *The Hindu* clarified that except for a contusion on his left shoulder, there were no other signs of injury. "Any blunt injury" could not be verified because there won't be marks left off.[1] It is to be noted that Susheel Kumar was admitted on the same day of alleged attack. Furthermore, he was admitted for acute APPENDICITIS. As per version of Dr Anupam Rao, Senior Medical Officer of the University of Hyderabad "after collecting all the medical report of Susheel Kumar and examining them, I could not reach the conclusion that he developed appendicitis due to the alleged assault. There was one line that there was a bruise on his left shoulder. I could not say if he was allegedly punched or beaten up. I did not examine him as he did not come to me and the hospital's report does not mention that he had any external or visible injury." The Indian Express which published this version of Dr Anupam Rao also published the view of Deputy Security Officer of the University of Hyderabad, (D.S.O.) Dilip Singh, who told, "I did not see ASA members beating Susheel. At least it did not happen in front of me."[2]

A Critical and Rationalist Search Light on Vemula Matter

To very large extent Vemula suicidal incident has been obscured, confused and tried to wipe out its hardcore impact due to too much politicalisation – some expressing too much sensitivity and others devoid of human sympathy. The political action and reaction may be only a matter of pity. Apart from that socio-legal and living law issues reveal that Indian society, though developed, is still not out of the clutches of evils of discriminatory, inhuman and paradoxical culture. The constitutional vision have got blurred and frustrated in actual practice and warning of Dr Ambedkar that politico-legal democracy would be meaningless in absence of social democracy is continuing to be true in its letter and spirit.

Vemula's Credential

Vemula was a brilliant chap which is evident from the views of his school teachers and friends as well as performance. B. Kondiah, the principal of Andhra Pradesh Residential College, Kodigenahalli expressing his experience with Rohith as school boy in 2004, when he was a lecturer there, expressed the view, "Rohith was very intelligent student who showed a lot of promise. Getting admission in this college is difficult since we admit only brightest rural students after an entrance test." Rohith's chemistry teacher, J.V. Krishanaiah expressed the view, "He was a good student passed with first class. He studied Biology, Physics and Chemistry. His English was also good, though he was better at Telgu." His best friend who had financed him when Vemula's scholarship of Rs. 25000 was stopped by the university, Ramji expressed his view that "Rohith was the bright guy I met, I am still not able to process his death."

His academic performance was superb. In class XII his score was 521 out of 600 i.e. an impressive more than 86%. He cleared CSIR fellowship twice as a general/merit category student without taking help of reservation. So, in CUH he had got admission on the basis of merit.

Thus, he was an exceptionally brilliant S.C. student. He was born out of inter-caste marriage between a Vaddera Backward Caste husband and a Mala Scheduled Caste mother. But, his mother Radhika was separated (deserted) and Rohith was brought up by his mother, he remained Scheduled Caste and died as Scheduled Caste suffering persecution. In what condition he was brought up his suicide note expressed (and it is well known credited rule that a dying person never tells a lie), ".....I always was rushing. Desperate to start a life. All the while, some people, for them, life itself is curse. *My birth is my fatal accident. I can never recover from my childhood loneliness.* The unappreciated child from my past. I am not hurt at this moment. I am not sad. I am just empty. Unconcerned about myself. That's pathetic. And, that's why I am doing this."[3] Though, he had not taken, need not taken due to brilliance, benefit of a Scheduled Caste but his all acts at CUH indicated/ are clear proof that he was true Ambedkarite – educate, organise and agitate. A very clear picture has been painted by Kalpana Kannabiran, Professor and Director, Council for Social Development, Hyderabad, in these words, "From all his writing and his associations, there is no doubt whatsoever that Rohith identified himself as a Dalit son of Dalit mother; as a Dalit Ambedkarite, scholar and organiser; and as a co-traveller encountering the oppressions, discrimination and exclusion experienced by his Dalit compatriots on the university campus and outside."[4] His dalitship is clearly established by the Supreme Court decisions – latest of them being *Rameshbhai Dabhai Naika v. State of Gujrat.*[5] In case of a marriage between dalit mother and non-dalit father, the presumption of the child to belong to the caste of father is not conclusive or irrebuttable.

The Supreme Court laid down the principle – "it is open to the child of such marriage to lead evidence to show that he/she was brought up by the mother who belonged to the Scheduled Caste/ Scheduled Tribe. By virtue of being a son of a forward caste father he did not have any advantageous start in life but on the contrary suffered deprivation, indignities, humilities and handicap like any other member of the community to which his/her mother belonged. Additionally, that he was always treated as a member of the community to which his mother belonged not only by that community but by the people outside the community as well."[6]

Mental Stress Due to Discrimination, Humiliation and Financial Deprivation

The mental stress due to hostile discrimination, police case, university authorities working under influence of some powerful forces punishing only ASA members are obvious in view of the following :

1. One month pre-suicide letter to the Vice-Chancellor
   – to supply 10 mg of sodiumaside to all the Dalit students at the time of admission......[and] nice rope to the rooms of all Dalit students."[7]
2. "I request your highness to make preparation for the facility [of] "euthanasia" for students like me. And I wish you and the campus rest in peace for ever."[8]

   The above shows that some grave injustice was done to him.
3. **The Two Call Letters: First from Police, Another from Warden, CUH**

Vide letter dated Nov. 5, 2015 Sub-Inspector of Gachiboli Police Station summoned Rohith to record his statement in connection with the complaint lodged by ABVP leader Mandanam Susheel Kumar. In reply Rohith said:

"I deny the allegations made by Susheel Kumar which are false. I humbly request you not to proceed against me because I will be affected unduly for appearing in the case and my career will be spoilt. I belong to SC community and implicating me in a criminal offence amounts to atrocity on an S.C. person."[9] He was scared of the police calling in station with motive to arrest instead of visiting campus to interrogate.

The other letter dated 18th Dec., 2015 was received from the warden which rea: "This is with reference to the letter dated December, 17 received from the office of the Chief-Warden regarding vacating the hostel room immediately. Therefore, you are directed to clear your mess dues of Rs 9, 482 and vacate the room by 4 p.m. of December 18. Failing which necessary action shall be taken in this case. Please treat this as most urgent."[10]

One can easily understand mental stress on Rohith whose Rs 25000 per month scholarship had been stopped, who had to sent money to his mother regularly by borrowing from one friend named Ramji, owing Rs 40,000 to him. To be under tremendous stress was but natural added with fuel to fire of grief and anxiety by letter of Union Minister charging with "castiest, extremists and anti-national" credentials.

Before fateful suicide on January 17 Rohit had expressed his grief and lament before his friends – C. Ramji, P. Vijay Kumar and Parasnath – in utter anguish that he had literally become homeless.[11]

Credentials of Actors Influencing Committal of Suicide by Rohith

1. The Vice-Chancellor

Prof. (Dr) Appa Rao is said to become Vice-Chancellor of the University with blessings of power that be. He outsmarted 35 others to become V.C.[12]

As per Article of Teesta Setalvad, a noted Journalist, the present V.C. Appa Rao was Chief-Warden in 2002 who had asserted caste Hindu view by shifting a Dalit off his duties in the hostel mess – how can "we" have an "untouchable" "polluting" our food?" to his caste-driven place, sanitation duty. Ten students were rusticated then.[13]

The role of the university headed by the Vice Chancellor Appa Rao also presents some indicators – See the sequence —

(i) Susheel Kumar posted on facebook "*ASA goons are talking about hooliganism.*"

(ii) On 3.8.2015 ASA members asked him to remove that and tender apology. Something might have happened, but not that serious. He complained of attack on him. He filed a police case. The police and Registrar in their affidavit to the High Court reported that the injuries were minor and put it down as a scuffle between students.[14] That was natural and factually correct without any interpolation.

2. The Proctorial Board, as natural, in performance of its duty, recommended warning to both the parties and dropped further proceedings.

3. Another Proctorial Board Report (which was unusual) recommended permanent rustication of five Dalit students from the University and Sub-committee of the Executive Council, without holding an independent inquiry, endorsed the punishment recommended by the second report of the Proctorial Board.
4. The Executive Council chaired by Prof. Appa Rao decided to take many exceptional decisions on its own. The five Dalit students were expelled from hostel which meant they could only attend classes and use library during office hour, they were not to "participate in student's union election, enter the hostels, administration building and other common places in groups."[15] It amounted really to expulsion and social boycott. The role of V.C. did not appear to be fair, as the then Vice-Chancellor had ordered a fresh inquiry, in September, 2015, but Appa Rao did not abide by official decision of the earlier V.C. and rushed to punish Dalit students. The V.C. could not give accurate and convincing reasons for the question put by Anuradha Raman – "Why the flip-flop?" The Proctorial Board's findings recommended warning that both the ABVP student and Ambedkar Association students should be let off[16] with warning, but only Dalit students from ASA were censured. His answer was evasive. He responded, "Besides, all this was decided by the Proctorial Board, before I took over. The Board is a statutory body and decision was upheld by the sub-committee of the Executive Council. It is not our mandate to reopen the board decision." What about the Proctorial Board's earlier report? Why sub-committee of E.C. did not hold separate inquiry?

It is good of V.C. that he did not think expelled students to be anti-national.[17]

5. There appear to be enough evidence as to unreasonable, unfair, hasty and one-sided decision of the V.C. in view of five HRD ministry letters to V.C. based on the pressure of Union Labour Minister who had termed ASA activities as "casteist, extremist and anti-national."[18] About the role of overactive ministers and others on party line-less said, better.

Vemula : Nonetheless, a Scheduled Caste Chap

Amidst the all round efforts to confuse and muddle the Vemula issue the Indian Express published on Feb. 14, 2016 issue a detailed story of the life journey up and downs and hard pressed of Mala lady to nourish her children by hard work, tailoring and embroidery.[19] If we read between the lines the version of her adopting mother and father in law and analyse contradiction in their version, struggle of life of Radhika and way, surrounding her own declaration as Mala and actual facts during the formative stages of the education of Vemula and his brother and sister, it will leave no doubt about Rohith that he was a scheduled caste. Look the facts –

1. Anjali Devi, a backward class women took away in adoption one year old Radhika from the S.C. family struggling with acute poverty and leaving her under a tree all the day while working for livelihood outside.[20]
2. Anjali Devi, after the birth of two more daughters reduced the position of Radhika to a servant, as human nature is. A neighbour of Radhika's parent, Danamma said with four own children – two sons and two daughters, Anjali, "ill-treated Radhika and Radhika was to work like a servant."[21] Anjali often abused her, making frequent references to her Mala (S.C.) caste. When Radhika was 14 or 15, Dhanamma recollects, "Anjali once wondered why she had even brought" this useless Mala girl home."
3. As per Anjali Devi, adoptive mother, itself[22] "her relationship with Radhika changed five years after her marriage, and worsened when Radhika decided to take her caste as SC – Mala.[23]
4. There is contradiction in version of the Grandfather of Vemula and Anjali. His grandfather Venkateshwaslu said, "I was shocked when Rohith committed suicide and I was even more shocked when it was claimed that he was a dalit. We still don't believe Radhika belongs to a scheduled caste (S.C.). *If we had known, we would not have allowed the marriage in the first place. My son says even he did not know about Radhika's caste until Rohith's suicide, I swear.*"[24] Contrarily, the adoptive mother of Radhika, Anjali said she had told about Radhika to the boy's grandfather. In words of Anjali, "we did not hide the truth about Radhika's adoption and told him that she was from an S.C. family but was raised as a Vaddera. He had no objection."[25] Thus, both sides are not telling the whole truth.
5. The most important part of the report is the observation of Anjali's statement about what happened when Radhika was

left with no option by her Drunkard, abusing and beating husband but to return back to her adoptive mother's house, where too she was not welcomed and had to *move into "S.C. Colony" and that is there she took on her S.C. identity. "The children had just started going to school."*[26] (emphasis added)

6. The above S.C. identity is reinforced by Rohith's friend Riyaz Shaikh who said that Radhika and her children were not only to do menial jobs at Anjali's house but also *"they were never allowed to forget that Radhika had been adopted* – the things are speaking allowed for themselves.

(a) Radhika embraced S.C. identity after rejection by husband's side and parent's side and remained in that. The fact of adoption with no sincere desire to treat as own child and take menial job reminding her of Mala caste is of no significance, as she had no benefit of B.C.

(b) So was case with her husband's side which provided no benefit to her as B.C.

Thus, Radhika is an S.C. after accepting her S.C. identity.

(c) The children are definitely S.C. They had no benefit of B.C. grandmother or father being Backward community members. They started study as S.C. woman's son, they continued to have suffered the same stresses and strains, handicaps, disadvantages and humiliation of a Scheduled Caste person.

(d) Rohith's persecution was only due to his identity as Ambedkarite and nothing else.

Major Premise: Those who have suffered disadvantages, stresses and strains, humiliation etc. as S.C. would be schedule caste person, would fall in S.C. category.

Minor Premise: Vemula started study, continued and died as son of a brave S.C. lady who had suffered all odds of life and was brought up in that condition and acted as Dalit leader.

Conclusion : Rohith Vemula was nobody else than a S.C. scholar and hardcore Ambedkarite. Others are speaking to suit their point of view at present without having cared to help in any way in upbringing of Rohith from the start of schooling and Radhika as a gentlewoman does not say bad experiences with such contenders because she doesn't want to hurt anyone's feelings. But her residing in S.C. colony and embracing of S.C. identity, nourishing children in that culture, change of Rohith's name from his original name Manik Chakravarti to Rohith, his following of Ambedkar's mission and active membership of ASA, leave no option but to conclude that Rohith was Scheduled Caste and died as an Ambedkarite in an atmosphere of acute mental stress and pressure from University administration.

Politicisation of Caste Matter

In India, there is hardly a issue, which sooner or later, does not become highly politicalised caste issue.[27] The suicide note of Rohith Vemula raises very broad, serious, and issue of national importance if the nation is to survive and develop on right path. The danger signal is that, "The value of a man was reduced to his immediate identity, and nearest possibility. *To a vote. To a number. To a thing.* Never was a man treated as a mind. As a glorious thing made of start dust. In every field, in studies, in streets, in politics, and in dying and living." The post-Vemula suicide press reporting reveal the sad affair of the universities being converted into nursery of the political parties. Vote is the real consideration. It is said of a Russian Communist Party leader that when a group of students approached him with request to help him in political matters, he bluntly refused and asked to go "saying your first duty is to learn, your second duty is to learn and your third duty is also to learn." Can't our politicians think on such line?

Vemula episode arose out of students' politics guided by political power that be. Had university administration been imaginative tragedy could have been averted. The extraordinary interest shown by the two union ministers aggravated the matter. It is true they could not have visualised the so serious consequence. Nor there is any fault to defend the persons charged with offence under S.Cs, S.Ts (Prevention of Atrocities) Act, 1989. But, to turn the whole issue to be politicalised on caste-line is sad story. It is bad to defend unfortunate state as earlier such incidents had taken place. It is equally bad to take political benefit by opposition parties. It is more serious to divert the issue and escape from real causes inviting some permanent solution. The climax reached by efforts to give counter-caste issue by caste – diamond cuts diamond. One Dilip Kumar went on to accuse, "There is a malicious attack by certain sections on Susheel, who hails from OBC community. He is being accused of making false allegation. He is being "victimised because of his caste."

The Union Minister Bandaru Dattatreya was defended not only by the ruling party, his caste men came to his rescue.

Kuruma Sangthan (backward caste organisation) declared on 21.1.2016 that, "Dattatreya is himself from the backward caste community and he is being accused by other community of causing the death of Rohith. We cannot be kept quiet. We will dictare our support and defend Dattatreya at a function tomorrow."[28]

Obviously in such an atmosphere, the mother of Late Rohith, affirming Rohith as S.C. was very much pained when she said, "it is and that after such a tragic death questions are being raised about his caste".[29]

Does it mean that if somebody has caste backing can not be touched?[30] Has a student no identity other than caste? Has not Vemula suicide given an opportunity to cautious exercise of power by those who matter?[31] Has not it given occasion to overhaul university system by U.G.C. and Union government – ensuring allotment of Research guide at the earliest after enrollment, ensuring payment of scholarship in time and so on so forth?

A.K. Roopanwal Commission : Bad to Worse – Adding Fuel to the Fire of Persecution

After the suicide of Rohith Vemula on January 17, 2016 situation in the country and more particularly Hyderabad Central University and J.N.U. Delhi got worsened. Amidst turmoil, uncertainty, confusion, divergent and tension situation, the HRD appointed a fact-finding Committee and on its report being unpalatable to the Ministry, a judicial commission was appointed. The Report of both are quite at variance.

Fact-finding Committee and its Report :

On January 19, 2016 HRD Ministry dispatched two-member fact-finding committee to Hyderabad Central University.

Outcome : In its report to HRD Ministry the fact-finding Committee (i) slammed university administration for flawed probe; and (ii) found an atmosphere of discrimination on campus.

One-man Judicial Commission and its Report :

On January 28, HRD Ministry set up one-man Judicial Commission headed by Sri A.K. Rooppanwal, retired judge, Allahabad High Court.

Terms of reference : To probe circumstances that led to Vemula's death. The reference related to the investigation of the happenings in the university, the role of the Vice-Chancellor and other authorities who recommended punishment to Dalit students and the circumstances that led to the suicidal act of Vemula.

Report : In its report on August 1, 2016, the commission accused Vemula's mother of faking the Scheduled Castes status; his mother was not Dalit; there was no political interference; Cabinet Ministers Bandaru Dattatreya and Smriti Irani were merely discharging their duties as public servants and Rohith ended his life out of frustration.

The moot question is : Was the term of reference so as the report indicates ?

The Indian Express front page report on Oct. 6, 2016 read :

The Whitewash : Probe alleges Vemula mother faked S.C. Status, blames him for his suicide. The Commission found the claim of Radhika to belong to Mala S.C. family improbable and unbelievable as her foster family did not disclose the names of her biological parents. What about the disclosure of adoptive mother who had said in so many words about the Mala S.C. couple poor migrant worker ? The report veer around the caste of Vemila which was not term of the reference nor relevant fact as Vemula had never taken the benefit of S.C. certificate and had always been admitted on merit.

The Scheduled Caste person is one who has suffered the stresses and strains of deplorable caste. In an interview published in **Frontline** June 24, 2016 Raja the younger brother said :

"We were never allowed to sit inside my Maths tuition class. We were n't allowed inside homes, and people did not use or touched the glasses we used – because Hindu College (Guntur) is full of Brahmins, it is controlled by Brahmin teachers. We both studied there.

I told my brother then that I was willing to quit and get a daily-wage job. He asked me not to do that. He said we are atleast able to study. Think of those who cannot even do that. We should help them by getting ourselves into high positions. We are born to help others in our community who are suppressed like us."[32]

It makes clear that (1) Rohith was Dalit Mala S.C. and as such was discriminated at school and (2) he was not so weak heart to succumb easily, as the Commission jumps to the conclusion.

Sreenivas Janyala report from Hyderabad dated 6 October, 2016 rightly exposed **Probed missed : Vemula took no S.C. benefits, mother's parent confirmed Dalit identity**. The report revealed that even not so much read woman Radhika expressed outrage at Commission's conclusion and accused it for trying to divert the issue to caste, "instead of investigating the causes that led to Rohith's suicide." She also questioned the outcome of the Commission as to personal frustration, not discrimination as the cause of suicide. She asked :

"When Rohith never opted for reservation or quota as dalit, and always applied under general category, why has his caste become so import ? Why does no one want to investigate what forced him to commit suicide ?"

It is also surreptitious to black out role of the other group of the students and declaring expulsion of Rohith from hostel most reasonable. If one believes in Commission's version the Ministers forcing University authorities to punish Dalit students and leaving other rival group, whom the Proctorial Board in the first instance (spontaneous action) had issued warning along with Dalit students were discharging their official duties. To choose one to punish and expel and to grant immunity to equally circumstanced other comes under what type of discharge of official duty ? If this amounts to discharge of official duty what else the discrimination (hostile discrimination) may be ?

It is this irrationality, unfairness and subjectivity of the conclusions of the Report that the Indian Express in its Editorial requested the new HRD Minister to reject the report of Roopanwala Commission and ensure just and fair play.

Rohith's Sacrifice for Good Cause

In her interview published in **Frontline**, June, 24, 2016 p. 104 Radhika, the mother of Rohith Vemula pointed out the loud message of Rohith through his sacrifice:

"He died for good cause. He may have thought that people will come out after his death and so would his family. He must have thought that there has to be some sacrifice and that's why he sacrified his life to uplift those who are oppressed. He wanted to unite many people. I definitely agree that a day will come when there will not be any discrimination, definitely."

The sacrifice of Rohith has not gone in vain. It has consolidated the cause of Dalit right. It has given courage to publicly boycott those who caused injustice and persecution of

Rohith Vemula. On October 1, 2016 V. Sukanna Velpula refused to accept Ph.D. degree in Philosophy from the hands of Professor Appa P. Rao, the Vice-Chancellor (instrumental in Rohith's suicide) and snubbed that he, "does not have moral right to grant degrees to students." He received degree from Pro-Vice Chancellor Vipin Srivastava.[33]

A strong plea has come for Rohith Act so as to ensure that Rohith should be lost to sacrifice. Radhika herself said :

"Dalit children should not feel discriminated against by upper caste children right from pre-school to Ph.D. This Act should protect them from that. It should protect them from feeling a sense of persecution or helplessness. Also, Dalit and Adivasi members on all university Committees on any issue should become mandatory."[34]

A Critique of Caste Discrimination as an Ongoing Phenomena

The post–vedic India has experience ugly faces of caste discrimination. Our growing sense has been that caste discrimination is wrong in principle, because it is incompatible with decency of a cultured society to treat one caste as inherently inferior to another. But, in practice it does not, we do not follow it. The ways of operation, values and execution of discrimination differ but it never stops. It is by nature that men have urge to live equally with human dignity and "sense of injustice revolts against whatever is unequal by caprice." Edgar Bodenheimer[35] rightly observes that there is "human urge for respect, for equal treatment, human desire to be free from domination by others." There is something special god gifted within everybody. He spontaneously begins to do that. But, socially conceited artificial bars do not allow him. If he remains weak, meek, submissively bearing injustice, being exploited and so on, everything is in order. As soon as he tries to excel according to god-gifted talent either on his own or in guidance of some through gentle, liberal and equality loving guide, society's upper caste people find threat to their monopoly to use creamy comforts and position. They search some irrational *alibi* to cut such brilliant downtrodden people to size. In modern society awakening has increased. Individuality has changed with a sense of group identity and with liberal fruit of education, even the dalits are becoming conscious of their rights, dignity and to protest what is wrong. Their dumbness has stopped; they have mouth to speak, expose

Table 13

	Period	*Victim*	*Caste*	*Cause of Grudge*	*Mode of Execution*	*Grade of Execution*	*Executing Agency*	*Reason*	*Impact*	*Overall impact*
1.	Treta	Shambuka	Shudra (Lowest in caste hierarchy)	Excelling in knowledge reserved for Brahmin class	Beheading (Killing)	Most crude and Grave form of Execution	King (State)	Threat to Elitist mono-poly	Discouragement to Lower–caste to excel in life	National Loss of Merit due to lack of competition
2.	Dwapar	Eklabya	Tribal	Excellency in Archery meant for Kshatriyas	Cutting of Thumb	Less Crude and Grave, But treacherous and everlasting	Individual – Guru - Drona – Parshuram	– Inferiority – Lack of Confidence to train his favourite pupil to equal or excel in archery	1. Discouragement to low born 2. Birth of untold merit less reservation in favour elite class	National Loss of Merit due to lack of competition

(Contd.)

(Contd. Table 13)

	Period	Victim	Caste	Cause of Grudge	Mode of Execution	Grade of Execution	Executing Agency	Reason	Impact	Overall impact
3.	Dwapar	Karna	Backward	Putting challenge to Kshatriyas by excelling in weaponary	(1) Denial of opportunity (2) curse to forget learning when most needed	Less crude, But denial of Education opportunity	Individual – Guru - Drona – Parshuram	Threat to 1. Concentration of weaponary to Kshatriyas 2. Limiting learning to Brahmins	Decay of know-ledge due to denial of Equal opportunity.	National Loss of Merit due to lack of competition
4.	Present Day Kaliyuga	Rohit Vemula	Dalit (S.C.)	Raising Voice of persecuted Dalits using intelligence	Deprivation persecution and abetment to end life	Sophisticated weapon to Deal with challengers to status quoism	State Agencies – University – Ministeries – ruling party student wing	Threat to status quoism and bigotry	Denial of opportunity crushing voice and search for social justice.	National Loss due to Alienation of Depressed and representative democracy

Una Episode – Beating of the Dalits for unskinning dead cow

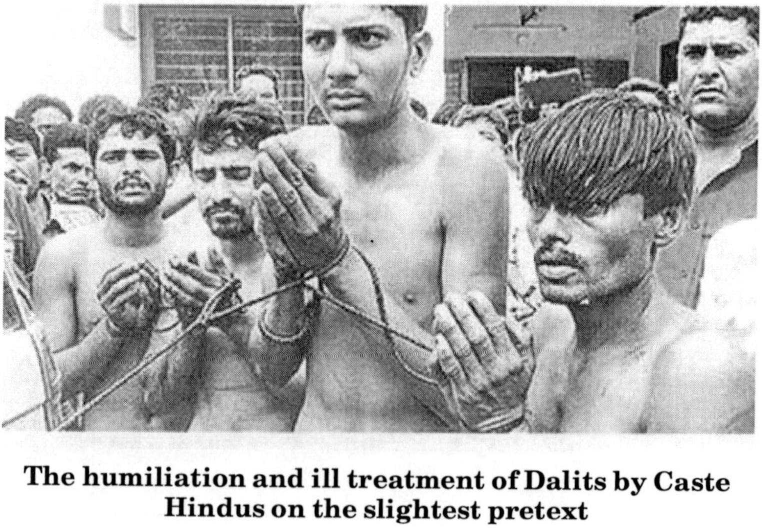

The humiliation and ill treatment of Dalits by Caste Hindus on the slightest pretext

and seek redressal and that is the problem. Educate, organise and agitate even for right cause becomes dangerous for them. The institution of learning are more prone to action and reaction due to knowledge of law, right and other things in reaction more sophisticated way are search to harm the genius of down-trodden people. A comparative chart of caste discrimination in historical perspective has been given from p. 282 to p. 283.

The story of Persecution of the Dalits is not ending still. Even in 2016 itself the news and televised news have appeared regarding beating of a Dalit Scholar in Central School, Muzaffarnagar, Bihar by two Caste students for the only fault of the Dalit student that he was execelling in studies and getting more marks than caste students; the news was published regarding beating of a preganant Dalit women for not performing certain works of the Caste person- the news also came regarding the disposal of the body of a Dalit woman after death- when her husband was not allowed to perform the funeral at Shamshan Place or in some vacant land, he set fire her to pyre of her corpse in front of his home. The two photos of Dalits persecution published in India Today, August 10, 2016 have been reproduced at p. 284.

Irrationality Based Prejudices and Dalit Discrimination, Persecution, Humiliation and Annihiliation

Prejudice is deep-rooted in Indian graded and degraded hierarchical society. Caste discrimination that disadvantages Dalits is unjust, not because people cannot choose their caste, but because that discrimination expresses prejudice.[36] Prejudice is based on irrationality. Irrationality has no time limit. As discussed earlier it was prevalent in Treta. Had rational thinking been prevalent Shambuka could not have lost life. The question would have flared up that if Shudra's Tapasya could be cause of the death of a Brahmin's son, why he could not be alive on the force of accumulated virtuousness of all the well-read gods of the earth (Brhamins). Shambuka was victim of deep-rooted social prejudices against Shudras. So was case with Eklabya, a tribal extra brilliant archer. The difference was that in Dwapar the institution was not involved - the individual prosecuted due to deep-rooted prejudice and inferiority complex. Time has changed. Science has produced miracles. People have become literate. The Constitution has set norms. Scientific temper and humanism have been declared fundamental duties.

But, prejudices, mores and complexes are the same. Though ignorance of law provides no excuse but it is rampant. It is common knowledge that the Supreme Court does not only decide cases, it declares the future laws. But, inspite of the bearing of stresses, strains and handicaps as test of dalit caste determination decided in so many cases and latest one being *Rameshbhai Dabhai Naika v. State of Gujrat*[37] (discussed earlier), the persons in power, who matter, what to say of men in street or less conscious persons are leaving no stone unturned to confuse, diffuse and kill the reason/cause of Vemula's episode. Some Union Ministers, inspite of Rameshbhai, Dabhai Naika's case being published in one of the national well reputed newspaper[38], repeatedly and intentionally propagated that victim was not S.C. but OBC. Two of them went to the extent of arguing that, "before Vemula suicide, there had been nine suicides on the campus [University of Hyderabad]. This was tenth suicide. Why not the first nine suicides become a big issue."[39] What did he mean? Can a bad precedent be used as defence of criminal act? Is our sensitivity towards human value gone far away from our inhered composite culture and the whole humanity as a family? The people who are in power justify the Bhojpuri adage – The stronger beats and does not allow to weep (Jabara Mare aa Rovahu Na De). Vemula episode's aftermath has crossed all the decency of a cultured society – it shows insensitive and politically motivated sympathy of some group, it shows all round irrational arguments to cover up the incident; it shows also the self-inflicted wounds of the dalits themselves for whom selling of souls away for sordid boon of ruling booty is more important than the cause of dalit dignity and right to live in safe manner equally with others – be they earlier fiery S.C. leaders now testing fruit of power[40] or S.C. wing of power that be finding Rohit's suicide as an act of atonement.[41] In a word Rohith's suicide was result of motivated mishandling of the issue under pressure of Union Ministers on party line.

Had scientific temper, sense of inquiry and justice prevailed the situation could be averted. *First*, the first report of the Proctorial Board would have been accepted and controversy would have died out; *Second*, if not first, the fresh inquiry would have been constituted, as suggested by the then V.C. before Dr Appa Rao's taking of charge; *Third*, coming to know the reality that the complainant was not correct, taking the reports from the doctor operating him of appendicitis, the complainant should have been suspended; *Fourth*, the scholarship of Rohith should not have been stopped; *Fifth*, the H.R.D. ministry would have responded that there were no anti-national elements on campus, as was conceded by the V.C. in the press interview; *Sixth*, the one month earlier letter of Rohith to the V.C. would have acted as alarm and preventive measures could have been taken; *Seventh,* after incorrect statement of H.R.D. Minister leading to resignation of 10 SC authorities of the university, hon'ble minister should have tendered apology on ground that the minister was fed with wrong information. So should have been done by the Union Labour Minister, as his letter exposing situation beyond proportion – calling University as "den of casteists, extremists and anti-nationals" had something (rather everything) to do in the episode resulting into university's unreasonable, unjust, unreasoned, irrational, vindictive and overall discriminating actions. Only two things based on fair mindedness and justice would have averted the situation from worsening – reliance on original Proctorial Board recommendation (which was immediate, spontaneous and in performance of responsible duty) and after the tragic incident tendering of apology along with punishing the real villain in the episode. In western countries Church has been apologising for miscomprehended earlier deeds from time to time. Our own culture+Gandhian piety requires such steps. What P.M. did in Lucknow on the occasion of Convocation of Dr Bhimrao Ambedkar University – Rohith's death is loss to Mother India, should have come spontaneously immediately after the incidence and it would have very soothing effect. Amidst the turmoil and Labour Minister's role under dock attracting F.I.R., he should have avoided sharing dias with him. The biggest message of Rohith incident is to ponder seriously on what Chetan Bhagat[42] says – Lack of Autonomy for Universities is a killer. To this one more addition; politicians, when occupy ministerial/official post they should start functioning with high head and broad chest (Matha Uncha Aur Seena Chaura) and be able to maintain a difference between election speech/commitment and requirement official duty as per oath of office taken under the Constitution.[43]

Our hearts begin to bleed when we hear some conscience pricking news like Mahesh Balmiki, a IIT, BHU 2nd year student of mining, who even mulled suicide when he could not pay off Rs 2.7 lakh which he had taken for studies and medical treatment. He could not sell even his Kidney to pay-off the loan. In his own words, "I visited around five hospitals in Varanasi and Alwar. The doctors there informed me that no one would take my Kidney as I am a Dalit." Sensing his attempt to end life his friends approached Sandeep Pandey, Magsaysay awardee social activist who arranged repay the loan of 2.7 lakh by involving BHU alumni. But Mahesh, a student described by his teachers "very bright" had to leave his study and take up a sweeper's job back at his village in Rajasthan's Alwar, for just Rs 4,000 a month.[44] Mahesh had scored 85 per cent in class X and despite many bouts of illness during examination he secured 70% marks in XII. He did extremely well in IIT entrance test and got a seat at BHU. But now he has no option but to clean and sweep. Mahesh Valmiki is bright S.C. chap as Vemula was. His observations are eye-opener towards the problem of deprived SCs/STs. "Sandeep sir helped me get rid of the loan through funds he collected from former IIT–BHU students. I have paid everything back. I think there are hundreds like Rohith Vemula (the University of Hyderabad Ph.D. scholar) studying at prestigious institutions in our country. Some are forced to end their lives. A few lucky ones get people like Sandeep Sir."[45]

How intolerant we are is evident from the incident of "U.S. Professor derided for supporting strikers." Immanual Ness, Professor at University of New York (Brooklyn College) who had come to deliver lecture in the Department of Political Science incurred ire of university authorities for visiting the place to pledge solidarity to protesting students. In words of Professor Ness, "those who invited me were not very pleased with idea and they turned hostile," and "some inflammatory and derogatory comments were made against the protesting student outfits."[46]

The world is changing fast. But, what is not changing is the caste-based hostile discrimination, deprivation and punishment of those raising voice of liberation and against discriminatory actions (agitating on conscience revolt).

The on-going scorn of some, as inferior in India, reminds us of one-hundred twenty years earlier distinction between political equality and social equality, made by Justice Brown in famous *Plessy v. Fergusan*[47] (1896) in context of the American race ridden society, if two races (Black and Whites) are two meet upon terms of social equality, it must be the result of natural affinities, a mutual appreciation of each other's merit and voluntary consent of individuals. Legislation is powerless to eradicate racial distinct or to abolish distinctions based upon physical differences and the attempt to do so can only result in accentuating the difficulties of the present situation. If the civil and political rights of both races be equal one cannot be inferior to the other civilly or politically. If one race be inferior to the other socially, the Constitution of the United States cannot put them upon the same plane."[48] So is the case with India. Constitution can be made, changed, law can be made or changed to equalise by abolition of untouchability, enactment of Protection of Civil Rights Act, SC/ST Prevention of Atrocities Act and many more ...., but the mind set of elite classes cannot be changed. It becomes more and more entrenched, irremovable and dangerous when added with bigotry and actions sans scientific temper and humanism loaded with what Max commented religion in politics acts as opium.

Society is developing, progress is made, education is spread but education, in instead of enlightening heart of our people[49] is darkening it with religious bigotry – be it Treta, or Dwapar or Kaliyuga. One can very well imagine how ostracised Dr Ambedkar might have felt in 1935 when he declared *"I will not die a Hindu although it was my misfortune to be born one"*. He made mark, wrote history with exceptional intelligence and diligence as Chairman Drafting Committee of the Constituent Assembly and gave us a most comprehensive document with splendid compromises. Before his death he embraced Buddhism. But, that was only changing the compartment and not the train. His mantra for Dalits' to Educate, organise and Agitate is proving costly to his brethren in posterity – who are thought only to bear silently humiliation, discrimination and persecution without any murmur. Vemula episode is symptom of our social outlook. There are many many untold stories of sufferings. In the highest seat of learning like Hyderabad University itself within a span of six years there have been six lives cut short of Dalits[50] and in one case – Venkatesh was not provided a guide and a lab, after three years, even when other students started their researches and published international papers." Many a things have come out openly. Many many cases of hostile caste discrimination and that too from high seat of learning and at the hands of teachers have been reported. Even cases of Muslims being discriminated have come out.

Will we take a lesson from Vemula episode and think seriously what P.M. Modi said – With the death of Vemula we have lost a son of our Mother India or what Union Minister Najma Heptullah said at Kashmir University –

"We should not divide the children in terms of upper caste, lower caste or Dalits. Our country has seen enough division. We should see the children as they are only as children, our heart bleeds for all, nor just for minority, and it does not differentiate on the basis of caste, creed or religion,"[51]

Since Dr Ambedkar had done in-depth research on Hindu social mores in the caste-ridden changing society with static entrenched prejudices, he did not fail to issue warning, a day before adoption of our Constitution in the Constituent Assembly viewing its successfulness if only political and legal democracy being given without firm footing in social democracy. But, we utterly failed to understand/honour his visionary prophetic message. And, discrimination remained to flow like the dirty waters of Karamanasha falling and polluting the pious waters of Ganges of the Indian composite culture. This led a committed and reputed legal scholar of par excellence, Professor Upendra Baxi, guessed/exposing a new happening of political appropriation of Dr Ambedkar "as a shining light in its own patheon" and suggest against the political tide that "Parliament would better celebrate Ambedkar by declaring war on unconstitutional evils like untouchability."[52]

Vemula's lamentation on the worth of human being reduced to vote speaks a lot of things. What Dr Ambedkar did through acute suffering of caste discrimination, endurance, benevolence, struggle to do something for unfortunate brethren and giving it a solid expression in the Constitution, Vemula has done by sacrifying his life to expose the utter failure of the Indian society to listen the human voice of the Constitution. It may provide opportunity to pick up the real causes of maladies exposed in some very informative and well intentioned objective exposition of facts/practices and suggesting solutions[53] e.g. Teesta Setalvad, "We all failed Rohith"[54]; Chetan Bhagat, "Indian Institutes of Politics — Lack of Autonomy for Universities is a killer ...."[55] Surya Kant Waghmore, "Rohith and the Sacred Holi Cow,[56]" Rama Chandra Guha "We, the Unequal" [57]; Sukhdeo Thorat, "Discrimination on the Campus"[58]; Satish Despande, "Death of the public University"[59]; K. Satya Narayana, "The Ghetto on Campus"[60], etc. The Hindu has done a tremendously laudable research work by publishing a series six caste fault lines.[61] So has it done by publishing The Sunday Magazine team's discovery of the new contours of discrimination. It rightly views that, "however much we try to brush it under the carpet, every now and then a Rohith Vemula forces our attention on the sensitive issue of caste in the country."[62] Interview with Lenin, a M.Sc. scholar revealed how he and his friend were declared 'trouble makers' without any rhym and reason and how SC students were given "10 to 12 marks out of the 25 marks of internal assessment and others were 20".[63] Santosh Kumar Selvaraj Ph.D. scholar, revealed how he was known by caste by everybody even they did not know that he was studying in which class.[64] Dr Vivek Kumar, Professor at J.N.U. revealed his pain of being addressed as Dalit Chintak and discrimination in publicity of good research works.[65] Ajay Rawat another Ph.D. scholar revealed mindset of people not allowing even choice of name of dalit children. To quote him "The take their name suggested by the upper caste. Names are allotted us on the basis of the day we are born or on a colour, like Bhure, Ram Bharose, Budhwari, we are not allowed the dignity of a proper name, so that our names can help identity us as Dalit."[66] And, yet another Ph.D. scholar, Prashant Ram Prasad told how he asked for water and was asked his caste.[67] In relation to the University of Hyderabad, The Indian Express published the outcome of the three inquiry committees – in all three Inquiry Committees Reports caste factor came out. Justice K. Ramaswamy Report stated in its report, "Because of the insensitivity towards problems faced by the students belonging to the aforesaid social groups, frequent occurrences of suicide are taking place."[68] The other two probes also revealed hostile discrimination at the hands of supervisor and apathy.[69]

References

1. The Hindu, 23.1.2016 p.12.
2. "ABVP leader lying about being attacked by ASA members?" ABP News Retrieved 29 January, 2016.
3. Suicide Note of Rohith. "Full text : Dalit Scholar Rohith Vemula's Suicide note – Times of India" Retrieved on 2016-01.20.
4. The annihilation by caste — The controversy over whether Rohith Vemula was a Dalit or not is a red herring, a disgraceful attempt to discredit his politics. The Hindu, 3.2.2016, p. 11.
5. (2012) 3 SCC 400 (d/on 18.1.2012. The bench consisted of Aftab Alam and Ranjana P. Desai, JJ. The decision was pronounced by Aftab Alam J.).

6. *Ibid.*, p. 424.
7. Quoted from Teestha Setalvad, We all failed Rohith, The Indian Express 22.1.2016, p. 12.
8. *Ibid.*
9. Quoted from, Srinivasa Janyala, Hyderbad, Rohith got Call from Cops, notice from Hostel, The Indian Express, 21.1.2016, p. 11.
10. *Ibid.*
11. *Ibid.*
12. See, Appa Rao, Out smarted 35 others to become V.C., The Times of India, 21.1.2016, p. 11.
13. Teesta Setalvad, We all Failed Rohith — Beyond the grief of the moment, we need to stop denying India's not-s-hidden apartheid, The Indian Express, 22.1.2016, p. 12.
14. K. Satyanarayana, The Ghetto on Campus, The Indian Express 4.2.2016, p. 13.
15. See, K. Satyanarayana, The Ghetto on Campus, The Indian Express 4.2.2016, p. 13.
16. *Ibid.*
17. *Ibid.*
18. Tribune News Service, Five HRD letters to Hyderabad Varsity blamed for Suicide, The Tribune 20.1.2016, p. 10.
19. In its N.E.W.S. North East West South Column dated 14.2.2016 at p. 16 the Indian Express published The Mother, The Daughter which cover the whole story.
20. *Ibid.*
21. *Ibid.*
22. *Ibid.*
23. *Ibid.*
24. *Ibid.*
25. *Ibid.*
26. *Ibid.*
27. The American adage is there is no political issue which does not become a legal one.
28. Suicide Express caste faultlines on campus, The Indian Express 22.1.2016 p. 11.
29. *Ibid.*
30. *Ibid.*
31. H.R.D. minister's version that five reminders were routine is completely inconvincing. There are evidentiary proof that representation/complaint sent to many important functionaries do not attract even acknowledgement, what to say of action? A circular be circulated to all ministries to the effect the story must not be repeated.
32. Frontline, June 24, 2016, p. 104.

33. The Hindu, Oct. 2, 2016 p. 8.
34. *Ibid*. p. 105.
35. Bodenheimer, Jurisprudence, p. 230.
36. This sentence is constructed on the basis of Dworkin's observation in Law's Empire at p. 395, "Racial discrimination that disadvantages black is unjust, not because people cannot choose their race, but because that discrimination expresses prejudice."
37. (2012) 3 SCC 420.
38. The Hindu 21.2.2016, p. 10 column, "Supreme Court Verdict of 2012 Backs Dalit Status".
39. Venkaiah Naidu, Union Minister for Development and Parliamentary Affairs while addressing Uttar Bharatiya Manch expressed such view, The Hindu 1.2.2016 p.13 column, 'Rid Campuses of Politics.' The same idea echoed in Chand Gehlot, The Hindu 3.2.2016, p. 9.
40. Udit Raj, Crocodile tears for Rohith – Activist Cry for Rohith but do they ever fight for true empowerment of Dalits? The Indian Express 25.1.2016, p.10.
41. The Hindu 4.2.2016, p. 9 column, "Rohith's Suicide was an act of atonement, suggests B.J.P. S.C. Morcha."
42. Chetan Bhagat, "Indian Institute of Politics — Lack of Autonomy for Universities is a Killer, literally so in Rohith Vemula's Case", The Times of India 23.12.2016, p.14. Meena Kandasamy rightly views – "What we see in the case of the university of Hyderabad is the deadly combination of caste supremacy and political pondering." The Hindu 19.1.2016, p.11 column. "He has left us with only his words" remark is truthful "Rohith Vemula death is the unforeseeable climax of struggle that he was spearheading against cateist, communal forces."
43. ".......I will faithfully and conscientiously discharge my duties as a Minister......... and that I will do right to all manner of people in accordance with the constitution and the law without fear or favour, affection or ill–will." Fourth Schedule–V.
44. Times of India, 23.1.2016, p. 9 News column, "IIT pupil tries to sell kidney to repay loan, but no takers for Dalit organ — Drops out to Earn Living as a Sweeper."
45. *Ibid,* And, the unfortunate aspect of Indian society showing illiberalism that such a social justice human being was targeted by B.H.U. administration terminating his contractual appointment in B.H.U. terming him anti-national. It reminds very reality oriented lines of Akbar Allahabadi – Rakeebon Ne Rapat Likhwai Hai Ja Ja Ke Thane Mein
Akbar Naam Leta Hai Khuda Ka Es Jamane Mein!

46. The Hindu 31.1.2016, p. 13, column "U.S. Professor derided for supporting strike."
47. 163 U.S. 537 (1896).
48. *Ibid.*
49. Pt. Nehru said Universities stand for humanism and learning. Learning gives benevolence; benevolence gives nobility, large heartedness and enlightenment. Education makes man cultured. And, cultural man as Betrand Russel put must necessarily be a "citizen of the universe, not only of one or two arbitrary fragments of space and time." For detail see, Anirudh Prasad, University Education Administration and the Law, Deep and Deep Publications, New Delhi, 2000 p. xv.
50. The Hindustan Times 21.1.2016, p. 8, published a column "Dalit suicides not new at University of Hyderabad" and cited the said examples.
51. The Hindu 21.1.2016, p.7, column, "Reason Behind Student Committing Suicide must be found: Heptullah."
52. "Constitution day after", The Indian Express, 3.12.2015, p.10.
53. The Hindu, 21.1.2016, p. 11.
54. The Indian Express 22.1.2016, p.12.
55. The Times of India (Chandigarh) 23.1.2016, p.14.
56. The Indian Express, 28.1.2016, p. 13.
57. The Indian Express, 30.1.2016, p. 12.
58. The Hindu 26.1.2016, p.10
59. The Indian Express, 1.2.2015, p. 9.
60. G. Satyanarayan, "The Ghetto on Campus", The Indian Express 1.2.2016, p. 13.
61. 1. "Ancient prejudice, modern inequality". The Hindu, 20.1.2016, p. 10.
    2. "Grim shadow of caste over Educational Institutions in T.N." The Hindu 22.1.2016, p.12.
    3. "Dalit Activism is now a reality across campuses in India" 23.1.2016 p.12.
    4. "Delaying Scholarship for Dalits is also Discrimination" The Hindu 24.1.2016 p.9
    5. "Discrimination at every step" 25.1.2016, p. 13.
    6. "At AIIMS, integration begins at the start itself" 25.1.2016, p. 13.
62. Caste on the Campus, The Hindu, Sunday Magazine 7.2.2016, p.1.
63. *Ibid.* In "Dalit activism is now a reality across campuses in India" dated 31.1.2016 many more instances have been presented as discrimination in assessment and RTI has revealed that many dalits got zero out of 30 marks
64. *Ibid.*

65. *Ibid.*
66. *Ibid.,* p. 2. It is rampant one may come across names like Mangru, Ghurahu, Thug, Bengali, Chirkut etc.
67. *Ibid.*
68. "Caste came up in three suicide probes", The Indian Express 8.2.2016, p. 8.
69 *Ibid.* On caste consideration dalit students felt a 'sense of alienation' and 'institutional discrimination'.

Part – Five
A CRITICAL APPRAISAL

Messages of the Image

1. Constitution as Indispensible as heart, keep it with Heart.
2. Emancipation through Participation in the Parliament.

12

CODA: An Evaluation of the National Profit and Loss With the Lesson for Posterity

It is very valuable, socially relevant and cohesive and politically most desirable to agree that all the institutions- social, political and religious are meant for the betterment and welfare of the people. Politically it is desirable to provide good governance; socially it is desirable to have cohesion and solidarity or inter-dependence; and religion is the cement of society which constructs a social structure based on love, compassion and mutual respect with the idea of otherness-love thy neighbour as thyself.

The book is pointer to the original trend- how the Vedic social structure was based on equality, classlessness and full opportunity to develop one's personality according to his own aptitude and ability. Even the three original Varnas-Brahmna, Rajanya and Vaishya-the twice-born were based on the principle of the division of labour and the member of the same family could engage in different callings depending on aptitude. In the course of time a fourth servile Varna known as Shudra was searched and yet on more later stage of constructing the hierarchical caste-structure a fifth category of outcaste, antyaja, chandala etc. was created. Even among such despised classes there was category of Untouchable and Unseeable. Be it based on Brahminical theory of purity- impurity or Kshatriyas power dominance, it was irrational, iniquibitous and inhuman from the very beginning. In post-Vedic and Upnishadic period

Brahmanas developed the hierarchical social structure with entrenched superiority and inferiority complex and declared themselves superior to the people of all other Varnas, as God of the earth. They deprived Shudras of all privileges of education, possessing money, living a dignified life, shelter etc. Shudras gained some respectability by Buddha and political protection on equal footing during the Gupta regime which was again deprived with vengeance during the Brahminical regime of Shunga kings.

The urge to live with human dignity is a natural urge. Finding no rays of hope of dignified life and overbearing the indignity, poverty and persecution, the untouchables started looking towards such religions where at least they could be treated as human being. The Hindu got alarmed and the reform in Hinduism started but every reformer sect was added as one more sect of Hinduism. Due to caste-ridden hierarchical structure the society was so divided that it became easier for foreign invaders to come and win without much of resistance. The intelligent Brahmins continued to enjoy privilege as advisors of such invader rulers and also continued their social deprivation of Untouchables.

I

The religious preachers, social reformers and political strategy makers all realised the heavy cost of the Indian graded and degraded system. In addition to attempts of individual religious reformers, three models emerged to deal with the problem of untouchability and provide the untouchable the dignified status. The first model is preached by Swami Vivekananda- the process of Brahmanisation of Shudras. He said: "We read that in Satyuga there was only one caste, and that was the Brahmin. We read in the Mahabharata that the whole world was in the beginning peopled with Brahmins, and that as Brahmins began to degenerate, they became divided into different castes, and when the cycle turns round, they will go back to the Brahminical origin."[1] In his scheme solution lies not in the process of bringing down the higher but by raising the lower upto the level of the higher. He pointed out that the ideal at one end is the Brahmin and the ideal at the other end is the Chandala, and the whole work is to raise the Chandala up to the level of Brahmin.[2] In his model education can play vital role and Pariah should be given special treatment for that purpose.[3]

The Second Model is presented by Mahatma Gandhi. Mahatma Gandhi believed Shudrisation of all. Gandhi said since we believe in **Varnadharma** let us accept the Dharma of service. Let us accept **Shudradharma**."[4] He made clear, "The Varna system has just now broken down .... There is no true Brahmin or true Kshatriya, or Vaishya. We are all Shudras, i.e. one Varna."[5] Gandhi further clarified that " Brahmins are rarity these days." As for Kshatriyas, there are, none left in India. If there had been any, the country would not have lost its freedom. India would not remain in her present condition if great learning and great valour could be found here."[6] The third model is Ambedkarite speaking of rationalisation of Hindu dharma on the bases of equality, liberty and fraternity. Dr Ambedkar was of considered view that piece-meal reform will never be effective because Mahatmas have come and Mahatmas have gone, but Hindu society continues to remain graded and degraded. He believed that nothing could be done except the radical overhauling of the Hindu religio-social system. In view of the vast and divergent Hindu religious literature including the Vedas, the Brahmans, the Aranyakas, Upnishadas, Sutras, Itihas, Smritis and Puranas, the system will remain as it has been. He summed up the impact Hindu Scriptures as multitude of commanding and prohibitions. He suggests cardinal items to be contained in religious literature, that is to say (1) There should be only one and a standard book of Hindu religion acceptable to all Hindus and recognised by all Hindus. All other books of Hindu religion such as Vedas, Shashtras and Puranas, which are treated as sacred and authoritative must by law cease to be so and the preaching of any doctrine, religious or social, contained in these books should be penalised; (2) Priesthood among Hindus should be abolished. But as this seems to be impossible, priesthood must at least, cease to be hereditary. Every person who professes to be a Hindu must be eligible for being a priest. It should be provided by law that no Hindu shall be entitled to be priest unless he has passed an examination prescribed by the State and holds a ***Sanad*** from the State permitting him to practice priesthood; (3) No ceremony performed by a priest who does not hold a ***Sanad*** shall be deemed to be valid in law and it should be made penal for a person who has no ***Sanad*** to officiate as a priest; (4) A priest should be the servant of the State and should be subject to the disciplinary action by the State in the matter of his morals, beliefs and worship, in addition to his being subject along with other citizens to the ordinary law of the land; (5) The number of priests should be limited, according to the requirement of the State. In his view all these measures are aimed to check abuses of the religious institutions. Dr Ambedkar viewed to answer the Yaksha Prashna of the Hindu Society.

Yaksha Prashna About the Hindu Society

Yudhishthira of Mahabharata clarified / answered all the questions put by Yaksha. Had the occasion come like this : What is the most astonishing issue about the Hindu Society ? The answer of Yudhishthira would have been : "all most all rational beings accept that untouchability has been the biggest ailment and divisive force in the Hindu society, yet since time immemorial no satisfactory solution has been searched out."

As has been pointed out earlier, Ambedkar was the first man to talk of one religious book and appropriate state regulation of secular matters relating to religion like appointment of qualified Arjakas without any care of caste, creed etc. Barring adoption of only one religious book, all other suggestions given by Ambedkar are being implemented. Article 25 (1) and (2) incorporate Ambedkarite view of State regulated and not absolute right to freedom of religion.[7] So does Article 26. Freedom to manage religious affairs is made subject to public order, morality and health. In a number of cases the Supreme Court has upheld the taking over of the management of the affairs of the religious and charitable places. Thus, in ***Bira Kishre v. State of Orissa***[8] the taking over of the management of Shri Jagannath Temple from Raja of Puri and vesting it in a committee and providing for Seva Puja was upheld. So was done in ***Shri Adi Visheshwara of Kashi Vishwanath Temple v. State of U.P.***[9] and taking over of management from Pandas and vesting it in trustees was declared not to affect the religious matter. In ***Seshamal v. State of Tamil Nadu***[10] the Act providing for certain hereditary religious offices non-hereditary and prescribing certain requisite educational qualifications for them irrespective of caste and creed was upheld. So was done in ***A.S. Narain Deekshitulu v. State of A.P.***[11] by upholding the validity of the Act providing for appointment of non-Brahmins as "***Santhikaran***" or "***Poojari***" in a Shiava Temple in Kerala[12] or 'Poojari' in Vaishnava Devi Temple in J. and K.[13]

The reform in Hindu religion on Ambedkar's intended line has started. It may take time but with State support - legislative, executive and judicial change towards secularity will bring reform gradually. The move to open temple for Untouchables and women and judicial support is good sign.

Dr Ambedkar attacked at the root of all the II evils resulting into pernicious caste-system. He very candidly and brilliantly exposed ill-impact of caste-system. "The effect of caste on the ethics of the Hindus is not simply deplorable. Caste has killed public spirit; caste has destroyed the sense of public charity; caste has made public opinion impossible. A Hindu's public is his caste. His loyalty is restricted only to his caste. Virtue has become caste-bound. There is no sympathy to the deserving. There is no appreciation of the meritorious."[14] Due to these causes Dr Ambedkar made strong plea of annihilation of caste.

There is agreement among Vivekananda, Gandhi and Ambedkar on the point of the evils of Hinduism (i) its pernicious dividing effect; (ii) cultivation through self aggrandized Brahminical culture and (iii) need of change. There is also agreement on the point that since upper caste caused the degrading condition of untouchables they should take initiative to remove it.

Vivekananda advised different ways to solve the problem of the Hindu graded and degraded society. ***First***, the upper caste cunningness should go, sooner they dig their grave better; ***second***, as in Bengali saying when Cobra sucks his poison the victim is relieved of poison, so Brahmins should suck the poison from society, which they have spread in the society; and, ***third***, the untouchable should be provided with opportunity to develop their ability through education, even spending more by preferential treatment to Pariahas (untouchables) and make them Brahmin through acquiring knowledge and make the society as the original society which consisted of only Brahmins. Gandhi's way was suggestive of the change of heart on part of caste-people (i) to give up the practice of untouchability and (ii) inculcate the spirit of service, the special trait of Shudradharma. The mode of transformation of Hindu Society suggested by both Vivekananda and Gandhi centred around upper caste reincarnation which never happened inspite of such preaching and well-wishing by many great men. Ambedkar was more practical and presented graphic historical picture.

1. The India of Brahminism or the Aryan society of the Vedic period; in reality was a barbaric phase, which could be termed as "Sunken priesthood".[15]

2. The India of Buddhism, with the Magdha – Mauryan empires embodying the pinnacle of human civilisation, where all Indians were treated as equal and with dignity. This era was dominated by Buddhist way of thinking which, "purged the Aryan society of its many evils and constructed a socio-religious domain that, for the first time, radically challenged the caste hierarchy of the Brahmnic ethos.
3. The India of Hindu counter-revolution, heralded historically with Pushyamitra Sunga's rise of power, and associated with Manu, the Hindu law maker who legitimised and codified the caste-system. The triumph of Brahminic Hinduism provided rigidity to caste system through spelled doom for untouchables – Manusmriti, Mahabharata, Ramayana and the Bhagwad Geeta.

Dr Ambedkar exposed that aggravation or minimisation of the evil of casteism was inseparably interwined with royal protection or royal neglect. He arrived at conclusion that without state sanction the evil of untouchability could not be wiped out. He himself experimented appeal to goodness of caste people by begging to accept him and his brethren as human being. He experimented wearing ***Janeu- Yagyopavit*** which resulted into beating and mass attack on untouchable. He made efforts to drink water from tanks which were open for drinking of animals, his men were beaten and so was to fate of temple entry. In the process he concluded – ***first***, incorrigibility of caste-evil can not be cured; it was evident from experience – Mahatmas have come, Mahatmas have gone, but evil of casteism remains the same; ***second***, on rational thinking as an educated person adopting scientific temper and sense of inquiry as preached by Buddha, he pin-pointed- what for religion exists ? And, sound answer, came in departing from the Vivekanandite and Gandhian way of clinging to Hinduism and hoping for change, which could not be brought earlier nor during their time. And, he applied his teacher John Dewey's considered view that, the task of social sciences is one of repairing moral and social beliefs and practices by encouraging the application of scientific methods and critical intelligence to them".[16]

Nothing unusual objectionable can be found in his move to plead for conversion. Even the great Hindu religious poet Tulsidas has preached :

Leave your most busoms like thousands of enemies, if Lord Rama and Sita are not dearest to them (***Jake Priya Na Ram***

Vaidehi, Tajiye Tahi Koti Bairi sam Yadyapi Param Sanehi; Tajyo Pita Prahalad Bhibhishan, Bandhu Bharata Mahtari......)" And, after great mental struggle for to remain in Hindu-fold or not for more than decades, in 1936, Dr Ambedkar taught, inspired, exhorted and guided his deprived, despised and dispossessed of human dignity brethren-

"Religion is for man; man is not for religion,

If you want to gain self respect, change your religion,

If you want to create co-operative society, change your religion,

If you want power, change your religion,

If you want equality, change your religion,

If you want independence, change your religion,

If you want to make the world in which you live happy, change your religion.[17]

After his declaration of conversion in 1936, Dr Ambedkar still waited for two more decades and it was in, 1956 that he embraced Buddhism with huge mass of Untouchables. In words of Namdeo Dhasal : "Conversion of Buddhism.... Freed the Scheduled Castes from mental and psychological enslavement,[18] or what dalit writer Shankar Rao Kharat says :

"I have accepted the Buddhist Dharma. I am Buddhist now. I am not a Mahar, nor an untouchable, nor even a Hindu..... I have become independent."

What was visible change in life of untouchables after Dr Ambedkar's embrace of Buddhism with his fellow Untouchables was that it did what others reformists – saints and Mahatmas including Vivekananda and Gandhi could not do. It inculcated among untouchables the desire to live with dignity, search for identity, hope in place of despair, voice for justice in the place of bearing injustice without whisper. Untouchables searched their own centre of worship deifying Ambedkar in two ways : ***first***, is the process of exaltation or ascension, which Ambedkar – merges with the Supreme and becomes a God himself and the ***second***, the process where Ambedkar descends on earth as an ***avatara*** – that is a god in human form – to combat the social evils.

Jungare in his song titled, 'Ambedkar : The Avatar of Bhimaraya' says :

"To this fortunate land of ours, appeared the avatar of Bhimaraya.

Through his grace, millions of the poor and downtrodden are bettered.

"To this fortunate land of ours, appeared the avatar of Bhimaraya.

When he was our leader, the whole world trembled.

The sinful Brahmin stopped preaching, the poor and down-trodden breathed freely.

"To this fortunate land of ours, appeared the avatar of Bhimaraya.

Whose grace touched the lives of millions of poor dalits.

"On this land appeared the avatar of Bhimaraya."[19]

Dhanajay Keer, Dr Ambedkar's biographer has culled out of Jhungare songs the conclusion that –

"The Unique life of Ambedkar has become a new source of learning and a new source of inspiration for devotees. From it has emerged a new deity and the lamp that will be burning in its temple in this land of temples."[20]

Or how untouchables feel:

I am now free. I have now become a free citizen of independent India.[21]

Now Buddhism mattered for untouchables ? Buddhism inaugurated a more rational mindset for the Dalits. It brought rationalism and humanism. Through Buddhism Indian Dalits found Ambedkarism as an expression of 'democratic – revolution'. Soon after mass conversion of untouchables in 1956 to Buddhism, Rajananda Gadapyle in his 'Jugate Pramjyota' (The Awakened Torch of Life) wrote :

The light of enthusiasm is spread everywhere
And the teaching of Buddha gives delight.
The evil days of slavery are gone
And the sorrowful songs are gone.
Bhim gave us the great hymn Buddham Saranam Gachchami
And by attaining the perfection of this hymn
We became riders of own chariots.[22]

Another song by Rau Bhim found connection between current possibility of dalit honour and old glorious past during the period of Buddhism. He sang :

Bring to this country once again
The blessed name
Which made land of thy birth sacred
To all the distant lands !
Let the great awakening under the Bodhi tree
Be fulfilled.

Let the open doors that were barred
And the resounding conch shell –
Proclaim thy arrival at Bharat's gate.
Let through innumerable voices,
The gospel of an immeasurable love
Announce thy call.[23]

The need of social adjustment through reawakening inspired by Ambedkarite Buddhism is that Ambedkar should be left as great social reformer and humanist, a torch-bearer of educate, organise and agitate and firm believer in work is worship and deadly against mystic hero-worship. As far as possible deification should be avoided and the torch of liberation of the human soul from ignorant slavery be carried on unrelentlessly and ceaselessly. So any move to make Buddha and Ambedkar God – heads be discarded and follow their preaching, act on conscience tested path and do something significant. Perhaps this is the message of Bhagwan Sawai's poetic expression to keep distance from Hindu mode of worship. He wrote:

Tathagat
I do not want you in your yogic posture as in the pictures
Before whom I could place my offerings of flowers and prayers
Pardon the slaves of fetishism
Who created Idols in your name and festivals.

The message of the book is that deification has done great disservice to humanity – people began to worship and forget the message of the great Gods Rama, Krishna, Shiva and others. Instead they imputed / attached some deeds to them which they would never have liked or encouraged. For personal selfish end the cunning learned people blacked out ***Sabri*** episode of Rama and the message of non-discrimination and glorified Shambooka – beheading to establish Brahminical superiority. They blacked out Supan story of Rajsuya completion declared by Krishna and even ability and conduct as basis of chaturvarna and reduced it to ***Jati*** based division. Even they constructed myth of the rebirth of God as Buddha and left no stone unturned to demolish him by fraternal embrace. The mystic image of God or incarnation theory make people enslave of deity and leave self help. Untouchable should remember Buddha as man excelling by deeds and likewise Ambedkar as liberator from caste evils. Ambedkar has given legal weapon to deal with caste evil-untouchability by abolishing it in all forms and declaring its practices as criminal act. They should consolidate mission of

Article 17 of the Constitution, enjoy privileges for betterment and sacrifice personal interests for community welfare as Dr Ambedkar did and he served the nation by ability as Chairman, Drafting Committee of the Constituent Assembly. They should never forget the message of Ambedkarite Buddhism-One is one's own refuge, who else could be the refuge[24] or educate, organise and agitate (act for claim of freedom), organise the society on the principle of liberty, equality and fraternity, strengthen nationhood and serve the cause of humanity.

III

The fault line of Gandhian approach was that he planned to demolish untouchability but not varnashramadharma. He looked promotion / absorbing of Untouchables into fourth Varna-Shudra. He thought Varnashramadharma to be an appreciable arrangement of social adjustment. In the "Harijan" dated 6.3.1937, he wrote, "What I mean is, one born a scavenger must earn his livelihood by being a scavenger, and then do whatever else he like. For a scavenger is as worthy of his hire as a lawyer or your president. That according to me is Hinduism. There is no better communism on earth. Varnashram Dharma acts even as the law of gravitation. The law of Varna is the anti-thesis of competition which kills."

Ambedkar was cautious of the ill of Gandhian approach as it was nothing but putting old wine into new bottle. Ambedkar pleaded for society based on equality, liberty and fraternity which was not possible in Varnashrama Vyavastha entrenched into hierarchical caste system. Untouchability was not only social problem; it had developed economic too. He agreed with Gandhi on the point that the problem of untouchability can be tackled by change in mind-set of the caste Hindus. But his logic differed, "Those who believe that untouchability will soon vanish do not seem to have paid attention to the economic advantages which it gives to the Hindus. An untouchable can not do anything to get rid of his untouchability. It does not arise out of any personal fault on his part. Untouchability is an attitude of the Hindu, for untouchability to vanish, it is the Hindu who must change."[25]

The study is pointer to the complex Hindu Caste problem and tackling of the issue of Untouchability and in this enterprise both Gandhi and Ambedkar become significant. Seven decade experience after the Independence in 1947 is indicator that (1) the mindset of caste-Hindus has not changed on the line suggested by reformists like Gandhi, Vivekananda and like. Still newspapers are full of news of cutting of leg of some Dalit, beating of pregnant Dalit women for refusing to remove carcasses, rape with Dalit girl, spitting on face and mercilessly beating of a Dalit student in Mujjaffarnagar Central School for securing better marks than caste students and so on; and (2) the purpose of legal sanction envisaged under Article 17 read with Protection of Civil Rights Act, 1955 (renamed in 1976 to remove semblance / remembrance of Untouchability in the form of original Untouchability Offences Act, 1955) and The Scheduled Castes and Scheduled Tribes Prevention of Atrocities Act, 1989 with appropriate changes has not been accomplished. Thus, Ambedkarite vision to abolish Untouchability and declare its practice in any form as crime, has also not worked well. It has done something but more is needed to be supplemented. For fruitful attempt to eradicate the untouchability in its roots and branch the academic and scholarly studies are so required as to avoid Gandhi- Ambedkar debate from confrontationist angle and a positive approach is needed to disseminate knowledge in society from Gandhi-Ambedkar rapprochment, complementariness and Joint attempts to solve the complex problem accepting that law can be significant instrument of social control but not the sole instrument. In order to fill a gap between law on the paper in Poundian sense or formal law in Ehilich's sense and their law in action or living law in addition to legal measures like Article 17 and PCRA, 1955 and SCST PAA, Act, 1989, other means of social control on Gandhian line is also needed. Social mores too need changes. And, therefore authors are of considered view that more and more research papers should be published on line suggested by Pantham and Zelliot's new version expressed in 1992. Here the views of both the writers are presented :

Thomas Pantham says :

"Despite basic differences between and serious conflicts over their respective political, social and religious philosophies and practical political strategies, both shared a genuine and deep commitment to the eradication of untouchability.[26]

In 1992 publication Eleanor Zelliot adds in the last as a foot note –

"........ there are indications that each was conscious of the other's necessary place in any final solution of the problem of Untouchability [Thus], the paths of Gandhi and Ambedkar, while they often diverged, ultimately converged, forcing on the Indian conscience the problem of untouchability as an issue of national concern....".[27]

IV

The status of Untouchables has been enhanced in the eye law – they have acquired constitutional status as well as the legal status. But, due to gap between the law on the paper or the formal law and law inaction or the living law prevalent in rural or semi-urban areas due to no change in social mores, the generalisation of Dr Ambedkar about the graded caste system that, 'a caste is an enclosed class. Hindu society is like tower which have several stories without a ladder or an entrance in which one was to die in the story in which one was born' is fully justified. There is no scope of the recognition of worth or ability. Dr Ambedkar himself had narrated story of melodious singing of ***bhajans*** in Bhajan-Mandali by the two untouchable Mahar good looking boys which attracted appreciation of all. But coming to know their caste, they were humiliated, beaten and penalised. Many serving untouchables are still unable to get good accommodations. If they get by not disclosing their caste and the landlord comes to know later, they are forced to leave the house. The generalisation of Justice Ramaswamy that, "the struggle begins for dalits from the cradle to the grave", still holds the field of dehumanising experiences of Dalits. Caste does not leave to follow even after death. Somewhere discrimination continues even at burial place. Some States have arranged separate burial places (***shamshan***) for Dalits which is constant reminder of the caste discrimination even after death. A very heart touching scene was presented in state of Haryana when a Dalit was not allowed burial of his dead wife at ***Shamashan*** place, nor in some cultivated vacant land and was compelled to dispose of corpse of his wife in front of his dwelling house.

The heart touching observation of Rohith Vemula that "my birth was a tragic accident" – is too fully justified in view of Dalit students not allowed to sit along other students in the class room; they are forced to sit in the last line or outside the room; they are given lesser marks in internal assessments and the news of Bihar Central School crossed all the limits of decency of the civilised civic society when the T.V. Channel showed on screen the brutal beating of a Dalit student by two brothers (sons of some criminal caste person in Jail) for his only fault that being Dalit he had scored better marks than caste-students. He was being tortured since long by spitting on face. But he dare not to whisper. After T.V. screening his maternal grandfather lodged F.I.R. which was followed by pressurisation on the victim Dalit to withdraw the complaint.

To endure and dare not to speak is developed due to ingrained inferiority complex and sense of insecurity on the part of Untouchables. How to remove this complex has been a great social problem. Some untouchables develop the habit of reading Gita and Ramayana in their children from the very beginning to overcome the inferiority complex. The conversation between Dr Ambedkar and his father is very instructive. When Ambedkar asked his father, why he insisted on reading the Mahabharata and Ramayana, which recounted the greatness of the Brahmins and the Kshatriyas and repeated the stories of the degradation of the Shudras and the Untouchables." The father of Dr Ambedkar proffered answer : "We belong to the Untouchables, and you are likely to develop an inferiority complex, which is natural. The value of [the] Mahabharata and Ramayana lies in removing this inferiority complex. See Drona and Karna – they were small men, but to what heights they rose ! Look at Valmiki – he was Koli (tribal population), but he became the author of [the] Ramayana. It is for removing this inferiority complex that I ask you to read the Mahabharata and Ramayana."[28] There is a point in it, though rebelling mind of Ambedkar could not be convinced.

A new problem is arising in society on assertion of Dalit rights throwing inferiority complex or insecurity. The Ambedkarite mantra of educate, organise and agitate inspires Dalits to claim equal treatment, dignity and freedom from exploitation and if done so it invites violent retaliation from upper caste through community boycott, torture, deprivation of employment etc. The present day requirement of Dalit protection is that such boycott by upper caste Hindus should be made punishable.

V

Opportunity is essential to the development of human caliber and its proper utilisation in the nation building. Intelligence and diligence added with opportunity bring success in life. Both Ambedkar and Justice Ramaswamy were intelligent and good students from the beginning. Both got support from worth loving teachers. Ambedkar got financial support from the ruler of Baroda and Chhattrapati Shahuji Maharaja of Kolhapur State and got education from abroad with more broad equalitarian vision and made all efforts to translate it into life mission for amelioration of all deprived classes – Untouchables, workers and women. He got opportunity to work as member and chairman, Drafting Committee of the Constituent Assembly and gave a Constitution with splendid compromises and a document of social revolution. His work was so impressing that Dr Rajendra Prasad, President, Constituent Assembly could not resist him from expressing the unparalleled contribution of Dr Ambedkar in words that his choice was the choice of right person, at right time and for right work. The work culture was so high that without caring the deteriorating health he completed with full ability the job of drafting the Constitution, answering all issues and leading compromises acceptable to all or near consensus of the members. In the process he remained uninfluenced by the personality cult and win over even the Gandhian predominant notion – in persuading to adopt unanimously the Ashoka's Dhammachakkapravartan as national symbol in the national flag instead of Gandhi's Charakha; preferring industrial development model in the place of cottage industries, resisting third tier of democracy at Panchayat level and so on which are proving more beneficial in the national development than the Gandhian model. Like all other countries, in framing of the Constitution our Constituent Assembly also consisted of the representatives of only 10 per cent elite people. Dr Ambedkar gave shape to the need and voice of remaining 90 per cent weak, meek and poor common people. So did Justice Ramaswamy he found opportunity to serve the nation as a Judge of the Andhra Pradesh High Court and thereafter as judge of the Supreme Court of India and proved to provide exemplary judicial service by putting record days of working, record number of disposal of cases, working even beyond prescribed working court hours and giving new dimension of justice-oriented sociological approach, making the Constitution on paper a living Constitution for weaker sections of the society. Coming events cast their shadows before. Justice Ramaswamy's qualitative judgments attracted report of the A.I.R. from the very first day and his disposal of cases without postponing for the next day proved exemplay for the court functioning. The noted jurist Dr Upendra

Baxi termed him as inaugural judicial actor, who deployed judicial activism for the depressed underclasses of contemporary Indian, inaugurated new spheres of social action litigation."[29] His judgment in ***State of Karnataka v. Appa Balu Ingale***[30] is judicial trend setter. He says, "Judges should respond to human situation to combat social evil" and "the court as the vehicle of transforming the nation's life, would respond to the nation's needs and add to interpret the law with pragmatism to further public welfare and to make the constitutional animation a reality."[31]

The contribution of Justice Ramaswamy would have been much more to the nation had he not been discriminated in the natural course of elevation to the bench first at the A.P. High Court and then to the apex Court. Had he been elevated in natural course without delay he would have adorned the Chief Justice of India's coveted post as the first Dalit CJI (instead of Justice Balakrishnan).[32]

The decorum of a Judge peeps through the life of Justice Ramaswamy. He was made victim of media mindset. In corruption episode of Justice V. Ramaswamy one magasine had inserted photograph of Justice K. Ramaswamy. He just ignored on pitiable mind set that, "this is indicative of the mindset of the people that the poor are generally corrupt."[33] The grace of Justice K. Ramaswamy is also exemplary as to the claim of date of birth. There are many instances of honourable justices claiming change in date of birth at the time of retirement and facing litigation on the point.[34]

In School certificate Justice Ramaswamy's date of birth was shown one year earlier (1932) than his actual date of birth (1933). He retired gracefully without claiming one year more.

Rohith Vemula was a brilliant chap. But nation could not find his contribution due to his falling victim of the hostile discrimination at the hands of power that be's mindset.

VI

The fruit of the participation of all sections of the society in the governance of the country makes the country grow immensely. The emancipation of Untouchables and weaker section of the society through affirmative actions or preferential treatment is a way to tackle the national problem. It is part of justice. It is a way to compensate not only for historical deprivation of some classes but also to push them getting them out of the present deplorable conditions which have resulted and accumulated due to the continued deprivation.

Non-discrimination and recognition of worth strengthens in nation doubly. First, the talented persons from lower strata of the society are encouraged to do more fruitful work and excel in life and second, even the upper class people try to compete by acquiring more and more worth. An atmosphere of fair competition is created which is better for the healthy growth of the country. In this backdrop one may easily imagine : Had Shambook, Eklabya, Karna, Vemula been appreciated for their excelling in life, helped by equal opportunity and encouraged to add more to their achievements, country would have gone much ahead, social cohesion, solidarity and co-operation would have flourished and invaders would not have dared to attack on our country nor country would suffer in future.

Inspite of their unequalled contribution in the nation building the untouchable caste stigma has not spared untouched Baba Saheb Ambedkar and Justice K. Ramaswamy in their due recognition through academic writings of others. As has been discussed in the book for a longer period Baba Saheb remained neglected. He could be adorned by Bharat Ratna after four decade of the inauguration of the Constitution and that too by 11th Prime Minister Sri Vishwanath Pratap Singh, a social justice P.M. Dr Baxi rightly doubts, if Baba Saheb would have accepted Bharat Ratna at such belated time had he been alive in 1990.[35] With the change of political climate of the country Baba Saheb became a vote attracting figure and has attracted all politicians, academicians and social reformers. But indepth researches are still lacking and the need of the hour is to analyse his own works in the light of world renowned juridical studies of social democracy, legal rights, distributive justice through affirmative actions etc. Justice Ramaswamy has also been neglected in the academic and legal circle. Barring his own autobiography – Ceaseless and Relentless Journey published by EBC, Lucknow, 2008, no other publication on his positive contribution through constructive and innovative justice-oriented interpretation as constitutional law judge different from mere CPC Judge is available whereas many advocates have published volumes on other Judges' contribution and memories. Much is needed to be probed about Justice Ramaswamy's contribution as a sociological Jurist Judge inspired by the Gandhian and Ambedkarite ideologies on tackling the socio-legal problems through a living interpretation of the Preamble, Directive Principles of State Policy and problems of social justice created by still static mores of the Hindu Society standing in the way of social transformation through Constitution.

The country needs proper appreciation of Vemula's sacrifice and national loss through his departing from amidst us. It gave an occasion to view, review and again think about the functioning of the university system – the delayed release of grant of scholarship and consequent financial hardship caused to the students; inequal treatment with talented Untouchable students – non-providing of appropriate guide, labs and due guidance and leaving them all the time to realise, demoralisation, humiliation and persecution. Justice Roopanwala Commission's report on Hyderabad Central University affairs not on the term of reference but diverted to give clean chit to some authorities or the persons relating to power that be is eye-opener to the working of even the so-called judicial Commission. First, was it wise, proper and legally permissible to appoint that Commission by the Ministry (HRD) whose Cabinet Minister herself was said to be involved in the university's inter –students group rivalry; Second, if the Commission crossed the limit of terms of reference, gave report without taking into account the relevant facts like version of Radhika's adoptive mother, herself a teacher, surroundings in which she brought up the children (whether amongst Scheduled Caste Basti or upper caste dwellings); School teaching atmosphere, and university affairs like spontaneous first action of Proctorial Board issuing warning to both the rival groups, and later punishing Dalits and completely leaving other group, falsity of the complaint of some student whose credential was discredited by doctor's version who operated him of disease and not beaten ailment, why the Report has not yet been rejected and fresh Commission consisting of different social segments representative has not been appointed? The causes leading suicide of a brilliant chap with Ambedkarite vision of social and community service has been side-tracked. Non-issue became the prominent issue and that too not appropriately probed. The position of university functioning remained where it was in the pre-Vemula suicide time. Unless the ill is diagnosed properly how the cure will be possible? And, one is compelled to join Justice V. R. Krishna Iyer's words :

"Those members handicapped by numbers or social disability have the right of special concern. It is there land and equalisation, through particular fillip, shall lift them to equality.

This process is equalisation to attain equality.

Full many a gem of purest ray serene,
The dark unfadomed caves of ocean bear,
Full many a flower is born to blush unseen,
And waste its sweetness on the desert air."
Thomas Gray[36]

VIII

More and more we read the Works and Writings of Baba Saheb Ambedkar more we get convinced about his unmistakable conclusions about the ill of graded Hindu social structure[37] and its continuance inspite of our freedom for all and constitutional commitment to wipe out every tear from every eye. One of his conclusion is that Indian social structure has been exploited by the priestly class as well as Banias. The richest persons (legal entity) are the temples constructed in the name of some deity and that richness is held by and distributed among priestly class. From womb to tomb there are a sixteen Sanskaras and on all the occasions priestly class gets some financial offerings. Even the Twenty-first Century scientific development has not closed the business of priesthood. It is flourishing beyond imagination. Superstition, dependence on considerations other than worth are spreading. Almost all T.V. Channels have employed some astrologer or the other who starts preaching in supernatural powers from the morning before dawn. Even the most popular and cheap benefactor, omnipresent, needing no formality in calling for help– Hanuman is being made costly and the services, goodwill and name of well respected, honoured Cine-actor, once famous for national ideas spirited film songs (*Mere desh ki dharati Sona Ugale Ugale Hire Moti.... Or Aai Mere Vatan Ke Longon Jara Ankh mein bhar lo pani, Jo Shahid Huye hain Unki Jara Yaad Karo Kurbani*) are appropriated for selling Hanuman Chalisa Yantra. Nationalism of the Cine-actor is lost in commercialisation, spreading superstitions, demeaning the most secular helper of human beings – Hanuman. This is the trailor of only one horror show. Superstitions are created, sold and propagated for the benefit of priestly class and Bania Jewellers. For spreading superstitions, ignoring self help- Gods help those who help themselves, nationalist goodwill is sold for the sordid boons. There is hardly a good astrologer who does not have buildings in Delhi, Bombay and other places, though many of them are themselves issueless. The mindset of the society is so build that modern scientific instruments are used for making more and more noises, pollution and health hazards in the society – more and more ***Durga Puja, Diwali Puja, Ganesh Puja, Chchaththi Puja*** more and more earning of priestly class and merchants. Recent ***Deepawali*** is source of unestimable earning of priestly class and Baniyas. In villages Banias give money, eatables and other necessaries to poor people. Recover the amount as they like. Purchase crops on lower price, sell on higher price. Business man is always flourishing. The lion's share of the capital of the nation is in the hands of less than two per cent people, known as big businessmen. This peculiar phenomenon goes on. Every year deities images are build, worshipped, money is thrown in the pocket of priestly class and Baniyas, image is immersed. In the process many people are drowned. Sometimes, one listens – ***Ganapati Bappa Moriya, Agale Barash Tun Jaldi Aa***, as if Ganapati Bappa has gone on leave or picnic tour. Is deity as savior of people not available when some image is immersed ? When gods are omnipresent and everytime present, one fails to understand why to immerse their images ? The circle goes on, emerging, remerging and again every year with more and more pomp and show ? Is it part of religion ? Does it furnish good acquaints of Jiva with Shiva (Brahm)? In spite of the Supreme Court's decisions in ***Church of God (Full Gospel) v. K.K.R. Majestic Colony welfare Association***[38] allowing ban on making too much noise in religious puja so as to disturb people of locality and create *noise pollution and in* ***Noise Pollution (V), In re***,[39] allowing ban on bursting of fire crackers between 10.00 P.M. and 6.00 A.M. even on Diwali, as bursting of fire cracker is not an essential part of Diwali celebrations and is against right liberty to live noise pollution free environment, the use of fire cracker-more powerful and on large scale is becoming the fashion of Diwali Pooja. Is it good ? Definitely not. Such practices are detractions from dharma, misuse of religion and definitely Adharma (to cause inconvenience to others). What is remedy ? Is derivative or use of intermediary between men and gods for one's welfare in consonance with the basic tenets of dharma? The answer lies in the brilliant study of Buddha and Ambedkar- the search of the real dharma – Do good, be good, believe in self help, search your refuge yourself- be enlightened, educate, organise and agitate for justice. The need of the present time is to develop scientific temper and humanism preached by Buddha,

Vivekananda and Ambedkar and enshrined in our Fundamental Duties.

The superiority complex among Hindu-fold is taking new turn-divisive forces are raising heads like phoenix from the ashes. The recent one is the acts done in the name of 'Hindutva.' In election 'Hinduvta' has been interchangeably used for Hinduism. Since 1995 Judicial verdict about Hindutva as a way of life different from Hinduism its use became frequent as a secular slogan advocating a cultural identity and nationalism. Hindutva has taken a dangerous turn. As in her recent petition in the Supreme Court seeking ban on the use of 'Hindutva' in polls, Teesta Setalvad argues that, "This has had devastating consequences leading to demands of homogenisation and assimilation of minority communities and SC/ST in the 'Hindutva' way of life. 'Hindutva' has become a mark of nationalism and citizenship. Such an interpretation has curtailed the faith in secularism, which is a basic feature of the Constitution."[40] A new type of organisation amongst Hindus is developing as Cow Vigilantism group. Many incidents of brutal beating and attack on the Scheduled Castes person have taken place while they had been exercising the unskinning of dead cows as their traditional occupation. No wonder the situation has got so aggravated that a PIL has been filed in the apex Court alleging that cow vigilantes were spreading hatred against certain sections like the Scheduled Castes and minorities. The Supreme Court has decided to examine cow vigilantism across the country in different States. The notices were issued to States and the Central Government to respond by November 7, 2016 about PIL filed against the practice of cow vigilantism.[41] The Guna episode of beating the Dalits has caused serious concern. Nearly two hundred Scheduled Castes persons embraced Buddhism. At many places the sense of insecurity is looming large and Dalits are facing crisis of earning livelihood due to the loss of traditional occupation of unskinning the dead animals (cows). Twenty first century is reverting back to old barbaric state of beheading and cutting the thumb. Dr Ambedkar faced discrimination but was never beaten for securing better marks than caste students. So was case with Justice Ramaswamy. Now-a-days a Dalit student may not be allowed to score better marks than even ruffian caste students. Spitting and beating scene of Central School Dalit Student by Davang caste students in Bihar, all students standing passive onlooker, relishing and enjoying the discomfiture of talented Dalit boy, shows a bad tendency and major fault-line in our post independence / Constitution India, Davangas may beat and allow not to speak for redressal (***Jabra Maare Rovahu na de***). The process of decadence which started in Brahminical era is not appearing to decay. More moral decadence and social degeneration is becoming rampant. The warning of Dr Ambedkar is more significant than earlier; "we must make our political democracy a social democracy as well."

References

1. Swami Vivekananda, Selections from Swami Vivekanada, Advaita Ashram,1944 p. 212.
2. Swami Vivekananda, Selections from Swami Vivekananda, Advita Ashram,1944. p.285.
3. *Ibid.*
4. Gandhi : Answers to Questions.
5. Gandhi To Haribandhu Pathak, 6 October, 1932 (in) CWMG, Vol. 57, p. 8.
6. Gandhi, Questions and Answers.
7. Article 25. Freedom of Conscience and free profession, practice and propagation of religion – (1) Subject to public order, morality and health and to the other provisions of this part, all persons are equally entitled to freedom of conscience, and the right freely to profess, practice and propagate religion.
   (2) Nothing in this article shall affect the operation of any existing law or prevent the State from making any law –
   (a) regulating or restricting any economic, financial, political or other secular activity which may be associated with religious practice;
   (b) providing for social welfare and reform or throwing open of Hindu religious institutions of a public character to all classes and section of Hindus....."
8. A.I.R. 1964 S.C. 1501.
9. (1997) 4 SCC 606; see also ***Kanaka Parameshwari Anna Satram Committee v. Commissioner***, H.R.C. and E. (1997) 5 SCC 303.
10. (1972) 2 SCC 11.
11. (1996) 9 SCC. 548.
12. N. Adityam v. Travancore Devaswom Board (2002) 8 SCC 853.
13. Bhurinath v. State of J. and K. A.I.R. 1997 S.C. 1711.
14. Annihilation of Caste Vol. I (in) Ambedkar's Writing and Speeches Published by Maharashtra Govt., 1987.
15. Vasant Moon (ed.) Dr Babasaheb : Ambedkar Writings and Speeches, Vol. III, p. 158. Dr Ambedkar said : "Much of the ancient

history of India is no history at all. Not that ancient India has no history. It has plenty of it. But it has lost its character. It has been made mythology to amuse women and children. This seems to have been done deliberately by the Brahminical order." Vasant Moon (ed.) Dr Baba Saheb Ambedkar ..... supra, Vol. III, p. 151.

16. Valarian Rodrigues, Buddhism, Machism and the Conception of Emancipation in Ambedkar, (in) Peter Robb (ed.) *Dalit Movements and the Meaning of Labour in India*; Oxford University Press, 1993, p. 305.
17. Cited in Eleanor Zelliot, From Untouchable to Dalit : Essays on the Ambedkar Movement, New Delhi, Manohar Books, 1992, p. 192.
18. Cited in Zelliot, supra, f. n. 17, p. 219.
19. Quoted from Debjani Ganguly, Caste and Dalit Life Worlds Post Colonial Perspective', Orient Longman, 2005, p. 194.
20. *Ibid*. p. 198.
21. Cited in Zelliot, supra, f. n. 17, p. 238.
22. Quoted from Debjani Ganguly, 'Caste and Dalit Life Worlds – Post Colonial Perspective', Orient Longman, 2005, p. 194.
23. Quoted from ibid, p. 195.
24. Dhammapada, XII, 4, Verse 160 : atta he attano natho Ka hi natho paro siya/ attana he sudantena Nathan labhati dullabham//.
25. Dr B. R. Ambedkar, What Congress and Gandhi Have Done To the Untouhables, p. 19.
26. Thomas Pantham, Against Untouchability- The Discourse of Gandhi and Ambedkar (in) Gopal Guru (ed.) Humiliation – Claims and Context, Oxf. Univ. Press, p. 179.
27. Eleanor Zelliot, 'Gandhi and Ambedkar : A Study in Leadership' (in) Ishtha Banerjee-Dubey (ed.) Caste in History, Oxf. Univ. Press, 2008, 2010, pp. 197-209 at p. 209.
28. Buddha and His Dhamma, CE, p. XXVI.
29. Upendra Baxi, Explorations in the Geographies of [Injustice] (in) S.K. Verma and Kusum (eds.) Fifty Years of the Supreme Court of India: Its Grasp and Reach, Oxf. Univ. Press, 2000, pp. 156-209 at p. 176).
30. A.I.R. 1993 S.C. 1126.
31. See, Chapter 10.
32. See Chapter 10 point XIII.
33. See Chapter 10 point XIII.
34. The notable examples are Justice Jyoti Prakash Mitter's and Justice A.S. Anand's cases.
35. U. Baxi, Emancipation As Justice, see also discussion in Chapter 7 of the book.
36. Quoted from V. R. Krishna Iyer "Unequal Justice to Professional

Courses" (in) Indian Law – Dynamic Dimensions of the Abstract, Universal Law Publishing, New Delhi, 2012 pp. 418-420 at p. 418.

37. Dr Ambedkar's multi-storied mansion simile without ladder has been supported by many sociologists exposing Brahminical influence. G.S. Ghurye writes, "Caste in India is a Brahminical child of the Indo-Aryan culture cradled in the land of Ganga and Jamuna and thence transferred to other parts of the country." Majumdar very aptly describes the caste-based social structure as pyramidal- at apex Brahmins and the bottom the untouchables.
38. (2007 7 SCC 282.
39. (2005) 5 SCC 733.
40. Ban Use of 'Hindutva' in polls : Teesta, The Times of India, Varanasi 22.10.2016, p. 12.
41. The Times of India, *Ibid.* p. 1.

13
Suggestions

1. The root cause of untouchables discomfiture need be removed. As Dr Ambedkar had explained, "Untouchability is not only a system of unmitigated economic exploitation but it is also a system of uncontrolled economic exploitation. That is, because there is no independent public opinion to condemn it and there is no important machinery of administration and restraint."[1] No change in set up and mind set is visible in seven decade period. The clue of solution was visualised in the observation of Justice O. Chinnappa Reddy : "Why not ask ourselves why 35 (now seventy) years after independence, the position of the Scheduled Castes etc. has not greatly improved ? Is it not a legitimate question to ask whether things might have been different, had the District Administrators and the State and Central Bureaucrats been drawn in larger numbers from these classes ?"[2] The idea of power sharing is the only solution. State should ensure more and more recruitments of the SCs/STs on all posts- from bottom to the top. The real power could be shared by the weaker sections only if the doors of the higher decks were opened to them.[3] The warning-cum-practical suggestion of Justice V.R. Krishna Iyer needs serious consideration and faithful implementation. Justice Iyer observed:
   "The higher echelons are real controllerates not menial levels. Obviously Article 16(4) was not designed to get more Harijans into Government as scavengers and sweepers but as "Officers" and "bosses", so that administrative power may become thc common property of the high or low, homogenized and integrated into one community."[4]
2. Now time has come to seriously think enough is enough of

divisive impact. We should take lesson from history. As men become wiser by experience, so should be the case of nation. What has been the effect of degrading certain classes – exploiting by the social and economic traditions of the country ? To quote Justice Kuldip Singh "This country remained under shackles of slavery for one thousand years. The reason for our inability to fight the foreign rule was the social degenerations of India because of the Caste system. To rule this country was not necessary to divide the people, the caste system conveyed the message, "Divided We Are – Come and Rule us."[5] History of Hinduism has made clear –

(i) Caste system has breeded gradation and degradation among the Hindu-fold.
(ii) It developed superiority and privileges of some higher caste people and inferiority, deprivation of wealth and means of livelihood to certain people.
(iii) It created resentment, reaction and isolation of different classes.
(iv) India became a divided country without nationhood.
(v) It made easier to Shaka, Hoona, Mughal, British to conquer and rule.
(vi) If the division and gulf between different classes remains without cementing, the country will not prosper.

Our most of the time is consumed to deal with trivialities. Police force is busy in dealing with problem of Untouchables' entry in some prohibited entry temple, entry of women in some temples, vigilantism, so on so forth. Has not time come to take some bold decision unswayed by populism and immediate power gain ? History will evaluate what is achievement of V.P. Singh, P.M. through implementation of Mandal Commission Report. Has it not served the social justice cause ? There is need of a ruler who can mould the public opinion like equalitarian Ashoka, the Great, who can speak to Hindus in definitive term that deeds done in the name of Dharma what are actually adharma in the language of Mahabharata, cannot be tolerated at any cost. As A.V. Dicey comments laws foster or create public opinion.[6] In the age of this globalised cut throat economic competition we are engaging even courts to solve the problem of Triple Talak, Women's entry in some temple or Dargah, Dalit entry in temples, unnecessary Dalit-Caste persons tussle resulting to atrocities. How long will it continue ?

3. As Dr Ambedkar exposed changing of name of dalits as 'Harijan' did not make any change. People knew that the so-called 'Harijans' are the same untouchables. So has been the impact of removal of the word 'Untouchability' from Untouchability Offences Act, 1955 and renaming it as Protection of Civil Rights Act, 1955 or use of secularised constitutional designations the Scheduled Castes and the Scheduled Tribes. People behave with the same contempt as they did earlier. It is so because the most of the Scheduled Castes are economically dependent on caste people. After Guna atrocities on SCs a very positive suggestion came from Sabarmati Sevashram telling the Gujarat Government to distribute vacant land among the Dalits. The exact availability of land was also indicated. Most of the vulnerability of Dalits is due to their being landless and vacant land are lying with States. Why not to distribute lands and provide effective occupation by Dalits ?
4. Dalits do not open lips against atrocities on them in fear of boycott i.e. deprivation of livelihood.[7] Dr Ambedkar's message worked; untouchables are getting education, they are organising and they have started agitating for their rights. They have developed some confidence. They have developed courage to practice – ***Vakta Ka Takaza Hai Toofan Se Jujho, Kab Tak Chaloge Kinare Kinare***. When they open their mouth and agitate for their claim, they invite another trouble. They face boycott by upper caste people, deprivation of job, right to fetch water from common tap, deprivation of right to purchase goods and necessaries of life from village Baniyas and so on. As Justice O. Chinnappa Reddy observed : "social hierarchy and economic position exhibit an indisputable mutuality. The lower the caste, the poorer its members. The poorer the members of a caste, the lower the caste and economic situation, reflecting each other as they do are the dues ***exmachina*** of the social status occupied and the economic poor wielded by an individual or class in the rural society".[8] In order to ensure no danger to livelihood, and the boycott of Dalits by caste people should be made an offence punishable by law.
5. Co-operation, not confrontation, rapprochment, not divergent approach and mutual understanding must be the basis of the solution of the caste evil in the Hindu society particularly and Indian society in general. Whereever a man goes caste

goes. Nothing is automatic in India. Untouchables embrace Buddhism for the sake of equality. But caste people still treat them untouchables. The superiority and inferiority complex has got so entrenched that the ill of brahminism has engrafted all the society- even the equality based religious units Islam, Sikhism, Christianity etc.. Conversion to Buddhism did not provide privilege of equality in actuality but on technical judicial interpretation many convents were disprivileged from contesting election from reserved category.[9] Pragmatism needs to be a guiding force. Both Gandhian and Ambedkarite models should help each other. Gandhi stands for higher caste benevolence. Those who have plenty should act as trustee and use their property for poor beneficiaries. Simple living and high thinking moved by ***peer parai*** (otherness) should be practice of those who wield power and pelf. Ambedkar should be role model for Dalits for getting relieved of interiority, armed with modernity-suited-booted with tie- Arise, awake and stop not till the goal of egalitarian Indian society is not achieved through liberty, equality and fraternity.

6. The message of Ambedkar and Ramaswamy to work hard ceaselessly and relentlessly in life, work for poor brethren with a touch of humanism, uplift and dignified life should be adopted by all. Introspection at all level should work. Dalit should assert themselves for vindication of their status. But should never misuse shield provided to them. Even one instance of misuse of SCs/STs Prevention of Atrocities Act, may greatly damage the cause of Dalit emancipation. Shield should be used for protection not for baseless retaliation. Honesty must be guiding force.
7. Dr Ambedkar defined Brahminism as an evil spread even in tower castes people, to say, Mahar thinks himself superior to chamar and does not inter-marry or like to inter-dine. So is case of all the castes. This mentality has to be changed. Learn good from others, where ever, available. But, discard evil of complexes. Charity must begin at home. In this respect (late) Ram Surat, M. P. from Gorakhpur set an example by marrying the daughter of a Halalkhor much inferior in local estimation than Chamar. All should try to get good traits of Brahmins and avoid brahminism and make success the dream of Vivekanand and Babasaheb who himself had many Brahmin good friends including one who taught him Sanskrit and his better half a Saraswat Brahmin Savita. He was critical

of Brahminism – an evil. It would be best homage to him to leave this evil.

8. Dr Ambedkar or Justice Ramaswamy never compromised with their integrity and dignity. Both worked for others. They never got benefit of reservation. Rather they suffered many a times on account of birth. But they worked for down-trodden, and other weaker section – workers and women. Given the opportunity they proved their metals. They knew the sorrow (*Dard*) of untouchables and translated it into the legal terms providing for prevention and protection. Ambedkar kicked Union Law Ministership, not for himself but for the cause of weaker sections – women, SCs/STs and OBCs. Is not it the pious duty of the Dalits, receiving benefit of reservation in the name of class, to work for their betterment ? Recent past increasing atrocities on SCs and silence on the part of SCs/ STs representatives in the Parliament and the State Legislatures needs serious introspection. Did Dr Ambedkar fought for it? Have the Dalit leaders got the opportunity to participate in Legislatures only for enjoying lucrative salary, position and raising hands approving what the leaders of their parties want ? They must know that after abolition of Untouchability almost all prominent members of the Constituent Assembly (who mattered) were against extending of more concessions to SCs including reservation in legislatures. Dr Ambedkar threatened boycott and did not participate in discussions for three to four days. The Assembly members were compelled to rethink and reservation and other special provisions were adopted. Reserved category public servant or representative (M.L.As or M.Ps.) represent class to which they belong. They are not meant to fall victim of new brahminism. Had they shown solidarity for Dalit cause and threatened to resign **en masse** after Guna atrocities, attracting long agitations, the result would have been different and recurring incidents of Dalit torture, humiliation and atrocities would have stopped. Should not such people remember and celebrate Baba Saheb's birth day reciprocating community cause for his sacrifices? Baba Saheb was, is and shall remain messiah of downtrodden. But where are enjoyer of benefits of the fruit of his sacrifice to pay real homage to that great humanist soul ?

Dr Ambedkar never clinged with office, worked for others, nation and posterity and died with anxiety of the fate of downtrodden and nation, Ramaswamy J. worked for betterment of down-trodden, social justice and human dignity. He refused his elevation to Chief Justice of Sikkim High Court because there would not be much work for him to which he was committed. Vemula sacrificed his life to awaken consciousness towards justice, liberty and dignity. A serious introspection is needed on the part of those who are taking the benefits of the grand deeds of the greatmen ensuring constitutional protections, safeguards and privileges.

9. The recognition of the special significance must be conceded to Dr Ambedkar's real grasp of the Indian problems. There is much truth in observation of Dr Baxi : "We all forget that it (the Constitution) was written in the blood and fury of partition and only Ambedkar had some sense of contradictions between the social and political inequality". Thus, the warning -cum- suggestion of Dr Ambedkar to search the ways to fill the gap between the constitutionally and legally devised equality and ingrained social inequality and also the judicial efforts of Justice K. Ramaswamy need serious thinking.

10. The social psychology, mind-set and social mores, need serious thoughts beyond Gandhi-Ambedkar vision of assimilative society. Both had encouraged inter-marriage and inter-dining. In his last days, Gandhi had stopped participation in such marriages in which one of the parties was not Dalit. But society could not take inspiration and translate it in the realities of life within all these days since Independence. As late as November, 20, 2016, The Indian Express news service reported, "3 of Dalits family shot in .." The obvious reason was inter-caste marriage between a Dhanak (S.C.) boy and a girl from the jat family (this is not an isolated incident, but recurring problem of the tradition bound narrow mindedness). In order to make Gandhian and Ambedkarite mission of social assimilation reality, ways and means need be devised to publically honour such marriages; newspapers should desist from glorifying such brutal murder cases by terming such sorrowful affairs as honour-killing. On the one hand public should be properly educated so as to get rid of complexes and irrational social mores and on the other, criminal law should be implemented with iron hand so as to ensure the rule of law.

11. Live and let live should be motto of the present day Indian way of life. Be good, do good, need be of religio-social model of life. Dignity of all will serve the country best. Talent of all sections of society should be utilised properly by providing equal opportunity to develop and equalisational justice, where required should ensure justice to the deprived and disprivileged and enable them to contribute in the nation-building.
12. India should take lesson from past experience of division, should leave that path which has proved to be perniciously disastrous and adopt new social mores of love, equality, dignity of all and nation building through worth, discarding birth.

    The opinion of Justice P.B. Sawant, expressed in the famous **Mandal case,** should be torch-bearer for the national recourse:

    "Those who point to the past achievements and the progress of the country, forget that these achievements and the progress are by a tiny section of the society who got opportunity to realise and use their talent. If all the sections of the society had such opportunity, this country's achievements in all fields and walk of life would have been many times more."[10]

Citing the examples of Vyasa, Valmiki and Ambedkar in the recent past, the learned judge speaks of the hard reality to be realised and let us wish:

Winter of hate and discorn should go
Autumn of love and solidarity should come.

Let us brood over the national cause seriously by now. India has been deprived of the contribution of how many Shambookas, Eklabyas, Karnas, Rohith Vemulas and how has the country benefited by the immense contributions of Ambedkars and Ramaswamys. When the time will come and our Dalit brethren will be able to sing with the Australian aboriginal poet?

To our father's father
The pain, the sorrow.
To our children's children,
The glad tomorrow.

References

1. Constituent Assembly Debates, Vol. IX-XII, p. 979.
2. *K.C. Vashantha Kumar v. State of Karnataka*, A.I.R. 1985 S.C. 1485.

3. *Akhil Bharatiya Soshit Karamachari Sangh v. Union of India* (1981), 1 SCC 246 at p. 274.
4. *Ibid.*, p. 274.
5. *Indra Sawhney v. Union of India,* 1992, SCC (L and S) Suppl. 1 at p. 176, para 337.
6. Law and Public Opinion in 19th Century England.
7. For detail study, see Anirudh Prasad and Chandra Sen Pratap Singh, "Reservation : Policy, Practice and its Impact on Society, Kalpaz Publication, Delhi, 2016.
8. *K.C. Vasantha Kumar v. State of Karnataka,* A.I.R. 1985 S.C. 1485.
9. For detail see, Anirudh Prasad and Chandra Sen Pratap Singh, Reservation : Policy Practice and its Impact on Society, Vol. 1, Chapter-5, Kalpaz Publications, Delhi, 2016.
10. Indra Sawhney v. Union of India 1992 SCC (Labur&Services) 1 at p. 209.

14

Postscript: A Ray of Hope

Since the manuscript of the book went to the press for publication many constructive and revolutionary reformative rethinking have appeared on the fore[1] and many informative literature[2] in conscnance with ethics of rapprochement have come to the knowledge of the authors, a few lines by way of addendum will make the study of the book more timely and of everlasting value.

On May, 2017 a news column appeared in The Indian Express (14.05.2017 p.1) through reporting of Pragya Kaushika under caption, "RSS outfit wants Manusmriti reworked to remove "anti-Dalit, anti-woman parts".[3] The report speaks of the move of the RSS's cultural affiliate **Sanskar Bharati** to work in collaboration with the Union Ministry of Culture to correct the historical wrong. According to Amir Chand, Joint organisational Secretary, **Sanskar Bharathi** the historical fact is acknowledged that Manu was born 8000 years ago and after 5500 years of his birth Manusmriti got different version. The present version is said to have been compiled 200 C E. To quote Mr. Chand, "We are debating the removal of portions from Manusmriti, which are anti-Dalit and anti woman...."[4]

In fact the same was the objective of Dr Ambedkar's Critique of Manusmriti and Mahatma Gandhi. His project was emancipator and Gopal Guru has rightly observed that, 'Ambedkar was a path finder who chose critique as a method of ethical preservation to gently pull in and retain members of caste society in the interlocutory framework of conservation'.[5] Gopal Guru views that collective project of Gandhi and Ambedkar was redeeming India with its affirmative energy which is eternal to Buddhism. He concludes that, 'in both the thinkers it was ultimately the ethical that was important for redemption, wherein conceptual politics was only the initial condition to realise the redemption of India.[6]

How redemption will materialise is a million dollar question?

Nobel Prize winner Gurudev Rabindra Nath Tagore had lamented m 1926 that 'by discrimination against the Namasudras the Hindus rendered themselves weak and vulnerable'.[7] Even after nearly a century discrimination and persecution has not stopped. Professor Upendra Baxi, a noted Jurist drew the attention of the nation towards 125 day Bhim Yatra (Dibrugarh se Dilli Tak) culminating in Delhi on April 13, 2016 into a stale message: "Stop Killing us"[8] So is the message of Guna episode and rec.ent Mazzaffar Nagar incidents and March of Ambedkar Army on Jantar Mantar, New Delhi in May 2017 itself. In **National Campaign on Dalit in Human Rights v. Union of India (2016 (12) SCALE 955)** the apex court accepted that there has been failure on the part of the concerned authorities in ensuring the objective of the SCs and STs (Prevention of Atrocities) Act, 1989 and thereby the laudable object of the Act has been defeated. The suffering of SCs and STs continued unabated. Consequently with a view to achieve the constitutional goal of equality for all the citizens, it directed the Central and the State governmentstrictly enforce the provisions of the Act.

The former Director of ICSSR, Professor Sukhdeo Thorat while receiving Ambedkar Foundation award for the year 2011 on 26.5.2017 at Vigyan Bhavan, New Delhi from President Pranab Mukherji could not resist his anxiety on Dalit plight. He told The Indian Express sideline of the event, "I accepted the award with great humility, but with mixed feeling of anguish and pain. (This is due to the)rising wave of atrocities on Dalits in recent times in Mirchpur (Haryana), Una (Gujtat), Ahmadnagar (Maharashtra), Saharanpur (UP) and other places."[9] He asserted, "The tribute to Dr Ambedkar through this award is to stop the increasing open mass violence against Dalits and secure the fundamental right of protection of life and personal liberty guaranteed in Article 21 of the Constitution."[10]

In this backdrop the move of the Sanskar Bharti in collaboration with the Union Ministry of Culture a welcome· move to be appreciated , encouragod and adopted from the core of the heart. This is because Dr Ambedkar's message is unity in diversity and not unity in perversity. Perversity may be eradicated slowly if the long awaited, ethical persuation of Dr Ambedkar and feeling in the core heart of Gandhiji is completed by re examining controversial parts of our scriptures meet effectively. A good beginning would prove to be half done. The remaining half can be achieved by cherishing the Ambedkerite ideals of social justice through equality, liberty, fraternity and democracy.

2017 Presidential election shows a move in the right direction of Dalit honour and ameliorator their position..The ruling party sponsored the name of Shri Ram Nath Kovind ,the Governor of Bihar and Dalit leader which attracted wide support not only from NDA alliance but also from JDU,a prominent opposition party. The opposition parties alliance too began to search a candidate from the Dalit community like Meira Kumar, the former Speaker Lok Sabha.

The following more positive mind set, chastenised by Ambedkarite visionary mission may annihilate caste system and restore the title deeds of humanity to SCs and STs.

1. As Prof. Upendra Baxi points out Dr Ambedkar was a doer, not a sloganeer.[11] The all round appreciation of the contribution of Dr. Ambedkar in the recent years should be translated into political will to implement his visionary aspirations as enshrined in the Constitution in its letter and spirit.
2. The human rights need to be taken seriously in light of taking human and social suffering equally seriously[12], as Justice Ramaswamy, as judicial incarnation of Dr Ambedkar did.
3. All the organs of State including judiciary should extend appreciative hands towards 'the winds of the change' and universal acceptance of human values and right to be treated as human.
4. Dr Ambedkar is becoming more and more inspiringly relevant today.
   History is repeating itself with winds of new changes. His pioneering role is trying to modernise Hindu society by ensuring gender equality and minimising masculinity is becoming most relevant in present with reference to reforms among the Muslims.[13]
5. Dr Amberkar's message to 'educate, organise and agitate' need real appreciation. What Dr Baxi suggests Ambedkarite message need true observance-'Organise negation '- the power to say "No' to caste based discrimination and

apartheid. And by 'agitate' to mean no seditious conduct but only the practise of articulation of human rights guaranteed by the Constitution and international law.[14] If the deprived people do appreciable acts that need appreciation not condemnation. What visioned by Rohith we should start thinking of soul not caste or body.

6. Te need of the hour is not to ensure Marxian Justice but to lean towards Ambedkarite Justice as Justice Ramaswamy translated into his judgments.[15]
7. As said earlier, a good gesture has started by Sanskar Bharati. Let it be given a real shape. In fitness of things great liability also falls on so far deprived people. Charity must begin at home. As Dr Ambedkar hated misuse of privilege that consciousness be avoided. Any semblance of use of SCs and STs (Prevention of Attrocities Act, 1989 may cause irreparable loss[16] to the cause of such people.

References

1. RSS outfit wants Manusmriti reworked, The Indian Express, 14.05.2017, pp. -2 (Pragya Kaushika)
2. Gopal Guru, 'Ethics in Ambedkar Critique of Gandhi', Vol. L 11 No. 15, Economic & Political Weekly, April 15, 2017 p. 95; U. Baxi, 1. Address at Delhi Universoty on the occasion of 125 1 birth year of Babasaheb Ambedkar. 2. Preface to casement with a view of S. Jaspat and others, 'Reading the Judgement of K. Ramaswamy J. Analysis of the Supreme Court Cases of K. Ramaswamy J. (1989-1987)
3. Supra f.n. 1
4. ibid
5. Gopal Guru, supra f.n.2 p. 95
6. Ibid. p. 100
7. Cited from Baxi, f.n. 2
8. ibid
9. The Indian Express dt/27.05.2017 p 08.
10. ibid
11. Cited from Baxi. f.n. 2.
12. ibid
13. Arnav Das Sharma,Learning From Ambdekar-His Struggle to reform the Hindu Society has lessons for the triple talaaq debate. The Indian Express 22.05.2017
14. Baxi, supra 2
15. Baxi, Preface to Casement with a view p. 18
16. Some unfortunate incidents of filing of complaints under 1989 act by some upper strata of SCs. take place. Such misuses are unapprovable and injurious to the cause of social justice itself.

Index

B